THE GREEN BRAID

Drawn from over fifteen years of peer-reviewed essays and design awards published by the Association of Collegiate Schools of Architecture (A.C.S.A.), *The Green Braid* presents the discipline's best thinking in written, drawn and built form.

Using essays that alternately revise and elucidate contemporary architectural thinking, this book situates sustainability at the center of best architectural design practices. By addressing sustainability within the context of architectural history, theory, pedagogy and design, *The Green Braid* provides an ideal studio companion for both students and professionals seeking to frame their architectural production in a sustainable manner.

Kim Tanzer is Professor of Architecture at the University of Florida and an architect practicing in Gainesville.

Rafael Longoria is Professor of Architecture at the University of Houston and co-editor of *A.U.L.A.: Architecture and Urbanism in Las Américas*.

Non-Fiction
720.47 G82b

The green braid : towards an architecture of ecology, economy, and equity.

DISCARDED
by the
Mead Public Library

THE A.C.S.A. ARCHITECTURAL EDUCATION SERIES

The intent of the Architectural Education Series is to produce Readers for use across the curriculum in architecture and design programs matching current lines of scholary inquiry with curricular needs. Each reader focuses on a thematic topic and is composed of chapters presented originally at A.C.S.A. conferences along with invited chapters. Leading edge design work and scholarship are included to give faculty, students and professionals resources for the studio and classroom.

SERIES EDITORIAL BOARD

Michael Benedikt, University of Texas at Austin
Luis Carranza, Roger Williams University
Thomas Fisher, University of Minnesota
Lisa Iwamoto, University of California at Berkeley
Fernando Luiz Lara, University of Michigan
John Stuart, Florida International University

ABOUT A.C.S.A.

The Association of Collegiate Schools of Architecture (A.C.S.A.) is a non-profit organization founded in 1912 to enhance the quality of architectural education. School membership in A.C.S.A. has grown from 10 charter schools to more than 200 schools in several membership categories worldwide. Through these schools, more than 5,000 architecture faculty members are represented in A.C.S.A.'s membership. A.C.S.A., unique in its representative role for professional schools of architecture in the United States and Canada, provides a major forum for ideas on the leading edge of architectural thought. Issues that will affect the architectural profession in the future are being examined today in A.C.S.A. member schools. Additional information is available at www.acsa-arch.org.

THE GREEN BRAID

Towards an architecture of ecology, economy, and equity

EDITED BY KIM TANZER AND
RAFAEL LONGORIA

Routledge
Taylor & Francis Group

LONDON AND NEW YORK

First published 2007
by Routledge
2 Park Square, Milton Park, Abingdon, Oxon OX14 4RN

Simultaneously published in the USA and Canada
by Taylor & Francis Inc
270 Madison Ave, New York, NY 10016

Routledge is an imprint of the Taylor & Francis Group, an informa business

© 2007 Association of Collegiate Schools of Architecture

Typeset in Sabon by Keystroke, 28 High Street, Tettenhall, Wolverhampton
Printed and bound in Great Britain by MPG Books Ltd, Bodmin

All rights reserved. No part of this book may be reprinted or reproduced
or utilised in any form or by any electronic, mechanical, or other means,
now known or hereafter invented, including photocopying and recording,
or in any information storage or retrieval system, without permission in
writing from the publishers.

British Library Cataloguing in Publication Data
A catalogue record for this book is available from the British Library

Library of Congress Cataloging in Publication Data
   The green braid : towards an architecture of ecology, economy and
   equity/edited by Kim Tanzer and Rafael Longoria.
       p. cm. – (ACSA architectural education series)
   Includes bibliographical references and index.
   (pbk: alk. paper) 1. Sustainable architecture. I. Tanzer, Kim.
   II. Longoria, Rafael.
   NA2542.36.G73 2007
   720′.47–dc22   2006102759

ISBN10: 0–415–41499–7 (hbk)
ISBN10: 0–415–41500–4 (pbk)
ISBN10: 0–203–96488–8 (ebk)

ISBN13: 978–0–415–41499–9 (hbk)
ISBN13: 978–0–415–41500–2 (pbk)
ISBN13: 978–0–203–96488–0 (ebk)

Cover photograph: Mesa Dowayalanee, seen through the Zuni Eagle Aviary. Photo by Claude E. Armstrong.

9000975873

CONTENTS

PHENOMENA AND TECHNOLOGY 135

BUILDING PRACTICES 193

CONTENTS

NOTES ON CONTRIBUTORS

D. Michelle Addington is trained as both an architect and an engineer whose teaching and research explore physical phenomena. An associate professor of architecture at Harvard's Graduate School of Design, she teaches courses in energy, the environment, advanced technologies, and new materials. She is co-author of *Smart Materials and Technologies for the Architecture and Design Professions*.

Barbara L. Allen has written extensively on issues of sustainability and environmental justice. Her book *Uneasy Alchemy: Citizens and Experts in Louisiana's Chemical Corridor Disputes* (2003) examined the politics of local knowledge and professional expertise. She is currently the director of the graduate program in science and technology studies at Virginia Tech's D.C.-area campus. From 1999 to 2007, Allen was the executive editor of the *Journal of Architectural Education*.

Brian D. Andrews joined the U.S.C. architecture faculty after teaching at the University of Virginia, Syracuse University and Clemson University, where he was the Robert Mills Distinguished Professor. His teaching and research revolve around drawing and representation, and currently he is working on a book about the Asilo Sant Elia by Terragni. Besides teaching, he has his own architectural practice in Los Angeles. Andrews and W. Jude LeBlanc continue to collaborate on speculative research projects and buildings.

Claude E. Armstrong (see Donna L. Cohen and Claude E. Armstrong)

Robert Barnstone is Associate Professor at Washington State University and is engaged in the exploration of boundaries between sculpture and building. He has sculpture installations in Paris, New York and Los Angeles. He recently completed the first plastic wood composite building in history at W.M.E.L. and is currently at T.U./Delft building a cardboard house. His work has been recognized in *AD*, *Onsite*, *JAE*, *Azure*, and *Sculpture* magazine.

Craig Barton is an associate professor and Director of Programs in Architecture at the University of Virginia. Prior to this appointment he was a Loeb Fellow at Harvard University's Graduate School of Design. He is editor of the anthology, *Sites of Memory: Perspectives on Architecture and Race*, published by Princeton Architectural Press in 2001.

Dana Buntrock, a professor at the University of California at Berkeley, published her first book, *Japanese Architecture as a Collaborative Process* in 2001. Buntrock is currently working on a second book (with photography by LeRoy Howard) investigating concepts of time incorporated into contemporary architecture in Japan and Korea.

Jeanine Centouri is a principal of UrbanRock Design in Los Angeles and a professor of architecture at Woodbury University. Her practice and research focus on the intersection between public space, public art, and architecture. "Finding Public Space in the Margins" received several awards including a *Progressive Architecture* Citation and a Best of Category in concepts from *ID* magazine.

Raveevarn Choksombatchai is an associate professor in architecture design at the University of California at Berkeley. She is a former partner of *Loom*, which she co-founded with Ralph Nelson in 1993. *Loom* was the recipient of three Progressive Architecture awards and citations, was selected for Emerging Voices in Architecture by the Architecture League of New York, and was nominated for both a Chrysler Design Award and the Cooper Hewitt National Design Museum's National Design Award in the area of environmental design.

Donna L. Cohen and Claude E. Armstrong have been practicing together since 1982, beginning with architectural projects for American artist Donald Judd. Since that time they have earned national and international awards for their design of contemporary architecture in culturally significant sites. Cohen and Armstrong are both on the faculty of the University of Florida College of Design Construction and Planning.

William F. Conway is an associate professor of architecture at the University of Minnesota. He has worked in architectural offices in Fargo, Boston, Rome, Italy and the office of Cesar Pelli and Associates. The recipient of a Fulbright fellowship and Winchester traveling fellowship, he was a visiting artist at the American Academy in Rome. Conway and Marcy Schulte established their architectural firm in Ames, Iowa in 1994. Their practice has been recognized for its work in the design of public places.

Norman Crowe, Professor of Architecture at the University of Notre Dame, is the author of *Nature and the Idea of a Man-Made World* (1995). His teaching and research focus on urban design and on environmental issues as related to architecture and urbanism.

James Dallman is a principal of La Dallman Architects. Through projects of intentionally diverse scale and program, the design studio transforms the public realm through infrastructural interventions and redefinition of public space. Most recently, the studio was awarded the second prize in the International West End Pedestrian Bridge Competition in Pittsburgh, as well as four American Institute of Architects Wisconsin Design Awards.

Felecia Davis is an assistant professor at the College of Art, Architecture and Planning in the Department of Architecture at Cornell University and co-founder of Colab Architecture in Ithaca, New York. Much of Davis's speculative work focuses on the intersections of built form and cultural practice that proposes architecture as a performative art.

Anthony Denzer is Assistant Professor of Architectural Engineering at the University of Wyoming. This article was drawn from his Ph.D. dissertation, "Gregory Ain and the Social Politics of Housing Design" (2005).

Ellen Dunham-Jones is the Director of the architecture program at the Georgia Institute of Technology. She serves on the Board of Directors of the Congress for the New Urbanism, the editorial board of the journal *Places*, and the executive board of ULI-Atlanta. She is currently co-writing a book on retrofitting suburbs.

Lisa R. Findley is an associate professor at the California College of the Arts in San Francisco, where she coordinates the M.Arch. program. She is also an architectural journalist and a contributing editor for *Architectural Record*. This article is an early version of a chapter of her book *Building Change: Architecture, Politics and Cultural Agency* (2005).

Thomas Fisher is Dean of the College of Design at the University of Minnesota. He has published twenty-four book chapters and 246 major articles in various journals, and has written three books: *In the Scheme of Things: Alternative Thinking on the Practice of Architecture, Salmela Architect*, and *Lake/Flato: Buildings and Landscapes*.

Ellen Grimes is an architectural designer practicing in Chicago. She is Assistant Professor at the University of Illinois at Chicago and a board member of the Center for Research in Urban Ecology. Current projects include the Great Restoration Experiment, a research infrastructure at the Midewin National Tallgrass Prairie.

Thomas Hartman is Associate Professor at Arizona State University. A graduate of the École des Beaux Arts and a former collaborator of Renzo Piano, his teaching, writing and design work explores the transformation of constraints into opportunities.

Jyoti Hosagrahar is Director of Sustainable Urbanism International, an independent non-profit research and policy initiative. She teaches at Columbia University and earned her doctorate from the University of California, Berkeley. Hosagrahar is the author of *Indigenous Modernities: Negotiating Architecture and Urbanism* (2005).

Mildred Howard is a mixed-media and installation artist working in San Francisco. Her work has been shown in dozens of solo and group exhibitions, is held in a number of public collections and widely published in academic and popular presses.

Srdja Hrisafovic is a docent senior lecturer at Sarajevo's Academy of Fine Arts and a principal of HandH Architects with over twenty years of teaching, applied research, working, and consulting in architecture, urban design, and environmental protection. Hrisafovic has advised local and regional governments in Bosnia and Herzegovina on issues of lighting and environment protection.

Lisa Iwamoto and Craig Scott are principals of IwamotoScott Architecture, a practice formed in 1998. IwamotoScott's recent projects include: Jellyfish House for the Vitra Design Museum exhibition Open House; mOcean, a motion-capture installation for SFMoMA, 2005 *ID* Magazine Awards issue, IN-OUT Curtain; 2:1 House in Berkeley, California, and Fog House. Iwamoto is Assistant Professor in the Department of Architecture at the University of California, Berkeley.

Grace La is a principal of La Dallman Architects and an associate professor at the University of Wisconsin-Milwaukee School of Architecture and Urban Planning. Professor La was awarded the 2005 UWM Distinguished Undergraduate Teaching Award, recognizing university-wide excellence in teaching, and received the 2002–3 Association of Collegiate Schools of Architecture National Faculty Design Award.

W. Jude LeBlanc is an associate professor of architecture at the Georgia Institute of Technology and practices architecture in Atlanta. His teaching and research interests include the relation of architecture to painting and film. LeBlanc and Brian D. Andrews continue to collaborate on speculative research projects and buildings. Their work has received several design awards, including Boston Society of Architects Unbuilt Architecture Awards, a *Progressive Architecture* Merit Award, and a housing award from *Japan Architect.*

Rafael Longoria is Professor of Architecture at the University of Houston and a principal of Longoria/Peters, a Houston-based architecture and urban design firm. He is a founding editor of *AULA: Architecture and Urbanism in Las Américas,* and has served on the editorial boards of the *Journal of Architectural Education*, CITE, and the Rice University Press. Longoria was recently inducted to Mexico's Academia Nacional de Arquitectura.

Stephen Luoni is Director of the University of Arkansas Community Design Center where he is the Steven L. Anderson Chair in Architecture and Urban Studies. He has taught at the University of Florida and the University of Minnesota.

Carlos Martín works in academia and government in the areas of technological and social change in building. Trained as an architect, construction engineer, and historian of technology at M.I.T., University of Michigan, and Stanford, Dr. Martín returned to the Department of Housing and Urban Development's Partnership for Advancing Technology in Housing (PATH) in 2004 after serving as the Salt River Project Professor of Energy and the Environment at Arizona State University.

Phillip G. Mead is Associate Professor of Architecture at the University of Idaho in Moscow. He has taught and practiced in California, Texas and Idaho and is a former student of Charles Moore. Currently Mead teaches modern architectural history, environmental control systems and studio where he integrates his research on the health impacts of light, air, views, and energy conservation into his projects.

Steven A. Moore is the Barlett Cocke Professor of Architecture and Planning at the University of Texas at Austin where he is Director of the graduate program in sustainable design and Co-Director of the University of Texas Center for Sustainable Development. He is the author of four books related to sustainable design. The most recent, *Alternative Routes to the Sustainable City* will appear in early 2007.

Ralph Kirk Nelson was a principal in *Loom*, founded in 1991 with Raveevarn Choksombatchai as an interdisciplinary art, architecture and environmental design firm. Among the firm's projects are the Women's Suffrage Memorial in San Francisco, and the Basil Café. Nelson received his M.Arch from Yale University.

David Orr is the Paul Sears Distinguished Professor of Environmental Studies and Politics and the Chair of the Environmental Studies Program at Oberlin College. He is also a James Marsh Professor-at-Large at the University of Vermont and the author of *Ecological Literacy* (1992), *Earth in Mind* (1994/2004), *The Nature of Design* (2002), *The Last Refuge* (2004), and *Design on the Edge* (2006).

Mónica Ponce de León is Professor of Architecture at Harvard University and a principal in the Boston-based design firm Office dA. In 2002 Ponce de León received the American Academy of Arts and Letters Award in Architecture.

James Rojas serves as Project Manager for the Metropolitan Transportation Authority of the City of Los Angeles, working on pedestrian and transportation enhancement projects. His work on Latino empowerment has been widely cited in architectural circles. He holds a Master of City Planning and a Master of Science in Architectural Studies from the Massachusetts Institute of Technology.

Jonathan Reich is an architect and Professor of Architecture at California Polytechnic State University in San Luis Obispo where he teaches an architectural design thesis studio and interdisciplinary courses in sustainable design which won the American Institute of Architects national award for "Ecological Literacy in Architectural Education" in 2005.

Dean Sakamoto is a critic and Director of Exhibits at Yale University, and a practicing architect. Based in New Haven, Conn. since 1986 he has garnered numerous awards for design and construction. He holds a B.Arch from the University of Oregon, and M.Arch from the Cranbrook Academy of Art and an M.E.D. from Yale University.

Lawrence Scarpa is a principal at Pugh+Scarpa in Santa Monica, California and an educator in design and construction technology with a special emphasis in sustainability. He is also a co-founder of Livable Places, Inc., a non-profit development company, and a member of the editorial board of *LA Architect*.

Marcy Schulte was a designer with the firm of Cesar Pelli and Associates from 1987 to 1991. Since that time Ms. Schulte has paralleled her work in practice with teaching. Her design studios and seminars at the University of Minnesota focus on the inquiry of cultural issues and urban settings in design. Schulte and William F. Conway established their architectural firm in Ames, Iowa in 1994.

Anthony W. Schuman is Graduate Program Director at the New Jersey School of Architecture and a past president of A.C.S.A. His articles on housing design and urban development appear in ten books and numerous scholarly journals and conference proceedings. He serves on the Montclair (New Jersey) Housing Commission and several community development organizations in Newark.

Craig Scott (see Lisa Iwamoto and Craig Scott).

Mahesh Senagala is the Associate Dean for Research at the College of Architecture of the University of Texas at San Antonio. In addition to sustainable design, he is interested in the intersections of Batesonian systems theory, emerging technologies, smart architecture, tensile fabric structures, Latin American literature, and existentialism.

William Sherman is the Chair of the Department of Architecture and Landscape Architecture at the University of Virginia as well as a practicing architect. His teaching, research, and practice is focused on the interaction of buildings and dynamic natural forces in their role as incremental components of the urban infrastructure.

Jennifer Siegal is the Principal and Founder of Office of Mobile Design, an architecture/design studio that is dedicated to the exploration and production of prefabricated and portable eco-logic structures. She was a 2003 Loeb Fellow at Harvard University's Graduate School of Design. Ms. Siegal is a professor at Woodbury University in Los Angeles and the editor of *Mobile: The Art of Portable Architecture* and *Materials Monthly*.

Harris Sobin is Professor Emeritus of Architecture at the University of Arizona, where he taught from 1970 to 2000. His published research includes work on Le Corbusier's development of energy-related design and on the architect's friendship with sculptor Costantino Nivola. He is currently preparing a book-length study provisionally entitled "From Science to Poetry: Le Corbusier and the Development of the New Environmental Envelope."

Kim Tanzer is a professor of architecture at the University of Florida, where much of her work focuses on the transmission and transformation of architectural knowledge through human action. She has received local and national recognition for her work in social sustainability. She maintains an architectural practice in Gainesville, Florida.

Nader Tehrani is Adjunct Associate Professor of Architecture at Harvard's Graduate School of Design. In partnership with Mónica Ponce de León, he heads the firm Office dA and has been practicing architecture in Boston since 1987.

Karl Wallick is an assistant professor at the School of Architecture and Interior Design at the University of Cincinnati where he focuses on issues of design and technology. In 2004 he was part of the SmartWrap project team at KieranTimberlake Associates in Philadelphia.

PREFACE

The essays and design projects selected for this book are primarily drawn from 15 years of peer-reviewed proceedings of the Association of Collegiate Schools of Architecture. Chosen from over a thousand contributions pertinent to the subject, they are intended to serve as holograms, each capturing a complete response to sustainability from a very particular point of view. Some are extremely timely, and serve today to record historic moments, while others escape considerations of fashion. Relatively few were written or designed by authors who considered themselves to be part of a sustainability movement. Rather, the essays reflect these scholars' and designers' commitment to design ethics consistent with what we today consider sustainability. Throughout the book we have paired essays with design projects to demonstrate the multiple ways of creating and disseminating knowledge—words, spaces, images— developed within our discipline. We have also invited four authors, David Orr, Ellen Dunham-Jones, Thomas Fisher, and Steven Moore to contribute essays. These essays, consciously interacting with the twining of the green braid metaphor—ecology, economy or equity—look holistically at contemporary architecture and environmental design issues.

The book has five sections. The first, "Meta-discourses in Pedagogy and Practice" focuses on the architecture curriculum and the role academic architects play in framing the sustainability discourse through their own teaching and practice. The second, "Phenomena and Technology" links the sensuous and the mechanical, with the goal of recognizing the earth's elements as poetic design opportunities and functional constraints at the same time. The third, "Building Practices" focuses on atypical, sometimes marginalized, sometimes romanticized, ways of fabricating architecture. It provides evidence that changing a paradigm requires action in addition to reflection, and that a sustainable practice is one that, even more than most, sees constraints as opportunities. The fourth, "Settlement Patterns," recognizes the crucial role location, spatial and political organization inevitably play in large scale developments' sustainability. No amount of "greening" can compensate for a disconnected, polluted or unjust development pattern. The fifth, "The Shared Realm," articulates most clearly the role architects play as part of a network of collaborators. These collaborators, the authors argue, include far more than consultants in allied fields. All people who have lived or will live amidst our creations are equally a part of each project's construction, and to some degree, we must make their desires ours for a project to succeed.

ACKNOWLEDGMENTS

This project began in the year 2000, with the appointment of a national task force on sustainability by Tony Schuman, then President of the Association of Collegiate Schools of Architecture (A.C.S.A). Co-chaired by Kim Tanzer and Jean Gardner, this group of about fifty academic architects from around North America worked to cohere various threads of sustainability discourses and to raise the profile of this crucial ethical position regarding the practice of architecture. Their efforts were supported by subsequent presidents of the A.C.S.A., including Frances Bronet, Brad Grant, Geraldine Forbes, Rafael Longoria, Steven Schreiber and Ted Landsmark. In addition, members of the A.C.S.A. Board of Directors, beginning in 2000, lent their encouragement to this vital effort. Among the task force's goals was the dissemination of the significant body of knowledge, generated by our members, to compliment the growing wealth of information regarding sustainability and green building emerging in other realms. This book is the result.

In addition to the essential contributions described above, this book would not have been possible without the leadership of Michael Monti, Executive Director of the A.C.S.A. His thoughtfulness, patience and good humor have been critical lubricants when we reached inevitable points of friction. He has been assisted by Kevin Mitchell of the A.C.S.A. national office, who has ably coordinated much of the day-to-day work involved in producing a complicated, collaborative project.

We wish to thank our home institutions, the University of Florida and the University of Houston, for their support. At the University of Florida, Gary Ridgdill provided early assistance on behalf of the School of Architecture. His goodwill has been followed by that of Mary Kramer and Martha Kohen, in particular. At the outset, Jeff Huber worked to inventory sustainability-related essays in the *Proceedings* of the A.C.S.A. Annual Meetings over the past fifteen years. As we developed the final collection of essays, graduate architecture students worked through a much longer set under initial consideration, and made helpful editorial comments. They are Jason Canning, Craig Ditman, Toni Duce, Elvir Gazic, Carla Harvey, Michael Honig, Shih-Ping Lin, Ryan Parrish, Quilian Riano, Helen Schultz, Freida Speicher, Jennifer Stencel and Erica Walker. Harun Thomas provided critical and timely editorial assistance. At the University of Houston, Zui Lip Ng provided essential graphic assistance, and Stephen Fox, Jean Krchnak, Fernando Brave, Patrick Peters, Margaret Culbertson and the fantastic group at the William Jenkins Art and Architecture Library helped more than they realize.

A key principle of sustainability is that all efforts are situated within and responsive to a larger system. As highlighted above, the editors gratefully acknowledge the large and generous network of colleagues, families and friends that has supported this project.

THE GREEN BRAID

INTRODUCTION
Networked ways of knowing
KIM TANZER AND RAFAEL LONGORIA

I prefer 'both-and' to 'either-or,' black and white, and sometimes gray to black or white.[1]

In selecting essays for this book we have embraced the concept of sustainability popularized through the 1987 UNESCO Report, *Our Common Future*, also known as the Brundtland Report, after its primary author, Gro Harlem Brundtland, Prime Minister of Norway.[2] The report asserts "sustainability is defined as meeting today's needs without compromising the ability of future generations to meet their own needs." In the nearly twenty years since the report was issued, critics have challenged several of its key elements, specifically alleging it capitulates to continued human development and emphasizes human needs at the potential expense of nonhuman environmental needs.[3] Nonetheless, the definition provides a minimal benchmark against which current human action can be measured. It also establishes, again, in a modest way, the principle that people have the responsibility to consider others' needs—particularly future needs—in conjunction with their own needs. It suggests that a chain of responsible relationships replace the autonomous individual actor.

A second set of criteria, also following Brundtland, provided a further filter for the essays selected for this volume. *Our Common Future* asserted that three integrated behavioral trajectories are necessary to achieve a sustainable future—ecology, economy, and social equity.[4] Often described as "the three Es" the concept is also identified as the "three Ps" Planet, People, Prosperity, or, using the term popularized by William McDonough and Michael Braungart, the "triple bottom line."[5] Whichever specific shorthand is used, the joining of environmental outcomes with economic decisions allows us to recognize the crucial role architects play in brokering material and financial choices. Similarly the regrettable results of social inequity, whereby the world's wealthiest inhabitants consume a hugely disproportionate percentage of the world's resources, leave the globe's poorest citizens scrambling to meet daily needs in ecologically degraded and degrading circumstances.

Reinforcing this triumvirate—the green braid that infuses sustainable architectural design—has several other advantages, as well. Architects too often resist engagement with economic aspects of our projects, believing the field is too mercurial or too banal to engage. However, without the abstract leveler of economics our work can be perceived as naively extravagant or, worse, injurious to planetary health in the short and long term. Emphasizing

1 Robert Venturi, Complexity and Contradiction in Architecture *(New York: The Museum of Modern Art, 1966),* 16.

2 World Commission on Environment and Development, Gro Harlem Brundtland, Chairman, Our Common Future *(New York: Oxford University Press, 1987).*

3 See, for example, Thijs de la Court, Beyond Brundtland: Green Development in the 1990s, *trans. Ed Bagens and Nigel Harle (New York: New Horizons Press, 1990).*

4 Brundtland, Our Common Future, *37–38.*

5 William McDonough and Michael Braungart, Cradle to Cradle: Remaking the Way We Make Things *(New York: North Point Press, 2002). See Chapter 5.*

the role of social equity in creating a sustainable planet calls into play the many architects whose work has sought to level the playing field, particularly in heavily populated urban areas. Some of these architects, typically working without specific reference to environmental consequences, have been contributing inadvertently to long-term sustainability by enhancing living conditions, advocating for economic advantages, reinforcing relatively dense yet humane living patterns and honoring cultural sustainability which often holds keys to ecological sustainability. Finally, coemphasizing ecology, economy, and equity allows the architects who have, for more than a generation, worked hard to maximize energy efficiency and to modulate solar gain to share their efforts with colleagues whose goals are shared but who lack these well-developed, highly technical environmental means. In short, the use of the green braid metaphor, requiring three intertwined threads be woven into each sustainable project, allows us to reframe our own discipline's exclusionary categorizing logic as a network of relations.

CLASSIFICATORY LOGIC AND THE PROBLEM OF PERSPECTIVE

Prominent discourses within the academy, especially the sciences, have come to rely on the persuasiveness of classificatory logic. This logic has allowed us to understand a specific idea or thing as a piece of a larger whole, and it has allowed scientists to pursue a rigorous and exhaustive mapping of all the world's knowledge. This ambitious project was prefigured by the work of Raymond Lull and other proto-scientists in the early Renaissance who laid out a tiered, prioritized model of the world's knowledge in the form of "memory theaters."[6] Once the system was established by the great scientific philosophers of the seventeenth century, new knowledge could be fit neatly within existing categories, while the categories themselves, many worked out in the eighteenth and nineteenth centuries through the development of progressively more specific disciplines, remained fixed. But an important component of the memory theater was lost in the process, and with it the ability for knowledge to relate across categories. Memory theaters were originally imagined as combinatory systems, allowing new relations to be considered through the fresh juxtapositions of ideas or things.

A parallel or, some would say, resultant, development to the hegemony of classificatory knowledge is the intellectual objectification of those things studied.[7] In order to fully understand an idea or a thing, the argument goes, one must avoid feeling a sense of relation to it. Fairness and thorough scrutiny require that the scientist exhibit objectivity, not empathy, toward the thing being studied. In the current language of cultural studies, Western knowledge requires the acting subject (the scientist or "self") separate him or herself from the object of investigation (the thing or "other"). Over centuries, the perceived scientific necessity to separate self from other, subject from object, has been generalized to a societal disconnect severing the individual from a larger network of relations.

6 *See Frances Yates,* The Art of Memory *(Chicago, Ill.: University of Chicago Press, 1966).*

7 *See Morris Berman,* The Reenchantment of the World *(Ithaca, N.Y.: Cornell University Press, 1981).*

4

Ironically, as members of human society reinforce such separation in many ways through daily action, scientists have changed course. In the early twentieth century, physicist Werner Heisenberg unveiled his uncertainty principle which stated that an elementary particle can be observed as either a particle or a wave, depending on the role of the observer. The concept that the observer is inextricably linked with the phenomenon observed is now well established among physicists, but other branches of science, other academic disciplines, and most of the human community have not yet adjusted their/our conception of the world to privilege relation over objectification.

The implications of this change of perspective are profound. While many writers, including some cited in this book, advocate for a knowledge of relations or networks, among the earliest modern authors to capture the spirit of the transformation now in progress was philosopher Martin Buber. In his famous 1923 book-poem he described the change from "I–it" thinking to "I–thou" thinking, which suggested a reverence for those things so often considered object, thing, or other. He wrote,

When Thou *is spoken, the speaker has no thing for his object. For where there is a thing there is another thing. Every* It *is bounded by others;* It *exists only through being bounded by others. But when* Thou *is spoken, there is no thing.* Thou *has no bounds. When* Thou *is spoken, the speaker has no thing; he has indeed nothing. But he takes his stand in relation.*[8]

Underlying all the essays in this book is the conceptual foundation Buber described so beautifully. The authors, through their scholarly research and design proposals, demonstrate and indirectly advocate for I–thou relationships between our planet and all its citizens.

THINKING SYSTEMS

Over the past century, several disciplines have recognized the limitations of the metaphorical tree of knowledge on which smaller and smaller branches hold increasingly rarefied and disconnected facts. This metaphor for classification fails to recognize the impact that apparently disconnected phenomena have on one another. Brief examples from several disciplines, each of which has historically contributed to architecture's disciplinary foundation, will serve as examples.

Albert Einstein famously complained "God doesn't play dice" when confronted with theoretical anomalies that suggested the universe is constructed of interconnected probabilities rather than causal chains. While physicists over the past eighty years have worked to develop theories that incorporate the element of uncertainty, identified by Heisenberg, into what Prigogine describes as a new extended rationality, architects have generally felt more comfortable with the world as described by Einstein, if not Newton and Descartes.[9, 10] Newtonian concepts of objectivity and temporality and

8 Martin Buber, I and Thou, 3rd edn, trans. Ronald Gregor Smith *(New York: Charles Scribner's Sons, 1958), 4.*

9 Ilya Prigogine in collaboration *with Isabelle Stengers,* The End of Certainty: Time, Chaos, and the New Laws of Nature *(New York: The Free Press, 1996).*

10 Cubism is thought to echo *ideas of simultaneity developed by Einstein, and some authors have attributed notions of simultaneity to the work of modern architects such as Le Corbusier. See Leonard M. Shlain,* Art and Physics *(New York: William Morrow and Company, Inc., 1991), 119–138 and 187–203 and Colin Rowe (with Robert Slutzky), "Transparency Literal and Phenomenal,"* The Mathematics of the Ideal Villa and Other Essays *(Cambridge, Mass.: MIT Press, 1988).*

Cartesian spatial logics, and the mindsets they incorporate, still prevail within the discipline of architecture.

Meanwhile physicists have come to identify self-organizing non-linear systems and nonequilibrium processes that operate probabilistically. They imagine a world of multiple, fluctuating fields evolving asynchronously at the microscopic scale of dynamic systems and the macroscopic levels of biological and human activities.[11] Heisenberg said, "The world thus appears as a complicated tissue of events, in which connections of different kinds alternate or overlap or combine and thereby determine the texture of the whole."[12] While Peter Eisenman's explorations of scale symmetry and chaos theory resulted in a series of compelling formal studies, quantum physicists are interested in participating in the convergence of different sciences that describe life.[13] Prigogine says, "We are observing the birth of a science that is no longer limited to idealized and simplified situations but reflects the complexity of the real world, a science that views us and our creativity as part of a fundamental trend present at all levels of nature."[14, 15]

Critical theory, too, seeks to understand the world without overly simplifying it. Critical theory is a term used in the humanities to capture the intellectual skepticism leveled at the privileged position given certain philosophical and literary texts in the twentieth century. Scholars who employ methods to critique, deconstruct or otherwise challenge existing intellectual hierarchies often argue that knowledge cannot be fixed in perpetual relations of power and prestige. Rather, it migrates through multiple channels of communication within and between texts, affecting and infecting other literary works. The phenomena of migrating knowledge and argumentation, typically occurring without regard for authorized and approved routes of acceptance, was described by Roland Barthes in his 1971 essay "From Work to Text" in which he says,

The intertextual in which every text is held, it itself being the text-between of another text, is not to be confused with some origin of the text: to try to find the 'sources', the 'influences' of a work, is to fall in with the myth of filiation; the citations which go to make up a text are anonymous, untraceable, and yet already read: they are quotations without inverted commas.[16]

Gilles Deleuze and Félix Guattari, in their often cited book *A Thousand Plateaus*, articulate the concept of the rhizome in contrast to the tree, the latter described as part of an arborescent system.

Arborescent systems are hierarchical systems with centers of significance and subjectification, central automata like organized memories. In corresponding models, an element only receives information from a higher unit, and only receives a subjective affection along preestablished paths . . .

11 Prigogine, The End of Certainty, 162.

12 Werner Heisenberg, quoted in Fritjof Capra, The Web of Life: A New Scientific Understanding of Living Systems (New York: Anchor Books, 1997), 30.

13 For a review of Eisenman's chaos theory studies see Peter Eisenman, "Moving Arrows, Eros, and Other Errors," in Precis 6: The Culture of Fragments, (New York: Rizzoli, 1987).

14 Prigogine, The End of Certainty, 7.

15 For a readable yet thorough lay overview of quantum physics see Brian Greene, The Fabric of the Cosmos: Space, Time and the Texture of Reality (New York: Vintage Books, 2004).

16 Roland Barthes, "From Work to Text," in Image Music Text, trans. Stephen Heath (New York: The Noonday Press, 1977), 160.

6

*Accepting the primacy of hierarchical structures amounts to giving
arborescent structures privileged status . . . In a hierarchical system, an
individual has only one active neighbor, his or her hierarchical superior . . .
The channels of transmission are preestablished: the arborescent system
preexists the individual, who is integrated into it at an allotted place.*[17]

17 *Gilles Deleuze and Félix
Guattari,* A Thousand Plateaus:
Capitalism and Schizophrenia
*(Minneapolis, Minn.: University of
Minnesota Press, 1987), 16.*

Instead, Deleuze and Guattari advocate for the rhizome, saying, "The rhizome
is an a-centered, nonhierarchical, non-signifying system without a General
and without an organizing memory or central automaton, defined solely by
the circulation of states."[18]

18 *Ibid., 21.*

The metaphor of the rhizome allows these and other critical theorists to
summarize their project, to loosen systems of classification and hierarchy
within what is often known as the Western literary canon.

"Ecology" is the term Ernst Haeckel coined in 1866 by fusing the Greek
words for household (*oikos*) and study (*logos*) to describe the study of nature's
household. In the past century the concept has grown into a field of study,
based in the natural and eventually the social sciences. Ecology explicitly
looks at the relationships between natural systems, studying the impacts of
change in one system on another system. A key feature is the concept of an
ecosystem, comprised of elements of many diverse kinds of plant and animal
life brought together by physical proximity. Such an ecosystem depends
equally on contributions from all types of diversity, from earthworms to large
mammals, from molds to trees. Ecology helps us understand that bigger is not
better, nor is harder, nor more complex better. Ideas of hierarchy, often put
forward by human beings as projections of our own characteristics in an
attempt to rationalize the goal of planetary dominance, are inconsistent with
evidence found by ecologists. McDonough and Braungart provide an example
of the necessary relation between simple and complex, small and large and
high and low creatures when they describe a forest ecosystem:

*Each inhabitant of an ecosystem is therefore interdependent to some extent
with the others. Every creature is involved in maintaining the entire system;
all of them work in creative and ultimately effective ways for the success
of the whole. The leaf-cutter ants, for example, recycle the nutrients, taking
them to deeper soil layers so that plants, worms, and microorganisms
can process them, all in the course of gathering and storing food for
themselves. Ants everywhere loosen and aerate the soil around plant roots,
helping to make it permeable to water. Trees transpire and purify water,
make oxygen, and cool the planet's surface. Each species' industry has
not only individual and local implications but global ones as well.*[19]

19 *McDonough and Braungart,*
Cradle to Cradle, *122.*

Another key principle of networked knowing we learn from ecologists
relates to complex causality. In ecosystems change does not happen in a linear
fashion. Unlike laboratory experiments, where one factor can be evaluated

in isolation, in an ecosystem a change in one factor, seemingly innocuous, can have disproportionate impacts on other elements of an ecosystem, or on the health of the ecosystem itself. Nonlinear change, the value of diversity, nonhierarchical organization recognizing the equal importance of many elements of a system and the very concept of considering species in the context of complex systems—all these are concepts brought forward by practitioners of ecology.

The three disciplines briefly recognized for their roles in developing concepts such as the network, rhizome, and system, share several common threads. First, they all espouse nonmechanistic, post Cartesian thinking. They focus on the whole rather than just the parts. They are contextual. Second, they believe ideas and matter to be nonhierarchical. The object of study is always nested within larger and smaller systems. Indeed the concept of object or point is reimagined as an episode within a larger trajectory, pattern or "line of flight."[20] All parts of the system are recognized to be equally important. They specifically conceptualize networks operating within networks. Finally, they understand that systemic behavior is influenced by feedback loops which reinforce effective trial and error behavior and quickly communicate misdirection. In this way they recognize that early experiments influence outcomes and that methodical, thorough research, because it is less opportunistic, may not provide adequate timely feedback in systems that recognize many variables.

20 *Deleuze and Guattari,* A Thousand Plateaus, *9.*

THE STRUCTURE OF SCIENTIFIC REVOLUTIONS

The preceding section briefly summarized several disciplines of historical significance to architectural thinking, and fundamental changes initiated within each discipline in the twentieth century. While the work of physicists, philosophers, and ecologists described above is widely accepted within each respective discipline, architects have not yet internalized the repercussions of a changed worldview into our own broader disciplinary thinking. For example, we refer to building systems (structure and various mechanical infrastructures) using the term popularized by ecologists, but we do not typically conceive of these building systems as interrelated. We embrace critical theory as a component of architectural theory, but habitually respond in what Deleuze and Guattari would describe as an arborescent fashion— subliminally promoting hierarchies and centers, in the form of centers of influence (New York, Los Angeles, London), spheres of influence (certain old and well-established universities), and personalities of influence whose work is disproportionately published in journals and promoted by word of mouth. We often cite the value of twentieth-century discoveries in physics on the work of the Cubists and certain early modern architects, but as a discipline we understand little of contemporary math and physics. Instead we refer back to the work of Plato, Descartes, and pre-Einsteinian physics to find touchstones for spatial order and the linear causality implied in program narratives.

In short, we have not internalized the networked worldview developed in these disciplines into our own fundamental knowledge base.

As Thomas Kuhn wrote in *The Structure of Scientific Revolutions*, such a transformation rarely occurs automatically.[21] Kuhn argues that disciplinary communities typically hold tight to the status quo and only relinquish control of shared knowledge bases when community members depart or when significant external forces emerge. It is worth reviewing in some detail Kuhn's analysis of the process through which scientific knowledge changes in the academy.[22]

Kuhn first identifies the concept of the disciplinary community. This consists of the producers and validators (through the peer-review process) of scientific knowledge. In many scientific disciplines this is a specialized group numbering in the hundreds. These knowledge producers and validators share what Kuhn describes as a disciplinary matrix, with several common features. First, the disciplinary matrix captures shared symbolic generalizations, "expressions, deployed without question or dissent by group members, which provide points at which group members could attach the powerful techniques of logical and mathematical manipulations in their problem solving enterprise."[23] Second, the disciplinary matrix holds beliefs in particular models that supply the group with preferred or permissible analogies and metaphors. By doing so these models help to determine what the validators will accept as an explanation and puzzle solution. Conversely, these beliefs assist the producers and validators to determine a roster of unsolved puzzles and to evaluate the importance of each in completing the discipline's picture. The disciplinary matrix thus serves to limit the scope of further investigations. Finally, the disciplinary matrix establishes values which provide the producers and validators with a sense of community. These values are especially important "when the members of a particular community must identify crisis or, later, choose between incompatible ways of practicing their discipline."[24]

Kuhn then describes the characteristics of a scientific crisis. In general, a discipline in crisis finds too many features of reality that cannot be explained using the prevailing model. Some degree of disarray results, as alternative explanations are offered and tested. Typically, those most invested in the existing paradigm are most resistant to efforts to replace it. As a result, among producers and validators the youngest and those otherwise marginalized are less invested in supporting the prevailing paradigm and more likely to pursue alternative models. When an alternative scientific model replaces an existing model, it is known as a paradigm shift.[25]

What precipitates such a paradigm shift? First, it is important to note that it is not always evident such a shift is occurring. Kuhn's research involved the analysis of contemporaneous scientific literature now recognized as central to historic changes. He found that such changes sometimes occurred over the course of decades, generations, or even centuries. Given that such shifts

21 Thomas Kuhn, The Structure of Scientific Revolutions, 2nd edn (Chicago, Ill.: University of Chicago Press, 1970), especially 52–76.

22 Kuhn specifically refers to scientific disciplines. We are taking the liberty in this essay to apply his analysis to the discipline of academic architecture.

23 Kuhn, The Structure of Scientific Revolutions, 182–183.

24 Kuhn, The Structure of Scientific Revolutions, 184–185.

25 Specifically, Kuhn says "When, that is, the profession can no longer evade anomalies that subvert the existing tradition of scientific practice—then begin the extraordinary investigations that lead the profession at last to a new set of commitments, a new basis for science. The extraordinary episodes in which that shift of professional commitments occurs are the ones known in this essay as scientific revolutions. They are the tradition-shattering complements to the tradition-bound activity of normal science," 6.

may not be obvious as they occur, Kuhn suggests several precipitating factors. First, within an academic community, defenders of the old paradigm might simply retire, thus losing interest in defending the models that have made their careers. Or, evaluators might be convinced by a compelling new explanation to a vexing problem, satisfying newly identified criteria. Similarly evaluators might recognize a "neater," "more suitable," or "simpler" theory to explain a known phenomenon, replacing the older theory. Finally, a new model might appeal to an individual's sense of the appropriate or the aesthetic.

MAPPING KUHN'S ARGUMENT ONTO THE DISCIPLINE OF ARCHITECTURE

What are the ramifications of Kuhn's argument for architecture's disciplinary community? Do we see evidence that architects have begun to acknowledge the value of sustainable thinking applied to our professional discourse? Are these values being applied in a systemic, networked fashion?

First, as Kuhn describes, the people who promote an outdated paradigm leave the university and therefore no longer guard their intellectual positions. The paradigm they promote essentially fades. Currently the professors who came of age at the height of the Cold War and during a time of apparently plentiful resources are retiring in record numbers across all disciplines within the university. In many universities during this time, the demands of the military industrial complex drove the research agenda.

In addition, we are now at the beginning of the end of a generation of architects who have strategically and assertively promoted theory and work through self-publication for almost half a century.[26] While this essay does not intend to denigrate the valuable service of communicating disciplinary knowledge performed by these author/designers, it is worthwhile to note that the entire process occurred at the margins of the academic system and without a formal peer-review process. This semi-private enterprise stands in contrast to most disciplines that operate within the context of the academy.

The retirement of baby boomers who were educated to trust technology, taught using curricular models that disperse and categorize knowledge rather than integrate it, and valued objectivity over empathy leaves a substantial gap in our disciplinary matrix. This gap is perhaps amplified by the relative lack of widely disseminated, peer-validated knowledge. Taken together, this seems a classic description of a fading paradigm.

Second, Kuhn suggests that an irreconcilable paradox between evidence and beliefs emerges within a discipline. As each day's news reports, evidence of environmental change on a planetary scale is mounting. The planet is demonstrating that our behaviors are unsustainable. Because architects participate in many of the decisions that are causing exponential planetary damage, it would seem that we have no choice but to reconsider what we build and what and how we teach, along with how we live. This powerful external

26 Such self publication, in the most positive sense of the term, would include Five Architects, featuring the work of the so-called New York Five (Peter Eisenman, Michael Graves, Charles Gwathmey, John Hejduk, and Richard Meier) by Arthur Drexler; Complexity and Contradiction in Architecture, by Robert Venturi; Oppositions, published from 1973 to 1984; Assemblage, published from 1986 to 2000; Deconstruction in Architecture, published by the Museum of Modern Art, co-curated and co-authored by Philip Johnson and Mark Wigley in 1987 and ANY (Architecture New York), published from 1993 to 2000. Indeed Philip Johnson's first effort to serve as a disciplinary validator was the very persuasive The International Style, published and co-curated by Johnson and Henry Russell Hitchcock in 1932.

trigger, combined with a generational changing of the guard, suggest that we have arrived at a fertile moment in the reconstruction of architecture's disciplinary matrix.

EXISTING AND EMERGING DISCIPLINARY STRUCTURES

It is necessary to briefly inventory our discipline's structures—the community-wide cultural forms that hold our discipline's knowledge. These structures, no less than the knowledge they contain, reflect certain values and unacknowledged habits of behavior.

The academy, the colleges and universities that teach architecture throughout North America, operate in two primary modes: teaching and research. The first is the delivery of education. Through the development of curriculum and the teaching of individual courses, faculty members distribute known information and ways of thinking to students. The world of academic architecture is neatly divided into "studios" and "support courses," each taught for prescribed numbers of credit hours and contact hours, typically in a sequence leading toward an increasingly complex understanding of the design and construction of a building. The subject matter is gathered into categories reminiscent of Beaux Arts curricula developed a century or more ago.[27] These categories have been further homogenized over the past half-century, in part due to the increasing influence of national accrediting standards.[28] Scale dependent subsets of what was historically known as architecture, such as landscape architecture, urban design, interior design, are often taught as separate disciplines.

Emerging trends in schools of architecture call into question the disciplinary segregation that has developed in recent decades. For example, community design programs, an outgrowth of the social activism of the 1960s, have found new life by providing visions for rapidly growing communities as a counterpoint to the private developers who often times promote their own large-scale planning initiatives. Community design often bridges architecture, landscape architecture and urban planning and design. Design-build programs, created in response to students' desire to see their designs realized, their anxieties about the building process, and their ambitions to help the larger world attain better living standards, are flowering within many schools of architecture. These programs confound institutional structures such as the semester system and stretch legal and professional roles within the academy. They also invert the traditional hierarchy of head over hands, by requiring physical and mechanical intelligence along with design skill and academic knowledge. Finally, many programs are finding that disciplinary categories developed in the past century are cumbersome and institutionally expensive. Thus a number of special programs, such as historic preservation or sustainability are found to span scale-based disciplines while other programs, such as architecture and landscape architecture, merge. The specialists hired to teach particular courses are finding themselves placed in new

27 Felipe J. Préstamo, "Architectural Education in Postindustrial America: An Application of the Tyler Model to the Development of a Curriculum Framework." Unpublished thesis, University of Florida, 1990, 57. The five main courses shared by early twentieth century American architectural curricula: 1) drawing, 2) graphics, 3) construction, including basic science prerequisites, 4) applied construction, such as materials and specifications and 5) history of architecture.

28 Michael A. Bunch, Core Curriculum in Architectural Education (San Francisco, Calif.: Mellen Research University Press, 1993).

combinations to pursue integrated multidisciplinary design issues of interest to students and the public.

Research is the generic term for the second mode in which the academy operates. Produced through peer-assessed writing, theoretical and built design projects and funded investigations, research allows faculty members to develop and disseminate new knowledge to other members of the architectural profession and to the public. Here, too, architects are increasingly working as part of collaborative teams on projects that cross disciplinary boundaries. Today architects design and write about landscapes while landscape architects design structures. Subject matter crosses more than just disciplines within environmental design, as professors of architecture work with environmental engineers, political scientists, cultural theorists or health care practitioners. While such interdisciplinary work is not new, it is again newly popular.

Within the architectural profession, traditions that have been stable for half a century are being questioned by a new generation of practitioners. Entrepreneurial practices are supplementing the client-initiated professional model. While many architects still wait for clients to contact them, court clients with the help of public-relations professionals, or respond to invitations to submit credentials, others are increasingly becoming developers, contractors, website designers or manufacturers. With the help of digital technology, architectural design can be practiced by partners working across the country, or by firms working around the clock and around the globe. A new generation of architects is designing everything from furniture to towns. Perhaps the most extreme case of scale swing is the work of graphic designer Bruce Mau, whose firm's designs range in scale from books to countries.[29] And, as suggested by the work of Mau, designers not trained as architects and individuals trained as architects but not acting in a professional capacity or with the advantage of licensure, are increasingly participating in the design of the built environment.

The turbulence described above—in changing academic subdisciplines, in the rearrangement of professional relationships and strategies for advancement, and in the incursion of non-licensed professionals into the heart of architectural practice—all suggest opportunities for a reformulated disciplinary matrix. How does the ethic and knowledge known as sustainability work in this changing context?

Currently, some schools of architecture and some established offices see sustainability as a set of technical parameters to be applied to design projects, like paint to an already built wall. We believe a far more substantial realignment, described above as a paradigm shift, is necessary. This will require that the discipline of architecture, in its academic and professional roles, move beyond a focus on ecology and energy conservation, important though they are. Instead, we should recognize that sustainability is being taught by more than just one or two faculty members per school and valued by more than

29 See Bruce Mau with Jennifer Leonard and the Institute without Boundaries, Massive Change (New York: Phaidon, 2004).

one or two practitioners with a technical bent in each office. The values and expertise of these academics and professionals is typically disconnected from a shared vision of sustainability. This broad vision is one we hope to frame through the essays within this volume.

TWO COMMON THEMES

While the proponents of sustainability currently teaching, learning and practicing come from diverse specializations—from environmental technology to architectural theory to construction methods to design—they share several common traits.

First, they understand and cultivate relationships between the "parts" such as teaching areas, disciplines, or the boxes within their institutions' organizational charts. They are comfortable with fuzzy boundaries. They establish flexible relations between self/other. They have empathy with others and therefore are committed to social justice. They have respect for our planet's ecosystems and recognize that we cannot "beat" the natural world.

Second, they engage in time-based thinking. Rather than viewing architecture as an unchanging object they conceive of architecture as the physical part of a fabric intended to change over the course of a twenty-four hour day, through changes in season, and across human history and the over the course of the lifespan of planet.

FROM RE-SEARCH TO FEED-BACK

The paradigm of networked knowing, which has emerged in physics, ecology, and literary theory, among many other disciplines, prioritizes lateral linkages over vertical chains of command. Such linkages allow nonhierarchical networks-within-networks to flourish by complimenting deficits with strengths. Like an ecosystem, this paradigm relies on redundancy. Its organization is organic and flexible, responding to challenges quickly.

A critical feature of flexible and quick response to systemic challenges is the concept of feedback. Here, too, architecture can adapt from disciplines such as physics, literary theory, and ecology and incorporate immediate learning into our production of knowledge. Currently, the results of architectural production sometimes remain unknown or underappreciated by architectural producers. Most pertinent to our subject are examples of built design projects that are not sustainable, particularly using the criteria of ecology, economy, and equity. Our discipline's evaluative methods tend to value the persuasiveness of form, and even of heroic personalities, at the expense of important feedback regarding weathering, community acceptance, budgetary limitations, and numerous other less imageable issues.

While too many designers ignore feedback that conflicts with imageable fascinations as described above, others await research that is too slow in coming or is viewed as proprietary—that is owned knowledge rather than shared knowledge. Particularly in recent decades architects have avoided consideration of diminishing natural resources, planetary change, and social inequities because of the appearance of abundance, particularly in the United States. At the same time, the feedback to architects traditionally provided by craftsmen and draftsman has been significantly reduced by changed construction practices, outsourcing, and other aspects of globalization.

This book hopes to join the growing chorus of architectural echoes, returning good information back to the producers of architectural knowledge, whether in built, drawn, or written form. The diversity of authors, designers, and projects included reflects the vast network of academics working within the field now known as sustainability. Through variety and overlap, it seeks to builds redundancy into a disciplinary system too often conceived as univocal. It seeks to reinforce an astylistic cross section of our discipline doing excellent and ethical architecture. It seeks to capture Heisenberg's "complicated tissue of events, in which connections of different kinds alternate or overlap or combine and thereby determine the texture of the whole."[30]

30 *See Note 12.*

ARCHITECTURE, ECOLOGICAL DESIGN, AND HUMAN ECOLOGY

DAVID ORR

We shape our buildings, thereafter they shape us.

Winston Churchill

From the thirty-fifth floor of a downtown office tower that dominates the new Atlanta skyline, one can see two problems that all architects of high-rise buildings face. The question is how to bring the thing to an end gracefully before gravity and money do so. Some architects just quit, hence the flat roof. But most embellish the finale in various ways with one kind of flourish or another, each somewhat more outlandish than the one built the year before. The result, what some call "an interesting skyline," is a kind of fever chart of the collected psyches of architects and their clients that shape the modern megalopolis. The results, however, are more than just show. These are the buildings that contribute greatly to traffic congestion, poverty, climatic change, pollution, biotic impoverishment, and land degradation. If less visually dramatic, the same could be said of the designers of the modern suburb and shopping mall. In both cases the problem is that the art and science of architecture and related applied disciplines has been whittled down by narrow gauge thinking.

The importance of regarding architecture in a larger context lies in the big numbers of our time. We have good reason to believe that humankind will build more buildings in the next fifty years than in the past 5,000. Done by prevailing design standards, we will cast a long shadow on the prospects of all subsequent generations. No longer can we substitute cheap fossil energy for design intelligence or good judgment. The implications for the education of architects and the design professions generally are striking. Let me propose three.

First, the esthetic standards for design will have to be broadened to embrace wider impacts. Designers ought to aim to cause no ugliness, human or ecological, somewhere else or at some later time. For education, this means that the architectural curriculum must include ethics, ecology, and tools having to do with whole systems analysis, and least-cost, end-use considerations. Further, educational standards need to include a more sophisticated and ecologically grounded understanding of place and culture.

Second, it should be recognized that architecture and design are fundamentally pedagogical. Churchill had it right: we are shaped by our buildings and landscapes in powerful but subtle ways. The education of all design professions ought to begin in the recognition that architecture and landscapes are a kind of crystallized pedagogy that informs well or badly, but never fails to inform. Design inevitably instructs us about our relationships to nature and people that makes us more or less mindful and more or less ecologically competent. The ultimate object of design is not artifacts, buildings, or landscapes, but human minds.

Third, architecture and design ought to be seen in their largest context that has to do with health. At the most obvious level 'sick buildings' reflect not simply bad design but a truncated concept of design. A larger design perspective would place architecture and landscape architecture as subfields of the art and science of health with more than passing affinity for healing and the holy.

Architecture is commonly taught and practiced as if it were only the art and science of designing buildings, which is to say merely as a technical subject at the mercy of the whims of clients. I would like to offer a contrary view that architecture ought to be placed into a larger context as a subfield of ecological design. The essay that follows might best be considered as a series of notes on the boundaries of this larger field of design. Earlier forays into this area by van der Ryan and Cowan laid the groundwork for a more expansive view of the design professions.[1] I intend to build on that foundation to connect design professions, and the education of designers to the larger issues of human ecology.

THE PROBLEM OF HUMAN ECOLOGY

Whatever their particular causes,[2] environmental problems all share one fundamental trait: with rare exceptions they are unintended, unforeseen, and sometimes ironic, side effects of actions arising from other intentions. We intend one thing and sooner or later get something very different. We intended merely to be prosperous and healthy but have inadvertently triggered a mass extinction of other species, spread pollution throughout the world, and triggered climatic change—all of which undermines our prosperity and health. Environmental problems, then, are mostly the result of a miscalibration between human intentions and ecological results, which is to say they are a species of design failure.

The possibility that ecological problems are design failures is perhaps bad news because it may signal inherent flaws in our perceptual and mental abilities. On the other hand, it may be good news. If our problems are, to a great extent, the result of design failures the obvious solution is better design, by which I mean a closer fit between human intentions and the ecological systems where the results of our intentions are ultimately played out.

The perennial problem of human ecology is how different cultures provision themselves with food, shelter, energy, and the means of livelihood by extracting energy and materials from their surroundings.[3] Ecological design describes the ensemble of technologies and strategies by which societies use the natural world to construct culture and meet their needs. Since the natural world is continually modified by human actions, culture and ecology

1 *van der Ryan and Cowan,* Ecological Design.

2 *Our ecological troubles have been variously attributed to Judeo-Christian religion (Lynn White), our inability to manage common property resources such as ocean fisheries (Garrett Hardin), lack of character (Wendell Berry), gender imbalance (Carolyn Merchant), technology run amuck (Lewis Mumford), disenchantment (Morris Berman), the loss of sensual connection to nature (David Abram), exponential growth (Donella Meadows), and flaws in the economic system (Herman Daly).*

3 *Smil,* Energy in World History.

are shifting parts of an equation that can never be solved. Nor can there be one correct design strategy. Hunter-gatherers lived on current solar income. Feudal barons extracted wealth from sunlight by exploiting serfs who farmed the land. We provision ourselves by mining ancient sunlight stored as fossil fuels. The choice is not whether human societies have a design strategy or not, but whether it works ecologically or not and can be sustained within the regenerative capacity of the ecosystem. The problem of ecological design has become more difficult as the human population has grown and technology has multiplied. It is now the overriding problem of our time affecting virtually all other issues on the human agenda. How and how intelligently we weave the human presence into the natural world will reduce or intensify other problems having to do with ethnic conflicts, economics, hunger, political stability, health, and human happiness.

At the most basic level, humans need 2,200 to 3,000 calories per day, depending on body size and activity level. Early hunter-gatherers used little more energy than they required for food. The invention of agriculture increased the efficiency with which we captured sunlight permitting the growth of cities.[4] Despite their differences, both showed little ecological foresight. Hunter-gatherers drove many species to extinction and early farmers left behind a legacy of deforestation, soil erosion, and land degradation. In other words, we have always modified our environments to one degree or another, but the level of ecological damage has increased with the level of civilization and with the scale and kind of technology.

The average citizen of the United States now uses some 186,000 calories of energy each day, most of it derived from oil and coal.[5] Our food and materials come to us via a system that spans the world and whose consequences are mostly concealed from us. The average food molecule is said to have traveled over 1,300 miles from where it was grown or produced to where it is eaten.[6] In such a system, there is no way we can know the human or ecological consequences of eating. Nor can we know the full cost of virtually anything that we purchase or discard. We do know, however, that the level of environmental destruction has risen with the volume of stuff consumed and with the distance it is transported. By one count we waste more than 1 million pounds of materials per person per year. For every 100 pounds of product, we create 3,200 pounds of waste.[7] Measured as an "ecological footprint," i.e., the land required to grow our food, process our organic wastes, sequester our carbon dioxide, and provide our material needs, the average North American, by one estimate, requires some 5 hectares of arable land per person per year.[8] But at the current population level the world has only 1.3 hectares of usable land per person. Extending our lifestyle to everyone would require the equivalent of two additional Earths!

Looking ahead, we face an imminent collision between a growing population with rising material expectations and ecological capacity. At some time in the next century, given present trends, the human population will reach or

4 *Smil*, General Energetics *and* Energy in World History.

5 *McKibben*, "A Special Moment in History."

6 *Meadows*, "The Global Citizen."

7 *Hawken*, "Natural Capitalism," 44.

8 *Wackernagel and Rees*, Our Ecological Footprint.

exceed 10 billion, perhaps as many as 15–20 percent of the species on earth will have disappeared forever, and the effects of climatic change will have become manifest. This much and more is virtually certain. The immediate problem is simply that of feeding, housing, clothing, and educating another 4–6 billion people and providing employment for an additional 2 to 4 billion without wrecking the planet in the process. Given our inability to meet basic needs of one-third of the present population there are good reasons to doubt that we will be able to do better with the far larger population now in prospect.

THE DEFAULT SETTING

The regnant faith, however, holds that science and technology will find a way to do so without our having to make significant changes in our philosophies, politics, economics, or in the directions of the growth-oriented society. Rockefeller University professor, Jessie Ausubel, for example, asserts that:

after a very long preparation, our science and technology are ready also to reconcile our economy and environment . . . In fact, long before environmental policy became conscious of itself, the system had set decarbonization in motion. A highly efficient hydrogen economy, landless agriculture, industrial ecosystems in which waste virtually disappears: over the coming century these can enable large, prosperous human populations to co-exist with the whales and the lions and the eagles and all that underlie them.[9]

9 Ausubel, "Liberation of the Environment," 15.

We have, Ausubel states, "liberated ourselves from the environment." This view is similar to that of futurist Herman Kahn several decades ago when he asserted that by the year 2200 "humans would everywhere be rich, numerous, and in control of the forces of nature."[10] In its more recent version, those believing that we have liberated ourselves from the environment cite advances in energy use, materials science, genetic engineering, and artificial intelligence that will enable us to do much more with far less and eventually transcend ecological limits altogether. Humanity will then take control of its own fate, or more accurately as C. S. Lewis once observed, some few humans will do so, purportedly acting on behalf of all humanity.[11]

10 Kahn and Martel, Next Two Hundred Years.

Ausubel's optimism coincides with the widely held view that we ought to simply take over the task of managing the planet.[12] In fact the technological and scientific capability is widely believed to be emerging in the technologies of remote sensing, geographic information systems, computers, the science of ecology (in its managerial version), and systems engineering. For one thing the word "management" does not quite capture what the essence of the thing being proposed. We can manage, say, a 747 because we made it. Presumably, we know what it can and cannot do even though they sometimes crash for reasons that elude us. Our knowledge of the Earth is in no way comparable.

11 Lewis, Abolition of Man, 67–91.

12 Scientific American, 1989.

We did not make it, we have no blueprint of it, and we will never know fully how it works. Second, the target of management is not quite what it appears to be since a good bit of what passes for managing the Earth is in fact managing human behavior. Third, under the guise of objective neutrality and under the pretext of emergency, management of the Earth is ultimately an extension of the effort to dominate people through the domination of nature. And can we trust those presuming to manage to do so with fairness, wisdom, foresight, and humility and for how long?

Another, and more modest, possibility is to restrict our access to nature rather like a fussy mother in bygone days keeping unruly children out of the formal parlor. To this end Professor Martin Lewis proposes what he calls a "Promethean environmentalism" that aims to protect nature by keeping us away from as much of it as possible.[13] His purpose is to substitute advanced technology for nature. This requires the development of far more advanced technologies, more unfettered capitalism, and probably some kind of high-tech virtual simulation to meet whatever residual needs for nature that we might retain in this Brave New World. Professor Lewis dismisses the possibility that we could become stewards, ecologically competent, or even just a bit more humble. Accordingly, he disparages those whom he labels "eco-radicals" including Aldo Leopold, Herman Daly, and E. F. Schumacher who question the role of capitalism in environmental destruction, raise issues about appropriate scale, and disagree with the directions of technological evolution. Lewis's proposal to protect nature by removing humankind from it, however, raises other questions. Will people cut off from nature be sane? Will people who no longer believe that they need nature be willing, nonetheless, to protect it? If so, will people no longer in contact with nature know how to do so? And was it not our efforts to cut ourselves off from nature that got us into trouble in the first place? On such matters Professor Lewis is silent.

Despite the pervasive optimism about our technological possibilities, there is a venerable tradition of unease about the consequences of unconstrained technological development from Mary Shelley's *Frankenstein* to Lewis Mumford's critique of the "megamachine." But the technological juggernaut that has brought us to our present situation, nonetheless, remains on track. We have now arrived, in Edward O. Wilson's view, at a choice between two very different paths of human evolution. One choice would aim to preserve "the physical and biotic environment that cradled the human species" along with those traits that make us distinctively human. The other path, based on the belief that we are now exempt from the "iron laws of ecology that bind other species," would take us in radically different directions, as "*Homo proteus* or 'shapechanger man'".[14] But how much of the earth can we safely alter? How much of our own genetic inheritance should we manipulate before we are no longer recognizably human? This second path, in Wilson's view, would "render everything fragile."[15] And, in time, fragile things break apart.

13 *Lewis*, Green Delusions.

14 *Wilson*, Consilience, 278.

15 *Ibid.*

The sociologist and theologian, Jacques Ellul, is even more pessimistic. "Our machines," he writes, "have truly replaced us." We have no philosophy of technology, in his view, because "philosophy implies limits and definitions and defined areas that technique will not allow."[16] Consequently, we seldom ask where all of this is going, or why, or who really benefits. The "unicity of the [technological] system," Ellul believes, "may be the cause of its fragility."[17] We are "shut up, blocked, and chained by the inevitability of the technical system," at least until the self-contradictions of the "technological bluff," like massive geologic fault lines, give way and the system dissolves in "enormous global disorder." At that point he thinks that we will finally understand that "everything depends on the qualities of individuals."[18]

The dynamic is, by now, familiar. Technology begets more technology, technological systems, technology-driven politics, technology-dependent economies, and finally, people who can neither function nor think a hair's breadth beyond the limits of one machine or another. This, in Neil Postman's view, is the underlying pattern of Western history as we moved from simple tools, to technocracy, to "technopoly." In the first stage, tools were useful to solve specific problems but did not undermine "the dignity and integrity of the culture into which they were introduced."[19] In a technocracy like England in the eighteenth and nineteenth centuries factories undermined "tradition, social mores, myth, ritual and religion." The third stage, technopoly, however, "eliminates alternatives to itself in precisely the way Aldous Huxley outlined in *Brave New World*." It does so "by redefining what we mean by religion, by art, by family, by politics, by history, by truth, by privacy, by intelligence, so that our definitions fit its new requirements."[20] Technopoly represents, in Postman's view, the cultural equivalent of AIDS, which is to say a culture with no defense whatsoever against technology or the claims of expertise.[21] It flourishes when the "tie between information and human purpose has been severed."

The course that Professor Ausubel and others propose fits into this larger pattern of technopoly that step by step is shifting human evolution in radically different directions. Professor Ausubel does not discuss the risks and unforeseen consequences that accompany unfettered technological change. These, he apparently believes, are justifiable as unavoidable costs of progress. This is precisely the kind of thinking which has undermined our capacity to refuse technologies that add nothing to our quality of life. A system which produces automobiles and atom bombs will also go on to make super computers, smart weapons, genetically altered crops, nano technologies, and eventually machines smart enough to displace their creators. There is no obvious stopping point, which is to say that having accepted the initial premises of technopoly the powers of control and good judgment are eroded away in the blizzard of possibilities.

Advertised as the essence of rationality and control, the technological system has become the epitome of irrationality in which means overrule

16 *Ellul*, Technological Bluff, 216.

17 *Ellul*, Technological System, 164.

18 *Ellul*, Technological Bluff, 412.

19 *Postman*, Technopoly, 23.

20 *Ibid.*, 48.

21 *Ibid.*, 63.

careful consideration of ends. A rising tide of unanticipated consequences and "normal accidents" mock the idea that experts are in control or that technologies do only what they are intended to do. The purported rationality of each particular component in what E. O. Wilson calls a "thickening web of prosthetic devices" added together as a system lacks both rationality and coherence. Nor is there anything inherently human or even rational about words such as "efficiency," "productivity," or "management," that are used to justify technological change. Rationality of this narrow sort has been "as successful—if not more successful—at creating new degrees of barbarism and violence as it has been at imposing reasonable actions."[22] Originating with Descartes and Galileo, the foundations of the modern worldview were flawed from the beginning. In time, those seemingly small and trivial errors of perception, logic, and heart cascaded into a rising tide of cultural incoherence, barbarism, and ecological degradation that have now engulfed the Earth. Professor Ausubel's optimism, notwithstanding, this tide will continue to rise until it has finally drowned every descent possibility that might have been unless we choose a more discerning course.

22 *Saul*, Voltaire's Bastards, *32.*

ECOLOGICAL DESIGN

The unfolding problems of human ecology, in other words, are not solvable by repeating old mistakes in new and more sophisticated and powerful ways. We need a deeper change of the kind Albert Einstein had in mind when he said that the same manner of thought that created problems could not solve them. We need what architect, Sim can der Ryn, and mathematician, Steward Cowan, define as an ecological design revolution. Ecological design in their words is "any form of design that minimize(s) environmentally destructive impacts by integrating itself with living processes . . . the effective adaptation to and integration with nature's processes."[23] For landscape architect Carol Franklin, ecological design is a "fundamental revision of thinking and operation."[24] Good design does not begin with what we can do, but rather with questions about what we really want to do.[25] Ecological design, in other words, is the careful meshing of human purposes with the larger patterns and flows of the natural world and the study of those patterns and flows to inform human actions.[26]

23 *van der Ryn and Cowan,* Ecological Design, *x, 18.*

24 *Franklin, "Fostering Living Landscapes," 264.*

25 *Wann,* Deep Design, *22.*

26 *Orr,* Earth in Mind, *104.*

Amory Lovins, Hunter Lovins, and Paul Hawkens, to this end propose a transformation in energy and resource efficiency that would dramatically increase wealth while using a fraction of the resources we currently use.[27] Transformation would not occur, however, simply as an extrapolation of existing technological trends. They propose, instead, a deeper revolution in our thinking about the uses of technology so that we don't end up with "extremely efficient factories making napalm and throwaway beer cans."[28] In contrast to Ausubel, the authors of *Natural Capitalism* propose a closer calibration between means and ends. Such a world would improve energy and resource efficiency by, perhaps, tenfold. It would be powered by highly

27 *Hawken,* Natural Capitalism, *1999.*

28 *Benyus,* Biomimicry, *262.*

efficient small-scale renewable energy technologies distributed close to the point of end use. It would protect natural capital in the form of soils, forests, grasslands, oceanic fisheries, and biota while preserving biological diversity. Pollution, in any form, would be curtailed and eventually eliminated by industries designed to discharge no waste. The economy of that world would be calibrated to fit ecological realities. Taxes would be levied on things we do not want such as pollution and removed from things such as income and employment that we do want. These changes signal a revolution in design that draws on fields as diverse as ecology, systems dynamics, energetics, sustainable agriculture, industrial ecology, architecture, and landscape architecture.[29]

The challenge of ecological design is more than simply an engineering problem of improving efficiency, reducing the rates at which we poison ourselves and damage the world. The revolution that van der Ryn and Cowan propose must first reduce the rate at which things get worse (coefficients of change) but eventually change the structure of the larger system. As Bill McDonough and Michael Braungart argue, we will need a "second industrial revolution" that eliminates the very concept of waste.[30] This implies, in their words, putting "filters on our minds, not at the end of pipes." In practice, the change McDonough proposes implies, among other things, changing manufacturing systems to eliminate the use of toxic and cancer causing materials and the development of closed loop systems that deliver "products of service" not products that are eventually discarded to air, water, and land fills.

The pioneers in ecological design begin with the observation that nature has been developing successful strategies for living on Earth for 3.8 billion years and is, accordingly, a model for:

- farms that work like forests and prairies
- buildings that accrue natural capital like trees
- waste water systems that work like natural wetlands
- materials that mimic the ingenuity of plants and animals
- industries that work more like ecosystems
- products that become part of cycles resembling natural materials flows.

Wes Jackson, for example, is attempting to redesign agriculture in the Great Plains to mimic the prairie that once existed there.[31] Paul Hawken proposes to remake commerce in the image of natural systems.[32] The new field of industrial ecology is similarly attempting to redesign manufacturing to reflect the way ecosystems work. The new field of "biomimicry" is beginning to transform industrial chemistry, medicine, and communications. Common spiders, for example, make silk that is ounce for ounce five times stronger than steel with no waste byproducts. The inner shell of an abalone is far tougher than our best ceramics.[33] By such standards, human industry is remarkably clumsy, inefficient, and destructive. Running through each of these is the belief that the successful design strategies, tested over the course of evolution, provide

29 The roots of ecological design can be traced back to the work of Scottish biologist, D'Arcy Thompson and his magisterial On Growth and Form first published in 1917. In contrast to Darwin's evolutionary biology, Thompson traced the evolution of life forms back to the problems elementary physical forces such as gravity pose for individual species. His legacy is an evolving science of forms evident in evolutionary biology, biomechanics, and architecture. Ecological design is evident in the work of Bill Browning, Herman Daly, Paul Hawken, Wes Jackson, Aldo Leopold, Amory and Hunter Lovins, John Lyle, Bill McDonough, Donella Meadows, Eugene Odum, Sim van der Ryn, and David Wann.

30 McDonough and Braungart, "The Next Industrial Revolution."

31 Jackson, New Roots for Agriculture.

32 Hawken, Ecology of Commerce, 1993.

33 Benyus, Biomimicry, 97.

the standard to inform the design of commerce and the large systems that supply us with food, energy, water, and materials, and remove our wastes.[34]

34 *Ibid.*, 73.

The greatest impediment to an ecological design revolution is not, however, technological or scientific, but rather human. If intention is the first signal of design, as Bill McDonough puts it, we must reckon with the fact that human intentions have been warped in recent history by violence and the systematic cultivation of greed, self-preoccupation, and mass consumerism. A real design revolution will have to transform human intentions and that larger political, economic, and institutional structure that permitted ecological degradation in the first place. A second impediment to an ecological design revolution is simply the scale of change required in the next few decades. All nations, but starting with the most wealthy, will have to:

- improve energy efficiency by a factor of five to ten
- rapidly develop renewable sources of energy
- reduce the amount of materials per unit of output by a factor of five to ten
- preserve biological diversity now being lost everywhere
- restore degraded ecosystems
- redesign transportation systems and urban areas
- institute sustainable practices of agriculture and forestry
- reduce population growth and eventually total population levels
- redistribute resources fairly within and between generations
- develop more accurate indicators of prosperity, well-being, health, and security.

We have good reason to think that all of these must be well underway within the next few decades. Given the scale and extent of the changes required, this is a transition for which there is no historical precedent. The century ahead will test, not just our ingenuity, but our foresight, wisdom, and sense of humanity as well.

The success of ecological design will depend on our ability to cultivate a deeper sense of connection and obligation without which few people will be willing to make even obvious and rational changes in time to make much difference. We will have to reckon with the power of denial, both individual and collective, to block change. We must reckon with the fact that we will never be intelligent enough to understand the full consequences of our actions, some of which will be paradoxical and some evil. We must learn how to avoid creating problems for which there is no good solution, technological or otherwise, such as the creation of long-lived wastes, the loss of species, or toxic waste flowing from tens of thousands of mines.[35] In short, a real design revolution must aim to foster a deeper transformation in human intentions and the political and economic institutions that turn intentions into ecological results. There is no clever shortcut, no end-run around natural constraints, no magic bullet, and no cheap grace.

35 *Hunter,* Simple Things Won't Save the Earth; *Dobb, "Pennies from Hell."*

THE INTENTION TO DESIGN

Designing a civilization that can be sustained ecologically and one that sustains the best in the human spirit will require us, then, to confront the wellsprings of intention, which is to say, human nature. Our intentions are the product of many things at least four of which have implications for our ecological prospects. First, with the certain awareness of our mortality, we are inescapably religious creatures. The religious impulse in us works like water flowing up from an artesian spring that will come to the surface in one place or another. Our choice is not whether we are religious or not as atheists would have it, but whether the object of our worship is authentic or not. The gravity mass of our nature tugs us to create or discover systems of meaning that places the human condition in some larger framework that explains, consoles, offers grounds for hope, and, sometimes, rationalizes. In our age, nationalism, capitalism, communism, fascism, consumerism, cyberism, and even ecologism have become substitutes for genuine religion. But whatever the -ism or the belief, in one way or another we will create or discover systems of thought and behavior which give us a sense of meaning and belonging to some larger scheme of things. Moreover, there is good evidence to support the claim that successful resource management requires, in E. N. Anderson's words, a "direct, emotional religiously 'socialized' tie to the resources in question."[36] Paradoxically, however, societies with much less scientific information than we have often make better environmental choices. Myth and religious beliefs, which we regard as erroneous, have sometimes worked better to preserve environments than have decisions based on scientific information administered by presumably "rational" bureaucrats.[37] The implication is the solutions to environmental problems must be designed to resonate at deep emotional levels and be ecologically sound.

Second, despite all of our puffed-up self-advertising as *Homo sapiens*, the fact is that we are limited as clever creatures. Accordingly, we need a more sober view of our possibilities. Real wisdom is rare and rarer still if measured ecologically. Seldom do we foresee the ecological consequences of our actions. We have great difficulty understanding what Jay Forrester once called the "counterintuitive behavior of social systems".[38] We are prone to overdo what worked in the past, with the result that many of our current problems stem from past success carried to an extreme. Enjoined to "be fruitful and multiply," we did as commanded. But at 6 billion and counting, it seems that we lack the gene for enough. We are prone to overestimate our abilities to get out of self-generated messes. We are, as someone put it, continually overrunning our headlights. Human history is in large measure a sorry catalog of war and malfeasance of one kind or another. Stupidity is probably as great a factor in human affairs as intelligence. All of which is to say that a more sober reading of human potentials suggests the need for a fail-safe approach to ecological design that does not overtax our collective intelligence, foresight, and goodness.

36 *E. N. Anderson,* Ecologies of the Hearth, *169.*

37 *Lansing,* Priests and Programmers.

38 *J. Forrester, "Counter Intuitive Behavior Social Systems."*

Third, quite possibly we have certain dispositions toward the environment that have been hardwired in us over the course of our evolution. E. O. Wilson, for example, suggests that we possess what he calls "biophilia" meaning an innate "urge to affiliate with other forms of life."[39] Biophilia may be evident in our preference for certain landscapes such as savannas and in the fact that we heal more quickly in the presence of sunlight, trees, and flowers than in biologically sterile, artificially lit, utilitarian settings. Emotionally damaged children, unable to establish close and loving relationships with people, sometimes can be reached by carefully supervised contact with animals. And after several million years of evolution it would be surprising indeed were it otherwise. The affinity for life described by Wilson and others does not however imply nature romanticism, but rather something like a core element in our nature that connects us to the nature in which we evolved and which nurtures and sustains us. Biophilia certainly does not mean that we are all disposed to like nature or that it cannot be corrupted into biophobia. But without intending to do so, we are creating a world in which we do not fit. The growing evidence supporting the biophilia hypothesis suggests that we fit better in environments that have more, not less, nature. We do better with sunlight, contact with animals, and in settings that include trees, flowers, flowing water, birds, and natural processes than in their absence. We are sensuous creatures who develop emotional attachment to particular landscapes. The implication is that we need to create communities and places that resonate with our evolutionary past and for which we have deep affection.

39 *Wilson*, Biophilia, 85.

Fourth, for all of our considerable scientific advances, our knowledge of the Earth is still minute relative to what we will need to know. Where are we? The short answer is that despite all of our science, no one knows for certain. We inhabit the third planet out from a fifth-state star located in a backwater galaxy. We are the center of nothing that is very obvious to the eye of science. We do not know whether the Earth is just dead matter or whether it is, in some respects, alive. Nor do we know how forgiving the ecosphere may be to human insults. Our knowledge of the flora and fauna of the Earth and the ecological processes that link them together is small relative to all that might be known. In some areas, in fact, knowledge is in retreat because it is no longer fashionable or profitable. Our practical knowledge of particular places is often considerably less than that of the native peoples we displaced. As a result, the average college graduate would flunk even a cursory test on their local ecology, and stripped of technology most would quickly founder.

To complicate things further, the advance of human knowledge is inescapably ironic. Since the enlightenment, the goal of our science has been a more rational ordering of human affairs in which cause and effect could be empirically determined and presumably controlled. But after a century of promiscuous chemistry, for example, who can say how the 100,000 chemicals in common use mix in the ecosphere or how they might be implicated in declining sperm counts, or rising cancer rates, or disappearing amphibians, or behavioral disorders? And having disrupted global biogeochemical cycles, no one can say with assurance what the larger climatic and ecological effects will be. Undaunted by our ignorance, we rush ahead to re-engineer the fabric of life on Earth! Maybe science will figure it all out. But I think that it is more probable that we are encountering the outer limits of social-ecological complexity in which cause and effect are widely separated in space and time and in a growing number of cases no one can say with certainty what causes what. Like the sorcerer's apprentice, every answer generated by science gives rise to a dozen more questions, and every technological solution gives rise to a dozen more problems. Rapid technological change intended to rationalize human life tends to expand the domain of irrationality. At the end of the bloodiest century in history, the enlightenment faith in human rationality seems overstated at best. But the design implication is, not less rationality, but a more complete, humble, and ecologically solvent rationality that works over the long term.

Who are we? Conceived in the image of God? Perhaps. But for the time being the most that can be said with assurance is that, in an evolutionary perspective humans are a precocious and unruly newcomer with a highly uncertain future. Where are we? Wherever it is, it is a world full of irony and paradox, veiled in mystery. And for those purporting to reweave the human presence in the world in a manner that is ecologically sustainable and spiritually sustaining, the ancient idea that God (or the gods) mocks human intelligence should never be far from our minds.

ECOLOGICAL DESIGN PRINCIPLES

First, ecological design is not so much about how to make things as it is how to make things that fit gracefully over long periods of time in a particular ecological, social, and cultural context. Industrial societies, in contrast, operate in the conviction that "if brute force doesn't work you're not using enough of it." But when humans have designed with ecology in mind there is a greater harmony between intentions and the particular places in which those intentions are played out that:

- preserves diversity both cultural and biological
- utilizes current solar income
- creates little or no waste
- accounts for all costs
- respects larger cultural and social patterns.

Second, ecological design is not just a smarter way to do the same old things or a way to rationalize and sustain a rapacious, demoralizing, and unjust consumer culture. The problem is not how to produce ecologically benign products for a consumer economy, but how to make decent communities in which people grow to be responsible citizens and whole people who do not confuse what they have with who they are. The larger design challenge is to transform a society that promotes excess consumption and human incompetence, concentrates power in too few hands, and destroys both people and land. Ecological design ought to foster a revolution in our thinking that changes the kinds of questions we ask from "how can we do the same old things more efficiently" to deeper questions such as:

- Do we need it?
- Is it ethical?
- What impact does it have on the community?
- Is it safe to make and use?
- Is it fair?
- Can it be repaired or reused?
- What is the full cost over its expected lifetime?
- Is there a better way to do it?

The quality of design, in other words, is measured by the elegance with which we join means and worthy ends. In Wendell Berry's felicitous phrase, good design "solves for pattern" thereby preserving the larger patterns of place and culture and sometimes this means doing nothing at all.[40] In the words of John Todd, the aim is "elegant solutions predicated on the uniqueness of place."[41] Ecological design, then is not simply a more efficient way to accommodate desires as it is the improvement of desire and all of those things that effect what we desire.

40 *Berry,* Gift of Good Land, *134–145.*

41 *The phrase is John Todd's, From Eco-Cities to Living Machines: Principles of Ecological Design.*

Third, ecological design is as much about politics and power as it about ecology. We have good reason to question the large-scale plans to remodel the planet that range from genetic engineers to the multinational timber companies. Should a few be permitted to redesign the fabric of life on the earth? Should others be permitted to design machines smarter than we are that might someday find us to be an annoyance and discard us? Who should decide how much of nature should be remodeled, for whose convenience, and by what standards? In an age when everything seems possible, where are the citizens or other members of biotic community who will be effected by the implementation of grandiose plans? The answer is that they are now excluded. At the heart of the issue of design, then, are procedural questions that have to do with politics, representation, and fairness.

Fourth, it follows that ecological design is not so much an individual art practiced by individual "designers" as it is an ongoing negotiation between a community and the ecology of particular places. Good design results in communities in which feedback between action and subsequent correction is rapid, people are held accountable for their actions, functional redundancy is high, and control is decentralized. In a well-designed community, people would know quickly what's happening and if they don't like it, they know who can be held accountable and can change it. Such things are possible only where: livelihood, food, fuel and recreation are, to a great extent, derived locally; when people have control over their own economies; and when the pathologies of large-scale administration are minimal. Moreover, being situated in a place for generations provides long memory of the place and hence of its ecological possibilities and limits. There is a kind of long-term learning process that grows from the intimate experience of a place over time.[42] Ecological design, then, is a large idea but is most applicable at a relatively modest scale. The reason is not that smallness or locality has any necessary virtue, but that human frailties limit what we are able to comprehend, foresee, as well as the scope and consistency of our affections. No amount of smartness or technology can dissolve any of these limits. The modern dilemma is that we find ourselves trapped between the growing cleverness of our science and technology and our seeming incapacity to act wisely.

Fifth, the standard for ecological design is neither efficiency nor productivity, but health, beginning with that of the soil and extending upward through plants, animals, and people. It is impossible to impair health at any level without affecting that at other levels. The etymology of the word "health" reveals its connection to other words such as healing, wholeness, and holy. Ecological design is an art by which we aim to restore and maintain the wholeness of the entire fabric of life increasingly fragmented by specialization, scientific reductionism, and bureaucratic division. We now have armies of specialists studying bits and pieces of the whole as if these were, in fact, separable. In reality, it is impossible to disconnect the threads that bind us into larger wholes up to that one great community of the ecosphere. The environment outside us is also inside us. We are connected to more things in more ways than we can ever count or comprehend. The act of designing ecologically begins with the awareness that we can never entirely fathom those connections and with the intent to faithfully honor that we cannot fully comprehend and control. This means that ecological design must be done cautiously, humbly, and reverently.

Sixth, ecological design is not reducible to a set of technical skills. It is anchored in the faith that the world is not random but purposeful and stitched together from top to bottom by a common set of rules. It is grounded in the belief that we are part of the larger order of things and that we have an ancient obligation to act harmoniously within those larger patterns. It grows from the awareness that we do not live by bread alone and that the effort to build a sustainable world must begin by designing one that first nourishes the human spirit. Design, at its best, is a sacred art reflecting the faith that, in the end, if we live faithfully and well, the world will not break our hearts.

Finally, the goal of ecological design is not a journey to some utopian destiny, but is rather more like a homecoming. Philosopher Suzanne Langer once described the problem in these words:

42   George Sturt once described this process in his native land as "The age-long effort of Englishmen to fit themselves close and ever closer into England" (The Wheelwright's Shop, 66).

Most people have no home that is a symbol of their childhood, not even a definite memory of one place to serve that purpose. Many no longer know the language that was once their mother-tongue. All old symbols are gone . . . the field of our unconscious symbolic orientation is suddenly plowed up by the tremendous changes in the external world and in the social order.[43]

43 *Langer,* Philosophy in a New Key, 292.

In other words, we are lost and must now find our way home again. For all of the technological accomplishments, the twentieth century was the most brutal and destructive era in our short history. In the century ahead we must chart a different course that leads to restoration, healing, and wholeness. Ecological design is a kind of navigation aid to help us find our bearings again. And getting home means remaking the human presence in the world in a way that honors ecology, evolution, human dignity, spirit, and the human need for roots and connection.

CONCLUSION

Ecological design, then, involves far more than the application of instrumental reason and advanced technology applied to the problems of shoehorning billions more of us into an Earth already bulging at the seams with people. Humankind, as Abraham Heschel once wrote, "will not perish for want of information; but only for want of appreciation . . . what we lack is not a will to believe but a will to wonder."[44] The ultimate object of ecological design is not the things we make but rather the human mind and specifically its capacity for wonder and appreciation.

44 *Heschel,* Man is Not Alone, 37.

The capacity of the mind for wonder, however, has been all but obliterated by the very means by which we are passively provisioned with food, energy, materials, shelter, health-care, entertainment, and by those that remove our voluminous wastes from sight and mind. There is hardly anything in these industrial systems that fosters mindfulness or ecological competence let alone a sense of wonder. To the contrary, these systems are designed to generate cash, which has itself become an object of wonder and reverence. It is widely supposed that formal education serves as some kind of antidote to this uniquely modern form of barbarism. But conventional education, at its best, merely dilutes the tidal wave of false and distracting information embedded in the infrastructure and processes of technopoly. However well intentioned, it cannot compete with the larger educational effects of highways, shopping malls, supermarkets, urban sprawl, factory farms, agribusiness, huge utilities, multinational corporations, and nonstop advertising that teaches dominance, power, speed, accumulation, and self-indulgent individualism. We may talk about how everything is ecologically connected, but the terrible simplifiers are working overtime to take it all apart.

If it is not to become simply a more efficient way to do the same old things, ecological design must become a kind of public pedagogy built into the structure of daily life. There is little sense only selling greener products to a consumer whose mind is still pre-ecological. Sooner or later that person will find environmentalism inconvenient, or incomprehensible, or too costly, and will opt out. The goal of ecological design is to calibrate human behavior with ecological realities while educating people about ecological possibilities and limits. We must begin to see our houses, buildings, farms, businesses, energy technologies, transportation, landscapes, and communities in much the same way that we regard classrooms. In fact, they instruct in more fundamental ways because they structure what we see, how we move, what we eat, our sense of time and space, how we relate to each other, our sense of security, and how we experience the particular places in which we live. Most important, by their scale and power they structure how we think, often limiting our ability to imagine better alternatives.

When we design ecologically, we are instructed continually by the fabric of everyday life—pedagogy informs infrastructure which in turn informs us. The growing of food on local farms and gardens, for example, becomes a source of nourishment for the body and instruction in soils, plants, animals, and cycles of growth and decay.[45] Renewable energy technologies become a source of energy as well as insight about the flows of energy in ecosystems. Ecologically designed communities become a way to teach about land use, landscapes, and human connections. Restoration of wildlife corridors and habitats instructs us in the ways of animals. In other words, ecological design becomes a way to expand our awareness of nature and our ecological competence.

Most importantly, when we design ecologically we break the addictive quality that permeates modern life. "We have," in the words of philosopher Bruce Wilshire, "encase(d) ourselves in controlled environments called building and cities. Strapped into machines, we speed from place to place whenever desired, typically knowing any particular place and its regenerative rhythms and prospects only slightly." We have alienated ourselves from "nature that formed our needs over millions of years [which] means alienation within ourselves."[46] Given our inability to satisfy "our primal needs as organisms" we suffer what he calls a deprivation of ecstasy that stemmed from the 99 percent of our life as a species spent fully engaged with nature. Having cut ourselves off from the cycles of nature, we find ourselves strangers in an alien world of our own making. Our response has been to create distractions and addictive behaviors as junk food substitutes for the totality of body–spirit–mind nourishment we've lost and then to vigorously deny what we've done. Ecstasy deprivation, in other words, results in surrogate behaviors, mechanically repeated over and over again, otherwise known as addiction. This is a plausible, even brilliant, argument with the ring of truth to it.[47]

Ecological design, finally, is the art that reconnects us as sensuous creatures evolved over millions of years to a sensuous, living, and beautiful world. That

45 *Donahue,* Reclaiming the Commons.

46 *Wilshire,* Wild Hunger, *18.*

47 *See also David Abram's remarkable book* The Spell of the Sensuous *(New York: Pantheon, n.d.).*

world does not need to remade but rather revealed. To do that we do not need research as much as the rediscovery of old and forgotten things. We do not need more economic growth as much as we need to relearn the ancient lesson of generosity, which is to say that the gifts we have must move, that we can possess nothing. We are only trustees standing for only a moment between those who preceded us and those who will follow. Our greatest needs have nothing to do with possession of things but rather with heart, wisdom, thankfulness, and generosity of spirit. And these things are part of larger ecologies that embrace spirit, body, and mind—the beginning of design.

Design in its largest sense joins a variety of disciplines around the issue of how we provision 6 (soon to be 8–10 billion people) with food, energy, water, shelter, health care, and materials and do so sustainably and fairly on a planet with a biosphere. Design is not just about how we make things, but rather how we make things that fit harmoniously in an ecological, cultural, and moral context. It is therefore about systems, patterns, and connections. It is also a part of a long-term conversation between ecologists and designers of the built environment and technosphere, the essence of which is whether design becomes yet one more clever way to make end-runs around natural systems or is disciplined and informed by an understanding of nature. At its best, design is a field of applied ethics that joins perspectives and disciplines that otherwise remain disparate and often disjoined. Problems of environmental justice, for example, are unsolvable unless a morally robust design intelligence is applied to the design of food systems, energy use, materials flows, and waste cycling in ways that do not compromise standards of fairness and human dignity. Justice, in this perspective, is a design problem, but it is also a criterion for design and a result of good design. But design itself requires both robust ethics and mastery of design skills and analytical abilities.

REFERENCES

Abram, D. *The Spell of the Sensuous*, New York: Pantheon, 1996.

Alexander, C., et al. *A Pattern Language*, New York: Oxford University Press, 1977.

Anderson, E. N. *Ecologies of the Heart*, New York: Oxford University Press, 1996.

Ausubel, J. "Liberation of the Environment," *Daedalus* 125, 3 (1996): 1–18.

Benyuns, J. *Biomimicry*, New York: William Morrow, 1997.

Berman, M. *Coming to Our Senses*, New York: Simon & Schuster, 1989.

Berry, W. *The Unsettling of America*, San Francisco, Calif.: Sierra Club Books, 1977.

Berry, W. *The Gift of Good Land*, San Francisco, Calif.: North Point Press, 1981.

Clark, William C. "Managing Planet Earth," Special Issue, *Scientific American* 261 (September 1989): 46–54.

Daly, H. *Beyond Growth*, Boston, Mass.: Beacon Press, 1996.

Dobb, E. "Pennies from Hell," *Harpers*, October (1996): 39–54.

Donahue, B. *Reclaiming the Commons*, New Haven, Conn.: Yale University Press, 1999.

Ellul, J. *The Technological System*, New York: Continuum, 1980.

Ellul, J. *The Technological Bluff*, Grand Rapid, Mich.: Eerdmans, 1990.

Forrester, J. "Counter-Intuitive Behavior of Social Systems," *Technology Review*, January 1971: 53–68.

Franklin, C. "Fostering Living Landscapes," in *Ecological Design and Planning*, edited by G. Thompson and F. Steiner, New York: John Wiley & Sons, 1997.

Hardin, G. "The Tragedy of the Commons," *Science*, December 13 (1968): 8–13.

Hawken, P. *The Ecology of Commerce*, New York: HarperCollins, 1993.

Hawken, P. "Natural Capitalism," *Mother Jones*, April (1977): 40–53.

Hawken, P., H. Lovins, and A. Lovins. *Natural Capitalism*, Boston, Mass.: Little Brown, 1999.

Heschel, A. J. *Man is Not Alone: A Philosophy of Religion*, New York: Farrar, Straus, & Giroux, 1990.

Hunter, J. Robert *Simple Things Won't Save the Earth*, Austin, Tex.: University of Texas Press, 1997.

Jackson, W. *New Roots for Agriculture*, Lincoln, Nebr.: University of Nebraska Press, 1985.

Kahn H. and Brown, W. *The Next Two Hundred Years*, New York: William Morrow, 1976.

Kellert, S., and E. O. Wilson *The Biophilia Hypothesis*, Washington, D.C.: Island Press, 1993.

Langer, S. *Philosophy in a New Key*, Cambridge, Mass.: Harvard University Press, 1976.

Lansing, S. *Priests and Programmers*, Princeton, N.J.: Princeton University Press, 1991.

Lewis, C. S. *The Abolition of Man*, New York: Macmillan, 1970.

Lewis, M. *Green Delusions*, Durham, N.C.: Duke University Press, 1992.

McDonough, W., and M. Braungart "The Next Industrial Revolution," *The Atlantic Monthly*, 282, 4 (October 1998): 82–92.

McKibben, W. "A Special Moment in History," *The Atlantic Monthly* (May 1998): 55–78.

Meadows, D. "The Global Citizen," *Valley News*, July 4 (1998).

Meadows, D., Meadows, D. and Randers, J. *Beyond the Limits*, Post Mills, Vt.: Chelsea Green, 1992.

Merchant, C. *The Death of Nature*, New York: Harper & Row, 1980.

Mumford, L. *The Myth of the Machine: The Pentagon of Power*, New York: Harcourt, Brace, Jovanovich, 1974.

Orr, D. *Earth in Mind*, Washington, D.C.: Island Press, 1994.

Postman, N. *Technopoly: The Surrender of Culture to Technology*, New York: Knopf, 1992.

Sachs, W., Loske, R. and Linz, M. *Greening the North*, London: Zed books, 1998.

Saul, J. R. *Voltaire's Bastards: The Dictatorship of Reason in the West*, New York: Vintage, 1992.

Smil, V. *General Energetics*, New York: Wiley-Interscience, 1991.

Smil, V. *Energy in World History*, Boulder, Col.: Westview, 1994.

Sturt, G. *The Wheelwright's Shop*, Cambridge: Cambridge University Press, 1984.

Suzuki, D. *The Sacred Balance*, Amherst, Mass.: Prometheus Books, 1998.

Todd, J. and Todd, N. *From Eco-Cities to Living Machines: Principles of Ecological Design*, Berkeley, Calif.: North Atlantic Books, 1994.

Van Der Ryn, S., and Cowan, S., *Ecological Design*, Washington D.C.: Island Press, 1996.

Von Weizsacker, E., Lovins, A., and Lovins, H., *Factor Four*, London: Earthscan, 1997.

Wackernagel, M., and Rees, W. *Our Ecological Footprint*, Philadelphia, Pa.: New Society, 1996.

Wann, D. *Deep Design*, Washington, D.C.: Island Press, 1996.

White, L. "The Historic Roots of our Ecologic Crisis," *Science*, 155 (March 10, 1967): 1203–1207.

Wilshire, B. *Wild Hunger: The Primal Roots of Modern Addiction*, Lanham, Md.: Rowman & Littlefield, 1998.

Wilson, E.O. *Biophilia*, Cambridge, Mass.: Harvard University Press, 1984.

—— *Consilience*, New York: Knopf, 1998.

Originally published in the Proceedings of the 89th Annual Meeting of the Association of Collegiate Schools of Architecture, 2001.

A NEW SOCIAL CONTRACT
Equity and sustainable development
THOMAS FISHER

1 Jared Diamond, Collapse: How Societies Choose to Fail or Succeed (New York: Viking, 2005). George R. Holley et al., Envisioning Cahokia, A Landscape Perspective (DeKalb, Ill.: Northern Illinois University Press, 2003).

2 "The Native people have been here thousands and thousands of years, but take a look at the land and you cannot find a trace of where they have been. Western civilization has been here maybe 200 to 300 years, and you can see everywhere it's been." Claude Demeintieff, Simply Living, The Spirit of the Indigenous People, ed. Shirley Jones (Novato, Calif.: New World Library, 1999).

3 Diamond, Collapse.

4 Ibid.

How can we live sustainably on the North American continent? We know the answer to that question, however unsure we are of how to achieve it, since indigenous people lived sustainably for several thousand years on this continent largely in concert with each other and in balance with the ecosystems on which they depended. They did not always maintain that balance. When living in fragile environments, such as the Anazazi Indians, or when living in too dense a settlement, as in Cahokia, they brought on the collapse of their ecosystems and the dispersal of their communities.[1] Yet, overall, indigenous people here knew what we have forgotten: How to live in such a way that the natural environment can sustain us and future generations.[2]

Emulating Native American practices seems impractical or foreign to most of us, so imbued are we with the idea of progress and so immersed are we in the technology that now supports us and separates us from nature. That technological progress, of course, has brought real tangible benefits, such as lengthening our lives and improving our daily comfort, making it hard to imaging living without it. But as is becoming increasingly clear that we cannot continue along the path we are on. The historian Jared Diamond shows in his book *Collapse: How Societies Choose to Fail or Succeed* what happens when humans have ignored their impact on the ecosystems upon which they depend: Their societies implode, leading to the abandonment of territory, the cessation of economic activity, and the starvation and even cannibalism of people. Diamond's critics have argued that we need not worry, that technology and the marketplace will overcome these problems, but Diamond documents how such dismissive thinking has gotten societies into trouble in the past. If we humans have any ingenuity, it may lie in our ability to fool ourselves into thinking that we can thrive despite the damage we do to ecosystems.[3]

Diamond lists a dozen warning signs that he thinks we need to address over the next fifty years if we are to avoid what could be the first-ever global environmental collapse generated by human activity. Diamond notes that we have begun to destroy at an almost suicidal rate our natural habitats, fish populations, biological diversity, and farmable soil. He also observes that we have begun to reach a ceiling on inexpensive fossil fuels, accessible fresh water, and plant growth per acre. Pollution adds to those problems, whether it is with increases in toxic chemicals in the air and water, invasive plant species devastating ecosystems, or ozone-depleting atmospheric gases. And rapidly growing human populations and unsustainable standards of living and levels of consumption make all of the other problems worse.[4]

Inequities underlie most previous collapses of human societies, something that we see all around us. For example, human-generated CO_2 in the atmosphere, now at 380 parts per million, is the highest ever recorded and is likely to go up to 500 or 550 parts per million, creating all kinds of instability in the global climate. The United States has had a disproportionate responsibility for this rise. The United States has 5 percent of world's population (and falling) but is responsible for 25 percent of world's greenhouse gas output per annum. We produce 20 metric tons of CO_2 for every American man, woman, and child, versus 9 tons for every European.[5] The inequity in our impact on the global environment is matched by inequity within our own borders. The Global Energy Network Institute's economic index ranks the United States at 40.8, putting us as one of the most unequal countries in the world, better than Mexico but worse than most other developed nations.[6] In the U.S., the richest 1 percent holds 38 percent of the wealth. One in five adults live in poverty, versus one in fifteen in Italy.[7]

If, as Diamond observes, inequities in societies seem to hasten the collapse of societies, once the collapse occurs, it affects rich and poor alike. This seems contrary to what we saw in New Orleans in the wake of Hurricane Katrina, when the people left behind were largely poor. However, the upper, middle, and lower classes died in New Orleans' flooding in roughly the same proportion in almost every neighborhood of the city.[8] As the scale of a collapse increases, it seems that money and power matter much less; with a global collapse, they won't matter much at all.

That does not discount the importance of inequities or the necessity of trying to rectify them. But it does suggest that nature may do what centuries of political revolution have barely achieved: the elimination of privilege. Environmental stress seems to affect the wealthy as much or more than the poor: the coastal areas of the world most vulnerable to flooding and storms also contain its most valuable real estate: expensive resorts, exclusive homes, and upscale communities. Also, as Diamond shows from the evidence of social uprisings in the face of imminent collapse, the wealthy have the most to lose and the least experience with hardship.

Whether rich or poor, we need to do what we can to avoid the global collapse Diamond and others see in our future. Some argue that the best way to clean up the environment and address material inequities lies with more economic growth, the very thing that since the industrial revolution helped create the environmental damage and global climate change we now must try to solve. We are told that the unfettered global marketplace will lift all boats, bring more economic activity to more people, and raise everyone's standard of living.

However, limits on the earth's carrying capacity make this option no longer feasible in the long run. According to Redefining Progress, humanity's average ecological footprint is more than 35 percent larger than the available space on the earth, with a 10 percent increase just since 1992.[9] To achieve truly

5 Tony Judt, "Europe vs. America," The New York Review of Books, February 10, 2005, 39.

6 Global Energy Network Institute website, <http://www.geni.org>.

7 Organization for Economic Co-operation and Development website, <http://www.oecd.org>.

8 Shaila Dwan and Janet Roberts, "Louisiana's Storm Took the Strong as Well as the Helpless," New York Times, December 18, 2005, 1, 32.

9 Redefining Progress website, <http://www.rprogress.org/new projects/ecolFoot.shtml>.

sustainable growth, it demands that we find a way to raise the standard of living of the world's poorest people, while reducing that of the world's wealthiest to a point where we can maintain ourselves over the long term.

EQUITY AND ARCHITECTURE

What does this mean for architects? While the architectural community is widely interested and generally engaged in sustainable design, the issue of equity poses an awkward dilemma. Because most architects depend upon the wealthy and powerful for work, we have little incentive to embrace the idea that we may never achieve a more sustainable future unless we also create a more equitable one. When William Rees, the famed ecologist from the University of British Columbia gave a talk at the national convention of the American Institute of Architects, he told the crowd of several thousand that the U.S. profession needs to reduce the environmental impact of buildings by 90 percent over the next fifty years. He received enthusiastic applause from the audience of architects, but from what I could see and hear from the conversations afterward, it seemed as if the enormity of what Rees said did not register with most in the audience.

Achieving such reductions will take much more than increasing the use of "green" materials or of energy conserving mechanical systems or appliances. A 90 percent reduction demands a wholesale change in how we live and how much we consume, something that few architects probably want to raise with our clients. Many in the profession might agree with Tony Judt of the Remarque Institute: "The American pursuit of wealth, size, and abundance—as material surrogates for happiness—is aesthetically unpleasing and eco-logically catastrophic."[10] But architects are often complicit in creating those material surrogates—buildings of great cost, size, and abundance—with our fees often going up accordingly. To create a more sustainable, equitable world, we may need to begin by taking a hard look at how we practice and at how we, as a profession, contribute to the problem.

10 Judt, "Europe vs. America."

Richard Farson, President of the Western Behavioral Sciences Institute and a former public member of the A.I.A.'s Board of Directors, mused on the following when he stepped down from the board in 2003:

I sometimes wonder what an American architect would say if approached by the leader of China seeking his or her help for the 800 million ill-housed, struggling Chinese. "Well, the way we believe residential architecture should be practiced is that each home should be custom designed, the architect should be an integral part of the process for each structure, from beginning to end, carefully surveying the site, designing a structure that is particularly suited for that site, working intensively with the client to understand that individual's special needs, making sure that the contractors are performing, and that the project is completed on budget. Normally it takes us about a year or so to finish such a project, and

*we can undertake perhaps ten a year. We don't condone selling stock plans.
But we could bring a thousand architects to work with you." The leader
would shake his head, concluding that such a program, even if China could
afford it, would take 800 years.*

Farson ended his talk by calling for architects to become "metadesigners,"
focused less on the design of individual buildings and more on orchestrating
a wide range of other disciplines to help address the problems of the built
environment. Even more controversially, he argued: "architecture should be
publicly supported in the same way that education and medicine are. Our
professional strategies should include making a case for major public funding,
to the tune of trillions of dollars over time."[11]

Large-scale public funding of the profession is not likely to happen soon,
but Farson's observations show how our dominant mode of practice may
no longer align with what the world needs from us. The architect–client
relationship parallels the doctor–patient relationship in medicine, in which
individual needs get addressed one at a time by the professional. But medicine
has also evolved another model—public health—to address the needs of large
groups of people. Architects have long had a relationship to public health,
but rarely have architects looked to public health as a model for practice.
Most practitioners in our field work in small businesses, like physicians,
rather than in industry and government, like the public-health community,
even though health, safety, and welfare stand as a central justification for our
licensure as a profession. As a result, our profession has not built the institutions and agencies that can help us bring our knowledge to large numbers of
people who need our expertise and yet who cannot, individually, pay for it.

As happened with the flooding of New Orleans, the devastation of broad
swaths of coastline along the Gulf of Mexico and the Indian Ocean, and the
leveling of millions of homes in northern Pakistan, architects lack a clear way
of addressing the large-scale threats to public health that can occur in the
built environment—threats that will become an ever more pressing problem
in the future, with ever more intense weather brought on by global climate
change. As M.I.T. scientist Kerry Emanuel has shown, tropical storms now
last half again as long and generate winds 50 percent more powerful than just
a few decades ago, the result of ever-warmer tropical seas.[12] And with rapidly
increasing populations living in vulnerable areas, we could see a whole new
category of the homeless, "environmental refugees," as Oxford scientist
Norman Myers calls them, with "as many as 200 million people overtaken
by disruptions of monsoon systems and other rainfall regimes, by droughts
of unprecedented severity and duration, and by sea-level rise and coastal
flooding."[13]

How should we respond to such a sobering prospect, affecting developed,
developing, and undeveloped countries alike? It may be, at least in the short
term, that architects can work best as independent, creative entrepreneurs

11 Richard Farson, "Is
Architecture as Important as
Education?" (paper presented at
A.I.A. Board Meeting, 2003).

12 Emanuel Kerry, Divine Wind,
The History and Science of
Hurricanes (Oxford: Oxford
University Press, 2005).

13 Norman Myers,
"Environmental Refugees,
An Emergent Security Issue,"
Organization for Security and
Co-operation in Europe,
<http://www.osce.org/documents/
eea/2005/05/14488_en.pdf>.

in partnership with the public and non-profit entities dedicated to helping the growing number of people rendered homeless or placeless because of environmental or economic dislocation. Some architects have begun to do just that. They have addressed different aspects of the sustainability-and-equity problem: the infrastructure needs of slum dwellers, the shelter needs of the homeless, the material needs of those with few resources, and the habitation needs of those on the move. What unites their work is not just a commitment to environmental sustainability and social equity, but also an underlying and often unstated vision of the future that brings us back to where we started: the idea that the most sustainable future for North America may look like a modern-day version of how Native Americans lived before Europeans arrived, building with what is at hand, improving the environment around us, and living so lightly on the land that we hardly leave a trace.

ADVOCACY ARCHITECTS

The United Nations' Millennium Development Goals call for significantly improving the lives of at least 100 million of the world's 2 billion slum dwellers by 2020, focusing on access to safe drinking water and sanitation.[14] With those goals in mind, architect John Gavin Dwyer and his firm, Shelter Architecture, have designed a self-contained structure able to provide global slum-dwellers what they often need the most: access to electricity, clean water, and toilet and bathing facilities.

Called the "Clean Hub," the 10- by 20-foot unit has a V-shape metal roof that collects rainwater, an adjustable array of sixteen photovoltaic panels able to generate up to 2,640 watts of electricity, a reverse-osmosis water system that cleans water stored in a below-ground reservoir, showers and sinks whose grey water gets recycled back to the reservoir, and waterless, self-composting toilets. The building itself has impact-resistant stress-skin walls and has secure entry doors, supported by a steel-tube and concrete-pier foundation that can adjust to sloped terrain and poor soil. The Clean Hub's expected thirty-year life makes it most suitable for the many semi-permanent slums around the world that lack basic infrastructure.[15]

Response to the needs of people who have lost their housing during hurricanes and earthquakes involves another kind of response. Cameron Sinclair and Kate Stohr's organization Architecture for Humanity has shown how much architects have to contribute in the wake of these disasters. When Hurricane Ivan destroyed 85 percent of Grenada's in 2004, and Hurricane Emily did further damage in 2005, Architecture for Humanity participated in a team that included Architectonica, Ferrara Design, and Grenada Relief, Recovery and Reconstruction (GR3), producing seventy prototype transitional housing units. Called Global Village Shelters and designed by Daniel and Mia Ferrara of Ferrera Design, the temporary houses are made from recycled corrugated cardboard impregnated to be fire retardant and laminated for water resistance.

14 United Nations website, <http://www.un.org/millennium goals>.

15 Shelter Architecture website, <http://www.shelterarchitecture. com/cleanhub.htm>.

Architecture for Humanity has also addressed the needs of people suffering from war or disease. In the organization's 1999 competition for housing for returning wartime refuges in Kosovo, architects such as Shigeru Ban designed an insulated and waterproof paper log house and Sean Godsell developed his "future shack," using a standard shipping container and an unfolding roof to provide shade. In 2003, Architecture for Humanity sponsored a design competition for a mobile HIV/AIDS clinic for Africa, with KHRAS Architects designing the first place entry, with a metal-framed, self-contained, lockable structure that also incorporates local materials.[16]

Other architects have begun to look at unconventional materials as low-cost, sustainable alternatives to what the market has to offer. Richard Kroeker and students at Dalhousie and Minnesota have worked with aboriginal and native communities to adopt indigenous approaches to construction using pliable wood materials in various woven and tied configurations drawn from what is immediately available on or near a site.[17] He has also begun to look at materials in the modern waste stream, such as unused telephone books held in compression to form bearing walls. Another architect working in this area is Wes Janz, whose students at Ball State, along with I-Beam Design, have developed ways to use the 1.9 million wood pallets destined for landfills in the United States for housing, drawing from the widespread use of pallets in squatter housing from around the world.[18] These examples revise the ancient idea that we build with what we have at hand, and that we empower people to build for themselves.

All of these efforts suggest a new kind of practice for architects, based on advocacy, activism, and attention to what the rest of the world wastes. However, these architectural inventions have, so far, remained largely research. If we are going to create a more sustainable and equitable world, we need to apply these lessons on a broader scale, to people of all types. How might these examples serve not only the world's billions of slum dwellers,

16 Architecture for Humanity website, <http://www.architecture forhumanity.org>.

17 University of Minnesota, College of Architecture and Landscape Architecture website, "Undergraduate Studio IV," <http: //www.cala.umn.edu/architecture/ STUDENTS/studentgallery_v2/ ug4.html>.

18 Wes Janz website, "Research," <http://www.bsu.edu/web/wjanz/ WesSite/research.html>.

19 Thomas Hobbes, Leviathan
(New York: Collier and Son, 1910).

and potentially its millions of environmental refugees, but also the developed world, where some of the greatest inequity and unsustainability occur? For that, we need to rethink the social contract we have related to equity and the environment.

THE NEW SOCIAL CONTRACT

Historically, we have thought of that social contract in two very different ways. The seventeenth-century philosopher, Thomas Hobbes, imagined life in the "state of nature" as one that he famously characterized as "nasty, brutish, and short," a condition of constant warfare "of every man, against every man." He argued that, because of these inequalities in nature, humans entered into a social contract to create powerful central authorities—the Leviathan, as he called them—in order to achieve the equality and security that he thought impossible living close to nature.[19] The eighteenth-century philosopher, Jean-Jacques Rousseau, imagined just the opposite. He envisioned the "state of nature" as one characterized by the peaceful co-existence of equals, who lived with abundance and with little need for property. Conflict arose, according to Rousseau, the first time someone put a stake in the ground and claimed land as their own, leading to the inequities of property ownership

40

and the need for a social contract that would protect people's rights, while maximizing our personal freedom.[20]

20 Jean-Jacques Rousseau, The Origin of Inequality *and* The Social Contract *(Chicago, Ill. Encyclopedia Britannica, 1988).*

Political theorists still study Hobbes and Rousseau, finding in this work justification for authoritarian or libertarian ideologies, respectively. But we can learn something else from them: what it means to imagine a "state of nature" in today's world, given the unsustainable and inequitable ways we now live in North America. Both Hobbes and Rousseau saw nature in much the same way: as a near-infinite resource that is there for our use. And both saw equity in terms of property and political power, a matter of law and regulation. We now know, however, that the natural environment is anything but infinite, and that our fate, as a species, is intimately connected with its health. At the same time, we now know that equity takes many different forms, only some of which has to do with property and political power.

A new social contract, based on how we know the world to be, would have almost the opposite characteristics of those we have inherited from Hobbes and Rousseau. It would be a contract that recognizes and rewards people according to how well they husband finite resources, improve the natural environment, serve those most in need, and give as much as possible to others. Equity would no longer be, as it was for Hobbes and Rousseau, primarily a matter of keeping greed in check, since that assumes that the primary motive of human action is to acquire as much property or power as possible. In the new social contract, freedom would not consist of how much property we can own, but instead a matter of how much we can live without, as Thoreau said, and equity a matter of how much we can live simply so that others can simply live, as Gandhi put it. In a future in which many of us may be on the move, living lightly has real advantages.

This, of course, sounds impractical, idealistic, and naïve in our ego-driven, winner-takes-all world, but it is anything but that. It is the most practical, pragmatic, and realistic alternative we face at a time when we have just a few generations to avoid the kind of environmental collapse and subsequent social turmoil that an increasing number see in our future. If we are to meet William Rees's challenge of reducing our impact on the environment by 90 percent in fifty years, and if we are to make marked improvements on the dozen factors Jared Diamond sees as our greatest threats, we need to transform what we value, how we share, and who we embrace in the global community.

Our history and recent practices suggest that we will default to either Hobbes's or Rousseau's idea of the social contract, with some advocating for a strong authority imposing controls through strict regulation and others calling for a libertarian loosing of restrictions in order to maximize individual freedom. But at a time of rapidly growing population—estimated to be between 9 and 12 billion people in the next century—and rapidly diminishing resources, neither of these older social contracts work. There will be too large and diverse a population for a singular authority and too few finite resources for an expansion of personal liberty. The new social contract will require of us to internalize that authority and that freedom: to learn, as an essential part of being human, how to value the group as much as the individual, future generations as much as the present, and other species as much as ourselves.

This new contract isn't really new. The three dominant ethical traditions in the West all align with this shift in thinking, as does the work of a growing number of architects. Virtue ethics, with its focus on character traits such as a prudence and justice, demands that we look to the well-being of others and that we live modestly and with humility. The work of the late Samuel Mockbee exemplifies this architecturally. His Rural Studio for Auburn University students has created a number of houses and public buildings for some of the most needy people in one of the poorest counties in the United States. Using recycled materials—such as used tires for walls, reused wind-shields for windows, and discarded license plates for cladding—the Rural Studio has designed and built some of the most powerful projects of the late twentieth century, showing how what Mockbee called the "old-fashioned virtue" of giving to others can be the basis for the creation of community.[21]

Deontological ethics, with its concern for doing what is right regardless of consequences, reinforces our responsibility toward other species and future generations, and our obligation to act with them always in mind. Such an ethic underlies most utopian thinking, and that tradition remains as a way of showing what a new social contract might look like. Michael Sorkin has taken such an approach, exploring, in a number of urban designs, new forms of sustainable communities. For example, his Penangs Peaks project—a mixed-use community of housing, offices, and various public and commercial facilities—will be self-sufficient in terms of water and waste management. The project envisions a series of foliage-clad towers arranged around a large park, showing how large numbers of people can live in urban settings with a minimal impact on the local environment.[22]

Finally, utilitarianism, with its goal of maximizing the happiness of as many as possible, demands that we include all other beings in its calculus of the

21 Andrea Oppenheimer Dean and Timothy Hursley, Rural Studio: Samuel Mockbee and an Architecture of Decency (New York: Princeton Architectural Press, 2002).

22 Michael Sorkin Studio Web site, "Penang Peaks," <http://www.sorkinstudio.com/ Penang percent20Peaks.htm>.

greatest good for the greatest number, with attention to the process and consequences of all that we do. Socially active architects, such as Thomas Dutton in his work in Cincinnati's Over-the-Rhine district with the Over-the-Rhine Housing Network, represent a more participatory approach. Dutton and his Miami University students have designed and renovated a number of living and commercial spaces, including a laundromat, two single-family townhouses and a number of apartments, for budgets in the $5,000 to $10,000 range. Dutton's students have also explored a kind of guerrilla urbanism, using utility trucks to bring information related to poverty to well-to-do parts of town, and using public parks for temporary exhibitions on social justice issues.[23]

Nor is the underpinning for this new social contract strictly secular and ethical. All of the major religious and spiritual traditions in both the East and the West recognize the values we now need to embrace if we are to avoid a global collapse, values such as moderation and self-restraint, charity and mercy. At heart of almost every religious text lies the message that happiness comes from giving away what we don't absolutely need, serving as often as possible the poorest and most disadvantaged, and helping others as much as possible, without expectations of anything in return. Myriad religious communities remain the mainstays of housing the homeless, and in so doing, show us what we will have to deal with as hundreds of millions of environmental refugees face similar conditions.

The social contract underlying such work will serve us particularly well in what lies ahead. As we saw in the aftermath of the flooding of New Orleans, it was charitable individuals who initially came to the aid of others without regard for who they were. Rugged individualism and enlightened self-interest may work as a social ethic in periods of abundance, but in the coming era of scarce resources, those who value cooperation, interdependence, and mutual aid and who see wealth in nonmaterial, ethical, and spiritual terms, will be the ones who thrive. Such were the values and the wealth of the indigenous people of North America, and if we want to live sustainably on this continent for generations to come, they will need to become ours as well.

23 *Tom Dutton website, <http:// www.uc.edu/cdc/tomdutton.htm>.*

43

ECONOMIC SUSTAINABILITY IN THE POST-INDUSTRIAL LANDSCAPE

ELLEN DUNHAM-JONES

THE BRAID

The metaphor of sustainability as a green braid conveys the crucial need for the integration of economic, cultural, and environmental sustainability. The braid's strength is derived from its weaving of the multiple strands. None of them are nearly so effective on their own and the fraying of one weakens the whole. This metaphor clarifies the challenge to designers of synthesizing performance in these three areas and signifies a sea change away from design methodologies engineered to optimize performance of only a single variable. In theory, the three strands both enrich and constrain each other. However, their integration in practice raises numerous questions.

For instance, because common goods like social equity and the environment lack market prices, economists reduce them to externalities and have difficulty accounting for them.[1] As a consequence, contemporary development patterns are driven almost entirely by short-term economic viability with very little concern for long-term impacts, especially on the other two strands. This problem is further exacerbated in today's globalized economy where digital networks and mobile capital distance design decisions from placemaking and enable increased spatial segregation between the costs and benefits of the various strands. Instead of braided interdependence, the postindustrial economy has unsustainably widened the gap between rich and poor people and places. In the process it has largely redefined the role of the designer away from emplacing the local culture of a particular place and towards the market segmentation of global brands, chain stores, and designer labels. In other words, much architectural design has similarly shed its obligation to the externalities. How do we distinguish progressive architectural practices in this context?

Architectural discourse on sustainability stands in staunch opposition to these trends, but has been similarly lopsided. It too often reduces economic sustainability to an unconsidered, albeit desirable, byproduct. The overwhelming focus on environmental strategies has tended to reduce issues of economic sustainability to trade-offs between initial, operating, and lifecycle costs of green construction and systems. Obviously, attention to project costs is important, but so are the project's contributions to local economic development and to the larger economic system's means of sharing costs and benefits. Michael Pyatok's housing projects incorporate spaces for low-income residents to use for revenue generation, but this kind of programmatic invention to assist users' long-term economic sustainability is rare. So how do we sustainably integrate the strands of the braid into design while

1 Varied attempts to account for such "externalities" are documented in Paul Hawken, Amory Lovins, and L. Hunter Lovins, Natural Capitalism (Boston, Mass.: Little, Brown & Company, 1999), and Robert W. Burchell et al., Sprawl Costs, Economic Impacts of Unchecked Development (Washington, D.C.: Island Press, 2005).

operating within the realities of an economic system that reduces "green" to a niche market?

The braid's expansion of the scope of the designer's task is matched by its simultaneous expansion of the scale. While it is possible to ask of a single building whether it is viable in the long-term, fair, and ecologically beneficial, the questions can only be answered by branching out well beyond the building into the larger communal and natural systems. This engagement with the larger place is essential to sustainability and begs greater consideration of sustainability at the urban and regional scale. Again, in theory, the strands can be more effectively interwoven at the regional scale where jobsheds, transportation systems, watersheds, and airsheds tend to align. New urbanism and smart growth have offered designers and planners promising design and implementation tools at this scale. However, again in practice, the regional scale is where the unsustainability of our current development patterns are most glaring: dominated by auto-dependent, income-segregated, land-consumptive urban and exurban sprawlscapes where buildings are treated as disposable assets more than as enduring investments. Ignored by architects, sprawl has provided more Americans with unprecedented access to the American Dream but is it viable in the long-term, fair, and ecologically beneficial?

below: Chunshu, Xuanwu District in Beijing, 2004. Image by Sze Tsung Leong.

In order to more effectively integrate the braid's strands, I will argue that architects today need to recognize and make more effective use of economic sustainability as a driver in sustainable design and to more critically position themselves relative to their role in the production of unsustainable late capitalist, postindustrial landscapes. For starters, this requires a better understanding of globalization, the landscapes of mobile capital it has produced, and architecture's ability to negotiate between these forces in the production of places capable of sustaining capitalism's relentless "creative destruction."

THE LANDSCAPES OF GLOBALIZATION, POST-INDUSTRIALISM, AND POST-FORDISM

The contemporary economic system goes by many names. With reference to world trade some of the terms commonly used are globalization, late capitalism, the end of ideology, neo-liberalism, and "the Washington consensus." In reference to the most dominant economies, especially that of the U.S., prominent terms that indicate new shifts include: the service economy, the new economy, the hour-glass economy, the information age, the tech boom, the exit-ramp economy, knowledge workers, deregulation, "irrational exuberance", outsourcing and post-Fordism.

Because I'm principally interested in the types of development patterns, landscapes, and buildings produced by this system, I've found it most useful to employ Daniel Bell's phrase, "the postindustrial economy" to collectively describe these new practices.[2] It was used in the late 1960s and into the 1970s both enthusiastically and with great fear and trepidation to describe a near-future technocratic society where information systems and telecommunications would lead to the replacement of "messy" constituency-oriented, participatory politics, by more rational, scientifically based decision-making and the equitable distribution of automated and now abundant goods to a satisfied, media-saturated populace. Bell in particular, distinguished postindustrial society from pre-industrial and industrial society in terms of the centrality to the economy of processing information instead of extracting raw materials or mechanical production. While pre-industrial societies settle in proximity to natural resources and industrial societies develop around factories and transportation systems, postindustrial societies' investments are less place-dependent. Instead of producing farms, coal mines, or cities, postindustrial societies produce highly educated, mobile people and organizations.

Globalization and computation have only further accelerated Bell's prescient forecast of a new society dominated by mass media and telecommunications. In today's postindustrial economy electronic access increasingly substitutes for physical access and speed, mobility and malleability are valued more than endurance and placemaking. I have argued that these values are particularly evident in several specific postindustrial landscapes: the rustbelts of former industrial areas, recent sprawlscapes, "global city" financial cores,

2 *See Daniel Bell*, The Coming of Post-Industrial Society *(New York: Basic Books, 1973) for the more enthusiastic endorsement of postindustrialism. For the more critical view, see Alain Touraine,* The Post-Industrial Society, Tomorrow's Social History: Classes, Conflicts and Culture in the Programmed Society, *trans. Leonard F. X. Mayhew (New York: Random House, 1971).*

46

and the free trade zones produced by the past few decades of mobile capital.[3] Interdependent economically, but spatially and socially segregated, these landscapes provide a physical means to understand the widened gap between rich and poor places. They tell the story of disinvestment in places like Flint, Michigan and reinvestment in the nonunionized sweatshops of China's Pearl River Delta. As global production increasingly shifts to such free trade zones (FTZs or special economic zones or export production zones,) the goods produced increasingly feed the consumer landscape of American sprawl. Coordination of the transactions between these vast new landscapes of production and consumption has enriched transnational retailers like Wal-Mart on the one hand and financial service providers on the other. This has given rise to both the glittering new banking and luxury condo high-rise financial cores in major cities around the globe as well as the massive distribution warehouses, big-box power centers, and other suburban retail formats of the commercial strip and highway interchanges at the ever-expanding periphery. Although these landscapes are highly segregated and specialized, they share several less than sustainable characteristics: a privileging of speed and mobility through auto-dependency, malleability through cheap construction, and a lack of public spaces—except for shopping.

3 Ellen Dunham-Jones, "Capital Transformations of the Postindustrial Landscape," Oase 54 (winter 2001): 8–35.

top: Commercial Strip, Northern Indiana, 2002. Image by Phillip Jones.

Reflections of mobile capital, they can be described as market segmentation at a global scale.

Every economic system produces winners and losers, but what are the consequences of this kind of segmentation at the global scale? Many critics have decried the homogenization of landscapes of similar types. The banking centers in Pudong, Dubai, and Canary Wharf are being designed, financed, and retailed by many of the same firms and resources, resulting in tremendous similarities in the physical environments. The links between these loci of capital are such that the price of a condominium in one may have more to do with the comparable price in another city's financial district, than with the rest of that condo's local city. The placeless uniformity of building products and development patterns in sprawlscapes are similarly notorious and well recognized. However, there has been far less attention paid to the economic development impacts of the segregation of the different landscape types from each other. What are the consequences of the postindustrial economy's tendency to distance producers, consumers, and the administrators of capital into distinct and separate landscapes? This can best be answered by examining the shift from Fordism to post-Fordism.

Building to a large extent on the global economic channels and power relationships established by various colonial regimes, today's post-Fordist business practices decentralize production and marketing around the globe, while centralizing administrative and financial power. The recessions of the 1970s prompted many American businesses to use newly available digital technologies to become far more flexible and market-responsive by better tracking information on supply and demand, automating or monitoring increasingly offshore production and coordinating the inputs from increased use of outsourcing and consultants. Just as manufacturers became more reliant on information technologies, information-heavy services such as finance, banking, law, healthcare, media, and entertainment, boomed in the 1980s while blue-collar manufacturing jobs were increasingly sent overseas. Robert Reich, former U.S. Secretary of Labor, describes this shift in terms of the pyramidal organizations of postwar corporate America being replaced by global spiderwebs.[4] As advanced economies shifted from a basis in industrial manufacturing to postindustrial services and information, Henry Ford's unionized workers and centralized assembly lines have been increasingly replaced by a globally dispersed system of digitally programmed small-batch production, automated or nonunionized labor, temporary contracts, and just-in-time deliveries, enabled by telecommunications and digital networks. More directed towards mass customization and varied product lines than the mass production methods of the first half of the century, post-Fordism uses advertising and styling to appeal to varied consumer niche markets and relies to a greater degree on built-in obsolescence and disposability. Its practices are intended to maximize speed, mobility, and flexibility.

While substantial foreign trade existed long before telecommunications,

4 Robert B. Reich, The Work of Nations (New York: Random House, 1992), 89.

the incomparable mobility of contemporary capital is unthinkable without digital networks to facilitate capital flows, the monitoring of investments, and coordination of global transactions.[5] These networks also allow multi-national corporations to seek profits through maintaining gross inequalities between producers' wages and consumer prices on a globally distributed basis.[6] This is a fundamental shift. Fordism struck a balance between the employer's need to have workers show up on time to run the assembly line and the workers' right to organize a union and bargain collectively. Under these conditions Henry Ford recognized (albeit begrudgingly) that it was in his interest to pay his workers enough that they could afford to buy one of his cars, (in other words allowing his producers to also become his consumers.) Instead, post-Fordism uses global geography to segregate producers from consumers. While Fordism contributed to the substantial growth of the American middle class and arguably the most equitable distribution of wealth ever seen, post-Fordist mobility is able to keep wages low and unions out by threatening to move somewhere else.[7] The resulting global system is politely called "uneven development" because of its maintenance of structural inequities between capital and workers, producers and consumers, developed and developing economies.

This is not to say that the laborers in Mexican *maquiladoras* or Indonesian footwear factories are not pleased to have a job, that their countries are not benefiting from some degree of technology transfer or that the system as a whole is not economically sustainable. It is merely to point out how mobile capital's constant threat to hire someone else or move its jobs elsewhere has diminished workers' abilities to increase wages over time and move up into the middle class and become consumers. Instead, low-skilled, low-wage earners increasingly compete for jobs in a global wage race to the bottom.

The flipside of uneven development is that those with unique skills are catapulted to the top. Economists Robert H. Frank and Philip J. Cook explain the asymmetry of the global economy in terms of star power. In their book, *The Winner-Take-All Society, Why the Few at the Top Get so Much More than the Rest of Us*, they argue that markets, media, and technology have so increased the exposure of those identified as the best in their field, that they can completely dominate their markets.

Since it costs no more to stamp out compact discs from Kathleen Battle's master recording of Mozart arias than from her understudy's, most of us listen to Battle. Millions of us are each willing to pay a few cents extra to hear her rather than another singer who is only marginally less able and this enables Battle to write her own ticket.[8]

While few of us could discern the difference in quality, the availability of access to the best causes a tremendous asymmetry in the market between Number 1 and Number 2.

5 *See Manuel Castells*, The Rise of The Network Society *(Malden, Mass.: Blackwell, 1996).*

6 *Nike sneakers are a common example used to display the gross disparities between wages and prices. In 1996, 25,000 Nike workers in Indonesia made 70 million pairs of shoes. While the shoes were sold for upwards of $100 a piece, the workers each got $2.23 per day. At the same time, Michael Jordan's endorsement fees were over $20 million. Walter LaFeber,* Michael Jordan and the New Global Capitalism *(New York: Norton, 1999), 107, 147. However, wages are not the only factor in post-Fordist industrial location strategies. Access to the host country's market is also often a significant determinant.*

7 *Real wages for Mexican workers in* maquilladoras *have fallen in the face of regional competition from Honduras, and Guatemala, as well as from the export processing zones of Southeast Asia. See Andrew Ross, ed.,* No Sweat: Fashion, Free Trade, and the Rights of Garment Workers *(New York: Verso, 1997). While labor conditions and wages remain poor for individual workers, the export processing zones—especially in Southeast Asia—are credited with stimulating a tremendous investment of foreign capital and triggering substantial economic growth for the region as a whole.*

8 *Robert H. Frank and Philip J. Cook,* The Winner-Take-All Society: Why the Few at the Top Get so Much More than the Rest of Us *(New York: Penguin, 1995), 2.*

ARCHITECTURE IN THE POST-INDUSTRIAL LANDSCAPE

We see uneven development play out in our discipline with star architects. Shortlists for high-profile commissions around the world are likely to have the same five or ten names on them at any given time. Star practitioners with global practices, such as Frank Gehry, are hired not to produce a place-based design that speaks of the particular qualities of the local architecture, but rather to deliver a high-design signature product that shows their client to be an elite global consumer. Extremely talented designers, they have become identifiable brands with particular niche markets. If the modern mass-produced *objet type* served a growing middle class, the proliferation of design choices under post-Fordism serve a more differentiated social structure where the media articulate market segments and rank desirability. Consumption choices are most uniform at the highest end of the scale where Rolexes, Rolls Royces and, increasingly, star architects are internationally recognized. A consequence of this is that in the global economy, architecture, like a watch or a car, becomes an imported, fashionable, commodity, more expressive of the promises than the performance of postindustrialism.

Indeed, despite post-Fordism's low commitments to its buildings and workers, the promises of the postindustrial economy and its digital technologies are extremely seductive. A wide spectrum of authors including Bell, Marshall McLuhan, Alvin Toffler, Jeremy Rifkin, Francis Fukuyama, George Gilder, Nicholas Negroponte, William Mitchell, and Thomas Friedman have variously contributed to the rosy expectations that computers, robotics, and telecommunications will bring about laborless abundance, equitable access to information, self-realization, even world peace. Although white-collar workers have been working more hours not less and authors such as Benjamin Barber and Samuel Huntington argue that globalization's confrontation between "jihad and McWorld" is heightening not diminishing the "clash of civilizations," postindustrialism's liberating promises remain culturally compelling. Wired individuals, not just post-Fordist multinational corporations, are fueled by speed, mobility, and flexibility to empowered positions in the postindustrial economy. Ever since Macintosh's introduction of the personal computer in 1984, the marketing of digital hardware and software has played to the progressive promises of individual-empowerment and the democratization of power. The thriving computer engineers in Bangalore and new market capitalists in China certainly would not disagree. Friedman's thesis that digital technologies have "flattened" the playing field and made access to the global market more equitable bodes well for economic sustainability for certain sectors, but the sustainability of postindustrialism as a post-Fordist system, under even the most optimistic scenarios remains very much at question.

Under these circumstances how can architecture best promote "even" rather than "uneven" development? Which is more progressive—for architects to give expression to a radical future of laborless self-empowerment

above left: Commercial Strip, Los Angeles, 2001. Image by Phillip Jones.

above right: Dead Mall, Avondale, Georgia, 2004. Image by Phillip Jones.

with fluid, malleable forms, (even if today such forms principally serve the elite?). Or to design place-based alternatives to the reality of wasteful, auto-dependent, socially segregated, privatized landscapes whether in Malaysia's Cyberjava or suburban Atlanta (even if the alternatives' neo-traditional styling does not appear progressive?). The dichotomy is unnecessary, but because contemporary architectural discourse and publications have been so dominated by assumptions that progressive architecture is principally a matter of representation, the less visible aspects of reform and economic impact often go under-recognized and underappreciated. For example, if one looks at the generation of non-placebased logics, global production methods, and cutting edge uses of digital technology, the radically different but equally postindustrial architectures produced by Wal-Mart and by Frank O. Gehry and Associates have more in common than one would suppose.

Both Gehry's office and Wal-Mart have pioneered innovative uses of digital technologies, (from CATIA software to the universal barcode pricing and inventory system, the world's first private satellite system). Gehry uses digital networks to produce one-of-a-kind masterworks from components custom-produced in various parts of the world. While Wal-Mart's prototypical box stores (many designed for a lifespan of only five years) couldn't be more different from Gehry's buildings, they're stocked with goods produced and delivered from various FTZs with similarly digitally coordinated precision and custom arrangements. Exemplifying post-Fordist production, Wal-Mart has been charged with bringing down wages and triggering outsourcing industry-wide.[9] If Wal-Mart's seductive low prices are a result of both ever-lower wages and retail's speediest, most efficient distribution system, Gehry's seductive digitally milled, compound curves erase the hand of the worker and

9 There are many sources of varying credibility for discussions of Wal-Mart. One of the best reviewed is by Charles Fishman, a senior editor of Fast Company, entitled The Wal-Mart Effect: How the World's Most Powerful Company Really Works—and How It's Transforming the American Economy (New York: Penguin, 2006).

can be read as representing the postindustrial promise of flexible, seemingly instantaneous, laborless abundance. Gehry's mastery of new technologies and his star status have resulted in his reproducing his signature forms and materials in project after project such that he too almost seems to be franchising. Like Wal-Mart, Gehry has become a brand. His buildings, like Wal-Marts, have little to do with the particularities of places. They perform within a global system where cities seek icons by star architects to emulate the Bilbao effect and announce their presence in the global economy. Instead of representing what is unique about a particular local culture, both Gehry and Wal-Mart are more expressive of a global consumerist culture—a culture that values speed, mobility, and flexibility and whose networks allow for both Wal-Mart's highly successful bottom-feeding as well as Gehry's *haute cuisine*. The problem is that for all that we may admire Gehry's evocation of the progressive promises of speed, mobility and flexibility, their regressive reality in Wal-Mart is far more pervasive in our society and upon our landscape. This brings us to a discussion of sprawl.

SPRAWL, THE DOMINANT POST-INDUSTRIAL LANDSCAPE

Most of the research on the impact of the global economy on urbanization has focused on global cities and their relations with subordinate regional and/or postcolonial hubs. Dividing the world into Immanuel Wallerstein's core, semi-peripheral and peripheral economies, and then relinking them through a network of urban nodes, this model of interconnected cores of

below left: Wal-Mart, suburban Chicago, 2002. Image by Phillip Jones.

below right: Flooded parking lot, Ewing, New Jersey, 2004. Image by Phillip Jones.

52

graduated significance effectively illustrates the capital flows and communications infrastructure between administrative and banking centers throughout the world economy. However, because the work of Anthony King, Saskia Sassen, Manuel Castells, and others focuses so much on banking, finance, administration, and communication, it retains a focus on urban centers and financial districts as hubs that neglects the far larger proportion of urban development outside the centers, the variously described landscape of edge cities, edgeless cities, technoburbs, and urban sprawl. Since the 1970s suburban development in the United States has outpaced central cities three-fold.[10] For example, despite a significant boom in medium to high-density in-town construction in recent years, metropolitan Atlanta is chopping down 54 acres of trees a day, for ever-lower-density subdivisions and ever-greater auto-dependency at the ever-expanding edge.[11] Architecture schools have similarly tended to ignore this development, giving far more pedagogical emphasis to how to relate architecture to either culturally rich, urban contexts or biologically rich, natural ones, than to the ambiguous *terrain vague* of the suburbs.

If cities are the principal urban form identified with industrialism, urban sprawl is the principal urban form of postindustrialism. Coincident with the advances in telecommunications and economic restructuring beginning in the 1970s and continuing today, urban sprawl exemplifies the decentralization, dispersion, and disconnection from local conditions that is characteristic of digital media and the global economy. Not unlike the spiderwebs of the global economy, sprawl's chain stores and franchises are local manifestations of much larger, globally networked enterprises. Its office parks tend to be occupied by businesses that are regional exporters. As the global economy reproduces interchangeable labor pools in its relentless search for cheap labor, urban sprawl reproduces interchangeable places in its search for cheap land. Designed to attract mobile capital through real estate investment trusts traded on Wall Street the developments conform to formulaic, single-use, auto-dependent typologies: malls, strip malls, office parks, garden apartments, and residential subdivisions.[12] Wall Street values short-term predictability more than long-term financial performance (let alone long-term environmental or social sustainability.) As a result, most of these product types are built ever more cheaply since the investment will be treated as a disposable asset, amortized in as little as seven years. In an unsustainable cycle, their value quickly diminishes as they are leapfrogged by newer versions further out. Within this system, varied uses are configured more in relationship to highway exits and perceptions of mobility and speed than to each other and the result is a landscape largely bereft of public spaces devoted to democratic ideals of civic or communal activity. Instead, what serves as public space is predominantly oriented to shopping. Meanwhile the private spaces of sprawl, especially the subdivisions, tend to be highly economically stratified. Like the global differentiation of landscapes, zoning regulations with lot-size

10 *See Ellen Dunham-Jones,* "Seventy-Five Percent," Harvard Design Magazine, *12 (fall 2000).*

11 *This statistic is based on analysis of Landsat Satellite data as reported by Stacy Shelton,* "Study: 54 Acres of Trees Lost Daily," Atlanta Journal-Constitution, *April 15, 2005.*

12 *See Christopher B. Leinberger,* "Retrofitting Real Estate Finance: Alternatives to the Nineteen Standard Product Types," Places *17, 2 (summer 2005).*

minimums perform significant market segmentation, segregating those with different incomes and exacerbating jobs–housing imbalances. Finally, the generic aspect of so many of the places and buildings in sprawl's vast landscapes reflect the general placelessness of the postindustrial economy.

It is perhaps no surprise that this quintessential postindustrial landscape is aesthetically, environmentally, economically, and socially unsustainable.[13] Or is it? A few arguments have emerged refuting the litany of criticism against sprawl. Historian Robert Bruegmann defends sprawl's social sustainability by arguing that its undeniable popularity is due to its provision of the American Dream to more and more Americans. He is dismissive of sprawl's critics as mostly elite snobs disdainful of the middle class. Less convincingly, libertarians like Randall O'Toole have questioned sprawl's poor environmental performance by pointing out the advantages of open space in low-density development and dismissing concerns over land consumption by pointing out the country's enormous reserves of unbuilt land.[14] Such defenses of sprawl generally ignore the multiple negative impacts of auto-dependent lifestyles and pit those advocating free markets and unhindered private property rights against zoning, planning, and environmental protections as big government solutions.

Development patterns and the provision of roads are central to all of these debates. They constitute the biggest local government expenditure and are one of the most effective tools the state has for fostering either sprawl or more compact growth. Using conservative forecasts, a recent book by Bob Burchell, Anthony Downs, Barbara McCann, and Sahan Mukherji on the economic cost of sprawl argues that Americans can no longer afford to pay the infrastructure, land depletion, and disinvestment costs of leapfrog development. In one telling example, they write:

In South Carolina, if sprawl continues unchecked, statewide infrastructure costs for the period 1995 to 2015 are projected to be more than $56 billion or $750 per citizen per year for these twenty years. Roads would cost 2.5 times what would be spent on primary, secondary and higher education infrastructure; three times what would be spent on health infrastructure, including all hospitals, institutions, and water-sewer treatment systems; ten times what would be spent on public safety, administration, and justice infraction infrastructure; and twenty-five times what would be spent on all cultural and recreational infrastructure.[15]

Alex Krieger argues that what has gotten us into this situation is that the benefits of sprawl (increased privacy, mobility, and access to nature) have accrued to individuals, while the costs of sprawl (degraded air and water quality, traffic, social segregation, land consumption, and disinvestment) have been born by society as a whole.[16] Although new research points to the growing transportation and health costs of sprawl to individuals and growing

13 See F. Kaid Benfield, Matthew D. Raimi, and Donald D. T. Chen, Once There Were Greenfields, How Urban Sprawl is Undermining America's Environment, Economy, and Social Fabric *(New York: National Resource Defense Council, 1999).*

14 See Robert Bruegman, Sprawl, A Compact History *(Chicago, Ill.: University of Chicago Press, 2005), and Randal O'Toole,* The Vanishing Automobile and Other Urban Myths: How Smart Growth Will Harm American Cities *(Bandon, Oreg.: Thoreau Institute, 1996).*

15 Robert W. Burchell et al., Sprawl Costs, Economic Impacts of Unchecked Development *(Washington, D.C.: Island Press, 2005), 4.*

16 Alex Krieger, "The Costs— and Benefits?—of Sprawl," Harvard Design Magazine *19 (fall 2003/winter 2004).*

market dissatisfaction with sprawl's limited housing types, the legal, financial, and development systems remain oriented to reproducing this form of accounting and its built consequences. This lack of sustainable sharing of costs and benefits between individuals and society is not only endemic to sprawl, but to the difficulties of weaving the green braid at all scales. How do we shift to a more interdependent sharing of costs and benefits? Is this a matter solely of public policy or can it be reconsidered as a design problem?

NEW URBANISM

Architects naturally tend to focus on the design of individual buildings and immediate spatial relationships rather than less visible, less physical impacts. However, so much of the lesson of sustainability is the need to better understand the impact of individual projects on larger systems. William McDonough's attention to systems performance rather than the design of a product has helped to establish his leadership in sustainable design. By treating waste as food, whether at the level of the molecule, the lifecycle, or the ecosystem, he redefines individual design commissions as opportunities for long-term sustainable economic development.

Such thinking applied to sprawl suggests that rather than simply designing a single, green project or building what is needed is an overhaul of the very systems by which sprawl is reproduced. This is in fact the agenda of the C.N.U. (Congress for the New Urbanism). Instead of assessing new urbanism based on the virtues or vices of the 700 or so individual new urbanist projects or their designers (as has been the tendency in architectural discourse), if one looks at the work of C.N.U. as an organization, the radicality of this larger re-design project becomes more evident.[17] Like its predecessor, C.I.A.M. (Congrès Internationale d'Architecture Moderne), C.N.U. produced a charter of principles that clearly lays out the organization's reformist ambitions. Over the past fourteen years, it has fundamentally redesigned the systems of development by strategically building alliances and new tools and standards to allow for the implementation of the charter's principles. While academic discourse focused on theory and maintaining autonomous critical distance, the new urbanists collaborated with E.P.A., H.U.D., U.L.I., A.P.A., A.I.A., Fannie Mae, N.A.H.B., I.T.E., the R.W.J. Foundation and most recently, the U.S.G.B.C., to intertwine more sustainable practices into, and to change the rules of the game of, development.

While C.I.A.M.-influenced single-use zoning reflected a legitimate need to separate noxious industrial uses from housing in the early twentieth century, C.N.U. recognizes how out of date such prohibitions against mixed-use are in the American postindustrial landscape and has redesigned the zoning codes of numerous towns and cities and triggered updates in countless more. Through model ordinances of zoning overlay districts, locally specific form based codes, pattern books and Andres Duany's smart code, C.N.U. has provided new tools to promote more urban and more place-based

17 *My observations (and biases) are based on my attendance at twelve of the fourteen congresses, four years as a task force chair and my position since 2005 as a member of C.N.U.'s Board of Directors.*

55

development patterns and buildings. Based on a transect of six different zones that go from most urban to most rural, these new codes replace the relatively crude and monolithic land-use designations of sprawl with finer grained differentiations between more dense, walkable, mixed-use urban cores and protected rural preserves. Integrated with masterplans in most cases, the codes link varied lot sizes with specific building types and specific street types so as to design in a variety of choices for different incomes and needs. Instead of a typical subdivision of cookie-cutter homes at uniform price points, C.N.U. uses design to integrate diverse households into mixed-income communities.[18] The finer grain of the smart code also allows for designed transitions from the building to the street, from the center to edge of a neighborhood and between neighborhoods.

Just as sprawl separates uses, it separates decisions about transportation design from land use and relies on mid-century street-design principles. The A.A.S.H.T.O. manual on street design bases all fundamental decisions on only two conditions: mobility and access. The base assumption is that rural roads between cities are designed for high speed and maximum mobility while urban roads within cities are designed for slow speeds, multiple curb cuts, signals, and turn lanes to provide maximum access. Unfortunately, suburban conditions are not addressed and arterials are designed for a level of service consistent with mobility even though they are inevitably rezoned for commercial and retail—albeit significantly spaced apart because of the curb cut limitations. As a result, suburban commercial strips end up providing neither convenient access or mobility. Instead, C.N.U. has led interdisciplinary efforts with the Institute of Transportation Engineers to redesign street standards that promote a much wider array of context-sensitive designs that correspond to the transect zones of the smart code. In addition to linking land use and transportation for the first time, the new standards recognize that in addition to accommodating cars, streets need to be designed for multiple modes including pedestrians, biking, light rail, etc. The multi-year effort is moving towards national adoption and will provide designers with significant opportunities to integrate more sustainable compact, planning with more sustainable transportation modes and build on C.N.U.'s successes with transit-oriented development.

This integration is especially significant at the scale of the region. In association with various smart-growth organizations, C.N.U. has advanced strategies for designing regions to perform more sustainably. Developed by E.P.A., smart growth recognizes that environmentally friendly "no-growth" positions are futile in high growth areas and tend to increase housing costs. Instead, smart growth links and balances the conservation of natural areas to the identification of targeted growth areas within a region. The latter may be existing areas in need of redevelopment or new areas already well-served by infrastructure. Smart growth policies limit government funds for new roads, schools, or other infrastructure to only be expended in the identified

18 H.U.D.'s Hope VI housing program has replaced approximately 100 of the country's most blighted public housing projects with new urbanist mixed-income communities. However, despite mixed-income intentions, many new urbanist projects have been forced by N.I.M.B.Y.-influenced local planning boards to eliminate the lowest-end units and increase the number of single-family homes.

above: New Urbanist Town Center, Prospect, Colorado, 2005. Image by Phillip Jones.

growth areas. Criticized by some as allowing government to overly interfere with the free market, smart-growth policies have nonetheless been adopted by republican and democratic governors as a means of promoting sustainable economic development. For regional designers, these policies are tools that can redirect growth back into existing nodes and corridors so as to assist in less auto-dependent redevelopment and, where possible, to make transit feasible. The admittedly ambitious goal is to retrofit sprawl into healthy polycentric regions.

Additional tools that C.N.U. has developed or promoted to advance economic, social, and environmental sustainability include:

- the development of alternative financing models and means to assess mixed-use investments;
- location efficient mortgages which allow homebuyers near transit to qualify for $60–$90,000 more in a mortgage if they own one less car than would otherwise be expected given the size of the unit;
- guidelines for greyfield redevelopment;
- guidelines for replacement of elevated highways with surface boulevards;
- the reliance upon charrettes to involve stakeholders in the design (as in the post-Katrina charrette for the towns of the Mississippi coast);

57

- collaboration with public-health officials to promote walkability as a tool to fight obesity and other health risks;
- and current collaboration with the U.S.G.B.C. and the Natural Resources Defense Council to develop L.E.E.D.-N.D., a new Leadership in Energy and Environmental Design designation for projects at the scale of neighborhood design.

All told, this extensive toolkit picks up C.I.A.M.'s reformist torch and applies it towards alternatives to sprawl. Its strategies are intended to equip designers and planners to operate within the existing market structure of the economy to design places that consumers willingly choose for their long-term viability, fairness and ecological benefits.[19]

New urbanism is far from living up to all of its principles and goals. But the C.N.U. has been remarkably effective at drawing attention to both the need and the market for alternatives to sprawl and the value of the slow, the in-place, and the fixed within lives dominated by speed, mobility, and flexibility.

PLACEMAKING AND ECONOMIC SUSTAINABILITY

The global postindustrial economy integrates diverse parts of the world economically, but at the local level produces unsustainable landscapes based only on short-term profits. They increase the segregation of rich and poor, are highly auto-dependent and land consumptive and are prone to abandonment rather than reinvestment and nurtured growth.

However, precisely because postindustrial landscapes have been so dominated by generic buildings and non-placebased market logics, the uniqueness of place and placemaking matter more than ever. Within the sea of placeless sameness, design becomes the prime tool for adding value to places. Precisely because life in the postindustrial economy is increasingly spent in front of a computer screen, there is a growing interest in spending one's time offline in attractive, distinctive, diverse places with opportunities for social interaction and engagement with nature. Precisely because of globalization, urban neighborhoods are thriving that provide both a rooted sense of place and an ability for individuals to feel connected to larger communal/political, spatial and natural systems beyond themselves.

The market for well-designed places provides the opportunity for architects to weave the green braid. Architects and architecture cannot reform the economic system to make it more sustainable. But at the local level they can resist its pernicious effects and exploit its support for placemaking. The challenge for architects is to use design—both at the urban and architectural scale—to counter the postindustrial landscapes with places and communities that sustain value, diversity, and environmental quality over time.

The ability of places to endure, thrive, and evolve over time is crucial to their ability to intertwine the braid's strands. The more we reuse existing buildings and infrastructure, the less natural resources we have to consume

19 *Although new urbanism regularly receives criticism from architects for its predominantly neo-traditionally styled buildings, I have argued that this use of popular styles is a strategic attempt to seduce the market into accepting the otherwise unmarketable public goods of higher density, mixed-use, mixed-income, public space, and public transit. See Ellen Dunham-Jones, "New Urbanism's Subversive Marketing," What People Want, Populism in Architecture and Design, ed. Michael Shamiyeh (Basel: Birkhauser, 2005).*

and the more opportunities we have for meeting a broad spectrum of social and cultural needs.[20] Yesterday's less sustainable suburban development types—the malls, office parks, and commercial strips—are increasingly being retrofitted into more sustainable, more urban places. Revitalization of existing places like this is extremely important, but so is designing new places that can survive the opening of a new mall, subdivision, or office park 5 miles away or around the world. This is where the current postindustrial landscapes have most failed.

The value of placemaking is a lesson not lost on the new urbanists' attention to improving the standards and practices that give value to the everyday landscape. Nor is it lost on Frank Gehry, who since Bilbao has been the go-to guy for an urban shot in the arm. These strategies, the making of enduring economically diverse neighborhoods and the making of timely icons, complement each other well as they use design to give identity and beauty to place. In the long term, if we have made places that future generations find worth sustaining, we will have succeeded in weaving the braid.

20 *Jane Jacobs writes of the importance of older buildings with low rents to house the non-profits, artists, and other community-serving uses that can rarely afford to locate in new construction in* The Death and Life of Great American Cities *(New York: Random House, 1961).*

MODELS, LISTS, AND THE EVOLUTION OF SUSTAINABLE ARCHITECTURE

STEVEN A. MOORE

The purpose of this chapter is to challenge, at the outset, the abstract model that conceptualizes sustainability as a triangle of competing interests. This model proposes that sustainable development is achieved through the self-conscious balancing of three competing interests within society, those of economic development, environmental preservation, and social equity—what are popularly referred to as the three Es. My argument is that this increasingly popular concept is historical (or political), rather than scientific, in significance. It is an idea that is socially constructed, not one that was discovered in our DNA. In this sense "sustainable architecture" reflects the structure of an ongoing human conversation that is struggling to envision a more life-enhancing future, not a formula certain to deliver it.

In the 1960s—the period that catalyzed public concern over the degradation of "nature"—the environmental movement recognized only two diametrically opposed interests, those of ecological integrity and economic development. In this initial opposition activists pitted themselves against the interests of economic development so as to preserve ecological integrity. It took nearly twenty years of public conversation—until the mid-1980s—for most North Americans to recognize that it was not only the seemingly allergic interests of business and nature that were impacted by development. Rather, citizens came to recognize that the relatively poor were being adversely impacted both by those who would consume natural resources and by those who would preserve them. Thus the third E, equity, was given a seat—albeit a smaller one—at the table.

Through the international discourse that followed publication of *Our Common Future*, better known as the Brundtland Report, in 1987, this triangulated concept has been generally accepted as the logic that informs the concept of sustainable development. As a result it has been adopted by many institutions as the a-priori tool through which sustainable development is first conceptualized and then measured. My argument in what follows is not to hold that this logic is somehow wrong or misrepresents the social history of its construction. At the very least the green tripod, as some refer to it, has proven to be a valuable heuristic tool that helps us to understand one aspect of a very complex problem. I will argue, however, that such a-priori or deductive logic can be less than helpful, even destructive, when employed by well-intended architects, planners, and policymakers as the template through which sustainability is imprinted upon real places.

The basis of my critique derives from my study of three city-regions that are associated in the literature with sustainable urban development: Austin,

Texas; Curitiba, Brazil; and Frankfurt, Germany. This lengthy investigation was stimulated by a 1999 visit to Curitiba during which I discovered conditions that challenged my own assumptions, and those implicit within the Brundtland Report, about the relationship between democracy and sustainable development. Although I had previously argued that democracy was a necessary, if insufficient condition for sustainability to show up in any city, Curitiba clearly presented evidence to the contrary. That city has made dramatic progress toward achieving sustainable development through technocratic means founded upon the authority of the military junta that seized power in Brazil in 1964 and that lasted until the late 1980s. The book that derives from this study is, then, chiefly focused upon the relationship between democratic processes, social equity and environmental preservation.[1] This chapter, however, focuses upon a subtheme of that book: the relation between cities, stories, and progress. In the end I find that it is human stories, not abstract models or lists of best practices that most dramatically influence ecological outcomes. But before considering how sustainability might better be understood as a progressive storyline rather than a fixed geometry of interests it will be helpful to trace the steps by which the tripod became the dominant model of sustainability.

1 *Moore,* Alternative Routes to the Sustainable City. *This chapter is partially excerpted and derived from the larger study to be published by Rowman & Littlefield.*

TRIANGLES AND TRIPODS

I have already credited the authors of the Brundtland Report with the implicit suggestion that sustainable development at any scale can only be achieved through the balancing of the three Es. That seminal text of 1987 did not, however, explicitly model the concept as a triangle nor did it stipulate specific action to be taken. By 1992, however, the United Nations Conference on Environment and Development (U.N.C.E.D.), held at Rio de Janiero, articulated an action plan for sustainable development to be achieved in the twenty-first century that is now commonly referred to as Agenda 21. Under a U.N. mandate to implement Agenda 21, it was the International Council for Local Environmental Initiatives (I.C.L.E.I.) that first conceptualized sustainability as a triangle of competing interests. In picturing sustainable development as a "three legged stool" these authors suggested that sustainability initiatives could not stand as a whole without equal support from the three constituent social networks that represent the interests of ecology, economy and equity.

Although the three-legged stool metaphor has been widely adopted, it has been most elegantly pictured by the planner Scott Campbell. In Campbell's diagram, illustrated in Figure 1, the three corners of an equilateral triangle represent the competing interests of the three Es and the sides represent a set of conflicts that occur naturally in any modern society. Campbell's argument is that the role of planners and architects in democratic societies is to mediate, and thus stabilize the conditions of conflict.

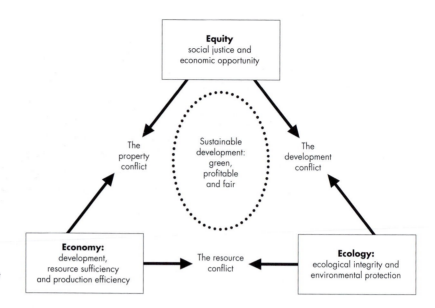

Figure 1 *The three Es of sustainability, after Campbell, Green Cities, Growing Cities, Just Cities.*

2 Godschalk, "Landuse Planning Challenges," 8.

3 Moore, "Disciplinary Blinders." *In this text and elsewhere I employed a tetrahedral geometry to model sustainable development.*

4 Moore, "Architecture, Aesthetics and the Public Health." *In this text I employed a circular geometry to model sustainable development.*

Others have adopted this vector-like logic, but have argued the need to include a fourth set of interests, thus transforming the triangle to a tetrahedron. This argument is based upon the historical precedent noted above. If environmental conflict of the 1960s began as a simple dichotomy between the two Es—ecology and economy—and grew to three Es by including the concept of equity as a legitimate variable in the conflict, why should we not have four Es and thus democratize the conversation to include yet other related interests. David Godschalk, for example, has proposed that the three competing values of sustainability—economy, ecology and equity—must be expanded to include "livable community values" if we are to construct a planning tool that will be helpful in negotiating and thus balancing the conflicts that emerge in real places.[2]

In similar fashion I have myself attempted to expand the three Es to include aesthetic interests as a necessary variable to be considered in the construction of sustainable places. By dropping the "a" from (a)esthetic, this strategy conveniently forms a tetrahedron of four Es. My logic in constructing this figure was to argue that unless healthy environments are also beautiful and compelling they will not be sustained by the societies they claim to serve. Even worse, I feared that architecture might be reduced to a positivistic field of measurement.[3] In some texts I revised the tetrahedron to other geometries so as to reveal new possibilities for conflict resolution.[4]

Having made such abstract arguments I am now free to critique the logic behind it. Although each of these abstract models (my own included) may be helpful in suggesting the many conflicting variables legitimately related to sustainability, empirical evidence suggests that any model, no matter how complex, fails to represent the nuance or contingency of history, past or future. In my study of Austin, Curitiba, and Frankfurt I found that all of these abstract models tended to obscure local discourses that thrived and/or languished in those places and thus distort the historical evidence. This is to say that although deductive models may help to explain some commonalities shared between cities that have already achieved some success in moving toward sustainability, such models only obscure the contingent process of *how* and *why* sustainability shows up in a particular city in the first place. And if this argument holds true, then my empirical findings suggest that extruding yet other cities through abstract models in an attempt to make progress toward sustainable development may do more harm than good.

What I did find in these exemplary cities, instead of the new and improved model of sustainable development I had hoped to find, is that each city has a very different story to tell.

SUSTAINABILITY AS AN URBAN STORYLINE

Like triangles and tripods the notion that sustainability is best understood as a narrative is not a new one. David Nye (1997), Barbara Eckstein (2003), James Throgmorton (2003), and others have developed this idea over the past ten years. From their work we understand that all societies construct stories about themselves. We do so not only to distinguish our tribe from others, but to explain to ourselves how our ancestors came to live in a particular place in a particular way. But such stories are not fixed. They are edited over time by new ideas that first appear as marginal social practices and only later become codified as explanations for those practices. As conditions change, as they inevitably do, the "foundation narratives" of all societies are periodically rewritten.[5] So, one way to understand the emergence of sustainability is not as a historically unique situation brought about by a singular case of over-consumption, but as a periodic and necessary rewriting of the foundation narrative of Western society. Our current era, as have others before it, requires a new storyline if we expect history to unfold in a trajectory we can accept on behalf of future generations and those who are now unable to speak for themselves.

Table 1 provides a simple analysis of six story lines that have shaped human understanding of the world at different times in history: the heroic, religious, scientific, C.I.A.M.[6], economic and the sustainable.[7] Although these are roughly chronological in order of appearance, none of them has ever entirely disappeared from view, nor is my list comprehensive. When new storylines show up they simply share the available space with those that precede them and with others that are less prominent. The sustainability story is just one layer of history that best describes the dilemmas of our time and it must be understood within the context of the other storylines that compete for our allegiance. It is the overlapping nature of these competing storylines that keeps local stories about sustainability in touch with larger global phenomena.

5 Nye, Narratives and Spaces. *Nye mentions sustainable development only in the closing passage of the book.*

6 *C.I.A.M., or the* Congrès International d'Architecture Moderne, *was held annually from 1928 through 1956. The organization articulated, and constantly revised the collective vision of its members. The manifestos issued under the CIAM are generally accepted to represent the orthodox views of modern architects toward the making of a truly modern world.*

7 *The structure and some terms in this table are derived from those presented in a lecture by Betty Sue Flowers at the University of Texas, October 12, 2000.*

	Premodern		Modern			Postmodern
Storylines	heroic	religious	scientific	C.I.A.M.	economic	sustainable
Ideals	excellence	goodness	truth	functionalism	growth (quantitative)	development (qualitative)
Behaviors	competition	obedience	experimentation	design	maximize	optimize
Actors	heroes	saints and prophets	scientists and philosophers	architects and planners	consumers and business	citizens
Modes of communication	legends	scripture and prayer	logic	drawings, models and manifestoes	images and numbers	feedback loops
Attitude toward time	immortality	eternity	timelessness	*Zeitgeist*	now	perpetual renewal

Table 1: Characteristics of alternative storylines.

Thinking about history as a succession of stories seems, at least at first, an outrageous notion. Is it possible that simply telling a new story will alter historical outcomes? To think so we would have to assert that the story to be told is a very powerful one indeed—so powerful that it will convince a majority of our fellow citizens that fundamental change of their ideals, behavior, heroes, modes of communication, time frames, and so on, is in their interest. But, stories do not cause history. Rather, they reflect real capabilities for history-making as much as they catalyze action. If stories are received as utopian fantasies, unrelated to daily life, characteristic behaviors, and plausible outcomes they will be rejected by citizens. What proved to be of most interest in my empirical investigation of Austin, Curitiba and Frankfurt is how stories of sustainable development come to be told, how they conscript others to retell the story to their peers, how they motivate citizens to live differently, and thus influence our evolutionary prospects.

THE STRUCTURE OF URBAN STORYLINES

My study of these three cities employed the methodological assumptions of *grounded theory* and ethnographic methods of data collection and interpretation borrowed from sociology and anthropology. In the process of interpreting the historical record and interviews conducted in each city I constructed terms that reflect the common structure, if not content, of the stories told in those cities. Simply defining these terms is helpful.

First, I propose that we should not think of sustainability as a *concept* as is done in common usage, or as a *discourse* as Dryzek[8] and Fischer[9] propose, or even as a *narrative* as Eckstein and Throgmorton[10] propose, but as a *storyline*. I prefer this term because it emphasizes the plot or trajectory of action rather than the style of the narrative. By investigating the lines of stories we can better anticipate how competing accounts might converge or diverge. This is to say that competing storylines may be in conflict yet project forward a limited horizon of possibilities. Storylines are, then, a shared way of making sense of the past and speculating about what might become true in the future.

8 Dryzek, Politics of the Earth.

9 *Fischer*, Reframing Public Policy.

10 *Eckstein and Throgmorton*, Story and Sustainability.

If competing storylines project a range of alternative futures, these are constructed, described and lived by citizens through different kinds of *public talk*. Every city has, of course, many different kinds of public talk, or conversations that take place over a long period of time. The citizens of Boston are, for example, the authors of many public conversations, some Irish, some Portuguese, some Catholic, some Puritan, some about the city's "big dig," and some about baseball played under the unique conditions imposed by "the green monster." Although each of these distinct public conversations include only some citizens, together they add up to public talk about the city's past and future that includes all citizens whether they can talk baseball stats or not. Benjamin Barber defines "public talk" as that which "always involves listening as well as speaking, feeling as well as thinking, and acting as well as reflecting."[11] In the study I adopted this definition, but add to it the idea that public talk is comprised of many competing quasi-public conversations that vie for our attention, allegiance and participation.

In my analysis of these three cities that aspire to develop sustainably I found that of the many kinds of public talk in which citizens are engaged— baseball talk, art talk, money talk, etc.—there are three that contribute most to sustainability: these are *political talk*, *environmental talk* and *technological talk*. This is not to argue that sustainability is comprised only of these variables, but that it turns up most frequently in these kinds of conversations. I'll briefly characterize each in turn.

POLITICAL TALK

Among architects it will not be controversial to characterize talk about sustainability as political. Given limited economic resources, how should we reasonably decide which of the many criteria put forward to define sustainability is correct or better—LEED, BREES, ISO 14400, Green Globe, etc? My point is that the disagreement between the expert authors of these various standards is not a scientific one, it is a political one. This is to say that choices about which criteria for sustainability are best are social choices about how we want to live, not scientific choices about what is true or more efficient. In my analysis of the three cities I concluded that each had developed distinct political dispositions in their historical development that reflect fundamentally different dispositions toward conflict resolution and what is socially valued.

The political philosopher, Benjamin Barber, has suggested a helpful taxonomy that categorizes three political dispositions within Western liberal democracies—these are defined in Table 2. Barber's categories are teleological to the extent that they imply a progressive order of development but, in his view are not yet inadequate forms of democracy. My point in constructing the table is to point out that each of the three cities I have studied exemplifies one of Barber's dispositions. I found that a majority of citizens in each city has very different political values and very different attitudes toward the

11 Barber, Strong Democracy, 177.

	Liberal-anarchism	Liberal-realism	Liberal-minimalism
Generic response to conflict	Denial—conflict emerges only because of the illegitimate authority of the state.	Repression—conflict is dangerous because it disturbs the contract certainty upon which growth depends.	Toleration—conflict is natural in a diverse society and stimulates individual creativity.
What is valued	Rights—individuals are perceived as having asocial origins and rights.	Wisdom—a few very wise individuals are required to administer social order.	Freedom—atomized individuals must be free to pursue happiness within market conditions.
Selected city	Austin	Curitiba	Frankfurt

Table 2: The three dispositions of liberal democracy.

conflicts inherent in assessing progress toward sustainable development. Where the real estate cowboys of Austin tend to deny the legitimacy of conflict in the marketplace, the technocrats of Curitiba tend to suppress conflict in the name of stability, and the cosmopolitan bankers of Frankfurt tolerate conflict in order to optimize cash flow. These attitudes tend to interpret global phenomena through very different kinds of stories.

ENVIRONMENTAL TALK

As I argued above, the dominant kind of environmental talk, or talk about sustainability that is found in Western cities is the "three-legged stool" or "planners' triangle" illustrated above in Figure 1. Here I'll argue that Campbell's discursive model is indeed a good fit for the political disposition of Frankfurt. The problem is that it less a fit for Austin, and largely unrelated to the political discourses and disposition of Curitiba. This is to say that one size, or one model, does not fit all. This discovery prompted me to adopt the broader description of competing environmental discourses developed by John Dryzek and illustrated in Figure 2. Dryzek developed these (and other) categories through the inductive methods of *discourse frame analysis*.[12] For the purposes of this short chapter I won't attempt to describe the characteristics of each kind of environmental talk encountered in my investigation, but simply note that all of the types that show up in Figure 2 also showed up in the cities studied.

This more complex, fine-grained and inductive view of environmental talk suggests that there can be many more than three competing values—economy, ecology, and equity—in any particular place that must be satisfied in order to realize sustainable development.

Where the citizens of Austin are decisively split between discourses that are radical and imaginative and those that are reformist and prosaic, Curitibanos rely upon elite experts to solve their problems and Frankfurters tolerate every imaginable possibility. These differing dispositions make for very different stories about the state of ecological integrity.

12 *Dryzek*, Politics of the Earth.

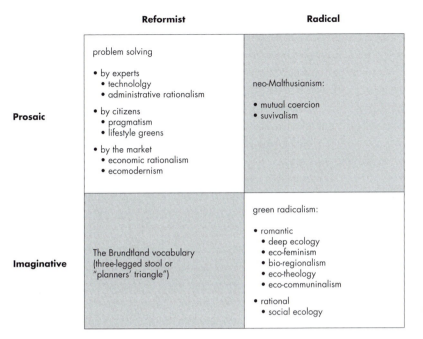

Figure 2. Categories of environmental talk.

TECHNOLOGICAL TALK

It is commonly argued that technology is the most distinctive feature of modern society. If we accept this characterization it suggests that human experience in the world is increasingly mediated by technologies of one kind or another. Talk about sustainable technology is, then, not only a matter of trading in one tool for another, it is talk about changing our living habits.

Choosing to understand unsustainability as an unnecessary and destructive social habit, as I have in this study, suggests that the reverse may also be true—that the condition of sustainability might spring from the conscious reconstruction of social habits. The problem with this proposition is that instilling in our fellow citizens the desire to modify their habits is not enough in itself to alter the situation. This is because repetitious social behaviors do not exist in isolation from the built world. First, social habits coevolve with the technological systems that enable them, and second, once technological systems like highways and automobiles are in place they limit our choices to live otherwise.[13] This is to say that the built world is the reification, or materialization of our social habits. If we are to consciously reconstruct malignant social habits, then we must also reconstruct our technologies and landscapes.

Yet another way to argue this point is to say that technology is not a necessary progression of artifacts but a scene of struggle that determines how we will live together and in relation to natural processes.[14] This is to say that reconstructing cities to be sustainable will require what Pfaffenberg refers to as a "technological drama"—a series of technological acts and counter-acts

13 Hughes, *"Edison and Electric Light."*

14 Feenberg, Questioning Technology.

15 Pfaffenberg, "Technological Dramas."

in which technological systems are regularized, adjusted, and reconstituted by sets of interested actors.[15] The case studies which constitute the better part of the book excerpted here are urban technological dramas of just this sort.

In my examination of the selected cases I found that ordinary citizens in each city developed over time interpretive frames, or attitudes toward technology that tended toward the technophilic (meaning that technology is inherently good) or toward the technophobic (meaning that technology is inherently bad). Ordinary citizens also had split attitudes toward the relation of technology to society. Some were deterministic (meaning that they saw technologies as controlling society) and others were voluntaristic (meaning that they saw society as free to choose whatever technology was deemed desirable). These are what I will refer to as "naïve" interpretive frames and are related to each other in Figure 3.

More sophisticated observers—activists, STS scholars, and historians, for example—tend to have more critical views that are neither technophilic nor technophobic, and neither deterministic nor voluntaristic. These various critical positions lie in the central cell of the figure.

To summarize what was learned from the interpretation of political, environmental and technological talk in the three cities, I'll hold that it is not abstract models derived from deductive reasoning (i.e., Campbell's illustration of the Brundtland model), or universally applied lists of "best practices" derived from inductive reasoning (i.e., the "green" architectural checklist developed by LEED) that will catalyze successful action. These deductive and inductive proposals certainly have heuristic value—meaning that they can introduce naïve or skeptical citizens to the general concerns of sustainability. Rather, I found that abstract models and cumulative lists are in themselves distractions from the social project of constructing future-oriented storylines from the unique perspective of people who live in a place. This kind of reasoning is what Charles Sander Pierce called "abductive logic,"[16] what

16 Pierce, On Arguments.

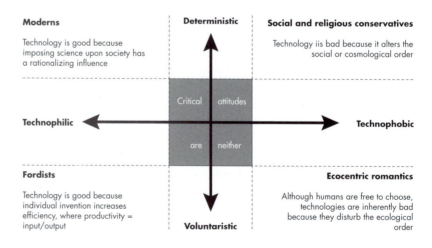

Figure 3. Naive technological discursive frames.

Donna Haraway calls "situated knowledge,"[17] and what Richard Bernstein—following Aristotle—calls "phroenesis."[18] Following these philosophers, my hypothesis is that *successful* storylines of sustainability—meaning those that lead to satisfying action—are constituted of political, environmental and technological talk that is home-grown from particular cultural and environmental conditions. Turning this hypothesis inside out would be to argue that when citizens of a particular place compare their situation to abstract models of sustainable development or lists of best practices what they encounter are local obstacles to be overcome by universal principles. But when they begin with local patterns of public talk and historical story-lines, what they encounter are opportunities. It is this latter possibility that leads most directly to satisfying action.

PROGRESS AND EVOLUTION

Movement toward the ending or horizon of a storyline is commonly under-stood as "progress." This term is, however, now received with skepticism and the criticism of those who have experienced or anticipated the dark side of Enlightenment rationality. In the view of postmodern philosophers, beginning with Heidegger, the very idea that science and technology will enable modern humans to predict and control nature is not our salvation but the very source of modern environmental and social degradation.[19] For postmoderns, progress never makes the world better, only more complex. Some postmodern architectural theorists go so far as to argue that the sustainability story is only a thinly veiled attempt to perpetuate the hege-mony of American corporate capitalism.[20] To embrace sustainability as the storyline of progress is, in the eyes of postmoderns, to stay firmly within the Enlightenment project of perfecting the world through the use of human rationality.

In response to these postmodern skeptics I must distinguish between the kind of human *rationality* that we associate with Enlightenment science and human *intelligence* itself. By the former I mean a particular way of reasoning, and by the latter I mean the ability to reason. Like many postmoderns[21] John Dewey was (occasionally) skeptical of traditional Western, or technological rationality, but unlike most postmoderns, he was generally optimistic about the potential of human intelligence to solve problems. He argued that "if human problems are to be solved it will be human intelligence that will have to do the job."[22] The story that Dewey put forward was that human nature is changeable, or developmental rather than fixed. This is to say human reasoning might be improved. Contrary to the fears of some postmoderns, then, all forms of rationality do not lead to the same consequence.

The emerging discipline of *memetics*, which derives most directly from the work of Richard Dawkins, proposes that human evolution is influenced not only by the laws of natural selection and genetic mutation but by the passing along of ideas from one generation to the next. Because ideas, or "memes,"

17 Haraway, "Situated Knowledges."

18 Bernstein, "Heidegger's Silence."

19 Heidegger, Age of the World Picture.

20 Shepheard, Artificial Love. Shepheard's critique of sustainability is hardly unique and derives from a generally Foucauldian aversion to the politics of modern institutions.

21 In general I use the terms "modern" and "postmodern" to distinguish philosophical attitudes not architectural styles. Where moderns accept the Cartesian dualisms of mind and body, culture and nature, or subject and object, postmoderns reject them.

22 Cited in Hickman, Philosophical Tools for a Technological Culture, 155.

23 *Dawkins*, The Selfish Gene.

affect not only human events but the physical environment, Dawkins argues that over time they also influence blind evolutionary choices.[23] For example, if we understand the idea of "rugged individualism" to be a "meme" of the American West that has been passed from generation to generation for the past century and a half it is perfectly reasonable to argue in Darwinian terms that a cultural landscape has been produced by rugged individuals that will in turn influence the possible choices of future generations. My point here is that the stories and "foundation narratives" we tell to each other have more than passing interest—they contain and/or suppress evolutionary possibilities. This is not to argue that human evolution takes place within such a short period of time as the era of rugged individualists but rather that the ecological impact of rugged individualists has been of geological proportion that in turn influences adaptive behavior and so on. An extension of this memetic logic would be to hold that it is not only the ideas which are passed between generations that have evolutionary impact, but also cultural habits or practices. In Dewey's assessment, thinking is biological in its origins. He held that, "Of human organisms it is especially true that activities carried on for satisfying needs so change the environment that new needs arise which demand still further change in the activities of organisms by which they are satisfied; and so on in a potentially endless change."[24]

24 *Dewey, "Existential Matrix,"*
35.

Dewey's position is not a form of environmental determinism, but a *relational* understanding of humans and nature that is entirely consistent with contemporary ecology. At its core is an understanding that humans interact with nature through technology. As human projects transform what we can call "first nature" into "second nature" not only are new technologies required, but humans too change in response to altered environmental conditions. In this scheme humans, nature, and technology are each granted shifting degrees of agency *ad infinitum*.

But here I must be careful not to leave the impression that human reasoning can direct evolution. Such logic would inevitably lead to the troubling proposal that Frankfurt is, for example, more evolved than Austin or Curitiba. Any such claim would require us to know the long trajectory of history from our position within it, which is not logically possible. To avoid such a simplistic view of either history or evolution we should distinguish between three models of evolution: those of Spencer, Lamarck, and Darwin.

Spencer's model proposes that greater complexity and progress are inevitable—his is a type of divine teleology first embraced by Enlightenment thinkers. In contrast, Lamarck's model proposes that human striving drives change but that progress per se is never guaranteed. Misguided striving might take us in a direction contrary to human interests. Darwin's model, however, proposes that evolution requires neither a historical force nor a direction of change.

I'll quickly dispense with Spencer's model of inevitable progress as wishful thinking, even if it is an attractive story still championed by many. Lamarck's model, however, seems closest to Dewey's position which is something of a problem because most contemporary evolutionary historians have discarded the idea that the striving of individuals can influence the long course of evolution. In spite of our ability to reason, skeptics argue, we can never predict the precise consequences of our actions. According to the more universally held Darwinian model, unconscious rather than planned selection is always at work in even the most carefully considered of human projects.

John Langrish, however, has proposed a neo-Darwinian model of evolution that does, I think, resolve the seeming conflict with Lamarck. Langrish's position combines Darwin's theory of natural selection with genetics, which appeared after Darwin, as a way of explaining what is carried from one generation to another. Langrish, like Dawkins whom I cited above, includes in the information carried between generations, not just the genetic code of DNA, but patterns of reasoning, or memes, which are transferred between generations and thus replicated through time and space. Larngrish thus argues that "the idea that Darwinian change is just 'chance' is wrong" rather, "[human] striving has to be seen as a necessary but insufficient factor in Darwinian change."[25] This is to say that striving to make things better is an essential human characteristic, but it doesn't assure that change will happen in the direction we intend. Progress is not assured by striving, yet striving does influence not only history, but the environment to which human biology adapts. A neo-Darwinian position would, then, accept not only the theory of *genetic* transfer, but *memetic* transfer as well.

This logic suggests that the social construction of storylines of sustainable development may in itself be an activity that foreshadows, if not determines, the appearance of the sustainable conditions we desire.

CONCLUSION

My study of Austin, Curitiba and Frankfurt concludes that there is no single or privileged route to the sustainable city. Extruding local conditions through the two, three, or four Es will not necessarily create sustainable conditions. Rather, each city is always in the making and remaking of itself through the historical process of storytelling. It is highly unlikely that the technocrats of Curitiba, for example, will suddenly adopt the model of high tolerance for social conflict that exists in Frankfurt or that the rugged individualists of Austin will suddenly adopt the model of rigid technocratic codes that enabled the miracle of Curitiba. Rather, progress toward sustainable development, if it is to continue, will be constructed by citizens engaged in rationally redescribing their own future. Toward this end what is needed are tools that will open up new public conversations, not models and lists designed to shut down old ones.

25 Langrish, "Darwinian Design," 11–12.

REFERENCES

Barber, Benjamin R. *Strong Democracy: Participatory Politics for a New Age*, Berkeley, Calif.: University of California Press, 1984.

Bernstein, Richard J., ed. *Heidegger's Silence: Ethos and Technology, The New Constellation: The Ethical-Political Horizon of Modernity / Postmodernity*, Cambridge, Mass.: M.I.T. Press, 1992.

Brand, Ralf, "Co-Evolution toward Sustainable Development: Neither Smart Technologies nor Heroic Choices," University of Texas, 2003.

Campbell, Scott "Green Cities, Growing Cities, Just Cities: Urban Planning and the Contradictions of Sustainable Development," *APA Journal* (summer 1996): 466–82.

Dawkins, Richard *The Selfish Gene*, New York: Oxford University Press, 1976.

Dewey, John "The Existential Matrix of Inquiry," in *John Dewey: The Later Works, 1925–1953* Vol. XII, edited by Jo Ann Boydson. Carbondale, Ill.: Southern Illinois University Press, 1991.

Dryzek, John S. *The Politics of the Earth: Environmental Discourses*. Oxford and New York: Oxford University Press, 1997.

Eckstein, Barbara, and Throgmorton, James ed. *Story and Sustainability*, Cambridge, Mass.: M.I.T. Press, 2003.

Feenberg, Andrew *Questioning Technology*, London: Routledge, 1999.

Fischer, Frank *Reframing Public Policy: Discursive Politics and Deliberative Practices*, New York: Oxford University Press, 2003.

Foucault, Michel *Discipline and Punish: The Birth of the Prison*. New York: Pantheon, 1977.

Godschalk, David R. "Land Use Planning Challenges," *Journal of the American Planning Association* 70, 1 (winter 2004): 5–13.

Guy, Simon, and Marvin, Simon "Models and Pathways: The Diversity of Sustainable Urban Futures," in *Achieving Sustainable Urban Form*, edited by Elizabeth Burton, Katie Williams, and Mike Jenks, London and New York: Spon, 2000.

Guy, Simon, and Moore, Steven A. *Sustainable Architectures: Natures and Cultures in Europe and North America*, London: Routledge/Spon, 2005.

Haraway, Donna, "Situated Knowledge: The Science Question in Feminism and the Privilege of Partial Perspective," in *Technology and the Politics of Knowledge*, edited by Andrew Feenberg and Alastair Hannay, Bloomington, Ind.: Indiana University Press, 1995.

Heidegger, Martin, "The Age of the World Picture," in *The Question Concerning Technology and Other Essays*, New York: Harper & Row, 1977.

Hickman, Larry, *Philosophical Tools for a Technological Culture: Putting Pragmatism to Work*, Bloomington, Ind.: Indiana University Press, 2001.

Holub, Robert, *Reception Theory: A Critical Introduction*, London: Methuen, 1984.

Horkheimer, Max, and Adorno, Theodor *Dialectic of Enlightenment*. Amsterdam: Querido, 1947.

Hughes, Thomas P. "Edison and Electric Light," in MacKenzie and Wajcman, *The Social Shaping of Technology*, Philadelphia, Pa.: Open University Press.

Langrish, John Z. "Darwinian Design: The Memetic Evolution of Design Ideas," *Design Issues*, 20, 4 (autumn 2004): 2–19.

Latour, Bruno, *Science in Action*, Cambridge, Mass.: Harvard University Press, 1987.

Lincoln, Yvonna, and Guba, Igon *Naturalistic Inquiry*, Newbury Park, Calif.: Sage, 1985.

MacKenzie, Donald, and Judith Wajcman, eds, *The Social Shaping of Technology*, Philadelphia, Pa.: Open University Press, 1999.

Misa, Tomas J., Brey, Philip and Feenberg, Andrew eds, *Modernity and Technology*, Cambridge, Mass.: M.I.T. Press, 2003.

Moore, Steven A. *Alternative Routes to the Sustainable City: Austin, Curitiba and Frankfurt*, Lanham, Md.: Lexington Books, Rowman & Littlefield, 2006.

—— *Technology and Place: Sustainable Architecture and the Blueprint Farm*. Austin, Tex.: University of Texas Press, 2001.

—— "Architecture, Esthetics, and the Public Health," in *The Hand and the Soul: Ethics and Aesthetics in Architecture and Art*, edited by Sanda Illescu, Charlottesville, Va.: University of Virginia Press, in press.

—— "Disciplinary Blinders that Enframe Sustainable Design," paper presented at the Society for Building Science Educators (SBSE) Annual Retreat, Sierra, Calif., June 2002.

Nye, David *Narratives and Spaces: Technology and the Construction of American Culture*, Exeter: University of Exeter Press, 1997.

Pierce, Charles Sanders. Memoir 19, Draft E: *On Arguments*. Pierce Telecommunity Project, Texas Tech University. <http://carbon.cudenver.edu/~mryder/mem19.html>.

Pfaffenberger, Bryan "Technological Dramas," *Science, Technology and Human Values* 17, 3 (1992): 282–313.

Rohracher, Herald, and Bogner, T. "Sustainable Construction of Buildings: A Socio-Technical Perspective," paper presented at the International Summer Academy on Technology Studies: Technology Studies and Sustainability, summer 1999.

Shepheard, Paul *Artificial Love*, Cambridge, Mass.: M.I.T. Press, 2003.

Strauss, A., and J., Corbin, *Basics of Qualitative Research*, Newbury Park, Calif.: Sage, 1987.

Taylor, Charles, *Modern Social Imaginaries*, Durham, N.C. and London: Duke University Press, 2004.

World Council on Environment and Development *Our Common Future*. Oxford: Oxford University Press, 1987.

Winner, Langdon "Do Artifacts Have Politics?" in MacKenzie and Wajcman, *The Social Shaping of Technology*, Philadelphia, Pa: Open University Press.

META-DISCOURSES

IN PEDAGOGY

AND PRACTICE

INTRODUCTION
KIM TANZER AND RAFAEL LONGORIA

The world needs more scholars and practitioners not only educated to prosper in their own careers but also prepared to fulfill social and civic obligations through the genius of design[1]

1 *Ernest L. Boyer and Lee D. Mitgang*, Building Community: A New Future for Architecture Education and Practice *(Princeton, N.J.: Carnegie Foundation for the Advancement of Teaching, 1996), 149.*

Historians of science locate responsibility for maintaining the intellectual status quo within the academy. They argue that, whereas disciplines within universities do develop new knowledge and technical innovations through theoretical and applied research, the knowledge transmitted to students is often one or more generations behind the leading edge. Even professors, who work in universities to develop new knowledge, are typically burdened by the conservative principles built into their own educations. These principles, fundamental to the organization and sense of hierarchy within any given discipline, are transmitted indirectly. Often they remain hidden and immune from constructive critique. The invisible infrastructure of academia—curricula, textbooks, credit hours, teaching techniques, grading practices—exerts a disproportionate and conservative influence over a discipline's next generation.[2] And so it is, we argue, within the discipline of architecture.

2 *See Thomas Kuhn*, The Structure of Scientific Revolutions *(Chicago, Ill.: University of Chicago Press, 1970), esp. Chapter 11 and Morris Berman*, The Reenchantment of the World *(Ithaca, N.Y.: Cornell University Press, 1981).*

To paraphrase Albert Einstein, we cannot use the same intellectual tools to solve problems that we used to create them. Thus, academic architecture, inadvertently responsible for promoting unsustainable practices for several generations (if not far longer), must look first at our discipline's invisible academic infrastructure, our pedagogical meta-discourses.

The essays that follow track the primary subdisciplines within architectural education: architectural history, theory, technology, and design. These areas, surprisingly intact from early twentieth-century *beaux arts* curricula despite formal and technological change, contain assumptions that lead to unsustainable built consequences.[3] Each essay posits a reframing of a disciplinary area, a redefinition of the meta-discourse. They share several characteristics infrequently found in typical curricula.

3 *Felipe J. Préstamo,* "Architectural Education in Postindustrial America: An Application of the Tyler Model to the Development of a Curriculum Framework," *(unpublished thesis, University of Florida, 1990) and Michael A. Bunch,* Core Curriculum in Architectural Education *(San Francisco, Calif.: Mellen Research University Press, 1993) summarize themes in twentieth-century American architectural education, though neither addresses the question of sustainability.*

They reject the notion of origin and authorship in favor of collaboration and borrowing. Felicia Davis's "One Week, Eight Hours" most overtly and poetically grapples with the role of the designer within an ongoing community narrative. Norman Crowe, by critiquing the overwhelming use of the history of styles to teach architectural history, opens the possibility of finding common themes across time. By looking across time and between cultures it is possible to recover underappreciated knowledge of building practices utilizing, for example, lower embodied energy. These essays treat contemporary architecture as a fragment in time, respectful of the past, hopeful toward the future.

The essays in this section also privilege the power of relationship over the tidiness of classification. Barbara L. Allen argues this point most persuasively through the concept of the cyborg. Part human and part machine, the cyborg is a hybrid self/other. While she uses the metaphor of the cyborg to articulate a position about technology, she equally advocates for a meaningful relationship between expert/architect and community. Each design project included likewise creates a setting for relationship rather than a study in object making. The designers serve not as objective observers but rather as participant-activists engaged in the flow of spatial practices.

The essays are stubbornly aformal and non-nostalgic. Anthony W. Schuman is most overt in his advocacy of action over aesthetics. While he does not condemn form making, he laments the tendency of some architects to lapse into the creation of formal analogues rather than struggling to address significant contemporary social problems raised through the theory of deconstruction. Crowe, too, advocates for useful knowledge over stylistic reference.

In these ways and others each of the contributions to this section strategically selects a leverage point within one of architecture's most pervasive meta-discourses and tries to change it, and with it the foundations of architecture as currently taught. Each contributor attempts to reintroduce the vital and braided roles of ecology, economy and social equity into the discourse of academic architecture.

Written in 1992 in response to the prominent role critical theory—and particularly deconstruction—played in schools of architecture, "We Are No[w here]: A Social Critique of Contemporary Theory" by Schuman seeks to recuperate the role of the socially responsive professional for architects. He opens the door left ajar by deconstructivists (self-named architectural theorists and practitioners aligned with the philosophy of deconstruction) to suggest that the role of critiquing repressive social practices must be diverted from form making to social action.

Schuman begins the essay by asking, "Does deconstruction in architecture represent a new cultural front in resisting hegemonic authority, or is the social theorizing simply a political gloss over more traditional esthetic concerns?" After reviewing the social history of modern architecture, and positioning contemporary practice relative to social and economic problems brought about by late capitalism and global market forces, Schuman furthers the ambition of deconstruction. He says, "In a deeply divided society, the idea of resistance cannot stop at the recognition of difference but must be applied to challenging the inequities that attend to this difference." While he expresses concern that the form language of deconstruction might tend to damage the fabric of the city, his real concern is that critique held in form alone might be insufficient: "Work which is grounded in the patterns of everyday life retains its physical coherence independently of its symbolic intentions. If the formal imagery is ignored or differently interpreted, all is not lost."

Norman Crowe calls attention to "the hidden influence of historical scholarship on design" in his essay of the same name. He points to the development of a linear concept of architectural history (following the model of art history developed by Wofflin and Panofsky) identifying some of its shortcomings and suggesting, as an alternative, the anthropological lens. He argues that a linear view of history unduly emphasizes the concept of progress, which tends to uncritically privilege the recent over the continuous. He also underscores the Western bias often adopted by architectural historians over the past two centuries, exemplified by Sir Bannister Fletcher in his seminal and widely used *History of Architecture on the Comparative Method*.

The anthropological lens, by contrast, seeks constants in human nature. Rejecting a reductive or nostalgic return to universals, he explains that such shared traits, "manifest themselves in all cultures, both modern and primitive, in ways so widely varied that the wellspring of their presence eludes cursory observation." He then suggests four aspects of design education which might be enhanced if architectural history was to be taught based on consistent features rather than evolving ones—regionalism, restoration and conservation, emerging technologies, and urban design and planning. His approach might make architectural history more useful without sacrificing intellectual rigor.

Speaking to the role of technologies in the architectural curriculum, Barbara L. Allen, in "Cyborg Theories and Situated Knowledges: Some Speculations on a Cultural Approach to Technology" advocates that students of architecture be given more than just instrumental, expert knowledge of technology. She suggests models such as Harraway's cyborg—part human and part machine—that allow us to reconceptualize technology as an extension of individual and community needs.

She provides examples of such technologies, including solar refabrications and a personal computer-based air-quality-monitoring systems, that have emerged out of community needs rather than experts' prescriptions. She implies that twenty-first-century architects, to work more effectively within an expanded conception of a client base, must recognize both the characteristics of certain technological solutions and the applicability of such solutions in particular contexts.

Three design projects, diverse from each other, share several common themes. First, all three projects are "built," that is, they have reached their final form. In each case, however, the form is atypical. An installation, a pair of portables classrooms and a website; none reflect the traditional expectation that architecture equals a building.

They are modest in scope yet have expansive ambitions. All three elaborate substantial theoretical premises. The small size of the projects may be explained by the challenge of creating critically programmed, aesthetically and technically resolved projects within the constraints of young academic practices. Each designer has turned this constraint to advantage by fully embracing a marginally architectural format to propose new architectural ideas.

Each project anticipates public use. While their premises may be embedded in a culture of academic exclusivity the results are intended to satisfy a broad spectrum of people. Each is, in its own way, literally inhabitable.

In short, each designer adopts an entrepreneurial attitude. They turn limitations into opportunities, supplement budgets with donations, re-envision physical circumstances with the power of practicality, imagination, and hope.

Their contributions to the paradigm of sustainability overlap and diverge. "One Week, Eight Hours," by Felicia Davis, reframes the difficult history of the shotgun house within the African American community as part of the Houston experiment entitled Project Rowhouses. By avoiding the iconography of the shotgun house in favor of the abstract quality of migrating light projected within a minimalist volume she emphasizes future speculations over painful memories. Yet light itself, recurring daily to project sunbeams across the installation's floor, gently and affirmatively reiterates the power of repetition and of memory. More pragmatically, by using light and shadow as her primary architectural media, she highlights these key design elements, often overlooked within traditional pedagogy and practice. She manifests literally the resonant shadows celebrated in Tanizaki's *In Praise of Shadows* and links it metaphorically with a range of sensitive cultural issues.[4]

4 *Thomas J. Harper and Edward G. Seidensticker, trans.,* In Praise of Shadows *by Junochiro Tanizaki (New Haven, Conn.: Leete's Island Books, 1977).*

The Mobile Eco Lab by Jennifer Siegal of the Office of Mobile Design and the Portable Construction Training Center (P.C.T.C.), designed and built by Siegel and Lawrence Scarpa (both done with teams of assistants), turn the concept of the portable school on its head. Whereas the portable is often viewed as a second rate substitute for a permanent building, these buildings celebrate their mobile typology, ephemeral sites and prosaic construction logics. The Eco Lab allows one space to be utilized by K-12 students throughout Los Angeles County, reducing greatly the energy and material usage required to provide permanent ecology education. The P.C.T.C., funded by the Venice Community Housing Corporation, works to address social sustainability from two perspectives. By providing job training to workers who will build affordable housing, it simultaneously addresses two critical components of poverty in a tremendously challenging economic environment. In addition to these broad social goals, the P.C.T.C. maximizes the use of modest square footage while providing students with natural lighting and ventilation.

The website and storyboards that comprise the project "Culture and the Re-Inhabitation of First Ring Suburbs," by Marcy Schulte and William F. Conway, take on one of America's most difficult problems, suburban sprawl. Schulte and Conway have located the opportunity for revitalization within post-World War II suburbs, which, if successful, avoids the necessity of building newer, often larger, homes in the greenfields currently surrounding major cities. They suggest four interrelated components of sustainable living—technology, material use, nature and community—and identify popular, understandable components that consumers can utilize to adapt older homes for contemporary life. The website is intended to provide specific choices to homeowners, developers, and architects, while two prototypical designs suggest inventive applications.

Taken together, these design projects are speculative proposals about an emerging form of design practice. They are inflected toward public acceptance and they utilize limited resources without sacrificing architectural presence. Though the architectural academy must undoubtedly maintain its ability to transmit knowledge about large scale programming, structural, material and spatial challenges, each of these projects provides a nimble counterpoint to curricula often overburdened with typologies from a time long gone.

CYBORG THEORIES AND SITUATED KNOWLEDGES
Some speculations on a cultural approach to technology

BARBARA L. ALLEN

INTRODUCTION

While technology is one of the most rapidly changing and frequently discussed subjects in the academy today, its meaning in architectural education, in other than a functional sense, has gone largely unexamined. Technological education should expand to become *dually focused* on both a socio-cultural approach to technology as well as cover the basics of function as it relates to design. In some architecture programs an inordinate amount of coursework is spent teaching the principles and conventions of traditional technology often under the guise of enabling the student to pass the licensing exam. This is not, however, what a university education is for. Technological literacy is more than passing a standard exam. Technologies change so rapidly that what is current one year may be obsolete the next. Something *in addition* to an instrumental approach to technology is called for if students are to have a deeper understanding of the technoscientific world they will face as professionals in the coming decades.

There has been much attention in the popular press paid to the decline of science and technology literacy in the United States. Educators studying technoscientific literacy have reached some important conclusions. For example, in an exhaustive study of the topic educator Morris Shamos found that most technoscientific education does not remain in any meaningful way with a student after they leave school. Second, he found that curricular change does very little to alleviate this problem.[1] And third, both activity-based and content-based technoscientific programs fared equally badly.[2] Keep in mind the kind of science and technology these scholars are studying is of the traditional sort; by adding fact upon fact, one truth or proper application can be found. It seems the problem lies not in the student's learning ability, but in how we define technology and science towards better and more meaningful ways of teaching and learning about technoscience as it relates to the human environment.

Often technology is discussed as if it were a free-floating set of ideas and applications that are removed from the material, social, and cultural practices through which they were established.[3] Technology viewed in this way is referred to as a black box; a hypothetical unit defined only by its function leaving the dynamics of its internal systems unexamined. The religious awe of technology as evidenced in the ideas of some international-style architects form yet another version of the black box. Mies van der Rone once said that

1 *Morris H. Shamos*, The Myth of Scientific Literacy *(New Brunswick, N.J.: Rutgers University Press, 1995), 132–134. He makes this claim for students in non-science disciplines. He also tries to make a division in his research between science and technology but fails to draw any definitive dividing lines between the two disciplines. For my purposes, I have chosen to label it a hybrid pursuit "technoscience," in order to avoid the largely un-illuminating science vs. technology debate.*

2 *The education models that Shamos studies looks at classroom lecture and lab situations for transmitting technoscientific knowledge. The proto-professional environment of the studio is not covered and would make an interesting comparison for the transmission of this kind of knowledge.*

3 *Joseph Rouse, "What are Cultural Studies of Scientific Knowledge,"* Configurations 1 *(1993), 11.*

"where technology reaches its fulfillment it transcends into architecture."[4] The problem with this belief is twofold. First it is deterministic; this belief assumes that technology has a drive all its own to reach some predestined state. And second, Mies van der Robe's reference to technological transcendence implies that an unearthly perfection is achieved in architectural form when technology is implemented in some ideal fashion. This form of metaphysical black-boxing is as equally uncritical as the instrumentalist's input–output version of technical systems.

Engineer Peter Rice, in refuting this deterministic version of technological systems writes that there is a "myth about technology. The feeling that technological choice is always the result of a predetermined logic, [sic] The feeling that there is a correct solution to a technical problem.... What is often missing is the evidence of human intervention, the black box syndrome."[5]

According to Kenneth Frampton, Peter Rice "understood only too well that a technological device is a cultural choice and not simply a matter of reductive logic."[6]

BEYOND THE CARTESIAN PARADIGM OF USE

Timothy Kaufman-Osborn, a theorist of technology, believes that we have unwittingly become victims of what he calls the Cartesian paradigm of use. In this view of technology the human being is conceived of "as an instrumental actor standing astride the world of discrete external objects awaiting manipulation in accordance with the dictates of the subjective will."[7] Instead, he argues, technology is not a "thing" to be manipulated but instead is part of who we are; an extension of what it means to be human. In the late twentieth century we are coevolving as organism/machine hybrids and lack the descriptive metaphoric tools for understanding our technologically embedded and embodied selves.[8] To fully illuminate his thesis, Kaufman-Osborn tropes the spider and her web as follows: The spider spins a web each night. The web has many uses. It catches food for nourishment and morning dew for hydration. It also protects her and her nest from predators, both as a trap and as a warning device that vibrates upon contact. "What is this thing? Is it an implement, or is it a system? A home or a trap? Is it inanimate or is it alive?" Kaufman-Osborne furthers his story-metaphor: "Like some odd contraption composed of so many elongated surrogate limbs, the web dramatically extends the reach of her otherwise circumscribed sensorium. A spiderweb is continuous with its creator in these senses and so confuses the mutually exclusive distinction a Cartesian draws between tools and their users."[9]

According to Merleau-Ponty, humans are the "fabric into which all objects are woven."[10] Using an example of a blind man he asserts that "the blind man's stick has ceased to be an object for him, and is no longer perceived for itself; its point has become an area of sensitivity, extending the scope and

4 Quoted in Kenneth Frampton's Studies in Tectonic Culture (Cambridge, Mass.: M.I.T. Press, 1995), 186.

5 Frampton, 386–87.

6 Frampton, 386–97.

7 Timothy Kaufman-Osborn, Creatures of Prometheus: Gender and the Politics of Technology (Lanham, Md.: Rowman & Littlefield, 1997), 101.

8 According to Kaufman-Osborn (p. 31), a metaphor is an artifact of language and as such acts as a tool to extend the range of knowledge and understanding. My own position is that language, or the ability to frame something in order to communicate about it, precedes and often shapes later action. Thus reframing agency within language can promote a change in agency and action "on the ground."

9 Kaufman-Osborn, 20.

10 Kaufman-Osborn, 235.

11 Maurice Merleau-Ponty, Phenomenology of Perception (London: Routledge & Kegan Paul, 1962), 143.

active radius of touch, and providing a parallel to sight."[11] Thus the division between human subjects and their objects which structures the Cartesian paradigm of use does not represent the activities of everyday life. While the arbitrary bifurcation of humans and technology may serve to efficiently transmit the mechanical workings of the latter it ignores the nuanced ways in which subjects and objects interact to shape contemporary life.

In Elaine Scarry's book *The Body in Pain: The Making and Unmaking of the World*, she proposes an intricate reciprocal relationship between humans and the artifactual world they make. She proposes that a room is:

an enlargement of the body . . . [its] windows and doors act as crude versions of the senses [enabling] the self to move out into the world and to allow the world to enter. But while the room is a magnification of the body it is simultaneously a miniaturization of the world, of civilization. Although its walls, for example, mimic the body's attempt to secure for the individual a stable internal space—stabilizing the temperatures so that the body spends less time in this act; stabilizing the nearness of others so that the body can suspend its rigid and watchful postures; acting in these and other ways like the body so that the body can act less like a wall—the walls are also important objects, objects which stand apart from and free of the body, objects which realize the human being's impulse to project himself out into a space beyond the boundaries of the body in acts of making.[12]

12 Elaine Scarry, The Body in Pain: The Making and Unmaking of the World (New York: Oxford University Press, 1985), 38–39.

Although her account contains residual Cartesianism, the person and the room are each accorded agency, culminating in an interrelationship that is difficult to dissect into proper subjects and objects.

To understand the political dimensions of technology, Foucault's notion of the inextricable relationship between power and knowledge provides a tool with which to analyze the socio-cultural context of technoscience within the built environment. Given that technology occupies a privileged place in our society and that technoscientific knowledge is highly regarded, questions the students might ask would be: How do certain technologies tend to concentrate or disperse power? Who is empowered and disempowered in the choice of certain technologies? What kinds of places are made possible by our technological choices in the built environment? And do these systems enhance personhood and citizenship in democratic societies?

In order to bring the social, cultural and political aspects of our relationship to technology together, theorist Donna Haraway invents her version of a cyborg. He/she is a hybrid of organism and machine constructed to describe our actual and potential lives at the end of the twentieth century. It is a metaphoric subject, an imaginary, meant to reconceptualize our world along the lines of the spider and her web or the blind man and his cane. She posits the cyborg as a material-semiotic actor, a composition that radically subverts the Cartesian paradigm of use. This boundary creature is a metaphor for recombinant and emancipatory uses of technology in locally meaningful ways, a co-evolution of humans and machines from a grassroots perspective. Unlike the spider, Haraway's cyborg is a deeply political actor, a renegade from corporatist conceptions of robotics and the like, committed to the realization of shared power and social justice. It is an imaginary intended to shape new horizons of thought and action into the next millennium.

Architecture schools need to teach the social, cultural, and political nature of technology as it shapes and is shaped by the built environment. Students should be given the basic tools of analysis needed to assess technology in more than instrumental terms thus becoming more effective designers and citizens in the complex world in which we live. While function-oriented technology education has been creatively reinvented by projects such as *Vital Signs*, the socio-cultural side of technology has remained unproblematized.[13] Through completely dismantling the black box, beyond monovalent functional explanations, the student can begin to ask second and third order questions about technology and the places they are designing for human habitation. They can begin to see interconnections between architecture and a multitude of other disciplines and practices that were before occluded by blind assumptions shadowed in the black box.

Kenneth Frampton in his book *Studies in Tectonic Culture* concludes that, due to the complexity of technological systems in the built environment, the architect will have to coordinate these systems with a new *cybernetic approach* to fully realize the interrelationships between them. In addition, through his lens of critical regionalism he envisions the architect's orchestration of technology as being *regionally inflected* while at the same time responding to the "transformed techno-economic character of building."[14] This, according to Frampton, will determine whether the profession will be able to reposition itself in the culturally diverse, global information age, or cease to exist at all. The *cybernetic approach and the regionally inflected approach* to architecture form the basis for the following two speculative accounts of a new cultural approach to technology.

SITUATED PRACTICES

Science and technology studies (S.T.S.) is an emerging field that examines the social, cultural and political nature of technoscience. This lens on technology is necessary if technology is to positively advance the goals of achieving a deeply pluralist and participatory democracy. A critical approach to an analysis of technoscience begins with questioning the very foundation of instrumental reason: abstract expert knowledge with its claim to rationality and objectivity.[15] In this schema, technical facts and artifacts are no longer understandable within the average person's sense-making capacity and experience; they are both created and deployed by the expert cultures that funded and generated them in the first place. Furthermore, this entire technoscientific construction reinforces the autonomous subject, who at a

13 *Vital Signs was a hands-on technology project developed at University of California Berkeley in collaboration with numerous other institutions. Its purpose was to further learning environmental control systems in a more engaging and meaningful fashion. There has even been some discussion among members of the Society of Building Science Educators of extending this format into teaching structures as well. These programs, however, are not the focus of this paper.*

14 *Frampton, 386.*

15 *The emergence of modern era science was predicated on a universal subject to empirically verify scientific truth-claims; this was the modest witness. This person was a transparent subject, a mirror of the truth they were witnessing, an embodiment of scientific objectivity. My version of the modest witness comes from Steven Shapin and Simon Schaffer's account of Robert Boyle's experimental practice in* Leviathan and the Air-Pump: Hobbes, Boyle and the Experimental Life *(Princeton, N.J.: Princeton University Press, 1985). It is further illuminated for current day use by Donna Harraway in* Modest_Witness@Second_ Millenium. FemaleMan_Meets_ OncoMouse *(New York: Routledge, 1997), 23–39.*

distance, manipulates his world; it reenacts the Cartesian paradigm of use in ways incongruous with lived, embodied experience. Recovering the epistemic authority of non-technically trained people is important if technology is going to be publicly guided instead of being used to coopt people into lifestyles that they did not choose. Teaching students about the context-laden nature of technology in the built environment will go a long way towards an understanding that there are choices to be made; average citizens and designers are capable of participating in shaping human/technology relationships.

Transforming the Cartesian subject in poststructuralist terms by problematizing the very notion of objectivity itself, STS scholar Donna Haraway introduces the idea *of a situated* subject with *situated* knowledge. This open ended, hermeneutically dependent technoscience questions the very foundation of one technological literacy. Haraway refers to these local inflections of global information as *situated knowledges*.[16] This is a fully embodied view of the world as seen from the perspective of the specific viewer. Because it does not conform to the Cartesian all-encompassing god's-eye view, it is necessarily partial and thereby privileged. It is privileged because it represents a decoding of global technology from a local perspective providing an opportunity for transformative use in radically contingent ways. From the ground, citizens redraw the boundaries of technology in ways that experts could never imagine. This is a regenerative practice leading to richer, more inclusive accounts of the world and greater participation in its making.

How can architects participate as cogenerators of regionally inflected technologies in the built environment? First of all, technology should be taught as multiple material, local, and global practices rather than only as immutable black boxes. Second, the field of technoscience has been extensively researched by many scholars within the disciplines of sociology, anthropology, philosophy, history, and political science. This material can provide a starting point for investigating technology in the built environment from other than an instrumental perspective. Mapping the concerns of architectural education onto this emerging field of STS will undoubtedly yield exciting new paths for design exploration. This will be one of architectural education's contributions to technology and innovation within the profession.

A few years ago a technologist well known for his groundbreaking environmental conservation work visited our school in south Louisiana. Being from a mountainous urban place he spoke at length about the importance of the "view" for both economic and cultural reasons. Part of the problem with "views" was having a technique whereby everyone could have one and at the same time have an energy-efficient place to live. He further elaborated his case about energy consumption and building orientation as well as presented new scientific approaches to glazing and heat gain. After a while a student raised her hand; she wanted to know what a "view" was. It became apparent that many in the class did not fully understand our guest's presentation as there are no panoramic views in this densely wooded, semi-tropical, bayou region.

16 *The concept of situated knowledges first evolved as standpoint epistemology in the work of Nancy Hartstock, "The Feminist Standpoint: Developing the Ground for a Specifically Feminist Historical Materialism," in* Discovering Reality: Feminist Perspectives on Epistemology, Methodology, and Philosophy of Science, *eds. S. Harding and M. Hintikka (Dordrect/Boston, Mass.: Reidel, 1983), 283–310. Donna Haraway revised the theory for postmodern technoscientific purposes in "Situated Knowledges: The Science Question in Feminism and the Privilege of Partial Perspective," in* Simians, Cyborgs, and Women: The Reinvention of Nature *(New York: Routledge, 1991), 183–201.*

He asked the students what local people place the highest value on in a residence if not a view. They responded that in this region many people have large extended families and a love of food, music and dancing at family gatherings. What people want in this area is the ability to open up their house to an outdoor room to accommodate this type of large active social gathering. On the part of the architect, this would mean rethinking energy-related spatial issues from a different perspective.

While this is a very simple example based on a small design problem, the single family home, applying situated knowledges becomes more complex as the scale becomes urban or regional. It does not follow that a simple technology applied to a small project is easily expanded. Technologies are not easily extrapolated in this way. This is where social studies and cultural theories of technology can provide a greater understanding of technoscience discourses as they circulate in a multiplicity of contexts. These theories are storied structures explaining the workings of an otherwise chaotic environment. They provide a means for the student's greater flexibility in traversing a variety design contexts and scales.

A few years ago Father Bill, the local priest on a nearby Indian reservation noted that his parishioners were becoming increasingly financially burdened by the rising cost of electricity. After researching the solar literature and talking with some local architects he realized that the tribe did not have the financial means available to properly solarize the reservation. What the people did have free access to were piles and piles of junk. Using some of the principles from the solar literature, the community began to build solar greenhouses and other solar additions using refuse from building sites and a variety of other discarded objects for construction materials. Proud of his accomplishment, lessening the people's reliance on the utility companies and giving them a sense of self-reliance, Father Bill told me that he "could even solarize a refrigerator carton!"[17] Reactions of some local architects in the area who were promoters of proper solar houses were less than enthusiastic about this eccentric approach to the subject. They felt that because the structures were visually chaotic and therefore unappealing to the trained "expert's" eye, that it would give solar design a "bad name." I disagree. These people have, using their situated knowledge and locally available means, refashioned solar technology in radically contingent ways that at the same time undermines the power of the seemingly impenetrable giant utility company.

CYBORG SUBJECTS

Art theorist William Mitchell states: "We make our tools and our tools make us: by taking up particular tools we accede to desires and we manifest intentions."[18] We see examples in the glossy trade magazines of architects like Gehry and Eisenman for whom computers are active generators of design concepts. Talk of the "end of history" and the "end of science" permeates

17 *This community is located on the Chittimacha Indian Reservation in Charenton, La., and its priest is Father Bill Crumley with whom I have spoken extensively.*

18 *William J. Mitchell,* The Reconfigured Eye: Visual Truth in the Post-photographic Era *(Cambridge, Mass.: M.I.T. Press, 1992), 59.*

popular culture; this is the idea that all the discoveries have been made and we are now simply inventing new applications for our ingenious tools and ideas. This is the world of the situated cyborg-subject. In the field of design, the possibilities for discovering new webs of connectivity between humans and their environments, coordinated by the architect and his or her computer prosthesis, are endless.

Donna Haraway takes the cultural manifestation of Frampton's "cybernetic approach" even further. She sees the computer as "metonymic for the articulations of humans and non-humans through which potent things like freedom and justice, skill, wealth and knowledge are variously reconstituted. The computer is a trope, a part-for-whole figure, for a world of actors and actants."[19]

19 Haraway (1997), 126.

It is productive to imagine artifacts as agents, enmeshed in a web or continuum with humans, acting together to co-create the complex places where we live. Rather than trying to dissect the parts, thus loosing the nature of the whole environment, we should ask questions that enable us to better understand the various ways in which humans and non-humans interact to form our environments. Understanding relationality, rather than reified objectness, would be useful knowledge; a knowledge in which everyone participates in its making. The pragmatist philosopher William James once said:

What really exists is not things made but things in the making . . . But put yourself in the making by a stroke of intuitive sympathy with the thing and, the whole range of possible decompositions coming at once into your possession, you are no longer troubled with the question which of them is more absolutely real . . . Philosophy should see this kind of understanding of the movement of reality, not follow science in vainly patching together fragments of its dead results.[20]

20 William James, A Pluralistic Universe (Cambridge, Mass.: Harvard University Press, 1977), 117–118.

Understanding postmodern hybrids such as the cyborg are important for the architect of the next millennium as the boundary between human and machine has become further blurred by new technologies; emergent characters and material-semiotic actors begin to reframe categories within the discursive practices of technoscience. The enlightenment subject predicated on methodological individualism is no longer the salient actor as client or inhabitant of the built environment; new agent-imaginaries for future designers must be envisioned.

Not far from my university is a small, rural, predominantly African-American town surrounded by numerous polluting industries. For many years the people were frustrated, not knowing when and if it was safe to: open windows, turn on air-conditioners, play and visit outside, plant gardens, etc. Many people barricaded themselves indoors in fear of their surroundings. In the 1980s right-to-know legislation was passed making the toxic release inventory from polluting industries available to everyone. It was soon on the Internet and people could simply "click" on their town and find out what was being released into their environment and what these effects were. But in order to plan their activities the residents needed to know which of the surrounding industries were polluting, with what, at any particular time. They applied for and received a grant for a neighborhood-controlled air quality monitor. The citizens were then informed in a timely way of hazardous pollution and its direction of travel. At this point the people had enough information, not only for day-to-day activities, but also for legal and planning purposes to insure a safe neighborhood for their families in the future. Between the global Internet and local applications of universal technologies these cyborg-citizens had turned the power of surveillance on its head; the people now had a tool for significantly reshaping their community. Recently, another neighboring African-American town having similar concerns has even used their locally inflected technical knowledge to incorporate their town and begin rezoning procedures as well as other infrastructure improvements made possible by their new citizen-controlled industrial tax base.

These communities' endeavors fit with yet another version of the cyborg actor located in spatial terms by African-American cultural theorist bell hooks. She proposes the notion of "homeplace" as a "site of resistance," a place coextensive with the techniques of productive struggle and emancipation.[21] Homeplace is both a literal and metaphoric construction of solidarity and identity, the joining of many into one, armed with the technologies of power and political agency. In hooks's conception, spaces, objects, and humans are subsumed within the web of homeplace, a space of both action and recovery. This culturally situated political sensibility that hooks calls "yearning" promotes " the recognition of common commitments and serve[s] as a base for solidarity and coalition."[22] According to Haraway "yearning in technoscience is for knowledge projects as freedom projects—in a polyglot, relentlessly troping, but practical and material way."[23]

21 *bell hooks*, Yearning: Race, Gender, and Cultural Politics *(Boston, Mass.: South End Press, 1990).*

22 *hooks, 27.*

23 *Haraway, 269.*

CONCLUSION

To conclude, for purposes of this argument, technologies can be artificially divided into two categories: material technology—the thing itself, and socio-cultural technology—how the thing is constituted by and constitutive of socio-cultural conditions and practices. These are large overarching categories that can inform the teaching of technology in architectural education in a number of ways. The first category, the technology or the thing in itself has been the predominant focus of courses taught in architectural schools. The social and cultural or *situated* aspect of technology is either mentioned only in passing or dismissed all together. Privileging of one form of knowing technology over another is a power move that effectively elevates expert, insider ways of knowing over local and nonexpert understanding of technology.

Another concept that serves as a corollary to situated knowledges is *standpoint theory*. This theory asserts that the knowledge originating at the grassroots should be given careful consideration towards an understanding of the function of technology in everyday life whereas knowledge from the experts should be scrutinized for the bias of using technology in the service of the professional or power elite. According to standpoint theory those who are in the elite circle of technoscience are often blinded by their beliefs about their work and its application; their insider status occludes knowledge that may question the very foundation of their work.[24] Outsiders, such as people living in inner-city neighborhoods, for example, are neither blinded by, nor funded because of, the promises of technoscience and tend to have different views of instrumentality. They are concerned with the way things actually work in everyday life. This local cyborg is an amalgamation of standardized technologies and local practices shifting what counts as knowledge from some rarefied foundational discipline to the experience of citizens in their environment. As architects, this awareness of the public's understanding of technoscience has been virtually absent from our curriculum. What we need are thick ethnographic accounts of everyday spatial practices as they intersect technologies towards a heterogeneous technological literacy.

Technology education should provide an opportunity for speculative practice, whereby students understand its contingent and situated nature. Technology can also offer critical points of entry into discussions of: social and cultural theory, environmental issues, and analytical and critical views of the history of the built environment. Technology in the broadest sense is an extended network, objectivity is situated knowledges, theory is storytelling, and socio-cultural issues saturate every technological decision about a project. The technologies in themselves are not lost; they are just not privileged outside of the context of their making.

In architecture we need to develop classes and seminars to broaden the student's understanding of our political/social/cultural relationship with technology within the built environment. We also need to devise studios within which both the design process and the design problem expand the student's awareness of the powerful interrelationships engendered by contemporary technology. By looking at technoscience as both discourse and practice, we move beyond the strict divisions and dichotomies that structured modernity such as: subjects and objects, natural and artificial, culture and nature, human and machine toward understanding technoscience as constitutive of who we are. This is the diffracting lens of the student-cyborg-architect practicing at the beginning of the twenty-first century.

24 *For an in-depth discussion and analysis of standpoint theory see Sandra Harding's* Whose Science? Whose Knowledge? *(Ithaca, N.Y.: Cornell University Press, 1991), 119–137.*

Originally published in the Proceedings of the 86th Annual Meeting of the Association of Collegiate Schools of Architecture, 1998.

WE ARE NO[W HERE]
A social critique of contemporary theory
ANTHONY W. SCHUMAN

FORMS OF RESISTANCE

In the short span of a generation, the expression of social concerns in architecture has come full circle. The 1960s program of an advocacy architecture that emphasized process over product and content over form has been challenged by deconstruction theory (as used within architectural discourse) which reasserts the primacy of form and denies both the importance of program and the idea of advocacy. While an earlier generation of postmodernists also sought to reestablish a formalist architecture, they did so in the name of the status quo. The deconstructionists, on the other hand, claim to endorse a set of radical social intentions (a critique of the institutions of bourgeois society) that can only be met by moving architectural theory beyond the failed utopian project of the modern movement. In this light, an approach to architectural design that starts with the workings of daily life— the creation of individual and communal place—is viewed as inherently conservative. As a charter member of the 1960s generation of radical architects I am asked to turn in my card.

The location of resistance in the realm of pure form—representation as criticism—may be seen as the endpoint of a process in which the ideology of the modern movement has been stripped of its social praxis by succeeding generations of architectural theory. In the twenty years between the publication of the *team 10 primer* (1962) and Peter Eisenman's *House X* (1982), the dialogue between social practice and architectural theory has been ruptured. Writing from the perspective of an academic with a background in community design and advocacy, I am hard pressed to explain to my activist friends what significance contemporary architectural discourse might hold for them. Conversely, architectural theory has lost its grounding in real-life issues of community development. This essay is an effort to investigate how this divorce occurred and to reclaim the territory of social concerns in architecture from the theoretical Coventry to which it has been consigned.

The retreat into form is in part a response to the disarray of contemporary society—the failure of science and technology to produce the social progress promised by the modern movement and the welfare state. This disillusionment, whether stemming from cynicism after the cruelties of Nazism, Stalinism, and Hiroshima, or from despair at the ravages of uneven development, is invoked to explain architecture's withdrawal from social engagement into autonomous formal discourse. Thus, for example, Eisenman establishes as a premise for his House X:

an explicit ideological concern with a cultural condition, namely the apparent inability of modern man to sustain any longer a belief in his own rationality and perfectibility . . . Of course when one denies the importance of function, program, meaning, technology, and client— constraints traditionally used to justify and in a way support form- making—the rationality of process and the logic inherent in form becomes (sic) almost the last 'security' or legitimation available.[1]

1 Peter Eisenman, House X *(New York: Rizzoli, 1981), 34–36.*

With the 1988 exhibition of "Deconstructivist Architecture" at New York's Museum of Modern Art, this refuge in form is saddled with ideological impli- cations. In grouping work by an unlikely cohort of architects on the basis of superficial design affinities, curator Mark Wigley denies any ideological intent—"the architect expresses nothing here"—and specifically disavows any connection between deconstructivist architecture and deconstruction philosophy.[2] At the same time, however, his catalogue essay blurs the distinctions between stylistic and ideological intentions, notably through his choice of critical vocabulary and philosophical references. The MOMA show contributes greatly to the present confusion in distinguishing among three concepts merged under the "decon" label: *deconstructivism* (an architectural style), *philosophical deconstruction* (a French poststructuralist interrogation of bourgeois philosophy), and *deconstruction in architecture* (an effort to synthesize architectural form and cultural criticism).[3] My concern in this paper is with the third of these concepts.

2 Mark Wigley, Deconstructivist Architecture, *ed. Philip Johnson and Mark Wigley (New York: Museum of Modern Art, 1988), 20.*

Does deconstruction in architecture represent a new cultural front in resisting hegemonic authority, or is the social theorizing simply a political gloss over more traditional esthetic concerns? K. Michael Hays, who as editor of *Assemblage* has consistently promoted deconstruction as a political project, is candid in identifying a serious weakness in the translation of deconstruction theory to architecture:

3 It is not my purpose here to analyze the intellectual origins or physical translations of deconstruction from literary theory to architecture. That task has been performed elsewhere and there are too many variant strains to summarize briefly. See Terry Eagleton, Literary Theory: An Introduction *(Minneapolis, Minn.: University of Minnesota Press, 1983); Margaret Soltan, "Architecture as a Kind of Writing,"* American Literary History *3, 2 (1991); Mary McLeod, "Architecture and Politics in the Reagan Era: From Postmodernism to Deconstructivism,"* Assemblage *8 (fall 1989); Louis Martin, "Transpositions: On the Intellectual Origins of Tschumi's Theory,"* Assemblage *11 (April 1990).*

[I]f an understanding of the affiliations between representational systems and structures of power has expanded our conception of architecture's domain and responsibilities, these projects have, for the most part, remained remarkably silent on specific questions of power, class, gender, and the actual experiences of subjects in contemporary society.'[4]

4 K. Michael Hays, "Editorial," Assemblage *5 (February 1988): 5.*

It is precisely this lack of specificity that makes the operation suspect. As long as design intentions are expressed in broad generalities they remain in a self- referential theoretical world and cannot be tested or criticized in any material sense. From a pedagogical standpoint, this reinforces dangerous habits in the design studio. Striking visual results are used to justify inattention to function, construction, environment, etc. Works whose intentions are particularly obscure benefit from an "emperor's new clothes" syndrome: No one wants to admit that they don't get the point. The implication is that design must *look* radical in order to *be* radical. A visual attack on the *form* of society is mistaken for a critique of the power relationships that provide its *structure*.

EVOLUTION OF THE THEORY/PRACTICE SCHISM IN SOCIAL ARCHITECTURE

THE MODERN MOVEMENT

It was the great invention of the modern movement that the task of architecture was to address the social problems of the age and its great conceit to suggest that these problems could be solved through architecture. This invention included both a social practice and a formal theory. The practice included a new client for architecture (the working class), a new program (housing for "the greater number"), a new patron (the welfare state), and a new role for architects (as head of municipal building programs). This practice was born and inscribed under a specific historical condition: The new social democratic government in the Weimar Republic following the fall of the Kaiser in World War I. In this context, one can appreciate the bursting élan of Oskar Schlemmer's Manifesto for the first Bauhaus exhibition:

The Staatliche Bauhaus, founded after the catastrophe of the war in the chaos of the revolution and in the era of an emotion-laden, explosive art, becomes the rallying point of all those who, with belief in the future and with sky-storming enthusiasm, wish to build the 'cathedral of socialism'.[5]

It is hard to remain impassive before modernism's embrace of this utopian project, however naïve it may appear in retrospect.[6] Less convincing was their argument that the egalitarian values of the new society could and should be codified into a new architectural language.[7] Even granted widespread support for the new building program—worker housing—its appropriate representation in formal terms was not self-evident. While standardized construction was a clear expression of industrialized production techniques, why should the resulting uniformity of façade be read as symbolic of equality and social democracy rather than of monotony and centralized authority?

The problematic nature of the representational system, however, did not necessarily interfere with the quality of the architectural result. By wedding modern architectural theory to traditional site-planning theory (from Camillo Sitte through Raymond Unwin to Ernst May), the first decade of the modern movement produced such triumphs of urban planning as the *Siedlungen* of May in Frankfurt and of Taut and Wagner in Berlin. It was only later, when the drive to rationalize urban planning through functional zoning was codified in the Radiant City tenets of C.I.A.M.'s Athens Charter, that the normative tendencies of modernism produced such disastrous effects on urban social life.

5 Oskar Schlemmer, "The Staatliche Bauhaus in Weimar," in The Bauhaus, ed. Hans M. Wingler (Cambridge, Mass.: M.I.T. Press, 1969), 65.

6 Recall, for example, Le Corbusier's famous dictum, "Architecture or revolution. Revolution can be avoided," from Towards a New Architecture (New York: Praeger, 1965), 269, or Mies van der Rohe's faith in rationalized production methods: "If we succeed in carrying out this industrialization, the social, economic, technical, and also artistic problems will be readily solved," from "Industrialized Building," G (June 10, 1924), reprinted in Programs and Manifestos on twentieth Century Architecture, ed. Ulrich Conrads (Cambridge, Mass.: M.I.T. Press, 1968), 3.

7 The modern movement in architecture was international in scope and had antecedents that may be traced to the eighteenth century. My focus here is on its development in Weimar Germany following World War I with the founding of the Bauhaus and establishment of organizations like der Ring and C.I.A.M. While all participants shared a belief that the new era required a new architecture, there were different views as to how this new form should be derived: a rejection of forms associated with the past; the logical expression of new materials; functional organization; and construction technologies. The symbolic representation of an egalitarian, social democratic society was not necessarily the explicit intention of every architect. Nonetheless, there was a consensus that the modern movement conveyed broad cultural significance. See Barbara Miller Lane, Architecture and Politics in Germany 1918–1945 (Cambridge, Mass.: Harvard University Press, 1968).

TEAM 10

It is significant that the first critique of the modern movement emerged from within its own ranks when a dissident group took over C.I.A.M. following the tenth congress in Dubrovnik in 1956. Known thereafter as Team 10, the group focused their critique on the tenets of the Athens Charter, with its insistence on separate use zoning of cities and tall, widely spaced housing blocks, the impact of which was already visible in the early 1950s. They offered an alternative approach based on patterns of human association (house, street, district, city) rather than functional category. While the Team 10 critique challenged the notion of master planning (for cities and societies alike) and the idea of a universal, normative architectural language to express these social ideals, they did not throw out the notion of social progress itself as their fundamental goal. Rather, they transposed the time frame of their operation from the future to the present, and its scale from the city and nation to the community and the individual. The values of the group were summarized by Alison Smithson, editor of the *team 10 primer*: "The architect's responsibility towards the individual or groups he builds for, and towards the cohesion and convenience of the collective structure to which they belong, is taken as an absolute responsibility."[8]

Thus while Team 10 abandoned the modernist conceit that architecture could transform society, they asserted an equally important, though less heroic, role for the profession: "to make places where a man can realize what he wishes to be."[9] This strategy led to a series of experiments with support and infill approaches to housing design (such as the projects of A.T.B.A.T. and, later, Habraken) that emphasized the particularity of each individual but ignored the broader class structure of society with its attendant inequality. Their approach thereby remains utopian in its suggestion that a supportive physical environment, independent of larger political and economic forces, can enable this process of self-realization.[10]

Team 10 represents a critical juncture in the development of social architecture. Because the group never directly addressed the question of political organization and tended to express its design approach more as a poetic methodology than a specific practice, their legacy invited divergent interpretations—one primarily social, the other formal. The most influential Team 10 figure in this dual legacy was Dutch architect Aldo van Eyck. A generation of student architects was captivated by van Eyck's insistence on both the small details of everyday life and the universal realms that verge on the spiritual—the "in-between" zones of seashore, dusk, and doorstep.[11] It was van Eyck who first called attention to the problem of representational form in the face of the complex heterogeneity of modern society that he called "vast multiplicity." "If society has no form," he asked, "how can we build its counterform?" Van Eyck's own response to this question was to promote a humanistic, almost anthropomorphic, architecture. "Start with this," he offered:

8 Alison Smithson, ed., team 10 primer (Cambridge, Mass.: M.I.T. Press, 1968), 3.

9 Ibid.

10 As Liane Lefaivre and Alexander Tzonis have argued, this emphasis on the ability to manipulate the immediate physical environment (in the form of participatory housing techniques) replaces the fetish of the universal norm by its opposite, the cult of individualism, denying in the process the collective nature of human society. See their article "In the Name of the People," (Dutch) Forum 25, 3 (1976).

11 For an account of the influence of Van Eyck and Team 10 on my generation of student architects at Columbia in the late 1960s, see Tony Schuman, "Form and Counterform: Architecture in a Non-Heroic Era," Journal of Architectural Education 35, 1 (fall 1981).

Make a welcome of each door and a countenance of each window. Make of each a place: a bunch of places for each house and each city . . . Get closer to the center of human reality and build its counterform—for each man and all men, since they no longer do it themselves?[12]

For some, getting closer to "the center of human reality" meant an immersion in community struggles around issues like housing, education, and parks. Groups like Urban Deadline in New York City, an outgrowth of the Columbia strike with whom I was affiliated for ten years, offered technical assistance to community groups on a variety of projects from vest pocket parks to storefront "street academies" for high-school dropouts.[13] We were part of the advocacy-planning/community-design movement that began in New York in the 1960s in response to the wholesale destruction of neighborhoods through federal urban renewal programs.[14]

POPULISM

If van Eyck was influential in pushing some of us toward more intense activism, his writings also encouraged a formal challenge to the reductive norms of modernism. Robert Venturi, in *Complexity and Contradiction in Architecture*, refers several times to van Eyck's evocation of timeless realms— threshold, inside-outside, twin-phenomena—in support of his own redis- covery of precedent and tradition, particularly as expressed in the formal language of mannerist, baroque, and rococo architecture. The book also introduces Venturi's defense of the commercial vernacular. "Indeed," he argues, "is not the commercial strip of a Route 66 almost all right?"[15] Although the introduction of popular design sources, as in the parallel pop art movement, reflects a pluralist view of American society, this view is interpreted visually. As Venturi observes, "true concern for society's inverted scale of values" can be expressed only through the ironic juxtaposition and interpretation of conventional elements.[16] Through subsequent writings, exhibits, and buildings, Venturi, Denise Scott Brown and their collaborators have elaborated a body of work inspired by the "ugly and ordinary" archi- tecture of mass-market consumerism. Although they have presented their use of the commercial vernacular as an ironical gesture aimed at moral subversion, it was never clear just what the target of the irony was, what critique of society was suggested by throwing popular taste back at the middle class in slightly distorted form. Venturi responds to the populist impulse of the 1960s, by removing it from the field of social action, by reducing it to the "signs and symbols" of popular culture and turning these to the purposes of high architecture.

POSTMODERNISM

If it was Venturi's originality to reassert a figurative dimension for architecture by incorporating popular images into the canons of high architecture, and his

12 Aldo van Eyck, "Kaleidoscope of the Mind," *Via I* (1968): 90.

13 The only published account of Urban Deadline is an article by founding member Alain Salomon in "Architecture douce," L'Architecture d'Aujourd'hui, 179 (mai–juin, 1975): 50–57.

14 Paul Davidoff's seminal article "Advocacy and Pluralism in Planning," American Institute of Planning Journal 31 (1965) galvanized and gave name to the incipient advocacy movement. The Architects Renewal Committee in Harlem (A.R.C.H.), founded by C. Richard Hatch in 1964, was the first of several community design centers. Although advocacy and community design organizations (and their clients) suffered from the withdrawal of community development funds during the Republican administrations of the 1980s, several survive. The most significant is the Pratt Institute Center for Community and Economic Development, in Brooklyn, which celebrated its twenty-fifth anniversary in 1990. In a three-day conference held in November 1990 to celebrate this accomplishment, architectural design was virtually absent from the agenda.

15 Robert Venturi, Complexity and Contradiction in Architecture (New York: Museum of Modern Art, 1966), 102.

16 Ibid., 52.

strength to exploit thereby the tension between past and present, his initiative brought in its wake a host of conservative interpretations. Dropping the polycultural brief from the debate, high architecture returned to high culture for its sources, as not only buildings but whole districts were refashioned in the image of Greece and Rome. This use of historical form carried with it a social message regarding the maintenance of privilege in a class society. It is no coincidence that postmodernism emerged in the United States during a period of resurgent private wealth and privilege with the multinational corporate headquarters as its emblematic building.

If postmodernism's rediscovery of figurative design and street-responsive urbanism may be described as resistant to the universal norms and spatial strategies of modernism, its representational vocabulary can only be defined as repressive. In assuming a universal fealty to the lessons of Greece and Rome, this approach speaks only to the dominant class in our society. A single cultural tradition emerged as the form-giver for a variety of constructions—shopping malls, civic centers, housing complexes, schools. The acultural norms of modernism were replaced by the monocultural forms of European classicism. As the African-American scholar Henry Louis Gates, Jr. wrote recently of parallel developments in literature, "The return of 'the' canon, the high canon of Western masterpieces, represents the return of an order in which my people were the subjugated, the voiceless, the invisible, the unpresented and the unpresentable."[17]

17 Henry Louis Gates Jr., "Whose Canon Is It Anyway?" New York Times, February 26, 1989, 45.

DECONSTRUCTION IN ARCHITECTURE

It is in this context that deconstruction in architecture emerges. As Hal Foster explains:

A postmodernism of resistance, then, arises as a counter-practice not only to the official culture of modernism but also to the "false normativity" of a reactionary postmodernism. In opposition (but not only in opposition), a resistant postmodernism is concerned with a critical deconstruction of tradition, not an instrumental pastiche of pop- or pseudo-historical forms, with a critique of origins, not a return to them. In short, it seeks to question rather than exploit cultural codes, to explore rather than conceal social and political affiliations?[18]

18 Hal Foster, "Postmodernism: A Preface," in The Anti-Aesthetic: Essays on Postmodern Culture, ed. Hal Foster (Seattle, Wash.: Bay Press, 1983), xii.

The deconstructionist critique is aimed at the idea of a normative representational role for architecture. Whether this criticism is of the instrumental progressivism of modernism or the hegemonic conservatism of postmodernism, deconstruction in architecture falls into the same trap by insisting that the critical power of architecture lies in its form. Having stated that multiple interpretations of built form are possible, desirable, and inevitable, deconstruction in architecture dissolves into political agnosticism, operating "to keep in motion the contingent and provisional status of meaning, thereby preventing any position, radical or conservative, from gaining absolute privilege."[19]

In denying the primacy of both program and context, in order to "destabilize" the institutions of bourgeois society including that of architecture itself, the deconstructionists restrict their field of operation. In their passion to negate the idea of fixed meaning, they produce work that is exclusively *about* meaning, work that is totally dependent on an immersion of the viewer in its competing "meanings" for its significance. The status of deconstruction in architecture as critical theory is weakened in practice because it never clarifies just *what* needs to be transformed or *how* that transformation might take place. In the process, the social program has been dropped from the brief. By defining themselves as *hors de categorie* in terms of ideological content they also place themselves *hors de combat* in terms of the social fray.

THE POLITICAL REALM OF RESISTANCE

HEGEMONY

More than any other art form, architecture exists in the material as well as the ideal world. Any discussion of resistance in architecture must move beyond language. Italian theorist Antonio Gramsci's concept of hegemony, which analyzes the conditions necessary for the exercise of power by the dominant social class, provides a framework for this discussion. He draws a useful distinction between the *coercive* (political) power of the state and its *consensual* (civil) power. The former relies on the legislature, courts, police, armed forces, and so on, to exercise power through domination; the latter relies on the ideological function of intellectual and cultural leadership to maintain class control through persuasion. In the campaign to overturn the bourgeois state, Gramsci thus identifies a crucial role for intellectuals: to develop a counter-hegemonic ideology that can make the oppressed conscious of their rights and of their own strength.[20]

Gramsci's emphasis on class conflict and class consciousness has bearing on social conditions in the United States today. Demographic trends document growing concentrations of wealth and poverty as a result of structural changes in the national economy. Whether this concentration is described in controversial terms like "underclass" or "Third World" or less charged words like rich and poor, its impact is increasingly visible and dangerous.[21] Our response to this uneven development will depend on how the issues are conceptualized. Here, the historic reluctance of Americans to acknowledge the class structure of our society is a serious obstacle to recognizing the depth of the problem.[22]

DIFFERENCE

When the idea of resistance is understood in a specific social context and historic moment—the United States under conditions of late capitalism marked by domination of the national economy by transnational corporations;

19 Jeffrey Kipnis, "Nolo Contendere," Assemblage 11 (April 1990): 57.

20 The emphasis here on one aspect of Gramsci's theory of hegemony—the role of intellectuals in creating class consciousness—simplifies his argument for the purpose of the present discussion. It omits, for example, his analysis of the role of the political party in organizing the counterhegemonic resistance. See Antonio Gramsci, Selections from the Prison Notebooks, ed. and trans. Quentin Hoare and Geoffrey Nowell Smith (New York: International Publishers, 1971). Also see Fredric Jameson, "Architecture and the Critique of Ideology," in Architecture, Criticism, Ideology, ed. Joan Ockman, Deborah Berke, and Mary McLeod (New York: Princeton Architectural Press, 1985).

21 The critical and popular attention to two recent books suggests the urgency of the theme: William Julius Wilson, The Truly Disadvantaged: The Inner City, the Underclass, and Public Policy (Chicago, Ill.: University of Chicago, 1987); and Kevin Phillip, The Politics of Rich and Poor: Wealth and the American Electorate in the Reagan Aftermath (New York: Random House, 1990).

22 The late cultural critic Benjamin DeMott appreciated the gravity of this deception:

An immense weight of subsidized opinion has gathered on the side of social untruth, and the means available to those who try to contend against the untruth are fragile. Social wrong is accepted because substantive, as opposed to sitcom, knowledge about class has been habitually suppressed, and the key mode of suppression remains the promotion of the idea of classlessness . . . We shall not shake the monster in our midst until we take serious account of the idea of difference . . . The task is nothing less than that of laying bare the links between the perpetuation of the myth of social sameness and the perpetuation of social wrong. We have all too little time in which to get o n with it.

Benjamin DeMott, "The Myth of Classnessness," New York Times, October 10, 1990, A23. This op-ed piece was based on his book The Imperial Middle: Why Americans Can't Think Straight about Class *(New York: William Morrow & Co., 1990).*

23 *Peter Eisenman, "En Terror Firma: In Trails of Grotextes,"* Architectural Design: Deconstruction H, 49, 1/2, *(1989), p. 43.*

24 *Eisenman's scenographic incorporation of the former National Guard/ROTC armory into his Wexner Center on the campus of Ohio State University exemplifies this ahistorical, depoliticizing intention. He makes visual reference to the prior presence of a massive masonry structure, but gives no indication of the political purpose this structure served. This is particularly problematic so near to the Kent State University campus where four students were killed by National Guard gunfire in 1970. See Diane Ghirardo's critiques of the Wexner Center, "The Grid and the Grain,"* Architecture Review, *(June 1990): 84.*

25 *Compare, for example, the respectful critical attention lavished on Eisenman's Wexner Center with the furious reaction to lyrics by rap groups like 2 Live Crew and the Geto Boys, whose menacing tone reflects the violence of ghetto life. Theirs is the voice of the underclass speaking for itself, unintellectualized and untheorized. It is not about repressed meanings; it expresses those meanings. In the words of* New York Times *reviewer Jon Pareles:*

Gangster rap is vulgar, violent, sensationalist. It prides itself on bluntness, and it doesn't provide

increased social and economic inequality by class, race, and gender; the proliferation of drug abuse, violence, and homelessness—it becomes possible to identify specific targets for this resistance. In a deeply divided society, the idea of resistance cannot stop at the *recognition* of difference but must be applied to challenging the inequities that attend this difference.

This is where architectural deconstruction fails. It celebrates "difference" in a value-free way that refuses to take sides in the real-life social struggle. Rather than adopting a position of *counter-hegemony*, the deconstructionists take an *anti-hegemony* stance. Theirs is an argument about repressed meanings, not about helping repressed social groups find a voice to articulate their own meanings. Even the notion of anxiety is removed from the material world to the intellectual realm. As Eisenman explains, "the object no longer requires the experience of the user to be understood. No longer does the object need to look ugly or terrifying to provoke an uncertainty; it is now the distance between object and subject—the impossibility of possession—which provokes this anxiety."[23]

This statement about anxiety reveals the problematic nature of deconstruction in architecture as a critical practice: How can a symbolic act of resistance operating purely in the realm of the cultural apparatus pose a challenge to the political power this apparatus supports?[24] When anxiety is aestheticized, it becomes digestible; the angst of the intellectual is more palatable than the anguish of the oppressed.[25]

THE PHYSICAL REALM OF RESISTANCE

FRAGMENTATION

The socio-spatial dimension of uneven development can be seen at a variety of scales. With the growing concentration of economic power in transnational corporations and the globalization of labor markets, segregation by economic function and conditions of daily existence can be seen in hemispheric north–south disparities, in national and regional shifts, and in urban neighborhoods. It is at the scale of the city that the fragmentation of contemporary life is most visible, the impact of cycles of investment and disinvestment most severe.

In opposing the false consciousness promoted by simplistic postmodern scenography, deconstruction offers an important critique of the hegemonic role of civil society in masking the impact of class dominance on repressed groups. But the particular alternative strategy posed by deconstruction in architecture—mirroring the fragmentation of modern society with jarring visual dislocations of habitual perceptions—denies the role of the city as the arena for social struggle. This confrontational approach reproduces the modernist attack on the urban fabric that was so damaging to the physical space of collective action.

THE CITY

When the struggle against repressive authority is construed in terms of action as well as ideology, the starting point must be to recognize the city as the physical realm of political resistance. As Hannah Arendt argues,

The only indispensable material factor in the generation of power is the living together of people. Only where men live so close together that the potentialities for action are always present will power remain with them and the foundation of cities . . . is therefore the most important material prerequisite for power.[26]

This urban concentration is necessary for a range of oppositional activities from picket lines, petition drives, and street demonstrations to mass rallies and armed resistance. The importance of this proposition has been demonstrated historically from the barricades of Paris in the revolution of 1848 (a point that was clearly grasped by Haussmann) to the fall of communism in eastern Europe. Consider, for example, this eye-witness account from East Germany:

The decision not to repress the large street demonstration in Leipzig on October 9 [1989] was the first major success of the young opposition movement . . . It became the voice of generalized discontent, and an eloquent voice. The chants, "We are the people" and "We are staying here" (to react to the exodus across the borders via Hungary) got international attention, and became the slogans for the thereafter-regular Monday night marches through the streets of Leipzig.[27]

Beyond the generic positing of the city as the sociospatial realm of resistance, there is a need to give this realm a specific physical form. Arguing against non-placebased definitions of the urban realm, Kenneth Frampton asserts that "the provision of a place-form is . . . essential to critical practice, inasmuch as a resistant architecture, in an institutional sense, is necessarily dependent on a clearly defined domain."[28] Frampton's discussion is focused on urban building types characterized by enclosure, such as the atrium or perimeter block. Fredric Jameson, extrapolating from Gramsci's strategy of establishing counterhegemonic enclaves within the dominant culture, speaks in terms of larger collective ensembles and is equally emphatic about the spatial dimension. When historical conditions prevent the creation of physical enclaves in the material world, he argues, the notion must be kept alive conceptually in the world of ideas.

What is at stake is the meaning of that "counterhegemony" which oppositional forces are called upon to construct within the ongoing dominance of the "hegemony" of capital . . . [C]ounterhegemony means producing and keeping alive a certain alternative "idea" of space, of urban, daily life, and the like.[29]

consolation or tie up loose ends. Unlike action movies, the raps refuse to let listeners off the hook. Both for what it describes, and for the unquestioned attitudes the raps reveal, it is often frightening—as well it should be. The world it describes is terrifying, and gangster rap distills that terror, not just as exploitation but as exorcism. But if it weren't scary, it would be a lie.

("Gangster Rap: Life and Music in the Combat Zone," Arts and Leisure, New York Times, *October 7, 1990, 29)*

26 Hannah Arendt, The Human Condition *(Chicago, Ill.: University of Chicago Press, 1958), 154.*

27 *Peter Marcuse, "Letter from the German Democratic Republic,"* Monthly Review *(July August 1990): 31.*

28 *Kenneth Frampton, "Towards a Critical Regionalism: Six Points for an Architecture of Resistance,"* in The Anti-Aesthetic, *ed. Hal Foster (New Press, 2002), 25.*

29 *Jameson, "Architecture and the Critique of Ideology," 68, 72.*

CONCLUSION: FORMS OF RESISTANCE

To be politically effective, architecture must concern itself with mounting *both* a cultural and a political resistance. Indeed, an important unfinished task of the 1960s thrust toward a social architecture is to engage the critical power of architectural language in the project of social transformation by linking formal image to material life. This constitutes as well the unfulfilled promise of deconstruction in architecture. At the same time we must be modest in our intentions and sober about the potency of architecture in the campaign to transform society. Architects make buildings; people make history.

An architecture which prods reflection through its form must also provide the physical arena for resistance through its spatial configuration and functional relationships. Work which is grounded in the patterns of everyday life retains its physical coherence independently of its symbolic intentions. If the formal imagery is ignored or differently interpreted, all is not lost. If, on the other hand, supporting conditions permit this dimension to be grasped, then architecture is fully engaged in the social project.

To facilitate this engagement, the derivation of architectural form must be rooted in daily life and social practice, including the architect–client relationship?[30] In this manner the resistant potential of architecture's symbolic systems may be more accessible to a diverse public and not limited to academic and professional audiences. An architecture of resistance must acknowledge that form carries social meaning only to the extent it is inscribed in social practice. Asked to assess the potential of architecture as a force of liberation or resistance, Michel Foucault cautions:

Liberty is a practice. So there may, in fact, always be a certain number of projects whose aim is to modify some constraints, to loosen, or even to break them, but none of these projects can, simply by its nature, assure that people will have liberty automatically, that it will be established by the project itself . . . [Architecture] can and does produce positive effects when the liberating intentions of the architect coincide with the real practice of people in the exercise of their freedom?[31]

Resistance is a life-affirming, creative act. In this light, the task of architecture, in collaboration with diverse clients, is to provide for a broad public the supportive environment which the studio provides for the artist. This constitutes, in the words of James Baldwin, "a refuge and a workshop and the place in which I most wanted to be when the time comes, as it perpetually does, to crouch in order to spring."[32]

Originally published in the Proceedings of the Eightieth Annual Meeting of the Association of Collegiate Schools of Architecture, 1992. An extended version of this paper appears as "Forms of Resistance: Politics, Culture, and Architecture," in Voices in Architectural Education: Cultural Politics and Pedagogy, ed. T. Dutton (New York: Bergin & Garvey, 1991).

30 *In the extended version of this paper and other earlier writings I have analyzed specific architectural projects which employ participatory design processes to accomplish this end. See, for example, "Architecture and Daily Life: The Revitalization of a French Neighborhood," Places 2, 1 (1985); "Participation, Empowerment, and Urbanism: Design and Politics in the Revitalization of French Social Housing," Journal of Architectural and Planning Research 4, 4 (1987).*

31 *Michel Foucault, "Space, Knowledge, and Power," in The Foucault Reader, ed. Paul Rabinow (New York: Pantheon Books, 1984).*

32 *James Baldwin, cited in brochure of the MacDowell Colony, Peterborough, New Hampshire, 1979.*

THE HIDDEN INFLUENCE OF HISTORICAL SCHOLARSHIP ON DESIGN
NORMAN CROWE

THE INFLUENCE OF HISTORICAL SCHOLARSHIP ON DESIGN

Architecture students learn about the history of architecture through courses in architectural history, usually taught by professional historians. However, the normative theoretical precepts that guide historical scholarship, and consequently guide those who teach architectural history to architecture students, are intended to satisfy the broader goals of historical scholarship, and were not necessarily created to satisfy the needs of designers. Because the intention of historical scholarship is not aimed at informing design, it is not unreasonable to assume that some of its influence on design is unintended. The purpose here is to look at some of those effects and to speculate upon what may be the effects on professional education in architecture of other approaches to historical scholarship.

First, a brief reminder of how historical material came to be included in architectural education. Formal courses in architectural history have been an integral part of the academic training of architects since 1819 when formal history courses were introduced into the reorganized École des Beaux-Arts, which would become the model for architectural education throughout the West and eventually come to influence the way architects are trained throughout much of the world.[1] Before 1819 and dating more or less back to 1671, the process for evaluating existing architecture as paradigmatic examples for new design took place in the form of public lectures and debates at the École des Beaux-Arts' predecessor, the Académie Royale d'Architecture, with the members of the academy coming together, "to publicly expound [in the Academy] the rules of this art [of architecture] drawn from the doctrine of the greatest masters and from those examples of the most beautiful buildings remaining from antiquity."[2] These theoretical discussions and debates, which were frequently very heated, concerned *how* architecture of the past should properly inform the task of designing in the present. The process included a formal approach to the notion of precedent—not entirely unlike the idea of precedent with which we are familiar in Anglo-American common law.[3] This is to say that works of architecture considered as appropriately paradigmatic served as both practical examples and as exemplars of a living, evolving body of theory regarded as integral with civilization. It was not until after 1848 that the history of architecture began to be presented in linear fashion, "from antiquity to the present" essentially as it is in most schools of architecture today. For students of the École, throughout much of the earlier period as well as after the introduction of a strict chronological presentation of history, the active study of specific examples of architecture

1 *Annie Jacques and Anthony Vidler, "Chronology: The Ecole des Beaux-Arts, 1671–1900", Oppositions 8 (spring 1977), 151–157.*

2 *Ibid., 154, 155.*

3 *This is not to suggest that there was any intentional relationship between English common law and the development of theory with regard to precedent in architecture within the École des Beaux-Arts. Each simply recognizes and subsequently codifies methods for discerning and employing certain practices rooted in the evolution of human culture.*

took the form of the *analytique*, which involved a careful rendering of an existing exemplary building. The *analytique* combined salient details, characteristics of site and setting, and overall form and the disposition of major elements, all presented in a carefully composed presentation of individual drawings, carefully rendered, at different scales on a single sheet of watercolor paper.[4]

Eventually, all schools dropped the practice of teaching the architecture of the past from the perspective of architects and changed to teaching it from the perspective of professional historians whose training was based in ongoing methods of historical scholarship. This meant that the criteria for the selection of examples from the past, as well as the evaluation of those examples, shifted away from the architect's search for appropriate paradigms to the historian's quest to understand the forces that guide historical processes, often with the aim toward prediction. This approach to historical material I will refer to here as "historicism." I use the term as consistent with Karl Popper's use of it in his writings on scientific method, especially from his *Conjectures and Refutations* and *The Poverty of Historicism*.[5] After the writings of Voltaire in the middle of the eighteenth century, historical scholarship began to shift to the examination of sequences of changing customs, habits, manner of governance and the like, and of course the study of the history of eventually architecture followed suit.

4 *A careful account of these methods may be found in Donald Drew Egbert,* The Beaux-Arts Tradition in French Architecture *(Princeton, N.J.: Princeton University Press, 1980).*

5 *Karl Popper,* The Poverty of Historicism *(London: Routledge & Kegan Paul, 1960), and Karl Popper,* Conjectures and Refutations *(New York: Basic Books, 1962).*

below: Analytiques. "Tower of the Winds" by Ricardo Arosemena, and "Erechtheion" by Marie A. Soundy, University of Notre Dame School of Architecture, Professor Paloma Pajares.

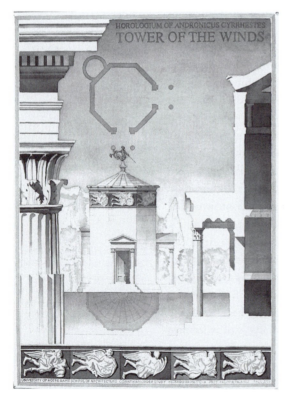

In art history, Wöfflin and, later, Panofsky are most notable for having provided critical examples for understanding art and architecture as sequences of styles, each style succeeding the one before it in a continuous response to emerging technology and changing circumstances throughout the broader social milieu. After the mid-twentieth century, Marxist-inspired theory began to effect the ongoing historicist approach as applied by art and architectural historians by focusing on the social dimension of historical determinism—eventually encouraging, for instance, the evaluation of works of architecture as expressions of gender-related issues, or of competing power structures such as the presumed existence of a worldwide economically based class struggle, or the presumed will of governments to hold and consolidate their power, or the intention of individuals to assert their presence in an increasingly dehumanized social landscape, and so forth. Historicist-based perspectives on the past—reinforced by theories of the inevitability of certain events in history (i.e., the historicism of Hegel) and methods of inquiry that emphasize objective detachment (the empiricism of Kant and rationalism of Descartes), and the notion of continuous progress (especially from Kant's teleological view of history)—forged a way of viewing historical events and artifacts that was characterized both by attention to continuous change and by a broadly held and often implicit assumption of continuous progress.

LIKELY INFLUENCES ON DESIGN

Now, while I have lumped the whole history of political, economic, and social scholarship since the advent of the Enlightenment—as well as the history of the inclusion of historical material in architectural education—into a few brief paragraphs, I must presume the reader is sufficiently familiar with modern intellectual history that this cursory recounting will serve as a sufficient reminder of the more important and influential sources of our collective wisdom about the past. Be that as it may, regardless of the actual sources of influence, we can recognize certain assumptions about past architecture that have characterized the thinking of designers throughout most of the twentieth century. These assumptions come, in the main, from the historicism that architects learned from their history teachers. I have condensed them into these three:

1 History presents us with a chronicle of progressive change, having occurred as a continuous cumulative development of thought and material accomplishments culminating in the present.

2 Therefore, the thoughts and material accomplishments of any particular era must be seen as necessarily relative to the development of society up to that point in history.

3 Because we can judge the present to be superior to the past in terms of achievements in social justice, material well-being, scientific understanding,

and human health and physical well-being, we may regard history, for the most part, as a record of progress.

These assumptions influence the way we design through the following parallel conclusions:

1 The history of architecture and urbanism is relevant to us today to the extent that it reveals certain principles of organization or characteristic responses to social, aesthetic, technological, and economic circumstances of the past for which we may find equivalent circumstances in the present.

2 However, because the history of social and material culture is progressive, the actual forms of the past are essentially irrelevant to the present. This is particularly true of past technological developments compared to later ones as well as with respect to unprecedented functional priorities that emerged in postindustrial civilization.

3 Therefore, it is incumbent on each of us, as designers, to interpret the present in terms of how it differs from the past and to reflect that in our architecture by revealing the uniqueness of each building design as both a reflection of its particular moment in time and the uniqueness of the particular programmatic requirements that animate it. Based on this, we recognize that the task of architects (their economic success as practitioners, or fame as architect-artists, or their place in history) is related to their ability to both understand and, especially, to separate themselves from previous influences so that they can fully address the situation of the present without preconceived encumbrances.[6]

THE PROBLEM OF HISTORICISM

The foregoing explanation might be read as a sort of modernist's credo. The success of this approach is associated with its ability to accommodate new technologies and to effectively yield to the demands (or to accommodate them, depending on the particular need or point of view) of economic circumstances in the ever-increasing commercialization of just about everything with which modern society is involved. Those are its virtues. Now I would like to shift to what may be regarded as the problems with the influence of historical scholarship on architectural design.

First, it has been pointed out that historicism so often has tended to encourage a fleeting expressionistic approach to architecture, one that is relevant to a particular moment in time and thereby quickly rendered irrelevant or obsolete by time's passing (in other words "the *Zeitgeist* paradox"), while at the same time tending to overlook broadly held and long existent social values in deference to current economic, technological, and commercial pressures and the latest trends of fad and fashion.[7] This is most obvious today in the assertion of Western commercial values by the pressures of economic globalization. In addition, the progressive view of history fostered

6 *For a discussion of vicissitudes of architectural history as presented in schools of architecture in the West, especially after the onset of the modern movement, see the special edition of the* Journal of the Society of Architectural Historians *on the subject of theories of architectural history and how they have manifested themselves in architectural education: 58, 3, (September, 1999). In an introductory essay to that edition, Stanford Anderson quotes Ludwig Mies van de Rohe on the rationale behind the study the history of architecture in the context of modernist theory: "The buildings of the past are studied so that the student will acquire from their significance and greatness a sense for genuine architectural values, and because their dependence upon a specific historical situation must awaken in him an understanding for the necessity of his own architectural achievement."* Ludwig Mies van der Rohe in The Octagon, *special issue, "Philosophies Underlying the Teaching in Our Schools of Architecture" (February, 1941), reprinted in Werner Blaser, After* Mies *(New York: 1977), 31–32.*

7 *Two careful observers of this problem with respect to architecture and urbanism are Colin Rowe and Carroll William Westfall: Colin Rowe,* The Architecture of Good Intentions: Towards a Possible Retrospect *(London: Academy Press, 1994) and Robert Jan van Pelt and Carroll William Westfall,* Architectural Principles in the Age of Historicism *(New Haven, Conn.: Yale University Press, 1991).*

by contemporary historicism as well as the globalization phenomenon tends to favor the architecture of the West over any other, to the extent that non-Western architecture would appear to lie outside the chains of influences—at least until it eventually yields to Western values driven by economic and technological circumstances. In other words, I refer here to the "Eurocentricity phenomenon" as it is sometimes called. This view was particularly well illustrated by the frontispiece from earlier editions of Sir Bannister Fletcher's *History of Architecture on the Comparative Method* where non-Western architecture is represented as offshoots of the main branch, essentially going nowhere. Finally, there is the popularly held belief— based on the rapidity with which change has taken place during the modern era—that humankind has virtually reinvented itself by restructuring its societies, their physical contexts, and the basic mores and social values that sustained human societies from a time somewhere in the mists of prehistory, thereby in effect denying the existence of a universal "human nature" as something shared by all societies around the globe and across time.

Any particular designer you may name will necessarily be biased for or against the specifics of what are characterized here as the negative and positive influences of historicism. The intention is to point out the general influences that tend to arise from the way history is presented to architecture students and not to suggest that the result is in any way monolithic. In fact, the effect is quite the opposite. While the result produces a disjointed effect on architecture (i.e., the proliferation of "styles" that have characterized modernism, each usually associated with an individual architect or a particular idea, such as structural and functional determinism, user-needs determinism, and so forth), it is sometimes celebrated under the banner of "pluralism." More precisely, however, it simply reflects a plurality of opinions by architects, which is not necessarily a reflection of the makeup of the broader community for whom the architects are designing. "Anything goes," is perhaps a better characterization of places like downtown Houston or the ubiquitous strip mall, industrial park, or high-end suburban development, for instance— and not "the triumph of pluralism." Inconclusiveness or relative incoherence in theoretical precepts, based in part on relativistic historical theory, tends to encourage an increasingly chaotic built environment. This is not to suggest that historical studies are solely responsible for the disjointed and chaotic character of today's more recent urban settings.[8] Popular deference to the automobile, economic competition between constituent commercial interests and the like all play a part, abetted as they are by a foundation in a relativistic design theory that in turn is encouraged by our normative approach to historical knowledge.

THE ANTHROPOLOGICAL LENS

Be that as it may, an informative exercise would be to approach historical material through a different lens, then apply that view to design in architecture

8 *It should be noted that, from the point of view that considers humankind as having reinvented itself in the modern age, the argument in favor of reflecting a disjointed, chaotic, frenetic environment assumes that today's environment is simply attuned to our new sensibilities. In other words, this assumes that things are the way they are because we like them that way, otherwise they would be different. This fails to take into consideration that the aggregate of social, economic, and political forces function outside the control of any individual, and that the individual has no recourse but to yield to their presence, "making the best of it" under less than ideal circumstances.*

to see, albeit hypothetically, what differences there might be. The lens I suggest comes from anthropology.[9] While anthropologists study social and political history from historians during their academic training like the rest of us, their approach to ethnographic material usually assumes a somewhat different focus. Unlike cultural and political historians, for instance, anthropologists are not necessarily interested in historical circumstances for their own sake. While historians search about the tree of history to see how each branch and its particular leaves contribute to the main trunk of history, most anthropologists content themselves with the study of societies that may have influenced absolutely no one outside the isolated domains of that particular society. Instead of looking for influences and change effecting "the march of history," they are frequently found looking for common expressions of characteristic ways of dealing with life among widely scattered and verifiably *dis*-associated, and consequently unique, societies. Anthropologists speak of "human nature" as a reliable constant among all humankind, recognizing that its expressions are widely varied from one culture to another. In other words, at the core of each cultural characteristic—each custom, ritual, habit, or practice—there is presumed to lie a deeper human proclivity, one that is endemic to all humankind—but dependent in its local form upon how a particular culture deals with that particular natural proclivity.[10]

A few brief examples of the anthropological approach will illustrate the point. Mircea Eliade, for instance, although a historian of religion, viewed religion through an anthropological lens. Rather than to chart the historical evolution of selected religions, he characteristically chose one or another ritual or belief from a particular religion, then searched for its presence and characteristic expressions in others. The result of such an approach suggests a unity of purpose, belief, and intent among all religions.[11] Some architects have been particularly interested in his work on phenomenological interpretations of place as reflections of meaning emanating from natural human sensibilities. Eliade's research also involved the study of human constants reflected in modern secular manifestations of the same human propensities found in religious beliefs and practices of former societies.

Another example may be found in the work of the principle theorist of structuralism among anthropologists, Claude Lévi-Strauss. He gathered examples of rituals, myths, and common social customs from his early ethnographic studies and from documented field work of other anthropologists, then analyzed the structure of each myth, ritual, and custom to reveal what he demonstrated to be hidden commonalities they all share.[12] The process known as structural analysis seeks to identify and isolate certain human proclivities shared by all individuals, revealed in very different forms in different societies.

Still another example comes from the work of anthropologist Peter J. Wilson. He is interested in the building practices of early societies in relation to geometric and organizational techniques developed in the service of the

opposite: Frontispiece, "Tree of Architecture," from Sir Bannister Fletcher's *History of Architecture on the Comparative Method*, 11th edition, 1943.

9 The discussion of the anthropological view of history here relies largely on James L. Peacock, The Anthropological Lens: Harsh Light, Soft Focus (New York: Cambridge University Press, 1986).

10 Anthropologists have studied changing conditions within a given culture as well, of course—perhaps the most well-known example being Margaret Mead's work on the impact of Western culture on Samoan society—but here again the focus is on an immediate setting, and not its long-term influence on other cultures.

11 See Mircea Eliade, The Sacred and the Profane: The Nature of Religion (New York: Harcourt Brace, 1959).

12 Structuralism as an analytical tool in anthropology is currently under criticism from techniques under the umbrella of deconstructionism. What is referred to as deconstructivism in architecture is related to deconstructionism in philosophy and linguistics. Structuralism and deconstructivism may be seen as revealing different truths about the same material. Therefore, I regarded them here, at least in most respects, as fundamentally parallel arguments.

13 Peter J. Wilson, The Domestication of the Human Species *(New Haven, Conn.: Yale University Press, 1988). Also see E. O. Wilson, Consilience: The Unity of Knowledge (New York: Knopf/Random House, 1998). In Consilience, E. O. Wilson concludes that the separation of science from the humanities as a result of post-Enlightenment thinking characterizes a failure to recognize the importance of a "unity of knowledge." We have resorted instead to a laziness, he alleges, taking the easy way out rather than to strive to reconcile these two parallel intellectual traditions. Anthropology, on the other hand, has sought to effect such a reconciliation for the most part in methodological and theoretical structures that guide practice.*

14 Peacock, The Anthropological Lens: Harsh Light, Soft Focus, *101.*

architecture of those societies, which in turn provided a basis for other inventions.[13] Among his conclusions are that there is a basic human proclivity for structuring the built environment in ways that distinguish it from the natural environment while alluding to the natural world at the same time. His work in this area, like that of many others, tends to reveal a basic human quest for a unity of knowledge to parallel the assumed existence of a cosmic unity in all of nature that lies beyond rational human comprehension.

All these examples reveal a quest for the details of an illusive body of natural human proclivities that manifest themselves in all cultures, both modern and primitive, in ways so widely varied that the wellspring of their presence eludes cursory observation. The upshot of such analysis, it is assumed, is that it reveals the constants of human nature by comparing unique manifestations of natural human proclivities as they emerge in various cultures and societies. The search is not for change, but rather its opposite, that is, consistency. In other words, a search for timeless characteristics of the human condition. There is still one more characteristic of the anthropological lens that bears mention here. It has to do with operational techniques or methodologies. James L. Peacock, a scholar who has written extensively on the subject of anthropological method, sums it up this way:

The anthropological perspective is holistic, and it strives toward an integrative paradigm. But within it two major divergent tendencies are apparent. One reflects the influence of the positivistic sciences; it attempts to achieve systematic and objective factual knowledge and generalization about humankind. The other reflects influences of the humanities; it attempts to characterize truths about humanity through descriptions and analyses that balance subjectivity and objectivity.[14]

RESOLVING SUBJECTIVE VERSUS OBJECTIVE CRITERIA FOR DESIGN

It would seem that anthropology has had to face a similar problem to architecture's with respect to the tension between subjective and objective truths. Anthropology, however, has found a more or less systematic way of resolving the problem of these opposites, while architecture, for the most part, has not. The history of the modern movement in architecture in particular may be characterized as a struggle to eliminate arbitrary decisions by turning to something like an architect's version of scientific method, all in the expectation of eventually drawing the inevitable subjective criteria into a reliably objective program brief. For architects and urban designers, in an era of increasing separation from a fundamental relationships between human society and our built environment and the built environment from nature, the search for totally objective and irrefutable criteria to guide us is inviting—although inevitably elusive. This, then, is to suggest that the anthropological lens may serve as a model for architecture in this regard, accepting the presence of humanistic bias and finding a comparatively disciplined place for it along side the more objective criteria of the program brief.

Most important, however, is the focus of the anthropological lens on permanence and the timeless. I believe that this is the place where the practice of architecture and especially urban design—that is, the design of cities—can begin to temper some of the excesses of relativism that have come to guide decision-making in design. At its base, the anthropological lens distinguishes itself from historicism this way: Because historicism assumes that "humanity is the ever evolving and ever changing offspring of history,"[15] modernism tacitly assumes that humankind lacks a fixed nature, therefore there can be no fixed norms to inform our actions so we must content ourselves with those norms and values that are relative to history at a given moment in historical time. The anthropological perspective, on the other hand, counters this view by assuming a fixed nature for humankind and so regards cultural differences as always emanating from principles of nature that are common to all humans everywhere. Posing the two views side by side sets universal and timeless principles in contrast to the realities of change. While one view emphasizes the relativistic and contingent, the other highlights the presence of universal constants. Ideally, their combination might eventually be refined into a kind of yin and yang for architecture and urbanism, a theoretical means to a balance of opposites in the pursuit of harmony.

How might these two forces, the relativistic and the contingent, if they were to influence design in equal measure, manifest themselves in architecture and urban design? That is, of course, anyone's guess, but I believe it would produce the most significant changes in four principle areas of practice: architectural regionalism, restoration and conservation, the interpretation of emerging technologies, and, especially, the character and direction of urban design and planning. I will take them briefly one at a time.

ARCHITECTURAL REGIONALISM

The anthropological perspective would encourage a direct relationship with intrinsic cultural traditions in the design of new buildings over the overt and unconditional expressions of corporate allegiances, international "styles," or avant-garde pretensions. In doing so, it would de-emphasize the role of the architect as artist who "rightfully" exerts his or her personal stamp of identity on the design (i.e., "signature architecture"), in deference to the intrinsic characteristics of a culture, subculture, society, or the particular geographic region where the design will ultimately reside (i.e., "critical regionalism"). Additionally, it is important to recall that regionalism, as a concept, is not exclusive to cultural and social differences alone. Historically speaking, the buildings and urban places of traditional societies were built of locally procured materials and their designs attuned to climatic conditions of the region with an economy of energy expenditure in both construction and long-term operation (heating and cooling, for instance). Anthropology, with its

15 *Van Pelt and Westfall,* Architectural Principles in the Age of Historicism, *4.*

attention to the natural setting of a community, would likely acknowledge the relationship between people and place through attention to economies of materials and energy-related characteristics of architecture and urbanism as much as it would emphasize the importance of emergent crosscultural technologies and economic conditions.[16]

RESTORATION AND CONSERVATION

The present practice of conserving historic structures as museum pieces to reflect the time of their creation would likely be questioned. The anthropological lens would encourage emphasizing the utility of old structures in the present, even to the extent that additions and renovations be rendered indistinguishable from the original, as opposed to the current practice of intentionally clarifying the new from the old to ensure the original be easily recognized from later modifications. The anthropological basis here comes from two directions. First is the suggestion that it is important for buildings, along with other artifacts, to reflect the passing of time rather than to promote the idea that their meaning and utility is relative only to "olden times" when people's values supposedly were unrelated to today's; and second, the anthropological lens would encourage the view that the past embodied a covenant for the future, linking past and present in a common quest for "the good city" or "universal truths" as part of a framework that nurtures the highest expressions of human nature.[17]

THE INTERPRETATION OF EMERGING TECHNOLOGIES

The historicist view, which encourages seeing history as a record of progress— while indisputable with regard to certain areas of endeavor—is all too easily construed to suggest that any and all technological innovation is inherently progressive. The anthropological lens would stress that technological developments are not ends in themselves, but rather are means to accomplishments for the greater good of a society. If a technological breakthrough is disruptive to the stability of a society and ultimately counter to traditional, inculcated values, that particular technology might well be regarded as inappropriate. The quest to realize ideals at the scale of community would be set against yielding to external forces such as worldwide techno-economic deterministic forces (that is, economic globalization and the McWorld phenomenon), solely because they appear to be part of an invincible, unchangeable, inevitable pattern of continuous change.

URBAN DESIGN AND PLANNING

It is in the area of urban design, I believe, that the anthropological lens would have its most valuable impact. While for a long time the doctrine of progress tended to validate nearly every innovation in modern urban planning—from completely unprecedented theoretical propositions such as "the city in a park" (for instance, Le Corbusier's *Ville Radieuse*), the shattered and chaotic "event

16 Recent studies concerning embodied energies in materials and methods of construction in relation to broader environmental issues reinforce this point. Scientists looking into problems of materials procurement and manufacture, in relation to the building industry, (i.e., problems of embodied energy in buildings) support the view that the economies of energy expenditure and resource conservation, as well as the generation of pollutants resulting from the building process and the manufacture and transportation of building materials and components, would be improved substantially by a return to more traditional building designs and materials. See Nicholas Lessen and David Malin Roodman, "Making Better Buildings," in State of the World 95: A Worldwatch Institute Report on Progress Toward a Sustainable Society, ed. Lester R. Brown (New York: Norton 1995), 95–112.

17 For a thoughtful treatment of the view of the past as embodying a covenant for the future, see John B. Jackson, The Necessity for Ruins and Other Topics (Amherst, Mass.: University of Massachusetts Press, 1980). In particular, see the chapter named after the book.

cities" of deconstructivism, and so forth to actual turns of events on the urban scene such as suburban patterns resulting in "endless" sprawl, the isolation of ethnic and racial groups into de-facto communities of the poor, the advent of gated communities for the affluent, and the wholesale reconfiguration of urban areas to facilitate the automobile—the anthropological lens, I believe, would encourage opting instead for the continuity of long-existing community structures so long as they are not inconsistent with the highest ideals of the broader society. This is based on the assumption that the natural evolution of culture takes precedence over innovations of the moment, whether they are technologically based or the products of the latest development in social engineering or economic theory. In other words, the anthropological lens, when it comes to cultural developments, is inherently conservative, therefore it signals caution at each new bend in the road, each new direction that could be seen as possibly counter to those existing social structures that are long evolved and inherently stable. Moral and ethical critique must, of course, be a part of such evaluations. If slavery, for example, is seen to be integral to a culture, timeless moral truths having to do with human rights that regard such practices as unacceptable must necessarily be applied.

In addition to these four specific areas of design, the anthropological perspective would likely effect general changes in normative design processes. Typology, for instance, would likely receive greater attention, given that most "types" carry cultural information along with them through time, helping to ensure the evolution of forms—as opposed to encouraging the complete reordering of forms in the face of newly construed requirements brought about by economic or technological changes. And I would like to believe that the anthropological lens would promote the identity of communities in such a way as to stress their uniqueness while at the same time stressing their commonalties with the broader culture and with other, even very distant and unrelated, communities, societies, and cultures.

CONCLUSIONS

All of that said, let me reiterate that what is outlined here is hypothetical. Still, the problems addressed are real. While the more or less exclusive application of the historicist's view of history may be seen as injurious to architecture and urbanism, so might be its opposite if applied in similar singular fashion. The changes suggested here would question many of the basic tenets of modernism, most of which have already been challenged from other perspectives beginning with the advent of postmodernist tendencies in architecture and in urban design and planning. It is broadly recognized that modernism in architecture and urbanism arose in large part from historicist forces that guided historical theory since the Enlightenment. To counter these forces with the anthropological perspective would help to ensure a better dialog and, consequently, a more effective critique of decision-making in design. The achievement of a harmonious relationship between opposites outlined above—whether it is the anthropological lens in contrast to historicism or a different set of conservative and progressivist constructs, whatever their origin—that is the real point of this argument. Especially, we must recognize that there is indeed a connection between how students of architecture are taught the history of architecture and how they approach design once they are immersed in the practice of architecture. This is to say that the place where the die is first cast is in the education of an architect, and if we are to change the culture of design to be truly inclusive, we must change as well how architects learn history.

Originally published in the Proceedings of the 88th Annual Meeting of the Association of Collegiate Schools of Architecture, 2000.

CULTURE AND THE RECALIBRATION OF FIRST RING SUBURBS
WILLIAM F. CONWAY AND MARCY SCHULTE

With typical renovation efforts aimed at the structure of the home—guided by cost, convenience or aesthetics—this project is based on the premise that neighborhood and home are linked. In turn, the proposed renovation of existing neighborhoods connects home and yard, lot, neighborhood, and region in an environmental and cultural ecosystem.

Developed in the postwar housing boom between 1945 and 1965, America's first ring suburbs are now home to a diverse working middle class and millions of aging structures. Reading this territory through the lens of culture provides a structuring logic for transforming existing conditions in light of contemporary life.

This project began as an inquiry at the Design Center for the American Urban Landscape under the direction of William Morrish. At the center, Morrish's work refocused urban thinking by linking neighborhood change to regional change. Relative to first ring suburbs "revitalizing existing neighborhoods can play a pivotal role in curbing urban sprawl and reclaiming natural resources."[1]

From this work we concluded that there were three fundamental issues that would inform our continued work.

1 The first ring suburb has changed. While the demographics of these neighborhoods has broadened since their construction in the 1950s and 1960s, the technology of the home (siding, windows, and insulation) have reached, and in some cases surpassed, their effective lifecycle. While many of these homes have declined in value, their relatively low purchase price provides a point of entry into a competitive housing market for first-time home-buyers.

2 While homeowners often use products from their local Home Depot® for do-it-yourself home renovation projects, a corollary to Home Depot®—a one-stop information source on green materials, home-based sustainability, design, landscape, and ecological practices does not exist. At the neighborhood scale, easy access to planning and public-policy practices that may better enable collective decision-making would be beneficial. The necessary information is out there, but it is diffuse, handicapping not only homeowners but also lending institutions, housing agencies, architects, landscape architects, and contractors.

3 The project opens questions regarding the traditional actions of the architect, of project definition, accessibility of design services, transmission of information, and construction administration and delivery processes.

top: Levittown family and their contractor cape, 1948. Photograph by Bernard Hoffman, Life Magazine, © Time, Inc.

above: Texas Family with Belongings, 1994. Peter Menzel, *North America: Material World, A Global Family Portrait* (San Francisco: Sierra Club Books, 1994).

1 *William R. Morrish, Re-Filling the Suburbs: A New Wave of Development in the First Ring.*

113

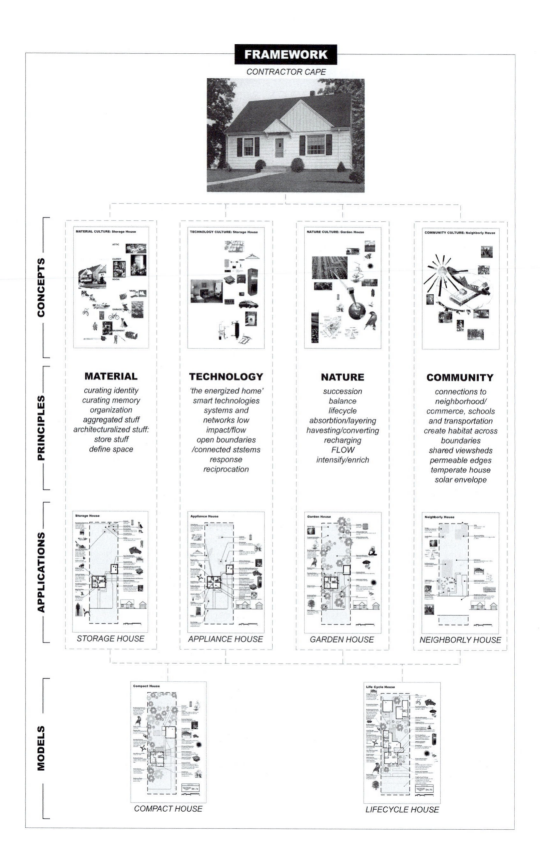

FRAMEWORK

CONTRACTOR CAPE

CONCEPTS

MATERIAL CULTURE: Storage House

TECHNOLOGY CULTURE: Storage House

NATURE CULTURE: Garden House

COMMUNITY CULTURE: Neighborly House

PRINCIPLES

MATERIAL

curating identity
curating memory
organization
aggregated stuff
architecturalized stuff:
store stuff
define space

TECHNOLOGY

'the energized home'
smart technologies
systems and
networks low
impact/flow
open boundaries
/connected ststems
response
reciprocation

NATURE

succession
balance
lifecycle
absorbtion/layering
havesting/converting
recharging
FLOW
intensify/enrich

COMMUNITY

connections to
neighborhood/
commerce, schools
and transportation
create habitat across
boundaries
shared viewsheds
permeable edges
temperate house
solar envelope

APPLICATIONS

Storage House

Appliance House

Garden House

Neighborly House

STORAGE HOUSE

APPLIANCE HOUSE

GARDEN HOUSE

NEIGHBORLY HOUSE

MODELS

Compact House

Life Cycle House

COMPACT HOUSE

LIFECYCLE HOUSE

WHY RECALIBRATION?

Throughout this work we have included language as a fundamental design element. Whether in the service of history, in the legitimizing texts of zoning ordinances and building codes, or in the service of public and design values, language plays a pivotal role in the design of our communities.

We have used recalibration to describe the project's conceptual resetting of the existing suburban condition. By employing research actions, including an inventory of the constituent built elements of the first ring, homes and neighborhoods, we set a baseline register for change. By adopting culture as a lens for our architectural and planning initiatives we look back at the regularizing practices used in the development of these tracts and project forward through the irregularities of demographic, economic, social, and lifestyle factors that will modulate their transformation.

The results of this design research were twofold. First, a design framework intended to guide decision-making for new physical structures and new urbanisms. And second, a delivery system that places the homeowner at the center with the ability to access and share information.[2] A digital database that enables access to information on green materials and products, home-based sustainability, landscape, and ecological, practices, and an online interactive site that allows homeowners to debate and offer changes to local zoning and planning documents.

opposite: The Framework. The framework structures, and makes accessible, information and ideas. It offers a basis for informed decision-making, and facilitates homeowner/neighborhood communication and strategies for implementation. Four tiers of text and images describe the translation of ideas from concept through the implementation.

- **Cultural Thematics:** four graphic plates describe the core thematics of Material, Technology, Nature and Community
- **Principles:** Brief action statements describe the value sets by which the thematics are put into play.
- **Applications**: Each plate arrays possible strategies, products and resources that could be implemented by homeowners to transform their home, lot and neighborhood.
- **Models:** an infinite number of designs that reflect particular household choices. Using the four Application palettes we have illustrated two projects, one modestly transformed — the Compact House and a more expansively transformed — the Lifecycle House.

2 The continued development of this project is supported in part by a grant from the Graham Foundation for Advanced Studies in the Fine Arts.

Website Garden House page and links to resources and products.

WHY CULTURE?

In the years following World War II, the methods of mass production and the logics of mobilization honed for wartime speed and efficiency were turned to domestic venues. Between 1945 and 1965 tens of thousands of living units were constructed in first ring suburbs.

As an idea and built reality first ring suburbs have had a dramatic impact in shaping American culture. In the 1940s and 1950s the popular media of magazines, movies, and television described the prototypical mid-century "suburban" experience for later generations. This was evidenced by the incorporation of new terms like picture window, rumpus room, carport, and cloverleaf to common usage.[3] The ubiquitous contractor Cape, an adaptation of the Massachusetts Cape Cod Cottage, was developed at mid-century for the postwar housing market. Widely adapted in new suburbs from the eastern seaboard to the Midwest, this diminutive and affordable house type was well suited for returning GIs and their young families.

Nearly sixty years later, the culture of the backyard barbecue, and stay-at-home mom has been supplemented with e-commerce, eco-awareness, sprawl, telecommuting, playdates and a quest for quality time. As metropolitan governments struggle with the population and demographic impacts on the region, first ring suburbs—with their aging housing stock, antiquated zoning ordinances, deteriorating infrastructure and ecological challenges—have frequently been overlooked as viable sites for engaging these dynamic changes.

Recalibration acknowledges the complexity of changing cultural conditions and our expectations for a quality physical environment. The approach accepts the first ring suburb—not solely as we find it today, nor strictly as it might have appeared in 1948—but through an understanding of the cultural conditions that have shaped it.

OPERATIONS AND DEVICES

While we have employed conventional operations and devices rooted in the architect's discipline to structure our work, this approach resets the terms of engagement with the first ring suburb.

1 **Make information and ideas accessible.** Architecture is presented as an interpretive medium offering accessible information to aid decision-making. Language, iconography, illustration, and representation are all essential.
2 **Develop/cultivate content.** Through the establishment of cultural thematics—material, technology, nature and community—the website organizes and offers links to products, research, and service providers.
3 **Provide a structure for communication.** The digital database and interactive site provide a localized communication tool that enables neighbor-to-neighbor discussion and debate regarding existing documents and processes (i.e., zoning, code, and masterplan) that impact their community.

3 Nancy Ann Miller, "Eero Saarinen on the Frontier of the Future: Building Corporate Image in the American Suburban Landscape, 1939–1961" (Ph.D. Dissertation, University of Pennsylvania, 1999), 101–2.

4 **Plan for implementation.** While incremental owner-by-owner changes are facilitated by this project, the logic for the renovation of such large tracts of American housing is nested within the mass-production practices that first brought these homes into existence. With the aid of committed communities, we envision successful disaster-reconstruction and airport-sound remediation projects as models for future block-by-block transformation within the suburbs of the first ring.

CONTENT: CULTURAL THEMATICS

Descriptions of the cultural thematics elaborates on the development of the project approach and content.

MATERIAL CULTURE: STORAGE HOUSE

The conventional relationship of storage to dwelling is a measure of quantity—how much storage, how many closets? From a cultural point of view, the consideration of storage and home involves not only the question of quantity but also the question of how—how identity is curated by individuals and families trough the acquisition and display of their possessions.

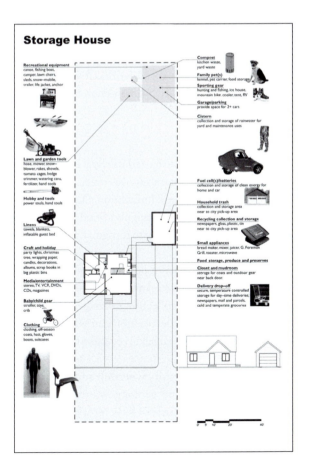

Detail view of Community Culture: Neighborly House Storage House applications.

117

As an "eco" household that actively engages the relationship of living/homemaking within the local environment—the house is reconceived. The storage of energy, heat, cold and water, foodstuffs, waste, and raw materials becomes an important part of recalibrating the organization of the home and lot.

The processes of consuming, conserving, disposing, and recycling transforms goods and products from one state to another. Recycling bins, compost, energy cells, building insulation, and kitchen cabinets represent an integrated set of decisions as the home increasingly acts as a weigh station for matter. Reuse is a question of how and when. Waste is a relative term.

TECHNOLOGY CULTURE: APPLIANCE HOUSE

In 1945 the Contractor Cape was marketed as a readymade home complete with an appliance package and the latest in heating technology. The technology of contemporary appliances, laptop, i-pod, satellite receiver, and high-speed internet access join the "new car" as status symbols of living well and moving forward. Contemporary expectations are coupled with concern for the consumption of resources, maintenance agreements, and user-friendly technology. Linked to quality-of-life issues, the networked smart home and the telecommute allow more control over our environment and our time.

The appliance house reduces energy consumption—linking temperature-control systems to building technologies and solar orientation—without forfeiting its place in a technologically advanced world. It is connected through intertie net-metering[4] systems to utility infrastructure in a dual role as customer and clean-energy provider.

NATURE CULTURE: GARDEN HOUSE

While the early development of first ring suburbs had its roots in the garden cities of Ebenezer Howard, the mid-century iteration was much diluted. The quarter-acre lot, the expanse of green lawn, and foundation plantings are its remaining signature elements. At the scale of the neighborhood, the primary blind spot of first ring developments was the failure to recognize and integrate local and regional site conditions.

The Garden House works to reconcile local topography, watershed, and habitat with underused lots. The fundamental relationship between ground cover, site drainage, roof forms and water-collection systems results in an integrated set of design decisions. Both new construction and site renovation strive for balanced inputs and outputs—the goal being ecological success over the long term.

Although property lines exist as crisp lines of ownership and tax responsibility on the city plat, they are invisible to geology, water table, solar window, view shed, and species habitats. Garden House property lines are eco-permeable delineations. The layering of plant materials, absorption of water, harvesting of solar energy, and integration of native species will

4 Intertie net-metering systems also known as utility-intertie or grid-tied is a system that makes it possible for individual property owners to connect their renewable energy system through an inverter directly to the utility grid. Under a net-metering arrangement a homeowner is able to draw energy from the grid when they need it and those who use solar systems run their electric meter backwards as they feed extra electricity back to their utility. This means that the utility "pays" the customer the retail rate for the electricity produced. See <http://www.utilityfree.com/solar/intertie2.html>.

118

contribute to an 'intensified nature' redefining the legacy of the garden suburb.

COMMUNITY CULTURE: NEIGHBORLY HOUSE

The ideals at work in shaping the 1950s first ring suburb were aligned with a set of assumptions about the American family, economy, workforce, and the automobile. Each lot and each family was conceived as an autonomous entity within the neighborhood plan.

Today, the changing demographics of the first ring include a greater diversity of household types, age groups, cultural and ethnic mix, two-income families, and single-parent households. Community culture and the Neighborly House reconnect the autonomous 'citizen' lot to the neighborhood.

While zoning ordinances and neighborhood codes typically serve as instruments of control and uniformity, we propose that the control of set-backs, accessory buildings, and density are shaped by a negotiated zoning language that promotes positive change and community. By facilitating access and participation in the amendment of controlling documents, individual choice and shared community interests are balanced in the development of individual lots.

Back yard transformation. The transformation of adjacent properties is made possible by negotiated amendments to zoning ordinances. In this case the implementation of two back-to-back 'Lifecycle House' projects are illustrated.

The integration and improvement of infrastructure, i.e., sidewalks, alleyways, and boulevards, provides connection to neighborhood commercial, recreation areas, schools, and public transportation for pedestrians and cars.

DEMONSTRATION PROJECTS: MODELS

Two demonstration projects illustrate the range of possible outcomes. It is our intention that projects developed from this framework would be infinite in number and disposition. Individual choice and the opportunities afforded by orientation and site conditions will shape decisions exercised by homeowners.

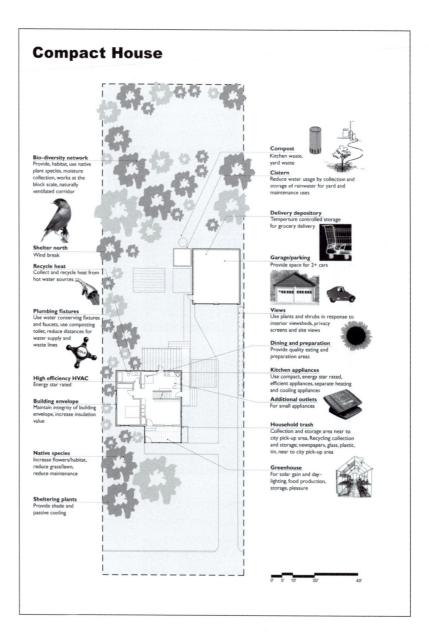

Demonstration project: Compact house.

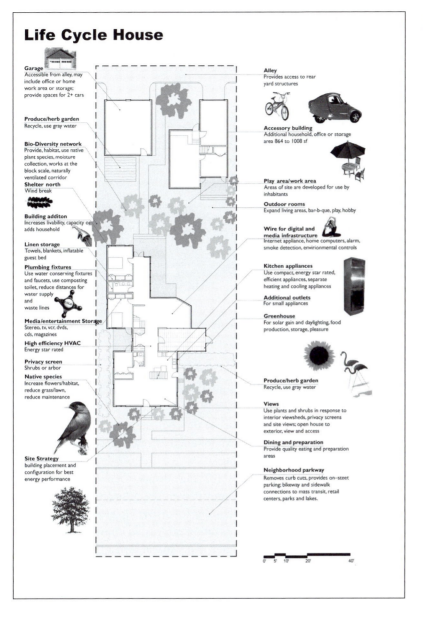

Life Cycle House

Garage
Accessible from alley, may include office or home work area or storage; provide spaces for 2+ cars

Produce/herb garden
Recycle, use gray water

Bio-Diversity network
Provide, habitat, use native plant species, moisture collection, works at the block scale, naturally ventilated corridor

Shelter north
Wind break

Building additon
Increases livability, capacity or adds household

Linen storage
Towels, blankets, inflatable guest bed

Plumbing fixtures
Use water conserving fixtures and faucets, use composting toilet, reduce distances for water supply and waste lines

Media/entertainment Storage
Stereo, tv, vcr, dvds, cds, magazines

High efficiency HVAC
Energy star rated

Privacy screen
Shrubs or arbor

Native species
Increase flowers/habitat, reduce grass/lawn, reduce maintenance

Site Strategy
building placement and configuration for best energy performance

Alley
Provides access to rear yard structures

Accessory building
Additional household, office or storage area 864 to 1008 sf

Play area/work area
Areas of site are developed for use by inhabitants

Outdoor rooms
Expand living areas, bar-b-que, play, hobby

Wire for digital and media infrastructure
Internet appliance, home computers, alarm, smoke detection, environmental controls

Kitchen appliances
Use compact, energy star rated, efficient appliances, separate heating and cooling appliances

Additional outlets
For small appliances

Greenhouse
For solar gain and daylighting, food production, storage, pleasure

Produce/herb garden
Recycle, use gray water

Views
Use plants and shrubs in response to interior viewsheds, privacy screens and site views; open house to exterior, view and access

Dining and preparation
Provide quality eating and preparation areas

Neighborhood parkway
Removes curb cuts, provides on-steet parking; bikeway and sidewalk connections to mass transit, retail centers, parks and lakes.

0' 5' 10'   20'   40'

Demonstration project: Lifecycle house.

While the original constructed uniformity of the first ring development was considered a value at the time it was conceived, the considerations of contemporary culture and ecological strategies are central to the resetting, the recalibration—of home, lot, and neighborhood. The recalibration of the Contractor Cape and first ring suburb envisions their transformation into vital eco-neighborhoods within a thriving metropolitan community.

Originally published in the Proceedings of the 90th Annual Meeting of the Association of Collegiate Schools of Architecture, 2002.

PORTABLE CONSTRUCTION TRAINING CENTER

JENNIFER SIEGAL AND LAWRENCE SCARPA

Utilizing a donated restructured trailer, the Portable Construction Training Center (P.C.T.C.) addresses many issues of sustainability. The function of the center is to improve the capabilities of the community while its structure is composed of adapted materials. Major emphasis was placed on simplicity, craft, material, and spatial meaning.

The P.C.T.C. was conceived for the Venice Community Housing Corporation, an organization founded with the mission to develop and maintain permanently affordable housing for disadvantaged and low-income individuals. This non-profit organization affords an opportunity for their student trainees to learn construction skills and in turn apply their skills to needed projects. The materials used in the P.C.T.C. were mainly donated from companies in the greater Los Angeles area. Other materials we recycled from the existing trailer and salvaged from other construction sites.

The 14 × 65 foot P.C.T.C. is a hands-on classroom used as the focal point in this construction training process. The P.C.T.C. allows space for the four basic construction trades: plumbing, painting and plaster repair, carpentry, and electrical.

The design concept encourages visual connections between apprentice and teacher. There is a 14 × 14 foot meeting space at the P.C.T.C.'s threshold that exhibits construction example boards and provides a well-lit location to gather between building sessions. Like a large porch, one entire length of the trailer folds open to reveal interior independent work stations. This creates a catwalk for the teachers which facilitates inspection and interaction.

In this 90-degree position, the operable translucent panels give shade and regulate the natural flow of hot and cool air. Additionally, the far end of the P.C.T.C. folds open to provide a wood shop, where tools can be disengaged to roll outside beyond the parameter of the trailer.

Portable, flexible, and operable, the P.C.T.C. is a symbol for alternative construction techniques and provides a place to teach them.

Originally published in the Proceedings of the 88th Annual Meeting of the Association of Collegiate Schools of Architecture, 2000.

Project credits:

Completion Date: August 1998

Owner: Venice Community Housing Corporation, Steve Clare, Director

Project Team: Alex Arias, Thomas Cohen, Guillermo Delgadillo, Maurice Ghattas, Han Hoang, Chayanon Jomvinya, Thao Nguyen, Jose Olmos, James Popp, Phung Thong, Juan Uehara

Assistants: Wendy Bone, Robert Chambliss, Ezell Edmond, Ann Murphy, Gary Windish

Structural Engineer: Gwynne Pugh

Photographer: Benny Chan

Donors: CBM Building Materials, Industrial Metal Supply Re-Sets, Burbank, Calif. Salvation Army, Westwood, Calif.

MOBILE ECO LAB
JENNIFER SIEGAL

The collaborative spirit in my design/build architectural studios emphasizes economy of means, reconsideration of construction techniques, and the adaptive reuse of materials and building components. Hands-on experience provides students with a fresh perspective on what is "appropriate" design at full scale. While considering various construction strategies, students often find predetermined notions of design solutions insufficient. In response, architects-to-be learn to rely on their personal experiences and their innate sensibilities. Through the ultimate realization of their work, students apprehend a more informed architecture.

The project's purpose was to explore issues of sustainability and mobility through the design/build studio. Inspired by Sant' Elia in his "Futurist Manifesto" catalog for the Città Nuova exhibition, we adhered to the belief that:

we no longer believe in the monumental, the heavy and static, and have enriched our sensibilities with a taste for lightness, transience and practicality . . . We must invent and rebuild ex novo our modern city like an immense and tumultuous shipyard, active, mobile, and everywhere dynamic, and the modern building like a giant machine.

The adopted studio language conveys a proactive design process that responds to the challenge of building for mobility. A measure of the mobile ECO LAB's

124

Project credits:

Completion Date: June 1998

Owner: Hollywood Beautification Team, Sharyn Romano, Director

Project Team: Ausencio Ariza, Larry Cheung, Thomas Cohen, Tinifuloa Grey, Chayanon Jomvinya, Jody Segraves

Assistants: Alex Arias, Guillermo Delgadillo, Han Hoang, Maurice Ghattas, Thao Nguyen, Jose Olmos, James Popp, Phung Thong, Juan Uehara

success is in its daily use and deployment throughout Los Angeles. The final construct, reflecting Sant' Elia's "Futurist" concerns, is built as a lightweight temporary structure: economical, experimental, and flexible.

The mobile ECO LAB was built in collaboration with the Hollywood Beautification Team, a grassroots group founded with the mission to restore beauty and integrity to the Hollywood community. Verbal and visual exchanges took place using computer animated drawings, traditional architectural drafting, and large-scale modeling techniques. Full-scale work was performed with a defined material palette (specifically that of a donated cargo trailer and cast-offs from film sets). The 8×35 foot trailer now travels throughout Los Angeles county to inform K-12 school-aged children about the importance of saving and protecting our planet. Like a circus tent, this mobile icon arrives at the schoolyard, where the lab's elevated walkways fold down and slide out of the trailer's body. It is immediately recognizable as a place for interaction, discovery, and fun.

As a working mobile classroom, the ECO LAB provides a base for a range of exhibitions all of which focus on ecology. Arriving at the threshold of the trailer, a child climbs up a set of folding stairs lowered by a nautical winch. When the stairway meets the ground, the attached springs and wheels swivel into place, absorb the compression, and provide access. Ascending the recycled expanded steel treads, the child enters a multimedia antechamber. A multimedia program explaining the "life of a tree" creates a path for discovery that weaves in and out of the expandable ECO LAB.

The multimedia chamber facilitates learning by providing a computer to surf the Internet on topics focusing on ecology. The young visitors hear a video describing a tree's growth cycle. Each child is then given a small container and tree sapling to be cared for along the path. Moving single file, the visitors emerge from the trailer onto a fold-down tiered catwalk. Advancing along, they gather soil for the sapling from planters lining the outside edge of the walk. At the top of the catwalk, they move back into the body of the trailer, and reemerge outside onto a stagelike platform that rolls out of the wheel wells. Here the children water their saplings and the teacher uses this space to discuss each child's role in the importance of planting trees and maintaining a sustainable environment. Progressing to the core of the ECO LAB, visitors gather in the dappled light shining through the woven wooden wall. The floor, engraved with a giant California oak leaf encircled by the words "you are ecology," provides the space for discussion and questions.

Originally published in the Proceedings of the 87th Annual Meeting of the Association of Collegiate Schools of Architecture, 1999.

ONE WEEK, EIGHT HOURS
FELECIA DAVIS

Beware of those who speak of the spiral of history; they are preparing a boomerang. Keep a steel helmet handy. I have been boomeranged across my head so much that I now see the darkness of lightness. And I love light. Perhaps you'll think it strange that an invisible man should need light, desire light, love light. But maybe it is exactly because I am invisible. Light confirms my reality, gives birth to my form . . . Without light I am not only invisible, but formless as well: and to be unaware of one's form is to live a death. I myself, after existing some twenty years, did not become alive until I discovered my invisibility . . .

Perhaps I like Louis Armstrong because he's made poetry out of being invisible. I think it must be because he's unaware that he is invisible. Invisibility, let me explain, gives one a slightly different sense of time, you're never quite on the beat. Sometimes you're ahead and sometimes you're behind. Instead of the swift and imperceptible flowing of time, you are aware of its nodes, those points where time stands still or from which it leaps ahead. And you slip into the breaks and look around. That's what you hear vaguely in Louis' music.

Ralph Ellison, Invisible Man, *1947*

BACKGROUND

Project Rowhouses (P.R.H.) founded in 1994 by the artist Rick Lowe is a large-scale community-oriented arts project. Located in southwest Houston in the third ward, a primarily poor African-American neighborhood, blighted by the razing strategies of urban renewal in the 1960s and late 1970s slowly has been turning itself around as the overall economy saw more prosperous times in the late 1990s. Rick galvanized the surrounding community and other arts organizations and corporate institutions and a coalition of artists in Houston to purchase the abandoned lots with twenty-two dilapidated shotgun-type rowhouses and cleared the lots of decades of debris and slowly renovated the houses one by one. It spans two blocks and consists of twenty-two identical houses. Seven on one block that house the Young Mothers program, a program that provides shelter and support services for up to a year to young mothers who are returning to school or receiving additional job training. A second block of fifteen houses, eight in front along the street and seven in the back form a court and provide additional space for a woodshop and workroom, classrooms for an afterschool and daycare program, and administrative support services for the Young Mothers program. The eight houses along the street have been renovated into gallery spaces for the Visiting Artists Program which hosts quarterly exhibitions by artists around the world and brings the attention of the international art world to this struggling neighborhood. Balancing both local and global programs, P.R.H. suggests a sustainable model that hopefully will be able to resist the forces of gentrification that its very presence invites through its grassroots connection to the surrounding residents of the third ward. In 2001, David Brown and William D. Williams of Rice University School of Architecture curated the fifteenth round of artist's installations at P.R.H. in the artists' spaces. Titled "Shotguns" after John Biggers' *Shotguns* painting and the series of paintings he made of shotguns in the third and fifth wards of Houston in the early 1980s, David and William invited seven artists to create a design for each of the gallery spaces. Their charge to the seven selected artists was to consider the shotgun-house type as a cultural artifact, to consider its significance in the collective memory, and to develop the relationship through the project to the work of John Biggers specifically his "Shotgun" series. This project, "One Week Eight Hours" was done over the course of one week, with two student assistants and the visitations of various children in the afterschool program.

The houses are very small, 31 × 17 feet wide typically, with front and back porches that are cut out of the main volume at the front at the street creating a recessed more protected area out front and an added porch along the back, facing an interior court, creating a much more sociable, intimate space in the back. The name "shotgun house" was coined because it was said a bullet could pass through the clear view from the front door to the back door without hitting any interior walls. They are quite simply built and recall a housing building type in western Africa brought to the United States as a remembered building method by African slaves. Most families living in the rowhouses did not stay in them forever and pass them along to their children, but rather saw them as someplace to rest on the way to somewhere else and as transitional places that were more about passing through than putting down roots. Invisibility here is related to a transient lifestyle, making these residents invisible to a system where wealth and visibility was generated by ownership. The lives they lead, stories and improvisational practices of survival and resistance in a hostile America was their children's rich inheritance.

INVISIBLE MEDIUM AND DRAWING IN THE BEAT

There were two phases to the project that used the house in two ways to effect two specific ideas about memory. The first phase used natural daylight and proposed memory as a struggle against forgetting, as an act of repetition, similar to the way one performs sounds to learn a new language. Tracing the impossible line between light and its absence as well as the projected shadows within the house was stating presence or an act of graffiti. In a second phase, these acts of graffiti were then rigorously photographed in natural light and then reprojected in a dark house that created a luminous timeful, rhythmic spectacle inside the house that then developed a proper or clean idea of memory; a formal cut or blockage to trigger remembrance a specific moment. Only the house interior was used to produce the effect of departure from the daily flow of time upon entry to the house and return to that flow upon exiting the house. The interventions to the interior of the house specifically concerned that which passed through it.

As a first-time visitor to Houston and P.R.H., inhabitation of the house was the principal way to understand the rhythms of place and to register the absence of those who had been here before. The installation was also seen as a space for use in an afterschool program where students would contribute their own light/shadow tracings and subsequent photographs. The installation was designed as an open and improvisational system that young people and lay people could participate in and was based on the photographic shot that documented the house as a full vessel. Inhabitation revealed a place full of others, some seen and present, many others unseen, including other artists and their traces, just underneath the white gallery paint and residents who resided in the house long before the place became P.R.H. Over the course of one week, an eight-hour day was divided arbitrarily into six intervals of one hour and twenty minutes, marking time at 9:00 A.M., 10:20 A.M., 11:40 A.M., 1:00 P.M., 2:20 P.M., 3:40 P.M., and 5:00 P.M. The plan was to observe the play of

b   c   d   e   f   g

h   k   l   m   a   b

Panorama Projector 2 3:40p.m. October 14, 2001

b   c   d   e   f   g

h   k   l   m   a   b

Panorama Projector 2 5:00p.m. October 14, 2001

Textile Serial Images

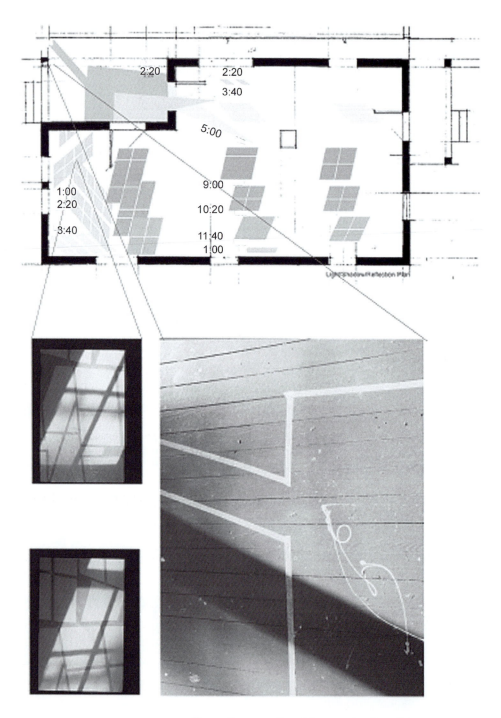

2:20   2:20
              3:40

              5:00

1:00   9:00
2:20   10:20

3:40   11:40
              1:00

Light/Shadow/Reflection Plan

Drawing on the House to the Beat

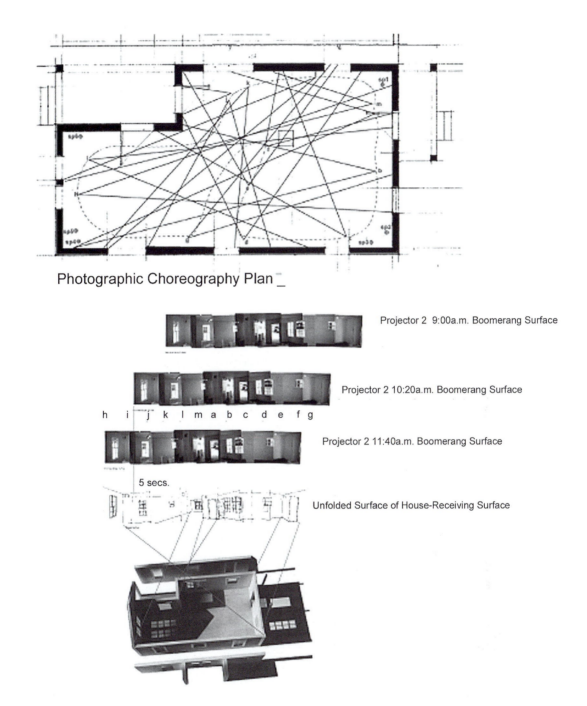

Photographic Choreography Plan

Projector 2 9:00a.m. Boomerang Surface

Projector 2 10:20a.m. Boomerang Surface

h   i   j   k   l   m   a   b   c   d   e   f   g

Projector 2 11:40a.m. Boomerang Surface

5 secs.

Unfolded Surface of House-Receiving Surface

Choreographic Unfolding of House/Five Second Shift

light, shade, shadow, and reflection on the shotgun's surfaces by drawing on and photographing the house at each interval over the course of a week.

During the first phase, drawings were made on the surface of the house where light penetrated, marked at the hour of a given interval. Because the light moved so quickly, it was difficult to actually capture and draw precisely whole moments capturing outlines on surfaces. The light and shadow were already someplace else by the time one started to trace it, leaving the careful systematic construction of intervals in shambles. Within this space set up between the drawing itself and the act of seeing it, one could speculate on whether the house was the same house or one rapidly replacing itself at the speed of light. Reflections pivoted from the house windows, complete with an invisible axis about which, point for point, primary light was recast into its ghostly twin. In the act of drawing one could develop an idea of what a shadow could be in terms of the future, time that had not yet gone through the house. Was a shadow simply a slave to the object that projected it? Could shadows be understood as another intersection of time? Was a shadow itself a projective element opening the house to a different space, removing the natural light allowing projections and a perpetual future?

During Phase 2 photographs were choreographed from six station points; slide projectors were later locked into the same six positions, where they sent out a continuous surface panorama using the photographic shots, creating a shifting, pulsing five-second skin of projected light across the interior of the house. One uncompleted goal of the installation was to work with a teacher at P.R.H. and with students in the afterschool program develop their own panoramic surfaces to be projected within the space. At the end of the week the windows of the "shotgun" were covered, cutting off the interior from the continuity of light to create new imaginary surfaces of projection and places for future speculation.

RELATIONSHIP TO JOHN BIGGERS WORK

This installation pulled forward some other ideas such as the implications of looking at places by the timefullness of space rather than the timelessness of space in relationship to different kinds of memory. John Biggers' paintings of "shotgun" houses from the early 1980s are very much about timefullness rather than timelessness. Their subject matter is about a process of triangulated practices and beliefs pivoting between Africa, Europe, and America. In the painting that served as a poster background for the conference, depth or space is indicated by the repetition of the "shotgun" house form, symbolizing the daily work that sustains home, family, and community. The overlapping elevations of the house establishes a flat, rhythmic, textile-like quality to the painting. Depth and time in the painting, perhaps space can be understood as a collapsing and weaving of the near and far, rather like a reflection in glass, which simultaneously allows one to see that which has passed and what is about to happen. Curiously, the space of the shotgun or

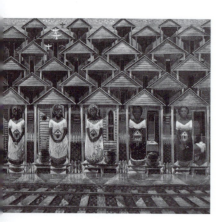

Phase Two Projected Panorama Fragments b-d Boomerang

the clear view from front to back that gives the house type its name is blocked by the bodies of women, themselves carrying miniature houses in their arms.

CONCLUSIONS

Drawing on architecture tracing the division between light and shadow makes a mark, a cut in time, that is otherwise invisible or impossible to actually have as a moment. Nevertheless it was this graffiti that becomes the memory, a complete fiction of what was actually happening at the time. Rhythm and repetition as structure and intervention, of drawing and of photographing, were direct ways of inhabiting the space and acknowledging the fiction of a cut in time to make a mark, to make a memory. The remembrance of the house is a process not representative of a singular or particular moment or specific individuals and their lives as in John Biggers' painting. The open house seen through daylight does not represent a single aspect of black culture but rather effects a process of being part of this diaspora, a process of passing through in time, understanding the tactical, improvisational nature of life. The darkened house is a medium that effects a cut in time or trigger providing space for the projection of the imaginary and trigger for multiple individual fictions.

Originally published in the Proceedings of the 90th Annual Meeting of the Association of Collegiate Schools of Architecture, 2002.

PHENOMENA AND TECHNOLOGY

INTRODUCTION
KIM TANZER AND RAFAEL LONGORIA

To meet the problem of climate control in an orderly and systematic way requires a pooling of effort by several sciences. The first step is to define the measure and aim of requirements for comfort. For this the answer lies in the field of biology. The next is to review the existing climatic conditions, and this depends on the science of meteorology. Finally for the attainment of a rational solution, the engineering sciences must be drawn upon. With such help, the results may then be synthesized and adapted to architectural expression.[1]

Before the advent of air-conditioning there was no choice—buildings had to respond to climate or become uninhabitable. In 1963 Victor and Aladar Olgyay's *Design with Climate* outlined the basic tenets of passive solar design and effective natural ventilation. Published at a time when the widespread use of mechanical cooling was accelerating, this research was particularly relevant to North America, since so many of its examples dealt with free-standing suburban homes.

The subtitle of the book, *Bioclimatic Approach to Architectural Regionalism*, encapsulates its attitude toward international style architecture. *Design with Climate* joined Robert Venturi's and Aldo Rossi's seminal texts from the same era in questioning the wisdom of the prevailing architecture and urbanism, forming the foundation for the postmodern critique.[2] In time, this critique would be further refined by Kenneth Frampton as critical regionalism.

Vernacular building traditions contain the accumulated wisdom of local strategies to deal with the sun, wind, and rain. But technological developments, the prevailing spirit of innovation, and the quest for a universal expression led some twentieth-century designers to believe that science could conquer climate. Le Corbusier certainly was enthusiastic about air-conditioning when he proclaimed in 1933: "The Russian house, the Parisian, at Suez or in Buenos Aires, the luxury liner crossing the Equator will be hermetically sealed."[3]

But however enthusiastic Le Corbusier was about expansive glazing and experimenting with mechanical systems, he was also at the vanguard of exploring natural ventilation and passive solar designs inspired by vernacular solutions. In "From *L'Air Exact* to *L'Aérateur*," Harris Sobin concisely traces the evolution of environmental control concerns in Le Corbusier's architecture and the lessons he learned from his own mistakes.

Octavio Paz defined modernity as the absence of prejudice.[4] Le Corbusier's deconstruction of "the problem of the window" into its three essential

1 *Victor Olgyay and Aladar Olgyay*, Design with Climate: Bioclimatic Approach to Architectural Regionalism *(Princeton, N.J.: Princeton University Press, 1963). Passage from the preface and acknowledgements.*

2 *Aldo Rossi*, The Architecture of the City, First published in Italy in 1966 *(Cambridge, Mass.: M.I.T. Press, 1984) and Robert Venturi*, Complexity and Contradiction in Architecture *(New York: Museum of Modern Art, 1966).*

3 *As quoted by D. Michelle Addington in "Good-bye, Willis Carrier,", this volume.*

4 *Stated during Octavio Paz series of lectures on modernity at the University of Texas at Austin, 1986.*

functions—to light, to air, to ventilate—and subsequent reconfiguration into various experimental devices is a brilliant demonstration of modern design methodology. Sobin's essay illustrates both the limitations and the promise of these innovations. As he concludes, Le Corbusier's experiments "helped focus the attention of a whole generation of architects worldwide on the desirability of achieving environmental comfort and efficiency, wherever possible, by natural and architectural means."

The energy crisis of the early 1970s called into question buildings that relied on cheap oil to function properly and accelerated the interest in energy efficiency. Phillip G. Mead's "Unhealthy Energy Conservation Practices" relates a cautionary tale of ventilation and illumination versus insulation, and the unintended consequences of single-minded energy efficient design, once more underlining the importance of a systems approach.

In "Good-bye, Willis Carrier," D. Michelle Addington documents the air-conditioning and construction industries' resistance to change, as she presents technological innovations that may show the way out of our conundrum. Using ventilation as a common theme, these three essays together make a convincing case for the complex and intertwined nature of sustainability questions: ecology, economy, and social equity must all be taken into account to arrive at a successful solution.

"Esthetics" has increasingly been identified as the indispensable fourth "E" in the making of sustainable architecture. Single-family houses have provided fertile ground for sustainable speculations—perhaps because their scale makes these issues more manageable; perhaps because they are the most frequent building type commissioned to academic architects. The four following houses give architectural expression to the intertwined "Es".

As its name implies, Thomas Hartman's "Compass House" rigorously marks the cardinal points. It illustrates a clever approach to design that reconciles proper solar orientation with urbanity by developing a kit of parts that is compatible with contemporary land-development practices and lifestyles. The variety of resulting courtyard configurations is well suited to the harsh desert climate.

Brian Andrews and W. Jude LeBlanc update the lessons of Gulf Coast vernacular architecture with a pair of "Scupper Houses" that manage to be thoroughly modern and traditional at once. Particularly noteworthy is the poetic way in which rain is harvested by turning the roofs into giant scuppers, and the careful consideration of the local ecosystem and regional culture.

"An Affordable, Sustainable House," by William Sherman is a proposal for Habitat for Humanity in Richmond, Virginia. It takes the vernacular typologies of the mobile home and the front porch and revises them to make a modest prototype that is easy to build. The long, thin plan effortlessly captures breezes and daylight while the roof channels wind and rain. The interior is configured to vertically stratify and evacuate the region's hot summer air, while simple strategies such as substantial insulation are mentioned as part of the overall architectural concept. The project sensibly proposes that well-conceived environmental strategies will make the house more cost-effective for its future owners. The goal of increasing social equity is also furthered by using easily obtainable materials intended to be assembled with volunteer labor.

Lisa Iwamoto and Craig Scott's "Fog House" is conceived as an instrument to magnify its inhabitants' awareness of natural phenomena. The house is carefully calibrated to the particular topography of its site, its magnificent views, and the climate and dramatic cycles of fog peculiar to the Bay Area.

Beyond "meeting the problem of climate control in an orderly and systematic way," each of these houses is a demonstration that sustainability and architectural expression of the highest order are fully compatible.

FROM *L'AIR EXACT* TO *L'AÉRATEUR*
Ventilation and its evolution in the architectural work of Le Corbusier
HARRIS SOBIN

Le Corbusier's mature modernist architecture evolved through three distinct periods: a purist or "high-tech" phase of the 1920s; a transitional or reassessment phase of the 1930s; and a primitivist or "low-tech" phase from 1945 to 1965. From an environmental-control standpoint, each of these periods was characterized by a focus on innovative, yet prototypical design solutions for a single, primary environmental "topic," "theme," or problem. For each period, the primary "theme" or "topic" changed, from light (purist period) to heat (transitional period) to air and ventilation (primitivist period). It can be shown that for each of these periods, Le Corbusier developed a building envelope system and an iconic element which "solve" the particular "theme" (or range of environmental problems) which characterized the preoccupations of that period. These solutions were generally additive, that is, the acquisitions of a prior period would persist into the next. At times, this would lead to direct conflict between a newly acquired solution and one evolved during an earlier period.

Throughout his career, it was characteristic for Le Corbusier to break an overall architectural problem into its constituent parts, then develop designs in which each element represented the solution to that particular part of the overall problem. Thus, for each of these primary environmental "themes" or "topics," Le Corbusier would typically develop an environmental symbol or iconic/totemic element, a sort of architectural *objet type*. These elements include the *fenêtre en longueur* (ribbon window) of the purist period, and the *brise-soleil* (sun breaker) of the transitional period. Each of these symbolic elements, while originally intended to be functional in character, also powerfully encapsulates, at a scale smaller than that of the building in which it was used, the environmental "theme" which marks each distinct period of Le Corbusier's modernist architectural work.

It is the intention of this paper to explore the background and evolution of the concept of ventilation in Le Corbusier's architecture and the systems and elements through which it was implemented. These elements begin in the purist phase with an early but experimental version of mechanical air conditioning (*l'air exact*) unavailable in Europe. By the primitivist phase, the architect had moved toward purely architectural solutions, to the point of making ventilation into a constituent and visible element of the undulatory window wall, in the form of the device to which Le Corbusier gave the name *l'aérateur*.

"MANUFACTURED AIR": 1920–1928

Le Corbusier's work of the 1920s showed a bold, innovative, and aesthetically influential approach to the environmental issue of natural daylighting, while his work of the 1930s revealed a new approach to solar control. By contrast, his approach to the issue of ventilation in buildings during both of these periods involved two diametrically opposed strategies, one purely mechanical but wildly utopian, the other commonplace, conventional, but without reliance on mechanical power. At this early stage in Le Corbusier's mature career, ventilation as an environmental issue was in fact relegated to a very low level of overall priority. Ventilation was to be dealt with either by falling back on resolutely traditional and natural methods (for small-scale buildings such as residential or other work of a modest scope, using conventional openable windows), or by totally mechanizing it (in large-scale projects by means of then-unbuildable air-conditioned and hermetically sealed buildings). The focus, during this period, clearly remained on daylighting or sunlighting of interiors. In 1929, Le Corbusier underlined this attitude, announcing that "la fenêtre est faite pour éclairer, *non pour ventiler*" ("windows are for light, not ventilation;" emphasis is Le Corbusier's).[1] During this early "high-tech" period, the machine constituted Le Corbusier's main metaphor for architecture, and it was not until after World War II that the theme of "ventilation" would emerge in his work as an aspect of architecture worthy of transformation into an environmental element, to be expressed as a separate, visible, architectural "statement."[2]

In the smaller-scale projects completed in the 1920s, two different types of operable windows were used, i.e., casement-style steel sash or sliding wood windows. Casement-type operating sections were by far the most common type of operable windows utilized in this period. These usually appear either as vertical panels within large areas of the *pan de verre* (glass window-walls), or as one-piece openable sash, in square shaped "punched" openings which occur in solid walls. The casement style also appears in the form of single tall and narrow vertical operating panels, inserted at intervals within runs of otherwise fixed industrial *vitrage d'usine* ("factory", or greenhouse glazing), made up of closely spaced vertical steel T-section mullions.

This industrial glazing is the same kind of window wall the architect used in his Citrohan house projects, as well as most of his villas of the 1920s. A variant (for which Le Corbusier took credit) on this type was to separate a single, operable, glazed panel from its usual location amidst a wall of such fixed industrial glazing and use it as an isolated element placed within a tall narrow slot. It would typically be punched out of an area of solid walling and was a window-type usually reserved for areas needing privacy but relatively little light, such as toilet rooms, bathrooms, or stairwells.

For large-scale projects, Le Corbusier by 1928 was advocating the use of two technically sophisticated mechanical systems: the *mur neutralisant* (neutralizing wall) and *l'air exact* (occasionally and interchangeably described

1 *Le Corbusier*, Précisions sur un état présent de l'architecture et de l'urbanisme *(Paris: G. Crès, 1929), 56.*

2 *The concept of "ventilation," whether mechanically or naturally, is associated with two major functions in architecture: (1) "code, or "dilution ventilation," concerned with the control of smoke, odors, dust, and allergens; or (2) "comfort air movement," concerned with reducing dry bulb temperature (through cooling of the building fabric), or effective temperature (through direct cooling through airflow of the surface of the body). It is not clear if Le Corbusier fully understood the distinction between these two functions before the Indian projects of the 1950s, at which time he began to confront both of these ventilation issues with the help of André Missenard, a French engineer, qualified thermal physiology expert and mechanical consultant.*

above: Le Corbusier, Villa La Roche, factory glazing. One vent open. © 2006 Artists Rights Society (ARS), New York/ADAGP, Paris/FLC.

141

as *respiration exacte*). *Air exact* was an elementary form of closed-circuit air-conditioning, invented (according to Le Corbusier) by the French engineer Gustave Lyon and designed to provide correctly humidified air at exactly 18 degrees Celsius (64.4 degrees Fahrenheit) in all seasons.[3] The former was adapted by Le Corbusier from double-glazing systems traditionally used in areas of Europe with extreme winter weather, such as Switzerland or Russia. It consisted of a double-layered cavity wall (glazed or opaque), filled with fast-moving hot or cold air depending on the season. This moving air was to be blown vertically between the two layers of the double wall from a central machine room.

Le Corbusier advocated these systems as the means for rendering the "glass box" habitable in all climates and seasons, providing the perfect machine-age environment not only in Europe but everywhere on the globe.[4] This claim was clearly based on a thorough misunderstanding of the physical principles involved. For example, neither doubling of a glass wall, nor a flow of cooled air between its two layers could have had any appreciable effect in reducing radiative transmission of solar heat into building interiors. Rather than detecting any flaws in these concepts, the architect proposed using the systems for two of his major large-scale projects in the late 1920s: a dormitory/shelter for Paris and a major governmental office building for Moscow.

The clients for both projects balked at anything as radical or untried as the sort of totally manufactured indoor climate Le Corbusier had in mind. One of the buildings (the Centrosoyus building in Russia) was built without incorporating either of the two mechanical systems, but included the double curtain wall (including openable sections).[5] The other building, the Salvation Army Shelter in Paris, was built without either the second glass skin (for the *mur neutralisant*) or the refrigerated cooling coils (for the *air exact*). As executed, however, the building retained its 10,500 square feet of south-facing single glazing containing only four very small openable sections. Nothing else was modified to compensate for either of the elements of the original design which had been omitted from the executed project. The building appeared to be an environmental success at its inauguration during the particularly cold winter of 1933–1934. But by the following summer, serious environmental difficulties had developed: the hermetically sealed all-glass, south-facing wall turned the building into an unventilated inferno. After a long and bitter legal battle with both clients and the Paris Préfecture, Le Corbusier was officially ordered, in March, 1935, to incorporate forty-one more openable sections in the south façade.[6] This experience undoubtedly encouraged the architect to accelerate his development of the *brise-soleil* device (a development underway since 1933). But it also must have served as a reminder of the critical importance of ventilation in buildings: *l'air exact* and the *mur neutralisant* henceforth gradually disappear from his later writings and projects.

3 *Ibid.*, 64.

4 *Ibid.*, 64.

5 *Jean-Louis Cohen,* Le Corbusier and the Mystique of the U.S.S.R.: Theories and Projects for Moscow, 1928–1936 *(Princeton, N.J.: Princeton University Press, 1992), 88–92.*

6 *Reyner Banham,* The Architecture of the Well-tempered Environment *(Chicago, Ill.: Chicago University Press, 1969), 155–162.*

"INTO THE WOODS": LE CORBUSIER'S REDISCOVERY OF NATURE: 1929–1945

By the beginning of the 1930s, Le Corbusier (and modern architecture in general) had experienced two serious rejections in major international competitions: the League of Nations (1927–1929) and the Palace of the Soviets (1931). The same years brought a major stock market crash (1929) and the start of the Great Depression. With these factors furnishing the economic and professional context, the architect appears to have begun to lose faith in his earlier machine-oriented philosophy. At this point, and in Reyner Banham's phrase, Le Corbusier "took to the woods."[7] Parallel to this loss of faith in the machine, there is also evidence of a new awareness of the human body and organic form, first seen in his painting. His architecture also began to change, shifting away from a reliance on mechanical solutions toward a greater acceptance of working within the often limited means at hand. Hermetically sealed, heavily glazed designs, using utopian high-tech mechanical systems gave way to passive methods, which allowed much more interaction between building interiors and the natural environment. Rough surfaces and natural materials increasingly took the place of smooth machine-

above: Le Corbusier, Salvation Army Building, Paris, 1929–1933. Main block (at center), originally clad with hermetically sealed, tautly stretched glazing; building was originally designed to be air-conditioned. After World War II, Atelier Le Corbusier installed a *brise soleil* providing needed shade for this very large and totally glazed façade. (Le Corbusier, *Oeuvre complète*, 1929–1934, p. 99). © 2006 Artists Rights Society (ARS), New York/ADAGP, Paris/FLC.

7 Harris Sobin, "Le Corbusier in North Africa: the Birth of the 'Brise-Soleil', in Desert Housing, ed. K. N. Clark and P. Paylore (Tucson, Ariz.: University of Arizona, Office of Arid Lands Studies, 1980), 153–173.

made finishes. Thin, tightly stretched planar elevations were replaced by more complex, sculptural façades, forming a protective transition zone between inside and outside.

Le Corbusier now began to travel widely, often to some of the world's preindustrial or less developed regions. Soon his writing, and then his architecture, began to reflect an almost obsessive interest in the vernacular building traditions of "primitive" cultures and regions, particularly in their use of form, and in their approach to environmental issues. Of special importance was a series of visits to North Africa, including Morocco, Algeria, and Tunisia, in 1931–1936. Observations made on these visits once again caused Le Corbusier to begin to question architectural solutions for generalized, worldwide application and to start to realize that an international style might not call forth an international climate! What he saw in North Africa suggested that a design approach suitable for hot climates and developing regions should consider the use of architectural methods of climate control. In particular, the Saharan oases and medinas were an absolute revelation, revealing the existence of a world of poetic replies to the question of how to create livable human environments in a harsh desert by simple nonmechanical means. These observations were soon to find their echoes in Le Corbusier's own projects, including three unbuilt but influential projects in the mid-1930s for Algeria, plus another in that colony which was executed in wartime.[8] During World War II, the resources of the highly industrialized economy of France were reduced to the level of a preindustrial society. Responding to the limitations of that context in 1942, Le Corbusier designed a self-build system, called the *Murondins*, for refugee housing and schools, using thick walls of sun-dried adobe blocks or pisé, and grass-covered sod roofs supported by branches over rough log beams. These structures, if built, would have relied entirely on simple wood stoves and natural ventilation.

8 Sobin, "Le Corbusier in North Africa," 157–159, 165–166.

REESTABLISHING THE CONDITIONS OF NATURE: 1946–1965

By 1945, Le Corbusier's philosophy of the 1920s had undergone an almost complete transformation. He had by now come to consider himself "an enemy of air-conditioning," and had come to believe that the unchanging quality of environments provided by mechanical systems was actively unhealthy.[9] In the postwar years, Le Corbusier attempted to synthesize his new philosophy and the technical acquisitions of the 1930s into a more fully integrated kind of architectural environment which was more nature-oriented, one able to take advantage of the challenges of a randomly varying natural environment and far more capable of responding to that environment and to its occupants' needs without relying on expensive machinery than did his earlier "high-tech" projects. He summarized this new attitude in 1953:

9 Le Corbusier, Carnet Nivola 1, March 23, 1951, Fondation Le Corbusier, Paris, 181.

To offset the effects of sedentary city life we need contrasts of various sorts—heat and cold, sun and shade, etc.—reaction to which provides an endless source of energy and vitality. Nothing is more dangerous than an absolutely uniform environment. Living in cotton wool . . . when you get up and open your door, you should be greeted by just that little shock of change, whether it be pleasant or unpleasant, which jolts you physically and mentally, providing a natural reaction . . .[10]

10 *Le Corbusier*, The Marseilles Block, *trans. G. Sainsbury (London: 1953), 24–25.*

These sentiments suggest a radical change has taken place in the architect's thinking, when compared to his earlier advocacy of a totally manufactured climate.

One of the first opportunities the architect had to put these ideas to work came in 1945, when Le Corbusier was commissioned by the Ministry of Reconstruction to design, at Marseilles, a large-scale collective housing prototype for postwar France. Completed in 1952, the Unité d'Habitation at Marseille was the first project of Le Corbusier to be built after the war, and the first executed example of the *brise-soleil* concept. A *bureau d'études* was set up for the project, possessing the sort of engineering expertise needed for a project of that magnitude. Its up-to-date H.V.A.C. design included mechanical exhaust for bathrooms and kitchens, connected to two main evacuation updraft ducts which terminated at the roof deck in prominent, funnel-shaped, concrete *cheminées de ventilation* which contained the exhaust fans.

The Unité also included a simple forced-air heating system, using a simple type of small diffuser called the véga, a patented device produced by the French firm, Etablissements Neu. The device is similar in concept and size to the type of adjustable small air nozzle used today in the passenger compartments of commercial jets. An adjustable finned metal "spider" is pivoted centrally within a framed circular air delivery opening, linked to that frame via a flexible ball joint. The spider is adjustable to modify airflow in any one of three ways: either adjusting the aiming angle of a single jet of air; or diffusing the airflow by splitting the main jet into two jets, one on either side; or closing off airflow entirely. As used at the Marseilles project, this very modestly scaled device may well have suggested to Le Corbusier the idea of inventing architectural elements capable of controlling and shaping ventilating airflow. Le Corbusier even had a véga installed in his personal work space at 35 rue de Sèvres, and he was photographed adjusting it about 1952. Shortly after his experience with the device at Marseilles, he began to experiment with larger scale elements which also functioned, at an architectural scale, as iconic expressions of natural airflow, ventilation, and human comfort.

In the early months of 1951, within a year of completing the Marseilles project, Le Corbusier began a long-term contract as chief architectural consultant for the design and construction of Chandigarh, a new capitol for the newly formed state of the Punjab in northwest India, a contract which called for him to make two trips to Chandigarh a year. Besides the overall city plan, his work included the design of four major government buildings, two museums, and two university buildings.

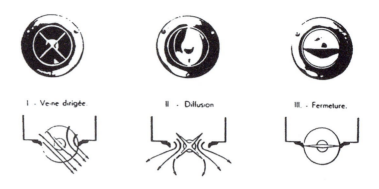

I - Ve-ne dirigée.   II - Diffusion   III - Fermeture.

above: *La bouche de ventilation Véga*, cover of sales catalog from French firm Etablissements Neu, featuring Véga diffuser, a unit typically used as forced-air heating supply.

above right: Véga diffuser: typical operating positions: 1. Narrow jet of directed/directable airflow; 2. Wide-spreading, or diffusing, of airflow, in two opposed directions; 3. Complete blocking of airflow. Ets. Neu catalog illustration.

right: Diffuser type Véga (upper left), in typical use as H.V.A.C. supply unit at the Unité d'Habitation at Marseilles (1945–1952). (Le Corbusier, *Oeuvre complète*, 1946–1952, p. 213). © 2006 Artists Rights Society (ARS), New York/ADAGP, Paris/FLC.

Once again, as with his visits to North Africa in the early 1930s, the direct, immediate, and very personal experience of a face-to-face contact with a hot climate provoked Le Corbusier to a sequence of observation, experimentation, and analysis, leading to a design response. Staying at the Taj Hotel in Bombay in November, 1951, while at the start of his second biannual visit to India, he conducted a series of experiments on the beneficial cooling effects of airflow, gauging the influence of various adjustments of door and window openings, using his own bodily reactions as the "measuring instrument." His conclusions, summarized in several sketches, was to propose an innovative type of window wall made up of three different components. These included (a) several ranges of large, openable solid wood panels, providing light when open and identified as "2" in the sketch; (b) a limited number of glazed "hole-in-wall" type windows and identified as "3" in the sketch, providing constant daylighting; and (c) a series of tall, floor-to-ceiling slots, narrow enough to qualify as "anti-theft," identified as "1" on the sketch and labeled as providing "ventilation."[11] This appears to be the first record of Le Corbusier's "invention" of a device which would soon become part of his standard design vocabulary, labeled as the *aérateur*, or "aerator."

11 *Le Corbusier, Carnet Nivola 1, November 27, 1951, 215.*

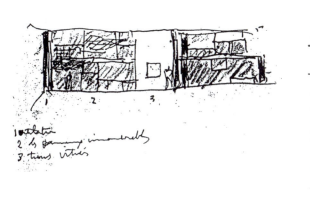

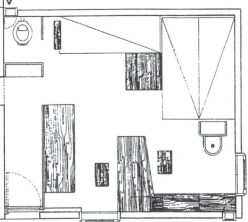

Le plan du Cabanon. V = fenêtres de ventilation

Within a few weeks of his return from India, toward the end of 1951, Le Corbusier was designing a one-room vacation *cabanon* for himself on the Côte d'Azur near Monte Carlo. It was in the design of this small unit that the tall, narrow ventilation slot, previously sketched in Bombay, made its next appearance: Le Corbusier appears again to have been "experimenting" on himself for the purpose of trying out new environmental ideas. An early plan of this small hut, published in Volume 5 of the *Oeuvre complète*, along with photos of the completed structure, showed two of the new devices, placed at diagonally opposite corners of the space. The devices are identified in an accompanying text as *ventilations-moustiquaires* (fly screened ventilators). The text goes on to add that the devices had "met all expectations. . . . the system will henceforth be applied in India for both public and private projects."[12] Each of the *éléments verticaux de ventilation* (vertical ventilation elements) is labeled on plan with small bold-face "Vs", and described in a legend as *fenêtres de ventilation* (ventilation windows). Hinged to the interior

left: Le Corbusier, sketch of window wall. © 2006 Artists Rights Society (ARS), New York/ADAGP, Paris/FLC.

right: Le Corbusier, plan of Cabanon. © 2006 Artists Rights Society (ARS), New York/ADAGP, Paris/FLC.

12 *W. Boesiger (ed.) Le Corbusier, Oeuvre complète 1946–1952 (Zurich: Éditions Girsberger 1953), 78–79.*

face of each slot is a full-height, hinged solid wood panel or door, for closure. The implication is that this arrangement would, through the use of the simplest means, provide a perfect cross-ventilation in rooms, even in the more challenging climates of India.

Le Corbusier had by now effectively "appropriated" the shape and (in part) the function of these "ventilation windows" from his own earlier use of narrow, vertical, casement-type operable elements, elements initially borrowed from the example of nineteenth-century *vitrage d'usine* (factory or greenhouse glazing). A major change from its earlier use, however, is that the element is now *solid*, rather than transparent, helping to clearly distinguish or separate it visually from light-giving elements of the façade.

If, as he said in 1929, "windows are for light, not ventilation," Le Corbusier had, by 1952, evolved what could be, within his own architectural vocabulary, an appropriate element for ventilation. Openable, it could provide ventilation to building interiors. And as a solid element, it was clearly legible as something distinctive from a light-giver. On a modest scale, this exemplifies Le Corbusier's philosophy of unraveling, or separating out, the functions of architecture, then giving visual expression to each distinction by isolating as independent elements the individual components of a building (as here, even the components of the wall), seeking a different form for each function.

The ventilation window made its next appearance in the first of Le Corbusier's major buildings for Chandigarh, the High Court of Justice (1951–1954).[13] In the High Court, this element is conceptually similar to that used at the Cabanon, only taller (7 feet 5 inches, from floor level), but maintaining the appearance of a narrow side-hinged flush wood door, located in a wood frame. By 1953–1954, the "ventilation window" had become a standard constituent element of Le Corbusier's architectural vocabulary. From this time forward, the "ventilation window" appeared in each of his major projects, whether or not the building is located in the tropics. In later projects, this element is often painted in bright colors, to call attention to both its opacity and its iconic qualities.

Its first application in a non-tropical location was at the Convent of La Tourette (1953–1960) in southeastern France.[14] In the period 1955–1956, when the most intense design development by the atelier was taking place on the La Tourette project, a group of other projects including the Maison du Brésil for Paris (1955–1957), and the next Chandigarh project, the Secretariat (1952–1957) were in more or less simultaneous design development. During this period, several important advances, offshoots and variations occurred in both the ventilation window and the *pan de verre* (window-wall) themes.

The progressive changes in the concept of the ventilation device can be seen in a sequence of two successive detail plan-section drawings for typical window walls of the individual monks' cells at La Tourette. The earlier drawing, dated September 12, 1955, shows a tall (6 foot 10 inch) vertical,

13 W. Boesiger (ed.) Le Corbusier, Oeuvre complète 1952–1957 (Zurich: Éditions Girsberger 1957), 56–77.

14 W. Boesiger (ed.) Le Corbusier, Oeuvre complète 1957–1965 (Zurich: Éditions Girsberger 1965), 32–53.

square element (10.5 inch × 10.5 inch on plan), labelled "*fente de ventilation en bois ou tôle pliée*" (ventilation slot in wood or sheet metal). The square element contains a hollowed-out, cylindrical interior within which rotate two airfoil or wing-shaped blades, spaced apart from each other and supported by a pivoting, star-shaped spacer or "spider" at the center. Pivoting the inner, drum-like component would have provided a more precise control of the volume of airflow than possible with the earlier, more primitive "side-hinged flap" version. This amazingly sophisticated "drum" version of the ventilation window also appears to the author to represent another significant advance. Because its movable element is located *within* the opening, rather than *beside* the opening, the new design would allow the user to "steer," or direct, the angle of airflow coming from the device and into the room. The idea of achieving directional airflow control in this way is reminiscent of the characteristics of the véga diffuser, which Le Corbusier had used in the Marseille Unité.

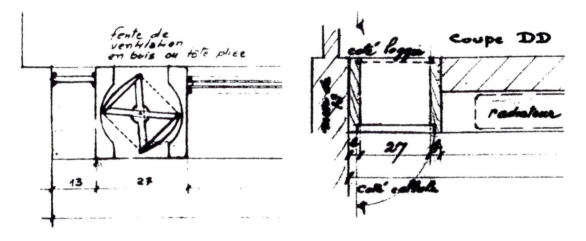

left: Le Corbusier, "drum"-type ventilator.

right: Le Corbusier, "side-hinged" type ventilator.

Within ten months, the first plan-section was voided and replaced by a later drawing, dated July 17, 1956, showing a simple "side-hinged" flap, opening inwards into the room, and labeled "ventilation door." Probably because of cost considerations, Le Corbusier had pulled back from the more sophisticated scheme, and reverted to the simpler "Cabanon" or side-hinged flap type of ventilation window, not only for the monks' cells, but also for most other locations in the project.

In the early part of 1955, the Atelier Le Corbusier redefined the window-wall idea itself, in the form of the so-called *pan de verre ondulatoire* (undulatory window wall). This system was henceforth used for main public spaces of buildings not protected by *brise-soleil*. The system consisted of full-length fixed glazing, held in place via vertical concrete *bâtis* (precast struts or mullions), spaced out according to ratios based on musical proportions and modular dimensions. At intervals, between selected pairs of struts, "ventilation windows" were inserted.[15]

15 *Boesiger*, Le Corbusier, Oeuvre complète 1957–1965, 78.

above: Le Corbusier, Couvent La Tourette (1953–1960), exterior view of *pan de verre ondulatoire*. Musically proportioned spacing of concrete struts or mullions, which hold both fixed glass and *aérateurs*. (Peter Bienz, *Le Corbusier und die Musik*, Wiesbaden, 1998, cover photo). © 2006 Artists Rights Society (ARS), New York/ADAGP, Paris/FLC.

above right: Le Corbusier, La Tourette, refectory interior view of *pan de verre ondulatoire*. © 2006 Artists Rights Society (ARS), New York/ADAGP, Paris/FLC.

16 *Boesiger*, Le Corbusier, Oeuvre complète 1957–1965, 78–101, 200–201.

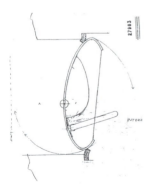

above: Le Corbusier, "airfoil"-type *aérateur*.

By early 1957, Le Corbusier had begun to use the invented word "*aérateur*" to refer to his ventilation windows. And at this time, a third type of *aérateur* was under development for the La Tourette project at the Atelier. This unit measured 12 foot high by 10¼ inches wide, fabricated of brake-formed, unpainted aluminum, with a combination wood stiffener and handle at handrail height, and with the unmistakable shape on plan of an open-sided airfoil, vertically and assymmetrically pivoted. The general configuration of this *aérateur* represented a return to the concept of the "drum" type of unit previously tried (and rejected) in 1956, that is, a type in which the movable element is located *within* the opening, and not hinged to one of its sides, presumably allowing it to more readily shape the direction of airflow into the room. This "aluminum airfoil" type of *aérateur*, which managed to combine the "primitive" technique of natural ventilation with a machine-age shape and finish, was reserved for major public spaces, usually within areas of *ondulatoire* glazing. The aluminum airfoil type was also utilized in two of the buildings then under design for Chandigarh, as well as in the main refectory at La Tourette.

Several of Le Corbusier's late projects utilized this asymmetrically pivoted type of *aérateur*, including two more major buildings at Chandigarh, the Secretariat (1952–1957), and the Assembly (1952–1960), the Maison du Brésil (student housing) at Paris (1954–1957), and Carpenter Center for the Visual Arts at Harvard (1959–1963).[16]

As the key component in an overall comfort ventilation system, the *aérateur* reached the zenith of its development in the Chandigarh Secretariat. Built without air-conditioning, (except for the ministerial suites), natural ventilation was even more critical to the building's environmental success. *Aérateurs* were liberally placed in the exterior *ondulatoire* glazing on both façades of the building. But there remained the problem of creating good airflow through both banks of office accomodation either side of the central, double-loaded corridor, while still preserving good acoustic privacy between the corridor and the offices. The final design, arrived at with assistance from the acoustical consulting department of Phillips Lamp Co., was to design special fixed *aérateurs* for use in along the corridor walls. These consisted of 17-inch wide openings, equipped with sound-baffles in the form of "Hs" on plan, with their interior surfaces lined with thick, sound absorbing material.[17]

CONCLUSIONS

In that portion of Vol. VII of the *Oeuvre complète* devoted to the Secretariat, Le Corbusier includes a short description of the *pan de verre ondulatoire*. Written shortly before his death, it reads as an "environmental last testament," summing up what he has learned about environmental factors (especially ventilation) and their control.[18] This text portrays the undulatory wall as the definitive answer to what Le Corbusier describes as "the problem of the window," fulfilling as it does the three necessary functions of the environmental envelope:

1 *éclairer* (to light);
2 *aérer* (to air);
3 *ventiler* (to ventilate).

Le Corbusier then goes on to explain how the undulatory wall fulfills each of these missions:

1 (Day)lighting is achieved by nonoperable *pans de verre*, glazed with clear or translucent glass, fixed into the concrete (struts or mullions);
2 *Aération* is obtained by means of "vertical full height *aérateurs*, or aerators, (11 inches to 17 inches wide, capable of being opened gradually, as desired, over their full height, providing an immense natural cross-ventilation, powered by differences in air density as between one façade and another, caused by temperature differences during the course of the day, depending on the position of the sun.
3 Ventilation, to be obtained "during hours of extreme heat in the tropics: we must counter the effect of air temperatures in excess of body temperature, by means of a powerful *courant d'air*, provided by fans placed on the floor or suspended from the ceiling."

This text does represent a real advance in Le Corbusier's thinking about ventilation, demonstrating that he has now realized that the concept actually involves two very separate functions. Yet here we have another, final example of the rigid, almost obsessional way in which he categorizes functions, designs an element to satisfy each function, then gives each element its own distinctive form and expression. *Aération* is so narrowly defined that the element designated to provide it, the *aérateurs*, can only be used to provide what amounts to dilution ventilation, and is not thought of as useful to create air movement

17 *Le Corbusier, interview by the author, September 30, 1961, Paris. Author's personal observations, April 1962, Chandigarh.*

18 *Boesiger,* Le Corbusier, Oeuvre complète 1957–1965, *100.*

for direct body cooling. By the same token, ventilation, or what amounts to cooling air movement, is only to be provided by fans (which are not even a component of the *ondulatoires*!).

As used by the Atelier Le Corbusier, the vertical *aérateur* remains more effective as the exposition or expression of a principle than as a real solution to the specific problem of natural comfort ventilation in buildings. When used as Le Corbusier used it, solely as a vertically oriented inlet device, the *aérateur* typically creates a narrow pattern of airflow on plan.[19] If the device is located near or adjacent to an interior cross-wall, the jet of incoming airflow will adhere to that wall, due to relative pressure differentials. Either result may often, of course, be preferable in cool or cold climates (e.g., France) or seasons, as it permits dilution ventilation without undesireable drafts. But in warmer climates, a more even pattern of distribution is desirable, available across as large a proportion of interior spaces as possible. From a functional stand-point, this suggests that if the element were oriented horizontally rather than vertically, an *aérateur* would be more effective as a provider of comfort air movement; but this would have violated the repetitive, purely vertical rhythm of elements in the undulatory wall.

In tracing the evolution of ventilation concepts in Le Corbusier's career, we can see, at a scale smaller than that of the buildings themselves, that the same kinds of dogmatic, absolutist, rigid and ideological thinking was at work, just as it was with other aspects of his design process. In the case of the *aérateur*, just as with other design elements, what begins as a building component based on an originally environmental rationale, comes to have independent aesthetic status, that is, it becomes a symbol, formalized into a "design statement" or a convention, quite detached from its original rationale.

Rather than providing effective functional building elements, most of those environmental conventions which were developed by Le Corbusier eventually more closely resemble expressions, representations, or metaphors for a particular environmental function or process. In later projects, they often conflict with one another (e.g., daylighting elements such as *pans de verre* or window walls combined with *brise-soleil*, together leading to excessively dark interiors), or simply fail to achieve their intended result (e.g., the *aérateur*'s excessively narrow airflow patterns). Nevertheless, they also helped focus the attention of a whole generation of architects worldwide on the desirability of achieving environmental comfort and efficiency, wherever possible, by natural and architectural means. By such means, Le Corbusier also helped dramatize an ideal of creating architecture capable of facilitating and reestablishing the essential contact between ourselves and the natural world, of seeking a greater sense of unity for that architecture with respect to both human needs and natural forces.

Originally published in the Proceedings of the 84th Annual Meeting of the Association of Collegiate Schools of Architecture, 1996.

19 *Harris Sobin,* Analysis of Wind Tunnel Data on Naturally Ventilated Models: Appendix A: Test Data Catalog *(Tucson, Ariz.: Harris Sobin Associates, 1983).*

UNHEALTHY ENERGY CONSERVATION PRACTICES

PHILLIP G. MEAD

Yet it is obvious that productivity and efficiency have no value in themselves, they have merit only as means to an end. In fact, excessive concern with productivity and efficiency interferes with the pursuit of significance.[1]

INTRODUCTION

"Today's problems come from yesterday's solutions." Systems thinker Peter Senge wrote this introductory comment in his primer *The Fifth Discipline* to illustrate the futility of simplistic resolutions.[2] Systems dynamics predict that the most obvious answers may improve matters over the short term, but only make things worse for the future. In examining energy efficiency practices since the 1970s oil embargo, it is clear that the building industry and the academy too narrowly attacked the energy crisis at the expense of broader health and welfare issues. A.S.H.R.A.E. conservation recommendations, efficient planning strategies and some passive energy strategies significantly contributed to building designs with restricted access to fresh air, natural light, and views of nature. These strategies encouraged efficient warehouse configurations with low exterior wall to high interior space volume ratios which fundamentally eroded basic human health ... not unlike tenement conditions of the late nineteenth century. This essay calls for a more responsible balance between the often-conflicting needs for energy conservation and basic human health.

Since ventilation represents 20 to 40 percent of a building's thermal load, A.S.H.R.A.E. in the 1970s took the most obvious way out of the energy crisis by lowering ventilation standards. For example, office building ventilation in 1977 was cut from 15 cubic feet per minute to 5 cubic feet per minute in 82.[3, 4] Twenty years later, after a proliferation of articles on ventilation and sick building syndrome, the 1997 *A.S.H.R.A.E., Fundamentals Handbook* shows its undying faith in ventilation efficiency when it writes the following: "Outdoor air introduced into a building constitutes part of the space-conditioning load which is one reason to *limit air exchange* rates ... to the minimum required."[5] This demonstrates that efficiency is of central importance while human health is of secondary concern.

But air quality appears to be a fraction of what makes a building "sick." In addition to respiratory illness, narrowly focused efficiency strategies have lowered the quality and quantity of indoor light. Within the past twenty years, medical studies have found that today's low levels of indoor light may significantly contribute to depression,[6] inattentiveness,[7] stress,[8] and compromised immunity.[9] Additionally, restricted access to *outdoor* spaces may significantly

1 René Dubous, So Human an Animal *(New York: Charles Scribner & Sons, 1968), 179. This book won the 1969 Pulitzer Prize.*

2 Peter Senge, The Fifth Discipline *(New York: Doubleday, 1990), 57.*

3 A.S.H.R.A.E. Handbook and Product Directory: 1977 Fundamentals *(Atlanta, Ga.: A.S.H.R.A.E., 1977).*

4 A.S.H.R.A.E. Handbook: 1982 Fundamentals *(Atlanta, Ga.: A.S.H.R.A.E., 1982).*

5 A.S.H.R.A.E. Handbook: 1997 Fundamentals *(Atlanta, Ga.: A.S.H.R.A.E., 1997), 25.3.*

6 Norman Rosenthal, Seasons of the Mind *(New York: Bantam, 1989).*

7 Lisa Heschong, "Daylighting in Schools: An Investigation into the Relationship between Daylighting and Human Performance," *condensed report submitted to the Pacific Gas and Electric Company, 1999.*

8 R. Kuller and C. Lindstern, "Health and Behavior of Children in Classrooms with and without Windows," Journal of Environmental Psychology 12 (1992): 305–317.

9 F. Holwich and B. Dieckhues, "The Effect of Natural and Artificial Light via the Eye on the Hormonal Metabolic Balance of Animal and Man," Ophthalmologica 180, 4 (1980): 188–197.

10 Michael Holick, "The Role of Sunlight in Providing Vitamin D for Bone Health," Biologic Effects of Light 1996, ed. M. Holick and E. Jung (New York: Walter D. Gruyter & Co, 1997).

11 Michael Holick, "Biological Effects of Light: Historical and New Perspectives," The Biologic Effects of Light 1998, ed. M. Holick and E. Jung (Norwell, Mass.: Kluwer Academic Publishers, 1999).

12 Roger Ulrich, "View through a Window May Influence Recovery from Surgery," Science 224 (1984): 420–421.

13 Morris Morgan, trans., Vitruvius: The Ten Books on Architecture (New York: Dover, 1960).

14 Leon Battista Alberti, On the Art of Building in Ten Books (Cambridge, Mass.: M.I.T. Press, 1988).

15 W. Jones and E. Withington, eds., Works of Hippocrates (Cambridge, Mass.: Harvard University Press, 1923).

16 Florence Nightingale, Notes on Nursing (New York: Appleton, 1860).

17 Holick, "Biological Effects of Light."

18 F. L. Wright, The Natural House (New York: Horizon Press, 1954). Wright scorned the unhealthful qualities of basements due to lack of fresh air and light. Irving Gill, "New Ideas about Concrete Floors," Sunset Magazine, December 1915. Gill wrote about the sanitizing qualities of his concrete floors. R. M. Schindler, "Care of the Body," Los Angeles Times, March 14 and April 11, 1926. Schindler wrote in place of Dr. Lovell on air-quality issues. Richard Neutra, Survival through Design (New York: Oxford Press,

increase rates of osteoporosis[10] and cancers of the breast and prostate.[11] For hospital patients, poor views due to smaller windows and lack of landscaping may slow recovery time and increase pain.[12]

ANCIENT AND MODERN TIES TO HEALTH DESIGN

Recent environmental medical research echoes the ancient writings of Vitruvius and Alberti who wrote extensively on how places and building design can affect bodily health.[13, 14] Both architects were significantly influenced by the environmental writings of Hippocrates who in the fourth century BC outlined the relationship of disease to unhealthy places and environmental conditions.[15] More recently, Florence Nightingale in the mid-nineteenth century strongly recommended the inclusion of light—in particular sunlight—and fresh air into hospital designs in her influential 1860 book *Notes on Nursing*.[16] In 1903, therapeutic light gained scientific validity when the Nobel Prize was awarded to Niels Finson for establishing the curative effects of light on tuberculosis.[17] These practices not only influenced the design of buildings and cities but the fledgling movement of modern architecture as well. From this era emerged the health-inspired work of Frank Lloyd Wright, Irving Gill, Rudolph Schindler, Richard Neutra, and Alvar Aalto.[18] All promoted the healthful incorporation of light, air, and views.

THE SEDUCTIVE EFFICIENCY OF MINIMIZED EXTERIOR WALLS AND WINDOWS

Traditional vernacular forms help provide a sense of place and serve as models for energy conservation. However, vernacular design does not guarantee healthy living conditions. Cold-weather vernaculars best show this conflict. Although the igloo, wigwam and the early New England homes are thermally responsive due to limited windows and minimized exterior walls, the designs are typically oriented inward, which may compromise basic health needs for light, air, and view. For example, the colonial New England house is considered appropriate for heat conservation because its rooms huddle around a massive central fireplace surrounded by walls of limited window size.[19] Colonialists could take comfort in this type of heat conservation, but in latitudes that rank the highest percentages of clinical winter depression in the United States, orienting spaces away from natural light in the winter most likely exacerbates depression.

Taking a clue from cold-weather vernaculars, Victor Olgyay recommends in *Design with Climate* that building plans in northern latitudes should be nearly square because of the high space to low exterior wall ratio.[20] Using graphic tables he demonstrates how B.T.U. efficiency slumps when building shapes become more elongated and thin. However, this strategy not only limits natural light, but in large buildings the strategy appears to justify a multitude of interior rooms whose only access to fresh air is through the H.V.A.C. system. If this system is contaminated or broken, those in rooms near the core don't have the option to open windows for temporary relief. Additionally, rooms near the core are cut off from stress-reducing views of nature and daylight access.

But thermal efficiency is not the only reason for minimizing exterior walls and compacting building plans. Worker productivity through shortened circulation routes is also a strong motivator. This rationale can be seen with the 1903 Royal Victorian Hospital in Belfast where it is clear that the values of medical productivity through worker efficiency are more highly prized over the quality of patient recovery. Prior to this time, the ideal hospital was modeled on the advice of Florence Nightingale who promoted plans like Lariboisière's 1839 Paris hospital pavilion with courtyards that abundantly harvested outdoor light, air, and views of gardens (see below left). However, this pavilion plan was deemed inefficient because it necessitated longer circulation routes for doctors and nurses. Additionally, if these plans converted to mechanical ventilation, longer duct runs would be necessitated. Thus, William Henman, the architect of the Royal Victorian solved this "problem" by shortening the circulation paths and mechanical duct runs by eradicating patient-centered courtyards and compressing the pavilion wings into a single fat warehouse mass (see below right). Not only did this reduce the amount of steps for doctors and nurses, but it also minimized exterior walls and windows. The hospital was now viewed as a factory . . . or as Henman called it, a "health manufactory,"[21] where patients could be seen as objects to be fixed in the most efficient manner possible. Henman was probably influenced by Frederick Taylor, whose factory time and motion studies and scientific management theories were beginning to gain popular acceptance in the manufacture of goods and services.

1954). Neutra wrote on various health-related design issues. Alvar Aalto's Pamio Sanitarium included design features that allowed beds and easy therapeutic access to outdoor sun, air, and views of nature. Aalto also designed more sanitary splash-minimizing sinks and chairs that allowed for patients to sit at such an angle as to make breathing easier.

19 Charles Moore, Gerald Allen, and Donlyn Lyndon, The Place of Houses *(New York: Holt, Rinehart & Winston, 1974).*

20 Victor Olgyay, Design with Climate *(Princeton, N.J.: Princeton University Press, 1973).*

21 William Henman, "The Construction of Hospitals," Journal of the Royal Institute of British Architects *(1896–97).*

below left: Paris Hospital plan by Lariboisière, 1839–1854.

below right: Belfast Royal Victoria Hospital Plan, Henman and Cooper, 1903.

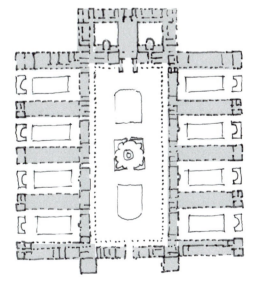

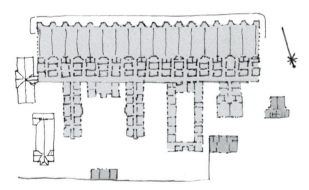

Minimized circulation schemes without garden courtyards picked up momentum after World War II, due in part to the replacement of environmental light and air therapies with the more efficient and effective biochemical drugs such as penicillin.[22]

Seventy-eight years after the construction of the Royal Victorian, the 1978 *A.S.H.R.A.E. Applications Handbook* also endorsed a similar compaction strategy while at the same time discouraging the use of windows. It recommended that "since the exterior load varies from 30–60% of the total air-conditioned load . . . it is desirable to keep the perimeter area to a minimum."[23] Conservation graphs comparing energy-wasting windowed spaces with more energy-efficient nonwindowed spaces further encouraged the planning of more interior rooms while limiting wasteful exterior rooms with windows. But beyond the seduction of thermal and administrative efficiency, minimizing exterior walls and windows is profitable for all buildings and climates because of the ease of planning and assembly. Compared to interior walls, exteriors require more detailing, trade coordination, building time, and energy intensive materials, due to the extra effort needed for waterproofing, insulation, and incorporation of windows and doors. In short, it takes a significant investment of human and embodied material energy to plan and build exterior walls.

MEDICAL EVIDENCE AGAINST MINIMIZED EXTERIOR WALLS AND WINDOWS

The health risks of limiting exterior walls and windows could be substantial. In addition to reports of poor air quality, Roger Ulrich's 1984 study of poor window views in hospitals could add to daily stress. Ulrich's 1984 landmark study of gall-bladder patients with window views to nature demonstrated that they both healed faster and took lower doses of pain medication than those patients who viewed a brick wall.[24] Ulrich's studies are significant because it confirmed and strengthened the commonly held belief that natural views pleasantly calm the mind which may improve conditions in other stressful settings like schools and offices.

The importance of windows and light is further demonstrated in Lisa Heschong's 1999 research report on windows and skylights in classrooms. Here she found a link with higher test performance in rooms with larger windows and skylights that minimized glare. In this study, she found that classrooms exposed to the largest window areas progressed 15 percent faster in math and 23 percent faster in reading than those with compromised windows.[25] Heschong's studies could tie into recent sleep disorder and depression research.[26] Inadequate indoor light as it relates to sleep disorders and anxiety could lead to higher levels of stress which raises the body's hormonal levels of cortisone and epinephrine. Both stress hormones compromise the immune system's white-blood-cell counts.[27] Inadequate levels of light as it relates to depression may conceivably contribute to other types of immune problems.[28]

22 Marni Barnes and Clare Cooper-Markus, "Research Report Applying the Therapeutic Benefits of Gardens," Journal of Healthcare Design and Development 8 (1996).

23 A.S.H.R.A.E. Handbook: 1978 Applications (Atlanta, Ga.: A.S.H.R.A.E., 1978), 3.7.

24 Ulrich, "View through a Window."

25 Heschong, "Daylighting in Schools."

26 Daniel Kripke, "The Uses of Bright Light in an Office Practice," in Sleep Disorders: Diagnosis and Treatment, ed. S. Poceta and M. Mitler (Totowa, N.J.: Humana Press, 1998).

27 R. Parsons, "The Potential Influences of Environmental Perception on Human Health," Journal of Environmental Psychology 11 (1991): 1–23.

28 N. Rosenthal et al., "Seasonal Affective Disorder: A Description of the Syndrome and Preliminary Findings with Light Treatment," Archives of General Psychiatry 41 (1984): 72–80.

Studies conducted on depressed patients have shown that certain immune system regulators like immunoglobulins and lymphocytes can be compromised making the depressed more vulnerable to illness and conceivably to building-related illness.[29]

One possible explanation for the link between light and depression may be evolutionary. Our brains and bodies have evolved with very high levels of outdoor light, ranging between 5,000 and 20,000 lux. With the onset of the industrial revolution, we began to spend the majority of time indoors which is five to 200 times darker. According to sleep researcher Dr. Kripke of the University of California, San Diego, humans function normally in the wake/sleep cycle, when exposed regularly to light conditions of 1,500 to 2,500 lux,[30] which is three to five times higher than the recommended 500 lux for today's office environments. According to Kripke and others who treat their patients with light boxes, these low levels do not significantly suppress melatonin, a neurotransmitter that signals the brain to sleep.

There is speculation that light also activates serotonin, the neurotransmitter that provides a sense of well-being. Both melatonin and serotonin are nearly identical on a molecular level and are known to transform into one another. During the day, too much melatonin and not enough serotonin can result in depression. Today's psychiatric prescriptions of Prozac and Zoloft in some way manipulate serotonin while light boxes measurably suppress melatonin. All have nearly replaced the former psychiatric drugs of Valium and Xanax.[31] So light and its relationship to melatonin suppression and perhaps serotonin production, as well as views of nature, could partially explain why Heschong's schoolchildren received higher scores in the daylit schools.

For those who suffer from Seasonal Affective Disorder (SAD), high-intensity lamps of 10,000 lux adequately relieve winter depression. However, these lamps along with typical interior lights lack the full spectrum of daylight. Incandescent light is skewed towards the red side of the light spectrum while cool white fluorescent has very high levels of yellow and green. Both of these specialized light spectrums are foreign to what our brain evolved with which consisted of a balanced outdoor full light spectrum. Some researchers have deemed this imbalance as "mal-illumination" referring to the different color spectrums as essential nutrients.[32]

Additionally, today's lighting standards may also contribute to anxiety and depression because current levels focus on low minimum light levels for *visual comfort* and task efficiency which is far below Dr. Kripke's recommendations. Current levels range from 300 lux for classrooms and computer stations to 500 lux for offices[33]—four to seven times less than the vastly higher, minimum levels of 1,500 to 2,500 lux recommended for normal bodily function.

29 Fredric Goodwin and Kay Redfield Jamison, Manic Depressive Illness (New York: Oxford University Press, 1990). Reports that depression studies have shown that one of the immune system's regulation devices, prostaglandin, is shown to be elevated in depressed patients. T. Kronfolz and W. Nascallah, "Leukocyte Regulation in Depression and Schizophrenia," Psychiatry Research 13 (1984): 13–18. Research finds that depressed patients have less circulating lymphocytes. Delist et al., "Serum Immunoglobulin Concentration in Patients Admitted to an Acute Psychiatric In-Patient Service," British Journal of Psychiatry 145 (1984): 661–665. Research finds that the level of immunoglobulins are lower in those suffering from depression than in normal people.

30 Daniel Kripke, phone interview by the author, May 25, 2001, Texas Tech University. In this interview, Kripke made reference to N. Okudaira and D. Kripke, "Naturalistic Studies of Human Light Exposure," American Journal of Physiology 245: R613–R615.

31 Michael Norden, Beyond Prozac, Brain-Toxic Lifestyles, Natural Antidotes and New Generation Antidepressants (New York: Regan Books, 1996).

32 John Ott, Light and Health (Old Greenwich, Conn.: Devin-Adir Co., 1973).

33 Benjamin Stein and John Reynolds, Mechanical and Electrical Equipment for Buildings (New York: John Wiley & Sons, 2000).

THE HEALTH BENEFITS OF OUTDOOR LIGHT AND AIR

In addition to the high levels of outdoor light, medical research is now claiming that the *lack* of outdoor full-spectrum light could be responsible for a number of maladies that go beyond sleep disorders and depression. Because 90 percent of our day is typically spent indoors,[34] studies are showing a relationship between a lack of outdoor light and higher rates of osteoporosis, jaundice, breast cancer, ovarian cancer, colon cancer, large bowel cancer, and prostate cancer.[35, 36] Most of this research is sponsored by science-based foundation grants and reported in hard scientific medical journals. Sunlight induced ultraviolet B light and its production of vitamin D3, a sunshine-, not dietary-induced hormone, helps bones and the immune system absorb calcium. This contribution to the immune system has resulted in a multitude of promising studies since the 1980s that show strong links to ultraviolet light and its role in combating heart disease and cancer.[37, 38] Reinforcing this research is a number of studies that show lower rates of both cancer and heart disease in global areas and times of the year where the sun shines strongest (higher altitudes, lower latitudes, arid climates, and the summer season).[39, 40] Although windows block out most ultraviolet light, thus eliminating vitamin D3 production, this prompts the need for more accessible and comfortable outside areas.

Not only is the outdoors a source of high amounts of full-spectrum light, but it is also in many cases, a source of fresh air. Compared to outside air, recycled indoor air in most sick buildings has higher concentrations of mold. According to asthma researcher Dr. Cynthia Jumper of Texas Tech's Health Science Center, sick indoor air conditions have been linked to upper and lower respiratory illnesses. Asthma in children has risen dramatically since the 1970s energy crisis where today one in twenty children are afflicted. Dr. Jumper speculates that tightly sealed buildings and lower ventilation standards are a major contributor.[41] As pointed out by Dr. Jumper's colleagues, Dr. Danny Cooley and Dr. David Strauss with their research of ninety-four buildings in forty-eight states, the fungi responsible for building-related illnesses and Sick Building Syndrome has significantly higher mold concentrations inside. As a result, these researchers use outdoor air as a baseline for measuring normal mold levels.[42] Because outside air is continuously moving, it can in most cases easily disperse harmful mold and gases.

In addition to fresh air, the outside generally contains higher concentrations of negative ions.[43] Although negative-ion research of the 1960s and 1970's faltered after subsequent research failed to replicate earlier studies, current research from Dr. Terman of Columbia University shows that high concentrations of negative ions are equally effective as light-box treatment for winter depression.[44]

The relative freshness of outdoor air, the opportunity to view natural scenes and the benefits of sunshine vitamin D3 appear to overshadow the danger of outdoor light's link with melanoma. Although abusive exposure to ultraviolet

34 American Lung Association web site, "Facts about Air Quality," <http://www.alaw.org/air_quality> (accessed 2002).

35 Full-spectrum light deprivation (in particular UVB light deprivation) and its detrimental effects on breast, ovarian, prostate, and colon cancer can be found in medical journals as early as 1980 in the International Journal of Epidemiology. Similar studies have appeared consistently through the 1990s in journals such as Cancer Research, Lancet and Cancer Causes and Control.

36 Holick, "Biological Effects of Light."

37 Rolfdieter Krause et al., "The Role of Ultrviolet Radiation on Cardiocirulatory Regulation and on Cardiovascular Risk," in The Biological Effects of Light 2001, ed. Michael Holick (Boston, Mass.: Kluwer Academic Publishers, 2002).

38 Michael Holick, "Vitamin D: Importance for Bone Health, Cellular Health and Cancer Prevention," in The Biological Effects of Light 2001.

39 Cedric Garland et al., "Serum 25-Dihydroxyvitamin D and Colon Cancer: Eight Year Prospective Study," Lancet (1989): 1176–1178.

40 J. Waterhouse, C. Muir, and P. Shanmugarantnam, Cancer Incidence in Five Continents, Vol. IV (Lyon: I.A.R.C. Scientific Publications, 1982). Follow-up studies tracked immigrants who moved from lower to higher latitudes and vice versa and found the subjects appeared to take on the risks associated with the new location.

41 Cynthia Jumper, M.D. and the author have taken part in three, one-day-long indoor-air-quality roundtable discussions between 1997 and 1999 at the Texas Tech

light (as demonstrated in the 1970s suntan fad) has been linked with melanoma, there is contrary evidence that significant *lack* of sunlight may also contribute to skin cancer.[45] Additionally, the hands and face, which are regularly exposed to the sun, seldom develop melanoma; it is the torso and legs, which are not normally exposed, that develop melanoma.[46] Finally, skin-cancer researchers Catherine Poole and Dupont Guerrt admit in their book *Melanoma Prevention, Detection and Treatment* that to most people, mild exposure to the sun is not detrimental and that mild exposure to the sun may protect from melanoma.[47]

CONCLUSION

It is often written that energy efficiency *is* healthy. From a global level this may be true, but on a more human biological level, the two can be at odds. Oftentimes, energy efficiency takes first priority while health needs are placed second. This may be a result of our educational values and standards. For example, N.A.A.B.'s 2001 accreditation criteria stresses human ecology, but it is written within the narrow context of energy efficiency. Of the thirty-plus criteria, the word "health" is briefly written once, but it is watered down and written within the same sentence as property rights and subdivision ordinances.

As future energy crises emerge, new regulations are inevitable. If again, energy strategies are too simplistic and not meaningfully paired with human health needs, then history may repeat itself in the form of unhealthy but efficient building design. From a biological point of view, recent light, air, and view research suggests that the rules of thumb and tools of energy efficient design be reexamined to include a more basic human ecology. The profession needs to think more like physicians and less like efficiency engineers if sustainable design is to be truly "sustainable." Through this reassessment, perhaps a more balanced vision of sustainability can emerge.

Health Science Center where Dr. Jumper has given the results of her asthma research and her views on building-related illnesses.

42 David Strauss et al., "Correlation between the Prevalence of Certain Fungi and Sick Building Syndrome," Occupational Environmental Medicine 55 (1998): 579–584.

43 Robert Iviker, Asthma Survival (New York: Penguin Putman, 2001).

44 Michael Terman, Jiuan Su Terman, and Donald Ross, "A Controlled Trial of Timed Bright Light and Negative Air Ionization for Treatment of Winter Depression," Archives of General Psychiatry, 55 (1998): 875–882.

45 F. Garland, M. White, and E. D. Gorman, Archives of Environmental Health 45 (1990): 261–267. Melanoma and other skin cancers have been linked with UVB light, but this research has shown that those who work mostly inside can have a higher risk of skin cancers than those who work outside.

46 M. Braun and M. Tucker, "Do Photoproducts of Vitamin D Play a Role in the Etiology of Cutaneious Melanoma," in Biological Effects of Light 1995, ed. M. Holick and E. Jung.

47 Catherine Poole and Dupont Gurret, Melanoma: Prevention, Detection and Treatment (New Haven, Conn.: Yale University Press, 1998).

Originally published in the Proceedings of the 89th Annual Meeting of the Collegiate Schools of Architecture, 2001.

GOOD-BYE, WILLIS CARRIER
D. MICHELLE ADDINGTON

> *At this moment of general diffusion, of international scientific beliefs,*
> *I propose: only one house for all countries, the house of exact breathing*
> *. . . The Russian house, the Parisian, at Suez or in Buenos Aires, the luxury*
> *liner crossing the Equator will be hermetically sealed. In winter it is warm*
> *inside, in summer cool, which means that at all times there is clean air*
> *inside at exactly 18°.*
>
> Le Corbusier, Precisions *(1933)*

More than half a century has passed since Le Corbusier extolled the virtues of centralized air-conditioning systems, and yet, even though the fervor has waned, the belief still persists that these systems produce the most achievable version of "man-made weather." The longevity of this technology has little to do, however, with its performance or adaptability, but rather with the prodigious timing of its development and introduction. The work of Alfred Wolff, Willis Carrier, and many others on latent heat control at the turn of the twentieth century enabled the rapid maturation of H.V.A.C. technology, propelling the industry so far ahead of classical theoretical research that it was effectively isolated from later developments in fluid mechanics and heat transfer. As a result, in spite of increasingly severe problems, the centralized air system has maintained its hegemonic dominion, and the majority of related research in the building industry has sought to fix problems within the technology instead of challenging the paradigm. Yet, the scientific under-standing of heat transfer, and particularly of fluid dynamics, has progressed so dramatically during the last century that if the precedent of the centralized air system did not exist, a radically different trajectory for thermal-control technologies may have occurred. How, then, can the industry return to the 'fold' to reconceptualize the technology in light of current theoretical understanding?

The centralized air system has remained the choice technology in thermal conditioning because of its ability to control both air temperature and relative humidity with the same supply air stream. Air temperature has always been somewhat straightforward to control, even in the case of cooling, with relative humidity floating as a dependent variable. Although Willis Carrier was but one of many engineers who was developing strategies for controlling relative humidity in the late nineteenth and early twentieth century, his "Apparatus for Treating Air," introduced in 1903, established the paradigm of an inte-grated system in which multiple thermal strategies were collapsed into a single technological response.[1] During the development of this apparatus, Carrier's frustration with existing psychometric data—the empirical tables that had

1 *Carrier's "Apparatus for Treating Air" used water spray for conditioning, with the water heated for humidification or cooled for dehumidification. Carrier was ridiculed by the mechanical engineering community for proposing that spray water could be used for dehumidification. As a result, the first apparatus that was sold was used only for washing air. It was not until 1906, after independent tests had been conducted, that a textile manufacturer installed it as the first central humidifying system. See Margaret Ingels,* Willis Haviland Carrier, Father of Air Conditioning *(Garden City, N.J.: Country Life Press, 1952), 20–28.*

been prepared by the U.S. Weather Service—led him to theoretically construct formulae for the determination of moisture in air. Introduced in 1911 as the "Magna Carta of Psychrometrics," these formulae with their configuration into a psychrometric chart tautologically tied the only available technology for controlling relative humidity into the theoretical method. As a result, even though aspects of the technology have evolved over the past century, the conceptual underpinnings of its highly integrated thermal strategy have not.

The use, however, of a single source to control both air temperature and relative humidity provides, at best, a compromise of the necessary heat-transfer actions: relative humidity control is due to the enthalpic sponge created by the air-temperature difference, and air temperature control is dependent upon the air-to-air mixing necessary to facilitate the diffusion of the moisture. The centralized air system, premised on this compromise between these two modes of heat transfer with very different drivers—vapor pressure differential versus temperature differential—will only perform properly when it is operated with conditions that produce perfect mixing. Variations in supply flow rate, temperature or pressure can upset this tenuous balance, particularly if the heat loading of the space is also varying. As a result, systems with constant compressor speeds, such as the constant air volume system (or C.A.V.), performed the most predictably and were the preferred H.V.A.C. system for decades.

From the beginning of the twentieth century to the early 1970s, electric power use grew by 400 times in the United States. During this supply side era, if the consumer was willing to pay for power, then the utilities readily provided it. Comfort and control were the primary factors influencing environmental systems design, with the result that most H.V.A.C. systems were designed with redundant secondary systems so as to smooth out any fluctuation that might accompany varying load conditions. The Arab Oil Embargo of 1973–1974, and its resultant severe energy shortages, changed almost overnight the attitude toward environmental control, as suddenly every building seemed to have a bloated H.V.A.C. system. The variable air volume system (or V.A.V.) gained popularity as it essentially maintained the same integrated infrastructure as the C.A.V. system, but with much less energy usage. Most new buildings designed after the embargo used some type of V.A.V. system, and many constant volume systems were retrofitted with V.A.V. controls.

The generous quantities of conditioned air that were supplied continuously by constant systems were summarily replaced by the penurious meting out of the V.A.V. system. Many of the load variations that had been easily compensated for in the original system became nearly insurmountable obstacles. In addition, a host of other energy conversation measures joined the widespread implementation of V.A.V. systems. These measures—duty cycling, peak-demand scheduling, economizer operation, occupancy determined lighting and nighttime shutdowns—all increased the thermal load variability.

Exacerbating this variability has been the dramatic rise in electrical equipment housed in buildings, adding very high point loads at various places and varying times. Even an oversized C.A.V. system with reheat would be hard pressed to compensate for these large swings.

Further compounding the energy usage issues were the inherent problems with indoor air quality resulting from the zealous implementation of energy-saving strategies. Buildings were sealed and tightened without any corresponding reassessment of their thermal behavior. As a result, poorly conceived insulation strategies coupled with inadequate ventilation contributed to a marked increase in indoor air pollution even though outdoor pollution had been steadily declining. According to John Spengler of the Harvard School of Public Health, the potential impact of poor indoor air quality on human health ranges from discomfort all the way to death, with Sick Building Syndrome, Legionnaire's disease, asthma and hypersensitivity pneumonitis as but a few of the illnesses that can be directly attributed to high concentrations of pollutants in indoor settings.[2] While many of these problems can and do arise from the use of constant volume systems, the varying ventilation rates and pressures produced by V.A.V. systems more readily create the precursor conditions for an unacceptable environment.

Nevertheless, both the H.V.A.C. industry and the federal government remained confident that the V.A.V. system, with its already complex thermal interrelationships, could be expected to minimize energy usage, maximize air quality, meet individualized comfort requirements, and respond to highly varying loads. Computer simulation and control were deemed the solution for managing these contradictory demands. In the C.A.V. era, crude approximations of the building's thermal requirements that could be manually calculated were often sufficient for determining the H.V.A.C. specifications, and simple feedback analog controllers were more than adequate for system operation. The coupling, however, of the more unstable H.V.A.C. system with a much wider range of cost-saving opportunities demanded not only more sophisticated calculations but also required advanced simulation studies to determine control strategies. In 1973, the U.S. Department of Energy (known then as E.R.D.A.—Energy Research and Development Administration) along with the U.S. Post Office and the Department of Defense, began funding the development of computerized energy calculation procedures, eventually releasing two programs to the public domain: BLAST in 1976 and Doe-2 in 1979.[3] These codes, along with many others developed by equipment manufacturers (Trace from Trane Company, Hap from Carrier), could perform analyses in which weather data and interior loading mimicked transient conditions for more accurate sizing of equipment than the traditional peak loads analysis. In spite of this added complexity and a substantial increase in input data, today's typical code can only perform a quasi-steady state simulation and in order to do this the transient heat gains and losses must be weighted into the calculations. The weighting factor

2 *See* Indoor Air Pollution: A Health Perspective, *ed. Jonathan M. Samet and John D. Spengler (Baltimore, Md.: The Johns Hopkins University Press, 1991), 15. John Spengler has also discussed the dramatic rise in asthma of American children since the 1970s. Current estimates are that 30 percent of children now have some form of environmental asthma, and he speculates that this results from the impact of increased humidity in homes that are tightly sealed.*

3 *J. Marx Ayres and Eugene Stamper, "Historical Development of Building Energy Calculations," A.S.H.R.A.E. Journal 37, 2 (1995): 47.*

method can only handle linear problems and, as such, the heat-transfer coefficients must be constants. More troublesome is that these codes depend upon given sets of H.V.A.C. parameters and are thus operating subordinate to the standard technologies. The codes were developed to facilitate the energy-conscious selection between alternative H.V.A.C. options and not to enable the evaluation of thermal behavior within a space nor to facilitate the exploration of new strategies for conditioning. Nevertheless, the "simulations" produced by these codes are presumed to be adequate enough models of the overall thermal behavior that current research is being directed toward using their results actively for system control.

Energy-management systems, of which the most sophisticated use energy analysis codes for part of the "brain," have become a standard component in many large H.V.A.C. installations. Connecting a phalanx of sensors to direct digital controllers, these automated systems, whether distributed or centralized, are considered to be the key to balancing the contradictory demands placed on the environmental system. Engineer Warren Hahn's enthusiastic testimony for computerized control is shared by much of the industry:

[The] system can directly compare flows, BTUs, and run time hours to schedule, optimize, or equalize the use of boilers, chillers, cooling towers, pumps, and/or AHUs. (It) can be used to schedule all HVAC operations on a daily, weekly, monthly, or yearly basis, including scheduling holidays, special events, and daylight savings time up to a year or more in advance . . . It can compare historical data to establish a pattern on which to build new operating parameters. In short, (the) system can do all that the ever-curious human mind can do, and it can do it on a continuous night-and-day basis without ever getting tired![4]

4 *Warren G. Hahn, "Is DDC Inevitable?"* Heating/Piping/Air Conditioning *60, 11 (1998): 95.*

The industry has jumped on the "intelligent systems" bandwagon, and building owners have been quick to believe the seductive image that a comprehensive network or new sensors and controllers will automatically provide seamless control under ever more stringent and varying conditions, even though the thermal conditioning strategy remains unchanged.

For all of the effort that has been directed toward salvaging the centralized air system, relatively little effort has been applied for alternative means to condition indoor air. A common axiom in the chemical industry is that a well-designed process can almost control itself. If this is true for environmental systems as well, then the trouble with the V.A.V. system does not lay with the need to further expand and sophisticate its control schemes. Rather, the question that should be asked is if the system's interactions with the space are properly conceived, and, if not, how then should the ideal thermal conditioning system behave?

As the H.V.A.C. industry was experiencing meteoric growth during the first half of the twentieth century, related theoretical work in fluid mechanics and heat transfer was at a critical turning point. Unlike most other branches of classical physics, fluid mechanics had not developed a theoretical structure that was able to account for generally observable phenomena. As a classical science, theoretical hydrodynamics had evolved from Euler's equations for a frictionless, nonviscous fluid, but it produced results that were contradictory to experimental observations. The empirical field of hydraulics therefore emerged to provide a method for solving the practical problems that hydrodynamics had been incapable of describing. It was not until 1904, when Ludwig Prandtl introduced the concept of the boundary layer, that these two divergent branches began to be unified.[5]

Theoreticians before Prandtl had recognized that the discrepancy between theory and experiment was due to the neglect of fluid friction in the theory. Even though the governing equations were capable of describing behavior in flows with friction, they were virtually impossible to solve mathematically due to their nonlinearity.[6] Friction had been neglected to enable their solution, and this assumption seemed valid as the viscosities of both air and water are small enough that the forces due to viscous friction should have been negligible when compared to gravitational and pressure forces. Prandtl, however, suggested this was only true in a free-flowing region far from a solid object, and he hypothesized that friction played an essential part in creating a thin boundary layer next to the object.[7] This conceptual separation of fluid flows finally allowed for the neglection of terms in each regime, thus greatly simplifying the mathematical complexity of the governing equations, and ultimately producing correlation between theoretical predictions and experimental results.

Boundary layer theory was first applied to problems of the drag produced when an object was moved through a fluid, such as the drag of a ship or of a turbine blade, and was limited to cases of laminar flow in an incompressible fluid. Eventually, it was extended to turbulent, incompressible flows and finally to compressible flows as the theory became an essential component in the development of aerodynamics. In 1920, G. I. Taylor proposed that the concept of a laminar sublayer could also be applied to problems of heat transfer, although most early work in this field was concerned with hot-wire anemometry.[8] Originally, researchers presumed that a thermal boundary layer existed that mirrored and was superimposed on the fluid boundary layer, but later investigations showed that the relationship between these types of boundary layers was much more complex. As a result, the application of boundary layer theory to heat transfer and to related mass transfer problems of diffusion and evaporation still remains as one of the youngest developing areas of classical physics.

Even though boundary layer theory enabled the analytical description of fluid behavior, the actual solution of the governing equations for predicting behavior was nearly insurmountable for all but the simplest of problems. Flows of constant velocity in a single regime (i.e., laminar or turbulent) near

5 The first translation of Prandtl's theory from German into English didn't occur until 1920. W. Margolis of the National Advisory Committee for Aeronautics (N.A.C.A.) translated an abstract titled "Theory of Lifting Surfaces."

6 These governing equations are known as the Navier-Stokes equations. They are partial differential equations that describe the conservation of mass, momentum, thermal energy, and chemical species.

7 See Hermann Schlichting, Boundary Layer Theory, trans. J. Kestin (New York: McGraw-Hill, 1960). It took many more decades before there was the recognition that boundary layers also formed in free air due to buoyancy effects.

8 See Hugh L. Dryden, "Fifty Years of Boundary-Layer Theory and Experiment," Science 121 (1955).

geometrically uniform and symmetric objects were most conducive for effecting a solution, whereas varying flows in crossover regimes demanded a numerically iterative process for approximation. Until the 1970s, empirical collection of data was the preferred method for characterizing complex flows; wind tunnels were used for evaluating aerodynamic behavior, and ship basins up to a mile in length were used for evaluating hydrodynamic behavior. N.A.S.A. realized that the compressible flow experiments necessary for testing aircraft configurations near the speed of sound were not only prohibitively expensive but were also extremely time-consuming so they pushed forward the development of computerized numerical analysis. In the late 1970s, the coupling of supercomputers with numerical iteration of the governing equations made computational fluid dynamics (C.F.D.) an applicable reality, and N.A.S.A. tested the new program in the redesign of an experimental aircraft after wind tunnel tests demonstrated unacceptable performance.[9]

Considered the third approach in the study of fluid mechanics, with experimental and theoretical analysis as the other two, C.F.D. is analogous to wind-tunnel experimentation while being derived from the governing equations. Essentially, C.F.D. performs numerical experiments, and additionally allows the researcher to investigate those physical aspects of fluid behavior that can not be explored in a laboratory setting. The advantages of C.F.D., however, were initially available to only a limited group of users. Accurate depictions of flows required millions of calculations using time-consuming marching algorithms. Unless a researcher was willing to simplify a problem to two dimensions, then supercomputers were the only digital equipment that could deliver the speed and storage capacity necessary for solving three-dimensional problems. The development in 1976 of the Cray-1, the pioneering supercomputer, was in direct response to N.A.S.A.'s need for faster C.F.D. solutions.[10] The nuclear industry soon joined the aerospace industry when they began to use C.F.D. to model jet flows during simulated faults. In the mid-1980s, the expansion of C.F.D. modeling into market-driven industries, particularly those producing turbo-machinery, automobiles and electronics, led to a proliferation of commercially available software but also fostered the refinement of the algorithms such that complex problems no longer required a supercomputer. By the end of the 1980s, C.F.D. was added to applications in environmental engineering: weather forecasting, air- and water-pollution studies, and fire/smoke behavior. It was not until the late 1990s that there was any significant application of C.F.D. for the study of the thermal behavior of air in buildings.[11]

Why did it take so long for this powerful method to percolate into the building industry? The fluid mechanics of a room are vastly more complex than those of an airplane, and comparatively speaking, much less consequential. An error made in the design of a wing for an experimental aircraft can cost millions of dollars and possibly take the life of a test pilot, whereas an 'error' made in the design of an H.V.A.C. system can usually be

9 The experimental N.A.S.A. aircraft was called HiMAT (Highly Maneuverable Aircraft Technology) and it was designed to test concepts for the next generation of fighter planes. Wind-tunnel tests showed that it had unacceptable drag near Mach 1. Continuing to redesign it and test it in wind tunnels was costing $150,000 per test and was also expected to significantly delay the project. Instead, C.F.D. was used to redesign the wing at a cost of $6,000. See John D. Anderson, Jr., Computational Fluid Dynamics (New York: McGraw-Hill, 1995), 3.

10 Ibid., 27.

11 By significant application, I am referring to the use of C.F.D. to facilitate the design of building systems and to determine performance parameters at a level commensurate to its application in other industries. According to J. J. McQuirk and G. E. Whittle in "Calculation of Buoyant Air Movement in Buildings: Proposals for a Numerical Benchmark Test Case" in Computational Fluid Dynamics (London: Mechanical Engineering Publications Limited, 1991), researchers have been exploring the potential of C.F.D. to predict air movement in buildings since 1974.

compensated for *if it is even noticed*. Unlike most other problems in fluid mechanics in which one or two mechanisms may dominate, building air flow, particularly when centralized systems are factored in, is a true mixing pot of behaviors: wide-ranging velocities; temperature/density stratifications; transient indoor and outdoor conditions; laminar and turbulent flows; conductive, convective and radiative transfer; buoyant plumes, mass transfer and randomly moving objects (people). This mix of mechanisms has effectively prevented any substantial empirical data collection on building air movement. Unlike the single mechanism dominated behavior of aircraft or ship drag which can be scaled down for laboratory or wind-tunnel simulation, the multiple mechanism present in a building environment often produce contradictory scaling parameters, particularly if buoyancy is included, with the result that there is no substantial body of validated experimental data for describing the parameters of air-flow behavior in buildings. Building air movement has always been described in the most anecdotal of fashions, and experimental measurements have value only for the buildings in which they were collected. Although C.F.D. modeling promised to bring both rigor and extensive data to performance assessment, the lack of any empirical foundation has significantly tempered implementation.

If building air behavior is difficult to characterize empirically, then it is even a more herculean task to model it for a C.F.D. simulation. Notwithstanding the array of input data establishing the physical definition of the problem, decisions are also required regarding the choice of algorithms, the terms to neglect in the governing equations, the numerical form of the convection operator, the configuration of the mesh, the relaxation method, the turbulence model used, the dominant thermal mechanisms, and so on. In short, in order to accurately model a problem for C.F.D. analysis, researchers must be as knowledgeable of numerical methods and theoretical fluid mechanics as they are of the specific physical characteristics of the problem.

Nevertheless, the burgeoning commercial potential of C.F.D. has led software designers to produce 'user-friendly' codes that eliminate many of the difficult steps and decisions. Meshes can be automatically generated from a geometric model, and defaults exist for the numerical procedures and the choice of equations. Any user with a P.C. and a commercial C.F.D. code can produce simulations with impressively complex temperature and velocity profiles that may have little requisite relationship to the thermal behavior and physical characteristics of the building other than a recognizable geometric section or plan. Even experienced and knowledgeable modelers are sometimes misled by the completeness of the solution unless they began with a clear projection of the expected behavior or possessed empirical data for comparison.

C.F.D. code validation, which is identified by N.A.S.A. as "detailed surface-and-flow field comparisons with experimental data to verify the code's ability to accurately model the critical aspects of the flow,"[12] looms as a major concern. A.S.H.R.A.E. has funded an ongoing research project to

12 A. J. Baker and R. M. Kelso, "On Validation of Computational Fluid Dynamics Procedures for Room Air Motion Prediction," A.S.H.R.A.E. Transactions 96, 1 (1990): 761.

quantify the "literate use of computational fluid dynamics methodology for accurate prediction of room air motion flow fields and pollutant transport."[13] Validation is of greatest concern for the modeling of specific complex spaces where test data can not be adequately collected. As a result, many of the early modeling efforts focused on simple spaces in which only one or two small parameters, such as window and diffuser locations, are varied and thus can be physically tested.

An alternative approach to the validation problem was put forth by the International Energy Agency (I.E.A.) who kicked off a multi-year, multi-country investigation into C.F.D. modeling in 1988. Their initial objectives were ambitious:

- to evaluate the performance of three-dimensional complex and simplified air flow models in predicting air-flow patterns, energy transport, and indoor air quality;
- to show how to improve air-flow models;
- to evaluate their applicability as design tools;
- to produce guidelines for the selection and use of models;
- to acquire experimental data for the evaluation of models.[14]

Most interesting was the product they expected to deliver: a database of precalculated C.F.D. cases on air-flow patterns within buildings that would *eliminate* the need for inexperienced modelers to perform C.F.D. analysis and full-scale experimentation. But their objectives were perhaps too ambitious; even though thirteen countries and six independent test labs participated, no significantly applicable direction for users or researchers was produced, and the group concluded that, "The experimental verification of proposed design methods has shown that complete validation is an impossible task: experiments are never perfect and all potential applications of a method cannot be foreseen. Therefore the performance of a design tool may only be evaluated for certain specific uses."[15]

Nevertheless, the database was still produced.[16] Several hundred cases were simulated, although all were of the same configuration: a single room office with a window. A decision tree interposition scheme was set up so that an engineer could input room dimensions, window size, number of occupants and computers, and the H.V.A.C. system type with diffuser location, and the C.F.D. simulation "results" would be automatically displayed.

Even if their objectives for this database were overly ambitious, the I.E.A. still conceived and directed the most comprehensive investigation into the C.F.D. modeling of buildings to date. And most researchers would concur that their method was well chosen given the state of the art in air flow characterization at that time. What went wrong? Is the problem of modeling air behavior in buildings so complex that the methods developed by N.A.S.A. are simply not sophisticated enough?

13 *Ibid.*, 760.

14 *International Energy Agency,* Room Air and Contaminant Flow, Evaluation of Computational Methods, ed. A .D. Lemaire *(Delft: TNO Building and Construction Research, 1993),* 2.

15 *Ibid.,* 76.

16 *See Q. Chen, A. Moser, and P. Suter,* A Database or Assessing Airflow, Air Quality and Draught Risk *(Zurich: Institut fur Energietechnik, 1992).*

The field of building air behavior is rejoining the science of fluid mechanics after a near century of divergence, but, as such, building C.F.D. modelers have grabbed onto C.F.D. methods without embracing the theoretical basis— boundary layer theory. Their lack of history in the development of C.F.D. has led to its application as a tool rather than a philosophical approach. The premise of perfect mixing, which forms the foundation of the centralized air system, still remains as the ideal such that the tendency is to consider the air within a room to be a single entity with multiple behaviors rather than as a simultaneous collection of multiple bounded entities of which each is dominated by only one or two behaviors. An analogy might be to consider the attempt to control the multiple behaviors in the perfectly mixed single entity model as being similar to attempting to make an airplane fly by controlling the conditions of the atmosphere rather than of its boundary layer.

Other than the cursory acknowledgment of the boundary layer on a wall surface (which is relegated to an equivalent resistance for heat loss calculations), the assumption is that the remaining boundaries in an air space can be neglected given that perfect mixing automatically dissipates them. If air behavior in a space isn't stable, then the problem is often attributed to the system's failure to produce perfect mixing, whether due to problems in discharge velocity, throw, diffuser location, etc. This inherent conviction that boundaries are inconsequential has led to the unilateral adoption of finite volume C.F.D. codes for modeling building behavior. C.F.D. codes currently support three types of discretization methods for describing a flow domain: Finite difference which breaks the domain into a matrix of discrete points; finite volume which breaks the domain into averaged volumes; and finite element which describes the domain through a matrix of connecting elements. Finite element is considered to be the most sophisticated in that it allows each individual element to vary independently. Finite volume is much less flexible as each discrete volume is dependent on the neighboring volume, rendering it difficult to incorporate derivative boundary conditions. The aerospace and nuclear industries depend almost exclusively on finite element methods as they are far superior for describing boundary layer behavior. The building industry gravitated toward finite volume methods as they were not only simpler to use and much less computationally intensive, but also because the finite volume is a natural analogy for the well-mixed air space in a room in which boundaries are inconsequential.

The operational boundaries within an airspace, however, are not only highly variable and transient, but can significantly influence the behavior of surrounding air. Numerous interspatial boundaries can exist within a single space: between laminar and turbulent flow, between isothermal strata, between convective currents and still air, between zones of different concentrations. Both the location of these boundaries and the rate of heat exchange across them have profound effects on the local air conditions.

Instead of eliminating them by diffusive mixing, what potential may be gained by taking advantage of these boundaries?

Perhaps the most interesting boundary within an air space is that between a buoyant plume and the surrounding air. Buoyant or thermal plumes form above heat sources, producing local upcurrents that entrain adjacent air. In a building, the heat from a human body is significant enough to produce a plume, and there are also plumes above computers and other electrical equipment. These plumes, if in a relatively calm aerodynamic environment, develop in the form of large-scale vortices. The air in the plume is turbulent, whereas the surrounding air is generally irrotational, and the entrainment takes place at the boundary between these two regimes.

Displacement ventilation, or low side wall distribution, attempts to take advantage of buoyant plume behavior to facilitate contaminant removal and to more efficiently dump heat loads. In this system type, low-momentum cool air is supplied near the floor and exhausted by the ceiling after being heated by sources in the room. The heat load generated by the occupants or equipment tends to stay contained within the cortex of the plume without diffusing into the greater air mass, while, simultaneously, contaminants in the room are drawn out of the general air mass into the vortex. The system was initially greeted with some suspicion in this country, but continued operational experience coupled with refinements have helped it establish a toehold, albeit small, in the H.V.A.C. arena. Displacement ventilation is a significant shift from the well-mixed approach, and its mechanisms announce a return to the fundamental basics of fluid behavior. More importantly, displacement ventilation demonstrates that one can take advantage of the thermal processes naturally taking place in a room rather than trying to eliminate them.

The difference between the conventional H.V.A.C. systems and the displacement system raises the issue of the appropriate technology. It was not through ignorance that the field of H.V.A.C. design split away from the science of fluid mechanics, but because an unprecedented technology was developed that dependably delivered the performance that people were demanding. While boundary layer characterization and control was creeping along slowly, the inhabitants of the world were able to enjoy the comforts of "man-made weather." And regardless of theoretical compliance, why would one attempt to control a multitude of discrete boundaries when a single system more than adequately met the user's needs? Perhaps even more significant was that there was no technology on the horizon that could provide the type of discrete behavior necessary for controlling air-to-air boundaries. Until now.

Microtechnology has already revolutionized communications and electronic systems due to the unique electrical properties of silicon. But electronic circuits do nothing more than switch and route electrons, whereas silicon possesses other properties that has helped to spawn an even more dramatic revolution in mechanical equipment by enabling micromachines that do real

17 Janusz Bryzek, Kurt Peterson, and Wendell McCulley, "Micromachines on the March," IEEE Spectrum, May 1994, 31.

18 Roger H. Grace, "Welcome, Introduction, and Overview" (introductory comments at M.E.M.S.: A Global Perspective on Markets, Technology and Applications Sensors Expo, Hynes Auditorium, Boston, May 16, 1995).

19 Pacific Northwest National Laboratory, The Potential for Microtechnology Applications in Energy Systems—Results of an Expert Workshop (U.S. Department of Energy Publication PNL-10478, 1995), 4.1, c. 2–c. 3.

20 Ali Beskok and George Karniadakis, "Simulation of Heat and Momentum Transfer in Complex Micro-Geometries," Journal of Thermophysics and Heat Transfer 8, 4 (1993): 647.

mechanical work. Three times as strong as steel, yet with a density less than that of aluminum, silicon also has the near ideal combination of high thermal conductivity with low thermal expansion.[17] More than simply outperforming traditional mechanical materials, this single crystal substance can be machined to micrometer dimensions, can perform electronically and mechanically simultaneously, and already has low-cost mass-fabrication facilities that can produce millions of elements in an area the size of a postage stamp. Microelectromechanical systems, or M.E.M.S., are one of the fastest growing commercial technologies, estimated to grow from a market of $700 million in 1990 to $12 billion by the year 2000.[18] Sensors and actuators were among the first M.E.M.S. to demonstrate the potential of silicon based micro-machines. The sensors, highly selective and capable of 16-bit accuracy, now enable the measurement and control of parameters that previously could only be estimated from other sources. Although M.E.M.S. sensors are expected to bring an accuracy and control to building systems that was never before possible, it is the development of M.E.M.S. energy systems that may deliver the unprecedented possibility to integrate scientific theory with new tech-nologies for the thermal conditioning of buildings.

In 1995, the Department of Energy concluded that the development of M.E.M.S. for distributed energy conversion systems in buildings was their highest priority in microtechnology research.[19] Among the benefits they highlighted were: reduced distribution losses and power requirements; improved efficiency due to individualized control; improved fundamental conversion efficiency from microscale processes; improved load efficiency due to the staging of conversion modules; and the elimination of C.F.C./ H.C.F.C. refrigerants. Under development were micro heat pumps, heat engines, compressors, evaporators, condensers and pumps, all sized with a maximum dimension of 50–1000 microns (the average diameter of a human hair is approximately 700 microns). Already commercially available are micro-channels and heat pipes for electronic circuit cooling. Of course, stepping up in a size from a circuit to an entire building seems somewhat ludicrous. An inherent assumption in fluid mechanics theory is that contin-uum behavior breaks down at small scales. As the size of an object approached the free path distance of the fluid molecules then slip flow will dominate, which essentially means that air ignores very tiny objects, and just "slips" by without exchanging energy. In 1993, the prevailing sentiment was that slip flow occurred at scales of 100 microns and less.[20] Advances in imaging, however, soon showed that continuum behavior is valid well into the nanometer range. As a result, scaling up from a circuit to a building became an issue of quantity rather than of technical feasibility.

Pacific Northwest Laboratory, who directed the micro-energy project for the Department of Energy, believed that the quantity issue was surmountable, particularly if full advantage was taken of M.E.M.S. capabilities to eliminate large centralized systems for smaller distributed installations. In 1994, they projected that if they could build a series connected micro-heat pump that was able to transfer 1 watt per square centimeter, then a 1 square meter sheet of heat pumps no thicker that wallpaper could easily heat and cool the typical home.[21] By 1996, they had already exceeded their expectations dramatically and were testing heat pumps capable of transferring 25 watts per square centimeter.[22] The technology was clearly achievable; less clear, though, was the system for actually deploying it in a building. Eventually the program was disbanded, even as the technology continued to become cheaper and more efficient. The reasoning? They were unable to replicate the interior conditions produced by the standard H.V.A.C. system. The century old precedent of perfectly mixed air still prevailed.

A new technology arrived at the same time that a new philosophical understanding of fluid mechanics was becoming established. C.F.D. and M.E.M.S. complement each other ideally, the former enabling a means to characterize the discrete behavior of fluids, the latter providing the ability to act at a discrete level. A breakthrough in the thermal conditioning of buildings should be imminent, yet focus and direction continue to be missing. When a similar convergence of a new technology—electromechanical equipment— with a new scientific understanding—psychrometry—occurred at the turn of the century, Willis Carrier stepped forward and revolutionized the heating and cooling of buildings. Who, today, can take Carrier's place?

As in most disciplines, the practice of mechanical engineering has become atomized into specialties. The C.F.D. skills and knowledge necessary for research at N.A.S.A. are of little relevance for the types of applications that require C.F.D. modeling in the chemical industry. Each specialty investigates problems that can be readily bracketed within a given domain of expertise. A C.F.D. modeler may search for a faster and more accurate means to characterize a fluid problem without questioning the problem, a M.E.M.S. designer may work to improve the torque-carrying capacity of a micrometer without knowing what the motor will be used for. That these researchers depend on someone else to establish the direction is perhaps best summed up by Professor Jeffrey Lang of M.I.T.'s microsystems lab: "We have an answer, and we're looking for a problem."[23]

It is not for architects to determine this solution, but rather to define the problem. For most of the twentieth century, the thermal environment was the responsibility of the H.V.A.C. designer, while the architect struggled only to integrate the physical, and static, shell of the conditioning system. What if it were in the architect's power to design the transient environment? To design the way a space feels rather than just how it looks? Would one want the fingertips to be warmer than the nose? Should different zones within a room be if different temperature to sequentially engage and disengage the body? Could thermal zones take the place of walls, or would one want to create a thermal shield around the body that moved with the body, but could be activated or deactivated at will, much like Archigram's Suitaloon? None of

21 Robert S. Wegeng and M. Kevin Drost, "Developing New Miniature Energy Systems," Mechanical Engineering 116, 9 (1994): 85.

22 Robert Wegeng, conversation with author, February 1996. Wegeng is one of the staff engineers responsible for P.N.L.'s research in micro-energy systems under a Department of Energy contract.

23 Jeffrey Lang, quoted in Doug Stewart, "New Machines are Smaller than a Hair and Do Real Work," Scientific American (1992): 95.

these scenarios are premised on the need for perfect mixing or centralized systems. And all of these scenarios are possible by coupling emerging technologies with a more fundamental application of fluid mechanics principles. There is, however, no Willis Carrier waiting in the wings who can single-handedly reinvent the technology for conditioning the environment. But there are scores of engineers ready to design systems for creating the environments that perhaps only architects are capable of imagining.

Originally published in the Proceedings of the 85th Annual Meeting of the Association of Collegiate Schools of Architecture, 1997.

THE COMPASS HOUSE
THOMAS HARTMAN

This project could be seen as an *homage to* as well as a *critique of* the single-family detached suburban dwelling. It is an homage to suburbia in that it attempts to acknowledge and sustain positive aspects of the suburban dwelling. It is a critique in that the design of the house becomes a process of identifying and exploiting the contradictory forces that shape the suburban dwelling from within as well as from without.

CONTEXT

The site for the project is generic. It assumes a relatively standard suburban plot of land located in the suburbs of the desert southwest. At the same time, the site is very specific; it is framed by precise zoning requirements as well as the extremely strong climatic characteristics of the region. Many areas of the United States offer equally unsuitable climates in the winter and summer months, suggesting an architecture of almost year-round separation from the outdoors. The climate of the desert, with its extremely hot summers and mild winters, suggests a radically different pattern of use. Approximately 8 inches of rain fall in a year. The harsh, dry summers encourage (or require) almost total isolation from the sun and the heat, while the winter climate invites the virtual disappearance of the architecture, extending activities to the site as a whole. In a climate of extremes, the consequences of particular design decisions are immediate. But at the same time, constraints might be pushed to the point where they become opportunities. The project seeks to exploit these opportunities.

METHODOLOGY

The project attempts to identify moments of opportunity among the nested relationships that exist between means of inhabitation and the form of individual units, and between the form of individual units and the form of collective structures (parts of cities). The methodology employed is one of identifying and isolating specific conditions in the dwelling that touch both the collective and the individual scales. These conditions become conduits through which changes in patterns of use might lead to changes in the form of suburbia, or collective forces might eventually be allowed to impact the house and act on the means of inhabitation.

The configuration of the house begins with the pairing of two constraints originating at extremes of scale. At the collective scale, the optimum use of subdivided land suggests that the house needs to be able to occupy plots of land with access from any one of the four cardinal points of the compass. Thus, four possible 75 × 100 feet sites are assumed, with street access from the north, south, east, and west. A constraint originating at the scale of the individual dwelling suggests that a preferential orientation between the environment (sun, wind) and activities within the dwelling should be established and maintained on all four sites, despite the fact that they require different orientations to the street. To resolve these contradictory demands, the dwelling has been broken down into a basic taxonomy of four spatial/programmatic conditions. Those that require a fixed relationship to the compass may be isolated from those that required a fixed relationship to the street grid. The four conditions include a public space, a cellular element, a solitary space, and a service element.

A virtual buildable area of 60 × 60 feet is left over when required building setbacks are subtracted from the 75 × 100 feet sites, allowing the basic elements of the dwelling to be configured identically on sites with different orientations. Three types of plants also occupy the site. The roof of each element collects rainwater, which is stored in a cistern and used to sustain a specific portion of the vegetation surrounding the house. The quantity and type of vegetation that each element of the house is able to sustain, as well as the size and configuration of the required cistern, have been determined by analyzing and exploiting data on monthly rainfall and water consumption by different plants. The relationship between roof area and planted area materializes the mathematical relationship between water availability and need. The cistern is needed to resolve a discrepancy between seasons of peak rain availability and seasons of peak water use. The cistern's dimensions, determined through analysis, materialize this temporal conflict. The house harvests the water to grow plants, which are then positioned for the enjoyment of the inhabitants.

FOUR ELEMENTS

The first element houses a solitary space (library?) one level above the ground, measuring 8 × 16 × 11 feet high. It bears a fixed relationship to the compass, with its short dimensions facing north and south. All but the north façade of this element are shaded with fixed louvers, lighting the space while diverting direct sun. This element collects 930 gallons of rainwater each year and stores it in a 455-gallon cistern, configured as a 16-foot high tower placed on the north side. The water is sufficient to sustain an African Sumac tree, which can be viewed through the large north-facing window.

The second element houses a series of cellular spaces (to be used as sleeping rooms, offices, guest rooms, playrooms, etc). This rectangular element also bears a fixed relationship to the compass, its short dimensions facing north and south. The long west wall forms an opaque barrier to the hot afternoon sun, and the long east wall is relatively open. An additional *constrained* fragment of the architecture, in the form of a system of demountable partitions, allows this portion of the house to be subdivided into as many as seven individual spaces, or as little as three spaces by stacking the partitions

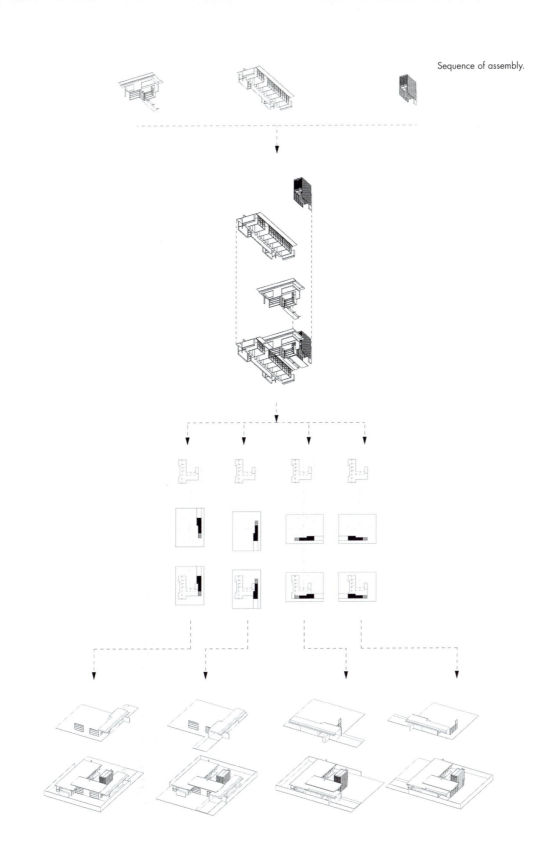

Assembly detail.

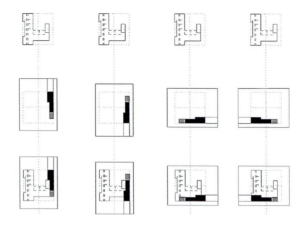

three deep to form thick walls. The 6,100 gallons of rainwater collected by this element are stored in cisterns at the north and south ends. Each cistern holds 920 gallons and is able to sustain ten bamboo plants configured as a "screen" on each end of the site.

The third element contains the main public space of the house and also bears a fixed orientation to the sun. It is configured as a rectangle with the short dimension facing east and west. Two parallel sliding glass walls spaced 8 feet apart form the north-facing wall. These constrained fragments of the building may be configured in various ways to literally project activities normally contained within the house into the outdoors during mild days or mild seasons. As the walls are manipulated into different positions, the two fireplaces within this zone are alternately indoors or out, fireplace or barbecue. The roof of this element collects an average of 3,700 gallons rainwater each year, which can support a 150 square foot plot of grass to the north. The 1,210 gallon cistern becomes a table or bench, 20 feet long, 4 feet wide and 2 feet high.

The fourth element is a service element, containing the garage, kitchen, and utilities. It provides the link to the street and the city infrastructure. Unlike the first three components of the house, which maintain a fixed relationship to the compass, the service element maintains a fixed relationship to the street. Its roof collects an average of 1,840 gallons of rainwater in one year, stored in a 550-gallon cistern which is used to sustain six bamboo plants.

CONFIGURING THE LANDSCAPE(S) OF THE COMPASS HOUSE(S)

These four spatial and programmatic conditions are configured separately as "standard" elements, and then reassembled on the four sites. First, the three elements requiring a fixed relationship to the environment (and the compass) are assembled to form a rough "L" plan open to the northeast. The service element is then positioned on each site, modified as necessary via operations of mirroring and rotation. The resulting assemblies produce four different houses, each providing a particular set of spatial and programmatic opportunities both inside and out. The strategy of separating the compass-attached elements of the house from the city-attached elements illustrates one way in which the conflict between collective and individual needs might be reconciled. The use of standard elements begins to address the economic advantages of repetition, while the variable combination addresses the issue of site-specificity.

INHABITING THE LANDSCAPE(S) OF THE COMPASS HOUSE(S)

The resulting four houses with their sites are seen as distinct landscapes . . . a set of topographic conditions that may be inhabited in a variety of ways. The process of assembly results in a mix of familiar situations as well as programmatically indeterminate or ambiguous situations. It is perhaps in this combination of the familiar and the unfamiliar that a questioning of the means of inhabitation might take place. The overlapping of the collective and the cellular elements provides one such situation within the house(s). The overlap provides an opportunity to adjust the relative quantity of cellular and collective space within the house, while the constrained elements that they contain provide subtle rules through which these adjustments might take place. The constrained fragments (moveable partitions, sliding walls) contained within the collective and cellular elements of the house are individually restricted to relatively few positions or are restricted to simple movements, but their combined use in these overlapping areas produces a complex array of possible spatial and programmatic opportunities. The manipulation of very simple constrained elements might go beyond spatial reconfigurations, provoking programmatic reconfigurations within the dwelling.

Additional ambiguous situations are produced in the exterior spaces surrounding the four houses. The familiar distinction between front yard (public) and back yard (private) is disrupted by the variable relationship of

top: Front elevation of North House.

bottom: Front elevation of South House.

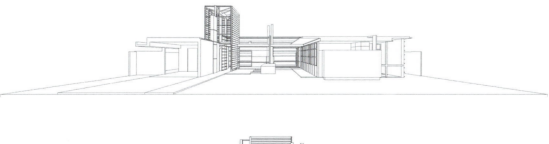

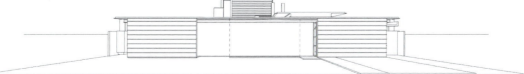

177

top: Front elevation of East House.

middle: Front elevation of West House.

bottom: Interior layout scenario.

the dwelling to the street. In the North House, the open façade of the solitary space as well as the court formed by the wings of the house are open to the street, while the West House presents virtually a blank wall. This variable relationship to the street redefines the public-private status of many of the open spaces surrounding the house, but begins to act on the public-private status of portions of the house as well.

Suburbia as a game of chess, not checkers.

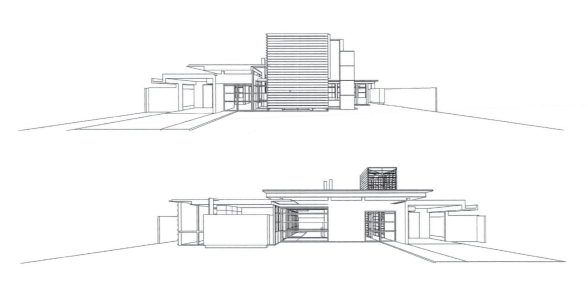

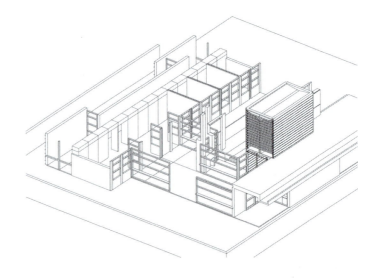

Originally published in the Proceedings of the 84th Annual Meeting of the Association of Collegiate Schools of Architecture, 1996.

SCUPPER HOUSES, OR THE DOGTROT HOUSE AND THE SHOTGUN HOUSE RECONSIDERED

BRIAN D. ANDREWS AND W. JUDE LEBLANC

We believe that the building industry is flawed in its capacity to produce quality environments and that this situation can be improved by a critical response to local geographies. We propose an architecture that resists the various leveling tendencies associated with modern building in favor of an architecture which is sensitive to particular locales. We maintain that architecture should remain a generalist field and we are testing the capacity of a design methodology to synthesize the most disparate information.

SHEDDING WATER: MOVEMENT AND STASIS

The roofs of these two northwest Florida houses are designed with inverted sloping gable roofs. These upside-down gables function as large scuppers. The ceiling shape, a result of the shared contour with the roof configuration, is a primary consideration in developing the internal spaces of the dwellings. The slow downward longitudinal slope of the ceiling is a constant reminder of the full downpours of the Gulf Coast. The faster lateral ceiling slope to the clerestory windows traces site lines to the open view of the sky.

As Alfred Barr observed of painting, that "it admits of movement only metaphorically," so too with architecture. Buildings tend, on the whole, to resist literal movement. But architecture is easily and often framed in terms of ideas related to motion and change, for example change over time regarding use or meaning, flexibility of use, changing constituencies, durability and duration, weathering, etc.

The five-sided silhouette of a triangle atop a square, the child's hieroglyph for a house, is often an expression and a symbol for solidity and stasis. The gable roof however, is also a response to, and an expression of, motion. The gable roof can be considered an uprighted version of the triangular prow of the speed boat. The former, a static, up-pointed wedge, designed to divide falling water, is similar to the latter, a horizontal wedge designed for propulsion, to slice through a liquid medium. In other words, the roof is a vehicle of potential movement and the boat is a vehicle of kinetic motion.

TYPES AND SITE

The roof represents a response to geographic location. An exaggerated roof configuration brings attention to the tropical locale. In addition to moving and shedding water these roofs work to make a dwelling. As dwellings among other dwellings both of these houses were developed in relation to known house types.

179

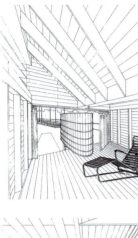

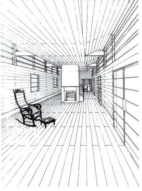

The house at parcel B is patterned after the vernacular "dogtrot" house. The dogtrot type is thought to be historically related to the center hall house. Both of these house types relate to the out-of-doors. The dogtrot structure with an open middle passage is common to hot humid climates. The through space of the center hall house is typically open at both ends connecting the hall with the front and rear yards. Historically, the decoration of such entry halls continued this allusion to the outside through details such as floral wall coverings or faux stone, and hall "trees." Either literally as in the dogtrot, or metaphorically as in the center hall house, an exterior space is positioned at the literal center of the dwelling.

The house at unit #5 is related to the spirit of the "shotgun" house. The interior rooms and areas are spatially and visually related longitudinally. This project varies from the shotgun model in its relation to the exterior. Typically, shotgun houses were placed close together with narrow sideyards. In this house a porch on the first and second floors open all interior space to a more spacious sideyard, reminiscent of the Charleston house type.

CONSTRUCTION, CLADDING AND PROPORTION

The construction and material makeup of both houses are identical: a wood platform frame on concrete piers. The floors, walls, and ceilings are sheathed in wood. The dwellings are covered on the exterior with cypress siding bleached to light silver-gray. The exterior louvers, the columns, and all wood trim are cypress. The interior walls are made of painted pine siding and the floors are natural cypress. The ceilings inside and out are painted pine. The abutting shell driveways are divided by a row of crepe myrtles.

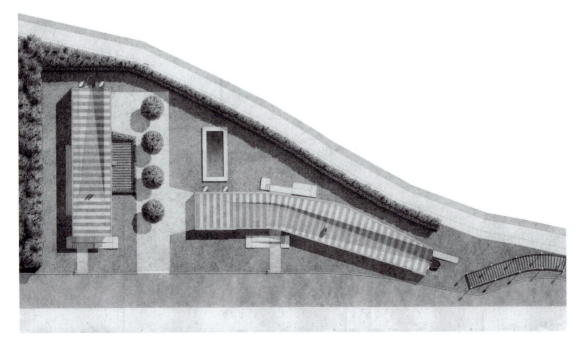

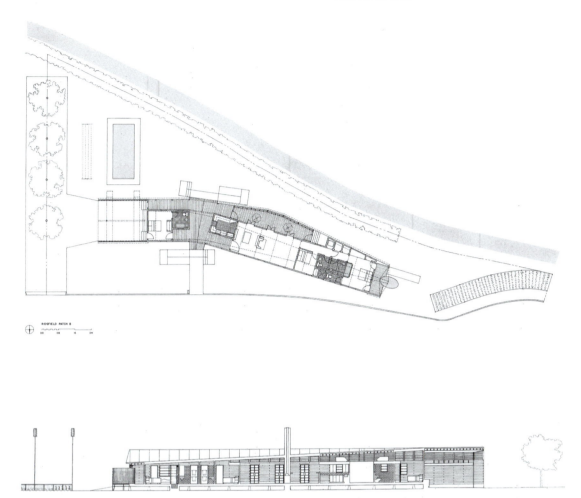

The primary rhythm of both houses in plan and section is an 8 foot bay over a 4 foot module, relating to standard material dimensions.

STORING WATER: USE AND CONSERVATION

Though a house may be a machine for living, it is rarely merely that. A house may literally be a collection of mechanisms, but as today's machines change so rapidly, this fact provides a poor poetic armature for a building meant to endure. In both of these houses the air-conditioner condensers are exposed as a reminder of energy exchange. To the degree to which machines appear in our work they are used as frank presentations not as fetishistic ends in themselves.

Traditional responses to this climate include high ceilings, louvered window openings, and ventilation near the ceiling. The gardens are watered with rainwater collected by the scupper/roof. The site plans show the location

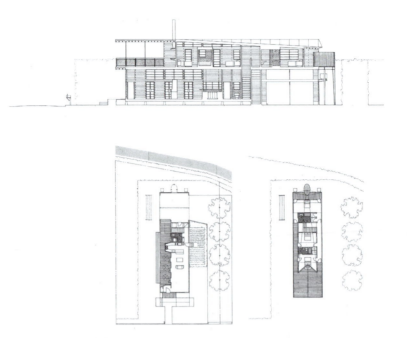

of these gardens which include compost areas. Clothes lines are planned to provide a supplement for electrical dryers. Purple martin birdhouses attract birds which consume vast numbers of mosquitoes, reducing the need for pesticide.

REFERENCES

Jordan, Terry G., *Texas Log Buildings: A Folk Architecture*, Austin, Tex.: University of Texas Press, 1978.

Scofield, Edna "The Evolution and Development of the Tennessee Houses," *Journal of the Tennessee Academy of Science*, 11(1936).

Holl, Steven *Rural and Urban House Types in North America*, New York: Pamphlet Architecture 9, 1982.

Originally published in the Proceedings of the 86th Annual Meeting of the Association of Collegiate Schools of Architecture, 1998.

AN AFFORDABLE, SUSTAINABLE HOUSE
Richmond, Virginia, 1993
WILLIAM SHERMAN

In many rural areas of the South, a type of building has emerged which combines two familiar rural fixtures: the mobile home and the prefabricated metal farm-shed roof (with an echo of a "higher" form of art). The mobile home, whose ancestry has been traced by J. B. Jackson to a number of vernacular American house types, is a model of economical dwelling (in the short term). The added roof modifies the microclimate, providing shade and a covered outdoor space. The design presented here was inspired by this act of ingenuity, combining a long, thin house in the tradition of early, climate-sensitive southern vernacular urban and rural dwellings, with the great sheltering roof to shade the sun, capture the breezes and collect the rain. As is the case in many American cities, the residential streets of this Richmond, Virginia neighborhood run east to west, creating long, narrow north–south lots. This orientation does not support typical strategies for passive solar design. In this climate, where the avoidance of air conditioning would be a major achievement, summer cooling can be accomplished with shelter from the west sun, wind-channeling sideyards, a deep south-facing porch, cross-ventilation and a breeze-catching roof, and (when all else fails) a simple exhaust fan. For heating, the efficiency of a simple hydronic system has been enhanced through proper insulation, judiciously chosen windows and doors with insulating glass, and may be augmented by the addition of roof-mounted solar panels. As a prototypical dwelling for urban infill conditions, this design attempts to balance the need for energy conservation with the best uses of the spaces created by existing patterns of American urbanism.

The philosophy of the materials and construction for this competition entry derives from its sponsorship by Habitat for Humanity, implying volunteer labor, as well as the intentions of sustainable design. It is one which

Trailer with Agricultural Shed, East Texas; Centre Le Corbusier, Zurich.

seeks to minimize construction waste, employ economical (if not always conventional) material assemblies and relatively simple construction techniques. The dimensions of the plan and elevations derive from the use of horizontal, staggered, 4 × 8 foot sheets of plywood for the exterior walls.

above: Model and longitudinal section.

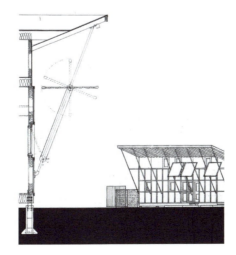

left: West wall section and elevation.

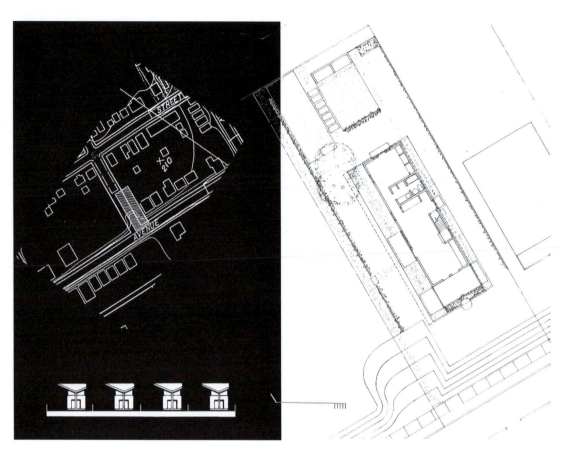

Site plans and repeated elevation diagram.

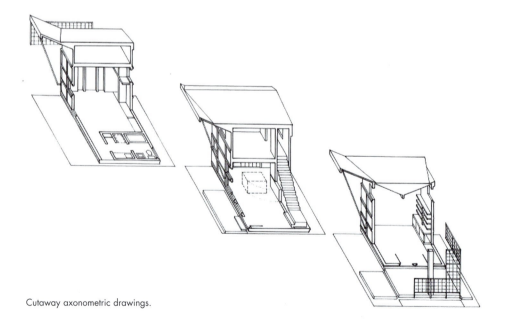

Cutaway axonometric drawings.

Where salvaged, recycled, or locally produced materials can be obtained to reduce costs and save energy, they are encouraged. It is intended that an effort be made during construction to capitalize on any special skills of the individual volunteer laborers.

There are two ways one might view the politics of sustainability: one which envisions the reform of economic behavior to create a new, environmentally responsible society and one which accepts the reality of contemporary culture by seeking to create a more healthy and efficient use of limited resources. In this context of affordable housing, the adoption of the first strategy, while noble in intent, may continue the long history of patronizing attempts to reform the behavior of the poor. The second strategy is closer to the one adopted here; the primary objective is a dignified, environmentally sensitive urban residence which will allow its inhabitants to make their own behavioral choices. The materials are "green," the climate is considered, the construction is simple, but the house is designed for the independent, all-too-human inhabitants of the contemporary city.

Originally published in the Proceedings of the 84th Annual Meeting of the Association of Collegiate Schools of Architecture, 1996.

PHENOMENAL SURFACE
Fog House
LISA IWAMOTO AND CRAIG SCOTT

Two photographs taken several hours apart looking toward the Pacific Ocean with and without fog.

Fog House seeks to engage the complex spatial and temporal dynamics of everyday life through the formal and experiential activation of surface and landscape. The project also attempts to blur the distinctions by which both surface and landscape are often conceived, such as that between surface and solid, landscape and building. Surface appears here as a medium to capture, reveal, and heighten latent, sometimes ephemeral, qualities present at the site.

The house's spatial quality derives from an effort to synthesize the specificity of the context with the particularities of the client's program brief: a private residence and home office for a biofeedback consulting practice. The site is located on the ridge between the Marin Headlands and the San Francisco Bay. It occupies a high point on the ridge from which it has access to 270-degree views. The panorama that wraps the house differs significantly on each side, and the perception and experience of the place changes as one turns and moves. To the east is San Francisco Bay, to the south the Golden Gate Bridge, to the west the Pacific Ocean, and to the north, Mount Tamalpias. While a place can alter dramatically in different seasons, the span of a few hours at this site can effect an incredibly quick and dynamic transformation as fog rolls in from the Pacific Ocean and sweeps up the hillsides. The fog often blankets the surrounding lower landscape, making the site an island in the clouds—a mass through which only the Golden Gate Bridge's towers protrude, until they too are finally engulfed in fog. This fog has a tangible presence, and it is possible to see it moving across objects in the landscape similar to the way clouds appear from an airplane. This movement offers the clearest and most physical manifestation of the site's phenomenal and fluctuating characteristics.

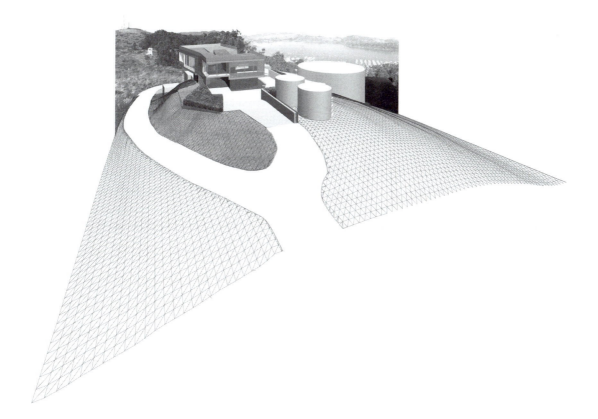

A driving concern for the project became how to directly and spatially engage the dynamic phenomena of view and fog. In response to the client's desire to be living in a "single story of a glass skyscraper," the initial diagram of the house proposed a simple glass volume out of which site-figured voids are carved. Drawing initially from the topography, the ground surface is conceptually and materially stretched through the house to engage near and distant phenomena. The exterior of the initial volume also inflects to respond to the dynamics of the surrounding conditions. It deforms to create particular alignments between internal void spaces and adjacent edges, such as that between the hedge at the eastern property line and the courtyard terrace.

The house is thus organized around two overlapping spatial voids created by an extension of interior and exterior landscape surfaces. One of these voids, emerging from the hillside, funnels and harnesses the fog to spatially interact with the interior. The second, beginning at the ground of the auto court and entry, is formed by a continuous surface that winds through the regular block volume, folding together building and landscape, interior and exterior, and defining internal spatial arrangements. This warped surface links diagonal spaces in the house, making it a viewing mechanism conflating bay and ocean. This surface works upwards to a roof garden, creating an artificial ground plane that recalls the auto court.

Bird's eye of project and site at top of hill.

189

The design is further conceptualized as a hybrid between figured earthwork (reminiscent of the bunker architecture of the Marin Headlands nearby) and hovering glass "skyscraper" box. In engaging the complexity of situation and program, these two paradigms interact to become a transformative whole. The interior formation of the voids is amplified by treating parts of the program as pochéd solids. Given the varying conditions of the view in different directions, the poché rooms are each distinguished by a particular landscape—Mount Talmapias in the master bedroom, the Golden Gate Bridge in the kitchen, for example.

This relationship of landscape to enclosure is, however, intentionally made problematic, even involuted. Solid-to-void relationships inside the house are inverted with the presence of fog. On a clear day, the house acts diagrammatically like an open glass box, pulling distant landscapes deep into the interior as views are extended outward. The living space and family room unite across the terrace in this condition. The two rooms separate in the afternoon, however, when low-visibility fog engulfs and splits the glass box's interior. As the fog makes "rooms," the house transforms into a set of carved and discrete spaces.

Stereolothography and laser-cut models were built to facilitate the study of solid to surface relationships, and to define the geometries of the surface that negotiate the opening for the fog and the sightlines made by the diagonal views. Later laser-cut models suggested a ribbed construction technique for

Plan of main living level.

Main Level
1. Living
2. Consulting
3. Dining
4. Family room / breakfast
5. Kitchen
6. Terrae
7. Entry
8. Master bedroom suite

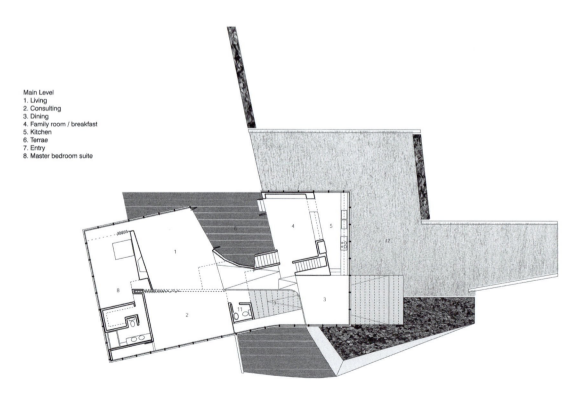

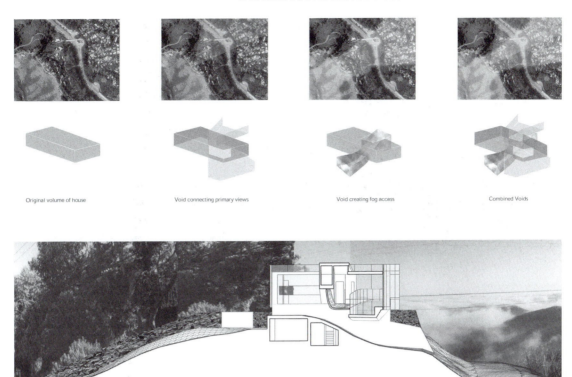

Original volume of house   Void connecting primary views   Void creating fog access   Combined Voids

this surface covered by smooth landscape and building material. While it was our general intention to suppress overtly legible tectonics in favor of seamless surface, we pursued certain distinctions that recall the relationship of earthwork to extracted skyscraper floor: The primary construction for the house is a concrete groundwork on which a steel structure sits. The reading of the box is reinforced by a continuous glass enclosure, but ultimately contested on the interior by the formation of fluctuating space.

top: Conceptual diagrams of view void and fog void.

above: Cross section through fog void.

Originally published in the Proceedings of the 90th Annual Meeting of the Association of collegiate Schools of Architecture, 2002.

View from living looking across
terrace without and with fog.

Project credits:

Designers: Lisa Iwamoto/Craig Scott,
IwamotoScott Architecture

Project team: Uggie Kim, Carl
Lorenz, Danny Sze, Etienne Kuhn

BUILDING PRACTICES

INTRODUCTION
KIM TANZER AND RAFAEL LONGORIA

If you're holding a hammer, everything looks like a nail.

(popular saying)

This section advances the thesis that the creation of a sustainable built environment will require more than strategic material selections and thoughtful building assemblies done by well-educated specifiers in conventional architectural practices. Without minimizing the importance of thoughtful incremental change within the architecture profession, we suggest that architects must fundamentally rethink our skills, specifically the nature of architectural services we provide.

The authors in this section all advocate a form of sustainability that could change the discipline more radically than will necessarily follow from simple adherence to a checklist of best practices.[1] In fact, while such checklists allow us to evaluate the consequences of our decisions and to make responsible buildings, they do not, in and of themselves, promote either excellent design or breakthroughs in sustainable design. The three architects discussed in these essays—Arthur Troutner, Terunobu Fujimori, and the firm KieranTimberlake—strategically concentrate on an element of what we today define as sustainability, without necessarily supporting evenhanded environmental responsiveness. It is their single-minded reinforcement of a specific property of particular material and its related process of assembly that sets their work apart.

Determination and the acceptance of risk might be the primary characteristics shared by all three. Today we might describe them, first and foremost, as entrepreneurs. As they unfold long-term success stories, the essays' authors, Jonathan Reich, Dana Buntrock, and Karl Wallick, are careful to include the travails each architect experienced while searching for new ways to engage the construction industry. A key part of each narrative is the moment at which the architect encountered a setback and the way he or she rebounded. As is the case of invention within all disciplines, such creative resilience is critical. Within the growing field of sustainable building practices, invention may be financially rewarding as well as ethically and aesthetically gratifying, but only for those who take risks.

Substantial creative thinking, beyond visual and spatial talent, is another common thread running through each of these essays. As Reich describes, Arthur Troutner came to view trees as sources of fiber rather than sources of timber. This conceptual shift let him conceive of new ways of accumulating fiber into structural shapes, which he patented and sold through his own company T.J. International. The firm KieranTimberlake is currently working

1 Checklists such as the Leadership in Energy and Environmental Design (L.E.E.D.) requirements are extremely valuable in guiding all architects and designers toward sustainably responsible projects. We argue that, while such checklists are necessary, they are insufficient in creating extraordinary work. Good values and good design are not incompatible, but good values will not alone create good design. As of this writing our discipline is more forgiving of good design that is unsustainable than of sustainable design that is not good.

to reframe the concept of the wall, using technologies such as digital fabrication and mass customization, now possible using simple digital printing techniques. Seeing the opportunity provided by today's thin technologies, they recognized the advantage architects would have if all such elements could embody design thinking. The qualities highlighted here, determination, extraordinary creativity and risk-taking, run through each essay.

"Poetic Engineering and Invention: Arthur Troutner, Architect, and the Development of Engineered Lumber," describes Troutner, a mid-twentieth-century architect from Idaho, as an inventor who directed his talent toward architecture. After learning to innovate on command as a member of the U.S. Army Air Corps during World War II, he returned to Idaho where he recognized the ultimate limits of forest resources. Jonathan Reich describes Troutner's multidimensional career—part product inventor, part manufacturer, part businessman, part architect—as he worked for the pleasure of creating and the reward of minimizing destruction of the forests of the west. Troutner was particularly concerned with reducing forest waste, which led him to invent structural beams composed of small pieces of trees laminated together. Other inventions followed, turning his good intentions into significant wealth.

As Dana Buntrock describes in "Terunobu Fujimori: Working with Japan's Small Production Facilities," Fujimori transformed an academic concern for Japan's small manufacturing facilities into a building method with persuasive aesthetic effect. Realizing that many of the small manufacturing facilities in Japan—makers of everything from windows to tiles to tatami mats—serve an important role in the economic vitality of local communities, Fujimori has sought them out for his own work and has used his academic credentials to publicize their aesthetic and economic value. In the projects described, Fujimori selects hand-split cedar boards for siding on the Jinchokan Shiryokan artifact museum and stone roof shingles to cover a private residence. In both cases and others, he uses traditional, often handmade finishes while standardized components provide the more typical mechanical and structural elements. His work is recognized for steering a precise course between modernism and traditional aesthetics and practices.

The current work of Kieran Timberlake approaches the role of surface from a completely different yet intriguingly sustainable manner, as Karl Wallick explains in "Making SmartWrap: From Parts to Pixels." Utilizing new and emerging technologies, KieranTimberlake has developed a prototypical process wherein the flow of design from architect to fabrication to installation is a seamless digital stream. Arguing that mechanical systems, which the firm characterizes as the building's infrastructure, are now thin enough to be literally printed on a surface, their experiment seeks to formulate a method to redefine the roles of professions and trades. Of particular interest is the one-to-one relationship between photovoltaics, capturing energy, and organic light-emitting diodes (L.E.D.s), casting light, on two sides of the same film.

The SmartWrap surface they've invented is so thin that it cannot fulfill some traditional functions of enclosure. Wallick suggests that they choose to view this as an opportunity, musing "[r]ather than wondering how SmartWrap becomes reoriented to our accustomed notions of enclosure it might be productive to reconsider how enclosure is reoriented to SmartWrap." Whether their proposal offers simply another chapter in the ongoing Semperian discourse regarding the textile wall or a more radical requestioning of the requirements of shelter, SmartWrap establishes a model of full-tilt ingenuity applied to the invention of sustainable technology.

The design projects included in this section also redefine constraints as opportunities. While all three proposals fit within the confines of traditional practice, unlike the career-defining research described above, the architects work to playfully yet responsibly reframe materials, spatial experience, and building processes. A common theme linking all three projects is the idea of recycling, expanded well beyond its typical role.

"Quilting with Glass, Cedar and Fir: A Workshop and Studio in Rossland, BC," by Robert Barnstone, describes a make-do aesthetic applied to the renovation of a wooden post-and-beam truck workshop into an artist's studio. Much attention is focused on the studio's skin, composed of recycled glass, surplus windows, and cedar lattice. Underlying the surface's jazzy, Mondrian-like articulation is a solid solar strategy, allowing solar gain from the primary southwest orientation and trapping it in a cleverly designed airspace. The studio's interior maximizes programmatic space within a minimal footprint. A sliding wall allows the artist to vary spatial possibilities without overbuilding. A second project, the Navy Demonstration Project, explores the metaphor of quilting and the process of recycling more thoroughly. Funded as a demonstration building for the U.S. Navy, Barnstone worked with a multidisciplinary team at the Wood Materials Engineering Laboratory to construct a building that tests various properties of engineered wood plastic composites. Both the design process and the resulting structure manifest quilted logic and offer rich possibilities to reuse wood and plastic.

Urban recycling is a key aspect of "Modernism Redux: A Study in Light, Surface, and Volume," by La Dallman Architects. This project is an example of an emerging phenomenon, the revitalization of 1960s high-rise residential buildings. In reaction to burgeoning urban sprawl, more city residents are choosing to remain or return to downtown living in formerly abandoned inner cities. This renovation, in addition to reducing demolition landfill and adding to the otherwise inevitable consumption of greenfields, literally reframes the interior shortcomings of an aging apartment. The architects describe editing walls to create an open plan, a response consistent with the exterior's horizontal ribbon windows. This, plus the use of bamboo flooring with a high degree of reflectivity, allows them to coax daylight deeper into the apartment.

"Solar Sails" by Mahesh Senagala offers a recycling strategy that works on several levels. Working from a competition brief provided by the Department of Energy (D.O.E.), Senagala proposes an addition of arrays of photovoltaic panels to the south wall of the Forrestal Building, which houses the D.O.E. in Washington, D.C. By placing four multistory "sails", dedicated to the four seasons, away from the building's face, he simultaneously creates a habitable interstitial space containing a grand staircase and an edge to a newly proposed pedestrian plaza. Like Palladio's renovation of Vicenza's Basilica, this strategy updates a major institutional building symbolically and functionally without recourse to demolition. It allows Senagala to correct flaws of the environmental strategy in a symbolically important existing building. His proposal also calls attention to the concept of solar recycling. Each of the sails is keyed to, and activated by, a season, marked as we complete our annual planetary cycle around the sun.

Each designer, by seizing on a challenge to traditional building practices—the use of recycled materials, a recycled building with continuous windows, or the retrofitting of an existing building with new technology—has made it spatially thematic and therefore persuasive. All give evidence of the importance of creative thinking in the design process and of the importance of conscious inflection toward a carefully selected sustainable strategy in creating excellent design work. In each case, such a strategy provides the key to refiguring a difficult project into a strong design.

POETIC ENGINEERING AND INVENTION
Arthur Troutner, architect, and the development of engineered lumber
JONATHAN REICH

THE FUTURE OF WOOD

An article in a recent mainstream architectural journal addressed recent debates about the use of wood in architecture. The debate goes something like this: First, nervousness is expressed about the use of wood and the depletion of the resource of older trees which are large enough to saw into boards and beams. A grim statistic is given that suggests that even if the remaining "old growth" were available to be logged, the supply would only see us through a few more years. The idea of forest management for sustainability is discussed in relation primarily to continuing (surprisingly) the supply of sawn lumber. Steel is considered and the debate continues over which is "greener," wood or steel. "Engineered" wood is suggested as an important alternative and some of the technical issues about it are discussed. The magazine reminds us that it first reported on the declining quality of available wood in December of 1990.[1]

In 1955 one person was already thinking about how wood could be combined with other materials to improve its strength and stretch its supply. He began a series of inventions that led to the development of engineered lumber. This person happened to be an architect, and his historic work places him squarely in the tradition of innovative development of building materials.

His name was Arthur Troutner and he was an architect, an inventor, and the co-founder of Trus Joist Corporation. He was arguably the most important single figure in the history of the development of wood technology for architecture because his work forever changed the way wood is thought of as a structural building material and the way the forest is thought of as a resource. He was also the architect of numerous buildings in the West. He built public buildings such as the Boise Little Theater, he designed the roof structure for the Kibbie Dome (the record roofspan in wood at the time), and he designed and built numerous innovative experimental houses to demonstrate the use of the wood technologies he invented. He held over fifty patents for his numerous composite wood products, their fabrication machines, a solar mirror boiler, a wind generator, wood transmission towers, and much more. Troutner's inventive work resulted from a combination of influences. Growing up in a remote place with scarce resources, experience in the innovative wartime aircraft industry, education in engineering and especially architecture, and a deep appreciation for nature and the landscape of the American West all played a role in the development of his thinking.

1 Holbrook, "Framing Techniques."

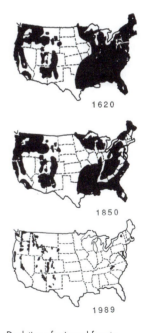

Depletion of primeval forests.

2. Primeval forests: 1620, 1850, 1989. Source: University of Oregon Survival Center (Eugene, Oreg.: 1990).

Construction of the Troutner House, Boise, Idaho 1955. Photo: Art Troutner. Used with permission.

"OUT WEST"

High in the mountains that rise abruptly out of the town of Boise, on a bitterly cold early March day in 1955, two men struggled to attach triangular brackets made of angle iron to a 2-foot diameter section of steel pipe that rose three and a half stories out of an exposed spine of rocks on a steep ridge. The vertical pipe was to be the central column of a sixteen-sided house that would be half embedded and half projecting from the promontory point of the ridge. When assembled, the sixteen angle iron brackets radiating out from the central column resembled a flat-topped dish that would form the bottom floor and support the house. The pipe rose out of the center of the construction ready to receive the second floor and then the roof. However there was some question as to whether there would be funds sufficient to get to the roof. The two worked with little discussion. They were brothers and attended the task with a quiet intense cooperation developed from years of needing to do difficult physical work in adverse conditions. One was a thirty-four-year-old architect named Art Troutner, the other was his brother Paul who was a stonemason.

Troutner had bought the land from a Basque sheepherder. The site looked into an empty draw that drained the slopes around a prominent feature of the Boise Front called "Table Rock," and then angled down to the south where it dropped away suddenly, revealing the green carpet of the town along the river below. Beyond the town, the desert stretched out 50 miles to the Owyhee Mountains. He liked the site because it was above and removed from town and all its confusion, and yet the town was visible as were the distant mountains he had worked in before the war. Though just 3 miles from town, the foothills right around his house were abundant with wildlife. There were deer, elk, bear, eagles, hawks, ground squirrels, rabbits, mice, and snakes. A family of red foxes lived in a den in the rocks under the house. The wildlife was familiar to him from years of hunting and fishing and traveling the territory. This is how it was in the West. He felt very comfortable there. It was a good place to make his home.

Thanks to the Boise River, the town is an oasis of green in the dry country of southwestern Idaho. Boise was named for its trees (boisé, wooded) by French fur trappers who removed most of the beavers from the rivers and streams in the region between 1808 and 1840. The beavers were made into fashionable hats in demand by well-to-do people "back east" and in Europe. This was the first example of "natural resource extraction" in the mountain west. In 1955 Boise was still a very remote place. There was no freeway. The good roads were two lanes that wound through the steep mountain ravines and stretched straight for miles across vast expanses of the high, dry, sagebrush covered Snake River plain. The nearest other city, Salt Lake City, over 350 miles away, took more than a day to get to by car, weather permitting. The small airport had limited service. There was little television. There was one high school, a small junior college, many churches, many bars, and a state prison.

Most people were employed in agriculture, construction, or in resource-extraction industries (mining and forestry), and were concerned primarily with providing themselves with the basic necessities of life. In remote places, where life can be harsh, it is unexpected to find someone devoted to experimental architecture at great personal cost. Troutner was not a rich man, and so his relatively isolated effort to practice architecture in an innovative way took some courage. From his brother Paul's point of view it was not at all unusual. The two of them were used to working outdoors and enjoyed making things. The relatively strange house they were building was just another in a long series of unusual projects his college-educated brother had got into.

Troutner was born in Pingree, in southeastern Idaho in 1921. Pingree is just across the Snake River from the Fort Hall Indian Reservation, home to the Shoshone-Bannock tribes. He was one of five children of a subsistence-level farming family that grew sugar beets and potatoes. He spent a lot of time hoeing weeds. Hunting game was another source of food, and this activity often took him into the back country for extended periods. Learning to live in the wilderness can develop in a thoughtful person a love for the land, an appreciation for the efficiency of nature, and a disdain for the messy waste that so often results from human settlement.

Construction of the Troutner House, Boise, Idaho 1955 Photo: Art Troutner. Used with permission.

CREATIVITY AND THE NECESSITY OF INVENTION

Living on a remote farm in Pingree, where scarcity was the norm, required a certain amount of invention everyday just to keep things running. By all accounts Troutner always had an especially inventive mind, but this impulse in him seems to spring from something besides necessity; perhaps from a different definition of need. When he was nine years old, he fashioned a miniature threshing machine out of junk he found around the farm. The toy actually worked. His mother recognized his mechanical intelligence and sent him to live in Boise where he could attend a good high school. To get around Boise he made a motor scooter out of an old Maytag engine. Troutner used to describe how there were certain times of day when his thinking seemed so clear that he could literally "see" an idea that eventually would become an invention. He would then become obsessed with developing it to the exclusion of day-to-day concerns. Often his inventive projects led to nothing. Maslow's hierarchy of needs would have us believe that people will take care of their basic needs before concerning themselves with tangential inventiveness. Troutner held more than fifty patents for things such as composite wood products and the machinery for making them, all of which made him and his company very wealthy. But he also held patents for such things as a toy rubberband gun, a hydro-planing sailboat, a vertical axle wind-powered generator, and a solar mirror furnace, and much more. He spent a great deal of time and money developing things that went nowhere, gaining him nothing but a healthy attitude about risk and failure. In his case, *play* was equal to necessity as a mother of invention. He found simple joy in devising creative solutions to problems of great complexity and approached them fearlessly. Some of these attitudes were innate in him and some were developed.

WARTIME INNOVATION

In 1942, the twenty-one-year-old Troutner enlisted and found his calling in the Army Air Corps. Because he had not gone to college, the option of being a pilot was not readily available. He was trained as a flight mechanic and soon made a mechanic crew chief and flight engineer. He worked on B-17 and B-29 bombers and P-51 mustang fighters. He sometimes had the job of modifying planes that were rolling off assembly lines at record rates. The assembly lines could not be retooled fast enough for changing developments in warplane design. To keep up with the demand for fighters and bombers, the same basic chassis would be adjusted and adapted with the addition of the latest equipment. Sometimes this customizing took place right on the assembly-room floor. Troutner's mechanical aptitude, inventiveness and can-do attitude fit right into this situation and he was encouraged. Solutions had to be quick and had to work. There was little time for exhaustive research and testing. Because the work involved aircraft, efficient strength to weight ratios were always required. Because so much talent and money were employed in the war effort, the latest in materials were made available. Troutner was introduced to many of these new materials and thrived in this setting.

Many of the new materials were developed to make up for shortages of standard materials. One principal method of development was to look for new ways various materials could be combined and processed. The water resistance and durability of softwood plywood, which had been invented around the turn of the century, was improved in 1933 by the addition of new synthetic urea-formaldehyde resin glues.[2] The vacuum form molding process was developed at this time, enabling veneer plywood to be formed into complex curves. Aircraft wings, fuselages, nose cones, turrets, and boat hulls, which might have otherwise been made of scarce metals, were made of this new "plastic" plywood.[3]

Larger than usual structures with very long spans were built of wood to conserve precious structural steel. Glue laminated timbers were employed to build the immense Hughes aircraft plant in Culver City, California. Giant hangers for the navy's fleet of dirigibles were built on the Oregon coast, using glue laminated arches that spanned an incredible 246 feet, 50 feet more than the previous record span with wood. A large navy yard machine shop was constructed to be three very tall stories (125 feet high) with columns made of laminated timbers and floors made of wood trusses. The entire structure was built using wood members no larger than 4 by 16 inches or longer than 24 feet. It was designed around prefabricated units to enable rapid on-site assembly.[4]

2 *Elliot*, Technics and Architecture.

3 *Friedel, "Scarcity and Promise."*

4 *Ibid.*

The United States has always viewed itself as a nation with a limitless supply of timber-producing forests. But in 1942, the enormous increase in demand for wood caused by the war outstripped the production capacity of the timber industry. There was a sudden timber shortage that caused a great deal of alarm. The war industry responded quickly with the development of ways to stretch the available supply of wood. The Homasote Company of Trenton, New Jersey came up with a panel material that was made of wood pulp and ground newspaper bound with resin, to be used in place of siding and sheathing for buildings.[5]

5 Ibid.

THE ARCHITECT IN THE MOUNTAIN WEST

Troutner had been shipped around the country in his capacity as a hotshot mechanic crew chief and flight engineer. He saw much of the material innovation that was being done and this experience had a significant influence on his thinking. He was impressed with the expertise of the formally trained engineers who were devising the solutions. So when he was discharged in 1945, he returned home to Idaho and entered the engineering program at the University of Idaho in Moscow, making use of the G.I. Bill. However, he soon switched to the study of architecture. He was motivated to switch because he found that engineering was too cautious and rule-bound once the urgencies and necessities of the war effort were removed. Architecture seemed to offer more opportunity for an open-ended and creative approach to problem-solving. He was neither very interested in the comfort of conformance with strict rules nor very good at strict procedure. He was exposed to ideas about interpretation and representation of place and culture in school, and he studied history of art, painting, and drawing. He was introduced to the work of Frank Lloyd Wright, whose work became a major influence on his ideas about architectural form.

Troutner graduated in 1949 and moved back to Boise. Almost immediately he began to design and build houses and small commercial buildings. His architecture developed along three major themes. The first theme was related to his understanding of nature and his love of the landscape of the American West. The sensibility of Wright's ideas about "organic architecture" that seemed to be anti-urban, individualistic, and an inventively sculptural integration of buildings in the landscape resonated with Troutner. The second theme related to Troutner's conviction that architecture is based on structure, and that structural form should be creatively manipulated in architecture to produce what he called "poetic engineering." He was fascinated with finding solutions to structural problems. The third theme related to his experience growing up in a family of subsistence farmers and in the military. He liked to refer to how the Native Americans of the great plains wasted very little of the bison they killed, thereby sustaining the herds while the white men's habits of killing in numbers far beyond need and taking only part of the animal contributed to its near extinction. His work tended to be both experimental

Troutner house in Gooding, Idaho, 1952.

203

and materially resourceful. He liked to use a combination of local natural materials and also new materials. A house he designed and built in Gooding Idaho in 1952 was curved in plan to provide maximum solar exposure through large south-facing windows. It was reviewed in the local newspaper, which referred to Troutner's use of stone from the local Oakley quarry "flint hard, the quartzite and mica revealed by expert cutting" and that the "unusual" home was "based on the concept of design that it is necessary to utilize fully the convenience and functions of modern mechanical gadgets and the new materials available." He continued to develop his ideas about architecture through a series of houses built for various clients as well as for himself, such as the sixteen-sided house near Table Rock in 1955, and he used several of the houses to showcase his invented products.

THE INVENTOR ARCHITECT

From early on, Troutner was being asked for designs that included longer and longer roof spans beyond the limit possible with sawn lumber joists. Large glu-lam beams seemed to him to be a waste of wood, and deep trusses seemed to waste space. He decided to try and invent a new structural system to suit the forms of the houses he was designing and building. He worked out a new kind of lightweight engineered open web system of connected trusses in the form of decking. He modified war-surplus aircraft parts to make the machinery necessary to fabricate the system and began producing the system himself. He called his invention "trus dek." The top and bottom chords of "trus dek" consisted of four 1 × 6 tongue-and-groove boards connected together with steel rods. The rods also served as the pin connections of four webs made of thin wall steel tubing in a Warren truss configuration. He produced the trus dek in sections that were generally 2 foot wide, 32 foot long, and 9 inches deep. He used the new system in several houses and charged a dollar per square foot for it to be installed. The most notable use of trus dek is in the Phillips House completed in 1958. The house was constructed as three folded plate triangles made of trus dek tilted up in a three-gabled A-frame configuration. There was little interest in the invention, despite Troutner's efforts to show it to people. Then one of the people to whom he showed it tried to steal the trus dek idea by attempting to file a patent on it. Troutner was able to save his invention, and he knew he was on to something. Unfortunately, there was nothing in the building industry quite like it, and thus it was viewed with some suspicion.[6]

In 1956, Troutner met Harold Thomas, who was a commission sales representative for several wholesale lumber companies. Thomas understood immediately that Troutner had a potentially very valuable invention on his hands. Thomas had a keen understanding of the market, and he convinced Troutner that what was needed was a long span joist instead of the trus dek. Troutner moved his operation into an old parachute and bombsite testing hanger at Gowen airfield near Boise. There he proceeded to develop a

6 *Bunderson*, Idaho Entrepreneurs.

Construction of the Phillips house using Trus Dek, Boise, Idaho, 1958. Photos: Art Troutner. Used with permission.

freestanding truss that utilized stress-rated single 2 × 4s as top and bottom chords and the same thin wall steel tubing as web chords in a Warren truss configuration. The first model was 20 inches deep, weighed 3 pounds per lineal foot, and was produced in lengths up to 50 feet. Troutner also designed the machinery for making this new invention, which he called the "trus joist".[7] His efforts left him broke. He had spent all of his money developing his inventions and building his own and other experimental houses. By 1959 Harold Thomas convinced Troutner to make him the exclusive marketing agent for the trus joist, and in 1960, with scant financial backing, they incorporated Troutner's trus dek and trus joist products into a company they called Trus Dek Corp. Troutner had the responsibility of manufacturing the product and Thomas marketed it. Sometimes Thomas would return from sales calls and help with the production.[8]

Even good ideas can take time to catch on, and acceptance of trus joists remained a problem. The idea that a lightweight, wood and steel truss joist could be mass-produced to be both a standard off-the-shelf item and also a custom-designed relatively high-tech structural element was revolutionary. The market for trus joists was in small-scale commercial and custom residential buildings. This market was not necessarily ready for sophisticated structural concepts, and contractors were reluctant to try anything new. There was a popular mindset that structures had to be heavy and massive to be strong. Troutner and Thomas had an independent lab run load tests. They took the risk of inviting the local building officials to the tests. Fortunately, the tests confirmed their calculations, which led to eventual code acceptance.[9]

Architects were easier to convince. Thomas would call on architects,

and when invited to state his business he would lay a small gold fringed red tablecloth on the architect's desk. Then he would produce a short section of the trus joist, set it on the tablecloth and stand back with his arms folded, not saying a word. Most architects would look at the product and study it with amazement. This sales approach proved to be innovative and effective.[10]

Joseph La Marche was a young architect working in Boise at the time. He was impressed with the trus joist and went to visit the shop at Gowen Airfield. He recalled the stamping and rattling noises of Troutner's Rube Goldberg-like production machinery. La Marche was the first to use the product in a commercial building. To assist architects in designing with the product, Troutner had typical construction details drawn up for architects to use, which when combined with load/span tables, made for a complete pre-engineered proprietary system. Trus joist was selling their expertise along with their innovative technology. The company broke even with $49,000 in sales its first year and was profitable thereafter. In 1964, its fourth year of business, the company sold over $1 million worth of product.[11]

Thomas' Trus Joist Sales Presentation. Photo: Courtesy of Trus Joist MacMillan.

OPEN-WEB TRUSS PROFILES

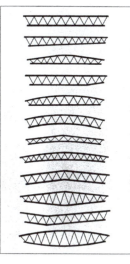

Trus Joist profiles. Courtesy of Arthur Troutner.

7 *Ibid.*

8 *Ibid.*

9 *Ibid.*

10 *Ibid.*

11 *Ibid.*

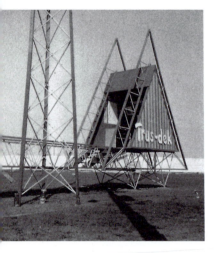

Trus Dek Corporation's pavilion made of truss joists for the 1962 Idaho State Fair. Photo: Nels Reese. Used with permission.

Meanwhile, in 1962–3, Troutner and his design team developed a series of kit cabin designs able to be prefabricated out of trus joists and delivered as an affordable package that could be erected quickly. This experience interested him in the mobile home industry. Mobile homes have always been a source of quick, inexpensive affordable housing in the West. One requirement of mobile homes is that they be lightweight. In 1968, Troutner invented a lightweight wood "I" joist, originally in a bowed profile for mobile-home roofs. The curved version proved too costly to produce, but the straight version was relatively inexpensive. The wood "I" joist was another breakthrough. With it, the company had a product that could fill a market that trus joists were too expensive for. Built in the shape of an I-beam, it consisted of 2 × 3 or 2 × 4 flanges with a plywood web dadoed into them and glued. It was less expensive than the trus joist and used less wood than sawn lumber. Introduced in 1970, it was an immediate success, used widely in multistory wood construction.

Nineteen-seventy was also the year Denis Hayes organized the first "Earth Day," signaling the beginning of the mainstream environmental movement. But even before the I-joist was introduced, Troutner had become very concerned with the waste of wood resulting from trus joist production. Though the trus joist and "I" joist used less wood to begin with, there was still significant waste resulting from their production because so much wood had to culled to get long enough pieces of stress-rated 2 × 4 for top and bottom cords. The supply of quality wood was quickly becoming less reliable. The lengths of trus joists one could buy at this time were limited more by

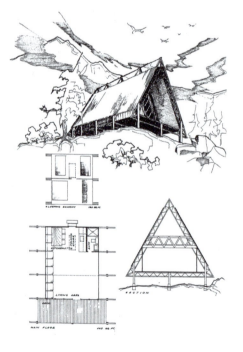

One of the Troutner designs for a kit cabin, 1962. Drawing: Nels Reese. Used with permission.

206

material availability than by strength. The company found itself with a growing inventory of odd length pieces. Troutner and Thomas realized that the supply of trees would not last forever and also that the waste was costly. They wanted to find a way to use all of the wood, to not have to throw any of it away. First they tried finger-joining the ends of random length pieces to create longer pieces. But they were still subject to the differences in grain and strength between various pieces of wood. Troutner wanted to find a way to make the wood more uniformly reliable.

He revisited the concept of reconstituting wood through glue lamination of thin veneers. Plywood was the best-known modern example of this; and the concept had been around for over a century. Furniture makers had long used glue laminated wood veneers. Steinway & Sons had used them for the curved sides of pianos since the middle of the nineteenth century.[12] The problem, however, was scale. No one had been able to devise a manufacturing process of glue-laminating veneers in a way that could make pieces large enough for structural uses. The big forest-products companies such as Weyerhauser had tried and given up, saying it was too costly. Troutner visited Weyerhauser's operation and is said to have commented that "expensive research leads to expensive results." He went to work with a small team to try and solve this manufacturing problem. They invented machinery that continuously glued and hotpressed veneers together, producing laminated veneer lumber billets 4 feet wide, 3½ inches thick, and 80(!) feet long. The product was introduced in 1971 and was called "Micro=Lam L.V.L." L.V.L. stands for the generic term "laminated veneer lumber." Its characteristics are impressive. The process diminishes the importance of the natural defects found in wood by randomizing them throughout the product. The glues are

12 *Elliot*, Technics and Architecture.

Troutner House, Hagerman, Idaho, 1985. Photo: Art Troutner. Used with permission.

up to 2.5 times stronger than lignin (wood's natural binder) so the resulting engineered wood can be 2.5 times stronger than sawn lumber. "Micro=Lam" is also uniformly predictable in its structural performance and more dimensionally stable because the moisture content is controlled throughout production. (Wheelwright) Micro=Lam allowed trus joists and I-joists to be more reliable and able to be produced in longer lengths. The product also found a market for use as headers and beams. Troutner demonstrated the structural capability of the material by designing and building a house in Hagerman, Idaho. The house features enormous cantilevers which might normally be expected to be built in steel, but Troutner designed them using box beams made of Micro=Lam. Troutner also designed and demonstrated high voltage electrical utility poles built out of the same Micro=Lam box beams in an effort to show how this kind of utilitarian item could be produced using fewer trees.

The big forest-products corporations considered Micro=Lam to be a niche product and continued to focus on providing conventionally sawn lumber. Few realized what Troutner knew in 1969; that the paradigm for building with wood had changed. No longer should trees be considered as sources of only sawn lumber. Instead, trees and also other plants needed to be considered as sources of fiber which could be engineered into lumber. It wasn't until the 1980s that restrictions imposed on logging because of environmental concerns convinced the big forest-products companies to move into engineered lumber in a major way. Oriented strand board (O.S.B.) using flakes instead of veneers to form large thin structural panels, and parallel strand lumber (P.S.L.) using long strands of fiber bundled to form planks and beams were developed by other forest-products companies, but not until the mid-1980s. Parallel strand lumber was developed by MacMillan Bloedel Corp. of Canada, however the product was not profitable until after MacMillan Bloedel formed a partnership with Trus Joist, and Troutner and his research and development staff were brought in to redesign the production processes.

Troutner Inventions, Trus Joist products.

Form-I
Industrial Products

MICRO=LAM
Laminated Veneer Lumber

Open Web Truss
Commercial Applications

Parallam
Parallel Strand Lumber

CONCLUSIONS

Arthur Troutner, an architect, pioneered the invention of technologies that revolutionized the use of wood as a composite structural building material. These inventions (trus dek, the trus joist, the wooden I-joist, and L.V.L.) are now valued by architects for several reasons: Their structural capability makes possible a variety of building forms; they can contribute to elegantly simple aesthetic design as structural pieces; and they are more efficient in the use of the resource of wood. Not only did Troutner conceive of the products, but in each case he also invented, or led the team that invented, the crucial technologies and machinery that made industrial production of these products possible. T.J. International Corporation, now a Fortune 500 company and the leader in this field, is the result of his work.

These developments in wood construction are as important as the addition of steel reinforcing was to concrete construction. In both examples, materials are combined to greatly extend their design capability. But Troutner's work led to fundamental changes in understanding as well.

Before Troutner's inventions, trees were always seen as sources of logs to be sawn into lumber. After Troutner's inventions, the understanding of wood as a resource changed. It is now understood that trees and other plants are sources of *fiber* which can be combined with a variety of materials to produce structural elements of great strength and efficiency.

Therefore, Troutner's work has not been merely innovative, though it would certainly be enough if that were all that it was. The implications of the work Troutner began in 1954 are of extraordinary importance now because the supply of large trees traditionally used for sawn lumber has diminished to the point where it is clear that their future and *the future of the use of wood for buildings will actually depend on the concepts he pioneered*. For this reason, he can be counted among the visionaries of our time because he understood that the future demand for wood as a natural resource would require new technologies. Troutner's work led to the lumber industry beginning to look less to federally owned forests and look more to the potential of tree farms for supply of raw material. His work greatly enhances the potential for wood to become a truly renewable and sustainable resource for building.

Many people who become wealthy do so out of a drive to succeed in achieving wealth. Although Troutner welcomed the financial rewards of his work, he seemed to have been motivated more by a love for invention and making things. The wealth that came his way was a byproduct of that. In this way he was more like a "successful" artist whose creative work continues long after his success. He continued working on ideas for the development of composite wood structural materials almost up until his death in 2001. His relationship to the corporate culture resulting from his company's success was seldom comfortable. His methods of working and his results were not always predictable. But Troutner's history with Harold Thomas and the company they founded illustrates the symbiotic interdependence between

Relative waste of wood.

A modified version of Trus Dek using Micro=Lam as top and bottom chords was used for the 400-foot roof span of the Kibbie Dome at the University of Idaho in Moscow. It was the longest wood roof span in the world when it was built in 1975 and the American Society of Civil Engineers recognized this project as its "outstanding civil engineering project of the year." Photo: Courtesy of Trus Joist MacMillan.

creative inventors and skilled businesspeople necessary for the success of innovation.

Troutner the architect/inventor is of historical importance as another key figure who exemplifies the relationship between technical evolution and design culture. His story also illustrates key ideas about the complicated relationship between Westerners' love of nature and the land, and their use of its natural resources. But over and above all else is the story of Troutner's fearlessly inventive creativity pursuing his idea of "poetic engineering," and this makes his story universally important.

The house that Art Troutner built on the hill next to Table Rock is now surrounded by a sprawl of mostly very large conventionally built suburban style homes. It seems sometimes that excessive consumption and overpopulation may ultimately outstrip any possible technical fix for resource scarcity.

REFERENCES

Bunderson, Harold *Idaho Entrepreneurs*, Boise, Idaho: Boise State University, 1992.

Davidson, Joel "Building for World War II: The Aerospace Industry," *Blueprints: The Journal of the National Building Museum* 11, 4 (fall 1993).

Elliott, Cecil D. *Technics and Architecture: The Development of Materials and Systems for Buildings*, Cambridge, Mass.: M.I.T. Press, 1992.

Fisette, Paul, "The Evolution of Engineered Wood I-Joists: Building Materials and Wood Technology," University of Massachusetts, Amherst, Department of Natural Resources Conservation (2000). Available <http://www.umass.edu/bmatwt/publications/articles/i_joist.html>.

Friedel, Robert "Scarcity and Promise: Materials and American Domestic Culture during World War II." *Blueprints: The Journal of the National Building Museum* 12, 4 (fall 1994).

Galluccio, Nick "Just a different glue . . ." *Forbes Magazine*, November 24, 1980.

Haskelite Manufacturing Corporation "Plymold advertisement," *Fortune Magazine*, September 1943.

Holbrook, Dana "Framing Techniques Change to Match Resource Quality," *Architectural Record* (September 1995).

Johnson, Peter *Raising the Roof: Creating the Kibbie Dome at the University of Idaho*, Moscow, Idaho: University of Idaho Press, 1998.

Kouwenhoven, John A. *Made in America: The Arts in Modern Civilization*, New York: Doubleday, 1948.

Maslow, A. H. *Motivation and Personality*. New York: Harper & Bros., 1954.

Reese, D. Nels "The Architecture of Arthur Troutner: Idaho Genius." Unpublished paper.

Sturges, William Gould "An Exploration of the Relationship Between Houses and Forests in American History," *Journal of Architectural Education* 46, 2 (November 1992).

Stegner, Wallace *The Sound of Mountain Water*, New York: Penguin, 1997.

Unknown author "Modern Home Built for Richard N. White Family Designed in Best Contemporary Trend." *Gooding Leader*, December 25, 1952.

Whiting, Henry *Teater's Knoll; Frank Lloyd Wright's Idaho Legacy*. Midland, Mich.: Northwood Institute Press, 1987.

Wheelwright, Steven "Trus Joist Corporation," Harvard Business School Case Study #9-675-207 Harvard College, Cambridge, Mass., 1975.

ACKNOWLEDGEMENTS

My research methodology for this work has consisted of interviews with the participants, review of historical documents, and study of other research and publications. My work has been supported by the Graham Foundation for Advanced Study in the Fine Arts, the University of Idaho Research Council, the Idaho Humanities Council, and the Idaho Heritage Trust. Thanks to the Association of Collegiate Schools of Architecture, the Architectural Research Centers Consortium, and the American Institute of Architects, I have had the opportunity to present my research at various academic conferences and meetings. I have also benefited greatly from the comments of those who have reviewed this work. They have included the notable scholars Edward Allen, Edward Ford, Max Underwood, Julia Robinson, Jeffrey Cook, Sandra Stannard, and others. I am very grateful for their advice and encouragement.

Originally published in the Proceedings of the 84th Annual Meeting of the Association of Collegiate Schools of Architecture, 1996.

TERUNOBU FUJIMORI
Working with Japan's small production facilities
DANA BUNTROCK

INTRODUCTION

Japanese manufacturing occurs in a dual economy. Much of what has been written focuses on the large scale; in this article I will illustrate the opportunities for the architect which result from working with small manufacturers and producers. In her book *The Technological Transformation of Japan: From the Seventeenth to the Twenty-first Century*, Tessa Morris-Suzuki demonstrates how two levels of production systems in Japan work in tandem and supply different segments of the market. These are defined as the "center" (large-scale sophisticated production supported by governmental activities and major corporations) and the "periphery" (small, localized production).[1] But these terms, while useful to someone who knows Japan, are also misleading: the area she refers to as the periphery actually accounts for a sizable segment of production; about 53.8 percent of Japan's factory workers are employed in firms of fewer than 100 workers.[2] Similar duality is found in the construction industry: Japan is represented by five of the world's largest construction companies, but 52 percent of licensed contractors are one- or two-person operations. In architecture, 35 percent of all designers are found in independent studios.[3]

Morris-Suzuki argues that Japan's flexible production processes date back to the development of industrialization in the early seventeenth century—

1 Tessa Morris-Suzuki, The Technological Transformation of Japan: From the Seventeenth to the Twenty-First Century *(Cambridge: Cambridge University Press, 1994).*

2 *Ministry of Finance,* Chuushou Kigyou Hakusho, 1995 *(Tokyo: Ministry of Finance Printing Office, 1995). Table 7 of the appendix.*

3 *Fumio Matsushita,* Design and Construction Practice in Japan: A Practical Guide *(Tokyo: Kaibunsha Ltd., 1994), 175.*

212

that is, roughly concurrent with industrial development in the West. However, as Japan had closed itself off politically and economically from the rest of the world, it thus developed a different approach to the role and significance of industrial production. There was less concern for labor-saving; governmental edicts of the time established a variety of programs which were explicitly intended to promote labor-intensive activities. Rather, there was an emphasis on value-added production; policies promoted the creation of small manufacturers which engaged in product differentiation.

The *tatami* mat, a symbol of many of the architectural differences between Japan and the West, is a useful illustration of this system: the actual producer of *tatami*, even today, will have a neighborhood workshop where he responds to customer orders by assembling a set of components made by other workshops, often those in other parts of the country.[4] These components include: the inner core of the mat, made of layers of straw and varying in size depending on the district in which it is produced; the outer covering, which may be selected for its strength in being rolled around an edge, for a tight weave, or for consistency of color in drying; and the ribbon used to finish the edges of most mats.[5]

The studio where the *tatami* mat is produced is generally found tucked in among single-family houses in residential neighborhoods; business is at least in part a result of community ties. Because of this, customers will often make the decision to purchase from their neighbor (at a higher price) instead of from larger production facilities to which they have no relationship, thus allowing the neighborhood facility to compete on other than economic terms. During the recent economic downturn, I have witnessed that many people who have not been affected will make decisions about purchases as much from the needs of their neighbor's business as from their own—in effect, offering financial support at a time when many small businesses might otherwise fail.

Because the capitalization of small businesses is represented in a single machine or set of machines, there is a demand for equipment which is flexible enough to respond to changing needs. This is considered at least in part to be the result of recent and rapid shifts in industrialization, essentially absorbing 400 years of Western technological development in only 150 years. Machinery used by these small producers is by necessity easier to retool, but these adjustments then become an opportunity for variations and customization which can be exploited by the architect or client.

Today, small producers use customization and product differentiation as a way to segment the market or to offer their customers service that justifies higher costs. However, this differentiation is found not only at the level of the smallest producers, but also at somewhat larger scales of production. In a manner similar to the neighborhood workshop, the small manufacturer of windows, metal screens, or custom-made furniture will also rely on relationships (often through a *keiretsu*, local bank support, or even old school ties) as the foundation for business, and will justify higher costs through the higher

4 *I see many women participating in manufacturing and production, but at the time of this writing, I had yet to see a woman involved in assembling* tatami. *Thus, the use of the male pronoun seems most appropriate.*

5 *Kumajirou Haketa, interview by the author, June 18, 1995, Tokyo, Japan.*

6 *The keiretsu system is described in any standard text or Japanese business. The following definition is taken from* Japanese Etiquette and Ethics in Business: A Penetrating Analysis of the Morals and Values that Shape the Japanese Business Personality *(Lincolnwood, Ill.: DeMente, Boyle; NTC Business Books, 1991), 163.*

Keiretsu kaisha—Keiretsu means "affiliated" or "series" and kaisha means "company." This term refers to the grouping of companies in Japan, including parent companies, subsidiaries, and subcontract firms, as well as those grouped around a certain bank or trading company. The system is an outgrowth of the economic structure of feudal Japan, when older employees of businesses were allowed to go out and establish their own companies while maintaining close ties with their former employers. Members of specific company groups cooperate with one another in various ways, in what often amounts to an exclusive network.

7 *Although in general manufactured products in the United States are still standardized, "manufactured customization" is emerging in this country as well. American systems of customization tend to rely on modularity or the use of computers, lasers, and other advanced technologies to create adaptable production systems. As a result, architects in the U.S. have access to more variety and lower prices in lighting systems, built-in coolers, window frames, elevator cages, handrails, and a wide variety of other products.*

value of customization or product differentiation.[6] In part, the context for these relationships is unique to Japan, a result of the greater proportion of privately held stock corporations, a limited and clearly organized set of relationships defined by the business and educational system, and the protection offered by a complex distribution system and import tariffs. Nonetheless, diversification in the market is also natural in an industrialized country where wealth allows large segments of the population to demand greater individual satisfaction or accommodation of the special needs of small groups.[7]

This customization can and is utilized by architects to appeal to popular taste and to promote innovation. Some architectural modifications are quickly apparent to the outside observer as signature elements: Arata Isozaki's "Marilyn curve" door pulls and furniture; the animal figures found in work by Team Zoo; or the fractal geometries of Kurokawa's more recent work. Less obvious, especially in the photographs which are the sole way many American academics know Japanese buildings, is the manner in which architects may readdress relatively prosaic areas of the building, redesigning the drainpipe, the mullion, or the roof tile. Large corporations often use the small producers, in conjunction with the marketplace, as a developing and testing ground for new materials and products. Thus architects who utilize flexibilities in production influence the products and materials available for a wider market.

PROMOTING LOCALIZED PRODUCTION SYSTEMS: TERUNOBU FUJIMORI

Terunobu Fujimori, a professor at the University of Tokyo, has only recently begun designing buildings, although he has been a popular architectural spokesperson and prolific scholar. He has authored dozens of books, writes regularly for newspapers and architectural journals, has interviewed major architects for a variety of journals and private publications, and is himself interviewed frequently on Japan's public television station, N.H.K. His decision to design seems to have been an outgrowth of the influence of his mentor Teijiro Muramatsu, who was known for his work on late nineteenth- and early twentieth-century architectures and the technology of production. Through Muramatsu's influence, Fujimori came to a growing awareness that if the opportunities of small-scale manufacturing are not integrated into contemporary design, they may be lost.

In his own research, Fujimori concentrates on modernist architecture. Today, modernism is perceived as calling for formal differentiation between buildings that embrace tradition and those that aspire to be contemporary, and in this context the work being produced by Fujimori would be difficult to classify. In Japan, his first building, the Jinchokan Moriyoka Shiryokan (*shiryokan* can be loosely translated as "historical artifact museum"), was initially thought to be "anti-modern"—a label that caused no little confusion since Fujimori frequently utilizes the works of Mies Van de Rohe or Le

Corbusier as a standard in assessing the accomplishments of contemporary architects. The perception that his work was "anti-modern" derived from the manner in which Fujimori exploited traditionally manufactured materials, deliberately setting out to use only handmade finishes.

Fujimori describes this approach as not being in opposition to modernism; it is very much in keeping with the pre-1923 tenets that Gropius proposed at the Bauhaus, calling for a unification of craft with contemporary planning; he defines himself more in terms of the later work of Le Corbusier (such as Ronchamp) and the Japanese architect and theorist Takamasu Yoshizaka, who worked for Le Corbusier from 1950 through 1952. (Yoshizaka later taught at Waseda University in Tokyo and spoke on the importance of uniting contemporary planning with tradition.) Even more striking a parallel to Fujimori's work is the Japanese Mingei movement of the early twentieth century, guided by Soetsu Yanagi. What each of these groups have in common (and others such as the Arts and Crafts movement inspired by William Morris might also be included) is a desire to respond to overenthusiastic social shifts towards standardization not by rejecting industrialization so much as by attempting to reintegrate and reinforce the importance of traditional production. Many, including those in the early Bauhaus and Yanagi, called for linking industrialized and traditional production in a manner which best exploits the opportunities of each. The influence of these groups on Fujimori probably accounts for the high degree of conscious thought evident at such an early stage of his built work.

北東立面図

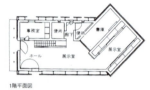

1階平面図

8 Kuma Kengo, "Nostalgia like
Nothing You've Ever Seen,"
Jinchokan Moriya Historical
Museum (Tokyo: Toto
Shuppan/Architecture Riffle, 2001).

9 Terunobu Fujimori, conversation
with the author, July 25, 1995,
Chino City, Nagano, Japan.

10 Coaldrake dates the saw to at
least the tenth century. See William
H. Coaldrake, The Way of the
Carpenter (New York: Weatherhill,
1990), 9.

The Jinchokan Shiryokan was completed in 1991. It is a small museum and repository for the artifacts collected by the Moriyoka family, which traces its history as supporters of the Suwa Shrine well over 800 years.[8] The building was published not only in several of the major architectural magazines, often prominently, but was also featured in the inaugural volume of a new series on architecture published by Toto—especially surprising in light of the size of the museum (only 1,988 square feet) and its relatively isolated location. During design and development, Fujimori relied on his former student Yoshio Uchida, also an architect and a professor at Toyo University, for practical support and advice on detailing and construction. This association continued for several years. Each of the designers has certain strengths; in my observation, Fujimori has been the person responsible for design decisions relating to opportunities of production, while Uchida took the lead on the construction site, having somewhat longer experience in practice. Because Fujimori is also the chief designer, this discussion will focus primarily on his contributions. In no way do I intend, though, to suggest that Uchida's contributions are unimportant; they simply were less significant in the context I am specifically addressing.

In the Jinchokan Shiryokan, Fujimori first proposed how tradition and regionalism might be united with a modernist approach to planning and materials. The museum is located in a remote, mountainous area of Japan with a long history, and Fujimori's concern for the region and its past are the basis for his essay on the project, published in Shinkenchiku. In his opening, Fujimori describes the cold water running into Lake Suwa and the blue mountains which embrace it. He then turns to the roots of the community, the Moriya family's history, and finally his own childhood in the area. From there, Fujimori goes into a lengthy description of the materials produced for the project, not only naming craftspeople and locations where materials are found, but going so far as to describe his own personal ties to these individuals through a former teacher, one of his students, etc. Surprisingly, he does not address modernist influences on the building, instead seeming to take it for granted that these would be apparent.[9]

At the time of this building, Fujimori sought to confine himself only to finishes which were refined by hand, including slate and other stone materials, a straw-embedded mortar coat which was applied by hand, wrought iron door pulls and locks, and handmade glass. (He was not entirely successful; firefighting materials are selected and located by local officials in Japan—clearly unsympathetic to the project's intent—and much of the electrical equipment is manufactured.) In one notable example, he utilized boards split in a manner that apparently predates the saw, but wrapped them around the building as a skin in a way which was distinctly Corbusian.[10] Using this material was a far from simple task; the first challenge Fujimori faced was finding someone still capable of splitting the equivalent of 50 tsubo (about 1,774 square feet) of board in this fashion, since it is a disappearing art.

Ultimately, through personal introductions, Fujimori was able to convince Chuu'ichi Yazawa to participate in the project. In the essay for *Shinkenchiku*, Fujimori describes Yazawa's day (due to his advanced age) as being "in the morning, on an intravenous drip, and in the afternoon, splitting wood in a way he had not been called on to do for half a century."[11] The use of traditional materials was not intended to be retrogressive; in the internal structure Fujimori utilized steel-reinforced concrete, metal decking, and expanded metal. Rather, there was a clear decision to link the advantages of hand-finished and manufactured materials, exploiting each for its benefits.

More recently, Fujimori has shifted away from purely handmade materials and has begun to incorporate production from small manufacturing facilities, in recognition of the challenges this sector also faces. While traditional neighborhood and family ties supported production in the manner I outlined earlier, the Japanese family is increasingly mobile, thus reducing the importance of community ties. Furthermore, the cost differential between locally manufactured goods and goods produced in standardized processes (especially goods produced overseas), continues to widen. This has led to a slight but continuous erosion of the sector served by small producers, and most likely will continue to do so. As late as 1921, 87 percent of Japan's manufacturers employed fewer than ten people; in 1995 46 percent of the workers employed in manufacturing work for companies of over 100.[12] Fujimori noted that some processes have almost completely been lost and others, while still having a healthy share of the production market, are in need of reintegration and support.

At this writing, Fujimori has one project, a house, under construction and two projects in the planning stage. The house, which is located in one of Tokyo's suburbs, is for Fujimori and his family, and thus refers not to the immediate context of Tokyo, but to the *furusato* (hometown) to which he is tied.[13] Suppliers are located at some distance from the construction site, so the building serves as an illustration not only of the opportunities of the production system, but also the manner in which Fujimori used production to connect the building to his personal history and his community. Two examples which underscore these ties and demonstrate the way in which Fujimori has been able to customize his materials, are his work with the sawmill, Kakudai Seizai, and a stone quarry, Kitazawa Teppeiseki. Both of these producers were also involved in Fujimori's first project, although perhaps each can be said to have a somewhat increased role in the current building.

In the early part of the twentieth century, most sawmills in Japan were local mills, often close to the forests. (In part this was due to the fact that Japan's most rugged landscape made shipping logs downstream far less feasible than was true, for example, in the American Midwest.) Large mills which operated in urban areas tended to cut primarily imported woods, and

11 *Terunobu Fujimori*, Hajimete no Kenchiku, Shinkenchikusha *(Tokyo: Shinkenchukusha, 1991), 267. Translation mine.*

12 *Historical data is from Tessa Morris-Suzuki, The Technological Transformation of Japan: From the Seventeenth to the Twenty-First Century (Cambridge: Cambridge University Press, 1994); contemporary data from the Ministry of Finance, Chuushou Kigyou Hakusho, 1995 (Tokyo: Ministry of Finance Printing Office, 1995). Table 7 of the appendix.*

13 *Typically, for example, unmarried children will still be registered as residents of their hometown, or even of the place their parents first lived when married. Eldest sons, such as Fujimori, are assumed to be responsible for the continuation of the family in the community, and it is anticipated that they will eventually return, albeit on retirement. For more on the topic, see Joy Hendry, "The House and Family System," Understanding Japanese Society (London: Croom Helm, 1987), 21–37.*

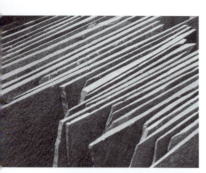

14 *Ryoshin Minami,* Power
Revolution in the Industrialization
of Japan: 1885–1940 *(Tokyo:
Kinokuniya, 1987), 261.*

15 *Ibid.*

16 *Ministry of Trade,* Heisei 5
nen kougyou Toukei Hyou
*(1993 Census of Manufacturers).
Tokyo, Research and Statistics
Department, Ministry of Trade
(1995), 7.*

the small mills—that is, under nine employees—accounted for somewhere around 90 percent of all sawmills in the country.[14] The importance of the small sawmill actually grew as access to power and small machinery made these facilities more competitive; government surveys show that small mills increased in number by 70 percent between 1919 and 1930, while large mills only increased 30 percent in the same period.[15] Even today, there are 18,566 lumber yards and mills in Japan, of which roughly two-thirds—12,147—are staffed by fewer than ten people.[16]

Even by these standards, Kakudai Seizai is a very small mill, run by a middle-aged married couple and the husband's father. Fujimori, who grew up not far from the mill, says that he began to spend time there watching wood be cut when he was as young as five years old. This mill is very much in keeping with the scale and capitalization of the small producer or manufacture; machinery is limited to a large bed for the log, which is driven along a track, and a single, stationary bandsaw. Heavy lifting was done by a truck-mounted articulated arm, the truck rented for the occasion, since logs of the size and weight Fujimori worked with were not usually milled at the site. Special saw blades were also rented as this wood was harder than what the mill generally cut. Fujimori and Uchida used simple notes on a letter-size sheet of paper to review how the logs should be cut. With the participation of the Kakudais and two students from the University of Tokyo, the first of two logs were removed from the truck bed and Fujimori directed its setting on the conveyor bed. When it was in place, he marked the narrow end of the log with chalk (primarily as a confirming device; this was not referred to during milling) and told the younger Mr. Kakudai how the wood was to be cut. Fujimori explained later that he did not feel it necessary to discuss his decisions with Kakudai because of his own long experience at the sawmill.

This is in marked contrast to the manner in which he consulted with head of Kitazawa Teppeiseki, which I will discuss further below.

Altogether, two large logs and one small tree from Fujimori's parents' garden were cut. The smaller tree had been set to dry in a mountain garden owned by his family. As a group, we went up to the garden in a truck and brought the wood back to the mill. This was to be used for window and door frames and was cut to uniform thicknesses.[17] The larger logs were intended for built-in cabinetry and furniture, and were milled to a variety of shapes and thicknesses; because of the way Japanese mill lumber, they retained a ragged bark edge which will be exploited in the finished furniture. At the end of cutting the second log, Fujimori and Uchida were surprised to discover that the rough sketches had been overly conservative and that there was a large piece from the center of the tree of about 5 centimeters in thickness remaining. After some consultation it was decided to keep this piece whole and determine later how they might use it.

In later discussions with the contractor on site, I was told that they preferred to make arrangements for materials themselves as they could control when they were delivered. (Japanese construction sites, being quite small, allow little room for storage.) Also, there is some labor saving to standardized wood sizes, although this was acknowledged to be more than offset by the beauty of less uniform materials. Nonetheless, since most contractors do tend to work with a variety of suppliers, there was not a significant resistance to the architect making other arrangements, and indeed, it relieved the contractor of any responsibility for material failure.

Fujimori's visit to the stone quarry around the same time was somewhat different. He has known Kitazawa only since 1991, when Jinchokan Shiryokan was built; at the time he had seriously been considered using French slate or a stone from southern Japan. Seeing an article in the newspaper about the museum, Kitazawa agreed to work with Fujimori to develop a roof shingle from "*teppei* stone," a flat, iron-based stone which splits naturally. (This stone is found only in the hills around Chino city in Nagano Prefecture and in an area of Gunma Prefecture. It is apparently exported to the United States under the name "*teppei* stone;" I have no satisfactory translation.) The shingle was first used on Jinchokan Shiryokan, and is being used as a roof and wall facing on the house. There are actually ten quarries in the area mining this stone, which is commonly used for stepping stones in gardens; many of the quarries which Fujimori approached were not interested in the project. A visit to Kitazawa's site, though, quickly showed him to be more entrepreneurial; there were experiments with stone garden furniture and flower boxes, children's pools, and imported stone from China. This may be due to the challenges of his quarry; he showed us an area where blasting by an earlier owner had damaged some of the stone, making it good only for limited uses.

Fujimori's visit to the quarry had two purposes. First, suppliers seem more frequently to make mistakes on materials requested in Japan, and the

17 Although in this case Fujimori was not concerned with recognizing the original siting of the wood in the way he finally employed it, it is easy to see from my description how an architect or contractor may, for example, orient materials to the compass in the same direction that they originally grew.

architect's visit to the site, prior to shipping, is intended to confirm that the appropriate materials are being cut. In the case of a single quarry, color and stone type are naturally consistent with what was originally selected, but the visit allowed Fujimori to confirm that the thickness and size of the shingles were accurate. In addition, Fujimori wanted to discuss with the supplier how the stone might be further treated by hand to get a rougher edge. (During processing, large stone sheets are cut by a circular saw and then hand split to their desired thickness; this leaves the stone with a flat, cut edge on all sides.) Kitazawa and Fujimori discussed possibilities at some length, with Fujimori experimenting while they spoke. In the end, Kitazawa also lent Fujimori a tool which would be suitable for this work.

Ultimately Fujimori was forced to decide that hammering all the stones by hand would be impractical; the amount of stone made this difficult to do without holding up construction. (Kitazawa estimated that the supply for the house would total between 8 and 10 tons, and the contractor said it required three 4-ton trucks, thus clearly exceeding 8 tons of material.) This kind of unresolved experimentation was also found in the Jinchokan Shiryokan, where Fujimori spent some time testing plaster finishes before giving up and accepting that he would have to use a mortar finish—although with embedded straw to give a texture similar to plaster.

There are several things to note about the manner in which Fujimori interacted with producers. First, the opportunity to experiment with materials during processing certainly allowed him to control thickness, consistency on color and grain, and size of the materials used to a much larger degree than one can expect with off-the-shelf components. Second, when the architect interacts with and tests materials on site, there is a greater understanding of what can be done, especially when one is able to consult with the producers as well. Fujimori seems to have been the first to use *teppei* stone as a shingle material, and during his site visits he was clearly concerned with refining its use. Third, small producers are able to accommodate unusual requests because they have the opportunity to rent the necessary equipment and materials, such as harder saw blades.[18] The manner in which Japanese architects are able to exploit flexibilities in the production system thus differs in several key ways from American experiences and offers architects a distinct set of opportunities.

Many other major architects in Japan, among them Maki, Kurokawa, and Isozaki, have exploited Japan's flexible production system in their work. The crucial difference between Fujimori and these architects is the manner in which he has created conscious connections between early developments in modernism and his own investigations, thus redefining what many in Japan perceive as modern.[19] Fujimori has created a theoretic context for the use of craft and small-scale production which assumes that more highly customized materials are most appropriate as finishes, while standardized materials can best be used for the unseen structure and mechanical components of the

18 The differences in liability laws are also important. This is discussed at more length in a piece written by the author, "Collaborative Production: Building Opportunities in Japan," Journal of Architectural Education, 50, no. 4 (May 1997): 219–229; and in my book, Japanese Archictecture as a Collaborative Process: Opportunities in a Flexible Construction Culture (London: Spon Press, 2001).

19 Fujimori's efforts can be compared to Kenneth Frampton's attempts to re-establish discussion of modernist architectures on the basis of tectonics. See, for example, Frampton's recent book Studies in Tectonic Culture: the Poetics of Construction in Nineteenth and Twentieth Century Architecture (Chicago, Ill.: Graham Foundation for Advanced Studies in the Fine Arts and Cambridge: M.I.T. Press, 1995).

building. In this way, differing production systems are rationally united with the areas of the building for which they are most suitable. Because of his importance as a theoretician, his proposals are being addressed seriously by practitioners in Japan.

EPILOGUE

When I wrote this essay, Fujimori's trajectory as a designer remained unclear. In the years since, he has experimented with various approaches to materials and construction, further exploring the challenge he set in these early works.

Fujimori designed several houses immediately after his own. The first was for Genpei Akasegawa, an author and artist. Akasegawa recognized that Fujimori's use of materials—plucking dandelions from Mount Fuji, hand-splitting shakes, and chipping the edges of stone—was unsustainable because of the high cost involved. He and Fujimori developed building finishes and components that amateurs could produce, accepting naïve craft and rough results rather than relying on the small fabricators who had supported Fujimori's earliest works. Cracked plaster and screens of split logs on skewers were made collectively by the Jomon Kenchiku Dan, a loosely organized crew of editors, potters, brewers, and writers.

The rapid success of Fujimori's residential work quickly led to larger commissions: an art museum in the Hamamatsu area and a dormitory for an agricultural college in Southern Japan, which received Japan's highest building award. But institutional work demanded reliance on commodities; Fujimori returned to building only small, private structures: a tasting room for a *shochu* brewery, a pottery studio, and a teahouse for a small temple in Kyoto.

That tiny Kyoto teahouse was a turning point, perhaps an inevitable one, since the teahouse as a building type embraces the craft and rough finishes

already a part of his work. Lately Fujimori has designed little else. But in spite of the esoteric focus of his work today, it continues to be treated as part of the architectural mainstream in publications and exhibitions in Japan.

More significant is Fujimori's impact on young architects not even mentioned in my 1996 essay. When I wrote of his work with hammered iron and rough mortar, most designers in Japan strove for sleek purity in glittering glass and aluminum. Today, Kengo Kuma is lauded for rural structures built with paper, adobe, and thatch (although I am perhaps more fond of the weathered boards and dilapidated automobile found at his 2004 Murai Museum in Tokyo), and Jun Aoki has recently completed an art museum that incorporates a long earthern wall designed to crack with age. Waro Kishi's 2003 Ono store in Kyoto features the wave-like texture of an ancient Japanese *adze* across chestnut and *zelkova*, and even the trend-setting Tokyoites at Klein Dytham Architecture designed a room wrapped in logs (the 2005 Gao). Ten years ago, Fujimori established a context for the reincorporation of traditional materials into the architecture of today, but others have eagerly followed.

ACKNOWLEDGMENTS

In the summer of 1994, I visited his first project, the Moriya Jinchokan Shiyokan, with Professor Fujimori. While I photographed the project, we spoke about his approach to its design and the perceptions of the project which others held. I was quite fortunate thereafter to be invited by Fujimori to observe the construction of a house for his family during the summer of 1995; he also had two other projects in the design stage at that time. Throughout the course of this experience I have not only had the pleasure of observing an intellectually rigorous approach to design, but I have quite literally been overwhelmed by the generosity shown to me by not only Professor Fujimori, but also by his extended family and by his professional associates.

Originally published in the Proceedings of the 84th Annual Meeting of the Association of Collegiate Schools of Architecture, 1996.

MAKING SMARTWRAP
From parts to pixels
KARL WALLICK

To tell the story of the white wall is to dwell on nuances, to dwell on and in the very thinness of the surface. Indeed, it is to follow those architects who have argued that the surface is the only place to dwell.[1]

INTRODUCTION: CONSTRUCTION VS. FABRICATION

The present state of building construction is mired between hope and stubbornness. Forms unthinkable without computer assistance are constructed using centuries-old methods of part-by-part construction. Research at KieranTimberlake Associates responded to these considerations by looking to extra-architectural industries and methods of mass-customization.[2] While buildings are still put together nail by nail on site, manufacturers of everything from toothbrushes to 747s explore new materials and methods of making. The prospect of mass customization, transfer technologies, and off-site fabrication should be givens for questions in architecture, just as issues of structure, enclosure, and use have been givens for a thousand years.

Architects should be building faster and smarter given the resources at our disposal. With infrastructural systems growing in scope, complexity, and cost in every project; architects are ceding control of the interstitial space for these systems to specialists. Wanting to challenge traditional methods, we sought a design and fabrication process which would allow more direct architectural oversight into the matter of infrastructure. The process would be one where the design of systems is as much an artistic element as the proportioning of windows. From this critique, we defined the central tenet for SmartWrap: reduce the struggle for infrastructure space by prefabricating as many of the systems as possible and generate an aesthetic from these constituent parts and their method of fabrication.

Today's abundance of cheap, mass-produced electronic devices drew our attention to deposition printing and roll-to-roll printing processes. With the increasing sophistication and size of available printing methods and new flexible technologies, the task of reducing infrastructural or interstitial space to a single printed plane by means of a mass-customizable wall system seemed possible. An entire wall system could be designed to contain multiple infrastructural systems, printed at a factory, easily and compactly transported, and then unrolled onto a structure. We wanted a wall to be installed in as few pieces as possible by a single crew of workers instead of the typical multitude of trades.

SmartWrap. Photograph by Elliott Kaufman.

1 Mark Wigley *White Walls, Designer Dresses (Cambridge, Mass.: M.I.T. Press, 1995).*

2 *KieranTimberlake Associates' research for SmartWrap ran parallel to three years of graduate studios at the University of Pennsylvania. Starting in 2000, the question was put to students: How can we build projects with more features and better quality for less time and money? The projects and dialogue generated by Courtney Druz, Tim McCarthy, and Richard Seltenrich were of particularly importance in exploring these issues. The principal researchers at KieranTimberlake Associates were: Stephen Kieran, James Timberlake, Christopher Macneal, Christopher Johnstone, and Richard Seltenrich.*

DESIGN: PROGRAM AND PARTS

An analysis of existing wall properties defined the program for SmartWrap: some degree of shelter, weather resistance, view out or in, natural and artificial illumination, information display, generation of power, transparent or translucent, and insulation comparable to existing wall construction. Obviously there are numerous other enclosure properties which we excluded from consideration. Qualities addressing security, structure, moisture, and time are worthy of attention but removed from our scope for purposes of expediency. We were impatient to fabricate a building component, not to invent a panacea for all of architecture.

To address these functions, SmartWrap would be comprised of a polyethlene teraphathalate (P.E.T.) substrate printed (although laminated in the prototype) with organic light emitting diodes (O.L.E.D.s), organic photovoltaics (O.P.V.s), phase change materials (P.C.M.s), thin film batteries, and printed circuitry.

Since we ultimately wanted to print, roll, and see through our wall; the substrate selection occupied a good deal of our time. Finding a clear material that would hold print was paramount for our ultimate goal and P.E.T. met that criteria. This polymer is more commonly seen as a thermoset in 2-liter soda bottles. Its mildew resistance, low moisture absorption, economy, UV resistance, and colorless transparency made it an ideal candidate for the substrate. It comes in 300 meter rolls and is flexible enough to be compatible with ink-jet and roll-to-roll printing techniques. Its downside is that it can only be tensioned in one direction. However, we felt that its potential for printing over-ruled this limitation. The interactive component is provided by O.L.E.D.s. We envisioned display of data, images, and illumination in an ever-changing patchwork of color. In the exhibit, the O.L.E.D.s face both in and out. We needed whatever was printed on the substrate to be flexible. Although currently O.L.E.D.s are assembled on glass carriers for consumer use, they have the potential to be flexible and translucent when printed on plastic. There are already existing research programs in pursuit of this goal. Organic molecules in the O.L.E.D. emit light upon the application of an electric current. Eventually we would have them printed directly onto the P.E.T. substrate; however, for the exhibit, DuPont supplied P.D.A.-sized O.L.E.D.s manufactured on glass slides.

The need for power generation is satisfied by thin-film photovoltaics (P.V.s). These would be roll-to-roll printed onto the substrate as well. Assuming proper site and weather conditions, there is a one to one relationship between the number of P.V.s needed to power the O.L.E.D.s. While initially discouraging, the great likelihood of improving efficiencies encouraged us to optimistically include thin-film batteries in order to store energy for cloudy days. The matrix for moving all this electricity around is silver conducting ink printed directly onto the P.E.T. substrate. The ink, while the simplest component in some ways, is the part most satisfying. Its application

SmartWrap elevation showing thin-film photovoltaics, organic light-emitting diodes, and thin-film batteries. Image by KieranTimberlake Associates.

and purpose could be immediately beneficial in an incremental development of a wall with embedded systems. Imagine being able to print a building's electrical wiring rather than punching it through structure or conduits. A universal network of electricity could be available anywhere on a wall.

Ideally, there would be only a single layer of SmartWrap. However, to address issues of thermal comfort, this layer is adjacent to a second insulating layer of P.E.T. containing an array of aerogel and P.C.M. pockets. The two layers are separated by a four inch airspace. The P.C.M.s used in SmartWrap come in the form of a powder. I.L.C. Dover mixed this powder with a small amount of resin in order to provide a means for the P.C.M.s to adhere to the P.E.T. The P.C.M.s work as a type of latent heat storage and were used to thermally moderate the interior surface. Aerogel is an insulating material which can be either transparent or translucent. In order to address issues of durability and flexibility, a translucent blanket form of aerogel was utilized. The thickness and fragility of aerogel limit its participation in any form of printing process. While only 2 inches of aerogel are needed to achieve a realistic R-value, the fact that it cannot be a coating and its need for encapsulation were factors that we have been unable to address yet. Because of this limitation, we decided to make a supplemental layer for SmartWrap that an architect could select depending on climate and application. As dissatisfying as it was to muddy the concept of a single printed surface, we felt that it

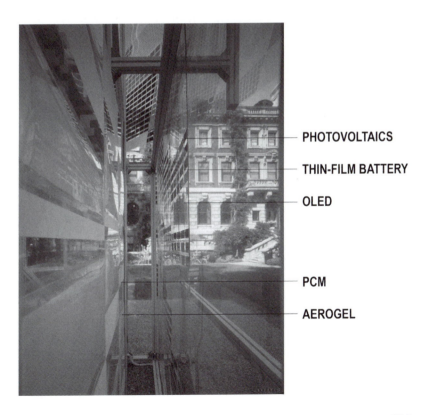

PHOTOVOLTAICS

THIN-FILM BATTERY

OLED

PCM

AEROGEL

View of wraps within the interstitial air space. Photograph by Elliott Kaufman.

would be irresponsible to exhibit SmartWrap as a prototypical building part without addressing the issue of insulation.

DESIGN: PROCESS

Like weaving a tapestry from infrastructure, the designer sits at a virtual loom selecting the proportion of P.V.s to O.L.E.D.s, how much clear view there should be, all the while experimenting with an array of predetermined or custom pattern filters much as one might manipulate an image in Photoshop, except rather than pixels of color, the architect's palette consists of pixels of infrastructure.

An essential and inherent characteristic of SmartWrap is that future applications would not all have the same type or proportion of components. The list of program parts is intended to be a menu to be considered in the design of individual wraps. Variability depends on the architect's criteria: site, orientation, climate, program and use, aesthetics, privacy and publicity, etc.

The production process is irretrievably intertwined with the process of design. Multiple building contractors would be traded for a single printer. By compressing the volume of a wall to a single plane, we could utilize concepts behind existing ink-jet technology which could integrate the engineer's efforts directly into the design process. The typical circuit diagrams produced by an electrical engineer would become part of the new wall substrate upon which a variety of devices could be deposited. The circuit drawing, with its array of devices, would go directly to a printer for production. In addition to the variability and customization afforded by printing processes, another benefit would be elimination of the interpretive burden placed on contractors. The technique would be exactly like an ink-jet printer except instead of depositing droplets of ink, we would deposit droplets of P.V.s or conductive circuits. Similar technology is already being put to use in three-dimensional printers used by industrial designers, prototypers, and in the production of micro-electronics. Later, we were to find out that the seemingly small issue of scale was an enormous obstacle.

FABRICATION: COLLABORATION

Having outlined a proposition, the real goal was to fabricate a prototype in order to test the theory of reforming architecture and construction processes. Only by immersing ourselves in collaborations with engineers and material scientists could we begin to understand the nature of producing a composite. In addition to this intellectual concern was the more practical one of cost. Product development depends on resources and as a fifty-person architectural firm, KieranTimberlake was already stretching its funds through the employment of four full-time researchers. If we wanted to make something, we couldn't go it alone. However, as unestablished prototypers, we were in need of a vehicle to help confer legitimacy, attract sponsorship, and to promote our prototypical wall. Interest was found at the Cooper-Hewitt National Design Museum in New York City which was trying to establish annual installations in their garden on Fifth Avenue. They liked the concept of SmartWrap and pushed us to expand the scope of the exhibit beyond the production of a prototypical material to one which also demonstrated our material's spatial potentials. Rather than displaying a single composite plane, we were now committed to the construction of an outdoor pavilion. The concept blossomed from being an experimental idea about a material and fabrication process into a full-blown architectural provocation.

FABRICATION: NINE MONTHS TO GO

With the Cooper-Hewitt committed to the project and a date, we were able to attract the type of collaborators necessary to implement the project.[3] The supportive responses received from potential collaborators assured us that we weren't the only ones interested in reform within the building-construction industry. One relationship begat another and a favorite consultant KieranTimberlake Associates had worked with for years were the first on board. C.V.M. engineers were concerned primarily with the pavilion's ground anchorage and the forces of SmartWrap (a big sail) on its supporting armature. They recommended we consult with Buro Happold in regards to the issue of SmartWrap's attachment to its structure. Buro Happold came up

3 Our collaborators included: DuPont, Skanska U.S.A, I.L.C. Dover, Inc, Bosch Rexroth Corporation, E.R.C.O. Lighting, C.V.M. Engineers, Sean O'Connor Associates, Buro Happold, Gabor M. Szakal Consulting Engineers, P.C., Celestial Lighting, and Lutron Electronics

Wrap attachment to frame. Image by Barry Halkin.

with the idea of using a luftgroove to attach the wrap back to the frame. A rod would be fastened to SmartWrap and then inserted into a slotted frame for the purpose of spreading the tensile forces over as large an area as possible. While there are drawbacks to this method, namely that four-sided framing of the skin and thereby full sealant or closure is not possible, it was the detail most compatible with the aluminum structure donated by Bosch-Rexroth. The benefits in terms of a simple and speedy installation due to the low number of connections became evident soon enough.

Products were lined up for all the components in the wrap, but there was no way we could print the prototype. The large-scale and unrealized infrastructure needed to support large-scale printing of P.V.s and O.L.E.D.s was still in the labs and minds of scientists. Lamination of the components to the P.E.T. was the realizable short-term solution which permitted us to meet our exhibit obligations. As for a fabricator, Buro Happold recommended I.L.C. Dover as a company with experience integrating textiles and technology.[4] As it happened, I.L.C. Dover already had a tremendous amount of experience with P.E.T., printed circuitry, thin-film photovoltaics, P.C.M.s, and aerogel. However, O.L.E.D.s were newer to them and they were interested in gaining experience in that area and with the general concept of intelligent fabrics. The O.L.E.D.s were critical to the exhibit's representation as a dynamic infrastructural system and so a partnership was formed. We had been discussing the project this whole time with DuPont and finally an audience was granted with the right person. O.L.E.D.s are a burgeoning industry and DuPont was trying to position itself as a leader in the technology. They turned out to be a prodigious collaborator. Besides donating the most expensive component of SmartWrap (the O.L.E.D.s), they also were producers of P.E.T. and the silver conducting ink we needed for the printed circuitry. With these major collaborators working with us, it became much easier to attract help for the remainder of the pavilion design.

4 Recent projects by I.L.C. Dover include airbags for the Mars Rover and, more famously, the astronaut suits for N.A.S.A. Their contribution in realizing SmartWrap cannot be overstated. They helped us through a myriad of technological hurdles in the drive to integrate the many components into a functioning prototype.

FABRICATION: OFF-SITE

The aluminum frame for supporting the wraps was donated by Bosch-Rexroth. This relationship turned out to be more than a material one, but gave us our first taste of digital design to fabrication enabling software. Bosch's website has plug-ins for Autocad which, in addition to being a three-dimensional library of all their stock shapes and hardware, also generates a parts list. All of the framing was delivered to the site precut, predrilled, and barcoded for identification.

As the exhibit opening loomed nearer, the issues of creating a context for displaying SmartWrap and explaining it to the public competed against the prototype for our attention. Fabricating an operating prototype at the dimensions of 11 feet wide by 7 feet high was daunting enough. Obstacles such as the quantity of O.L.E.D.s available, overloading circuits, waterproofing the silver ink, techniques of lamination and silk-screening such a large panel—

all were hindered by the issue of scale. The idea of making enough functional wrap to enclose our small 16 × 16 × 24 foot high garden pavilion was out of the question for our collaborators. So to convey our spatial aspirations for SmartWrap, we would design and print over 200 feet of simulated wraps to enclose the pavilion. Finding a local printer who could handle 8-foot-wide rolls of P.E.T. and was willing to experiment was challenge enough, but it turned out that the cardboard core supporting the roll obtained from DuPont would not fit on the printer's spindle. Fortunately, there is an entire industry which deals with just such problems: material expeditors recored the 1,000-foot roll supplied by DuPont onto five smaller cores. Finally, our pointillist array of function came together, and the simulated wraps were printed in the manner that we envisioned the actual prototype would be printed: in one pass on a single roll.

With all of the supporting elements for the exhibit mimicking the processes of fabrication we admired in other industries, it was somewhat disappointing that the active panel construction was fairly old world. Most of the scientists we talked to at DuPont were surprisingly optimistic about the efficacy of our vision for a printable wall. However, we knew from the outset that this ultimate goal of printing a wall was a future eventuality dependent on years of research. As such, the infrastructural components of SmartWrap were hand-laminated by I.L.C. Dover. They worked tirelessly to help us resolve the array of electronics into a functional and poetic assembly. Most circuit boards are fairly small; the largest circuit boards we could find were electronic white boards, but none were interested in collaborating with us. So our only printed component was the conductive network of silver ink . . . and it was silk-screened like a giant T-shirt. Two more setbacks occurred with the production of the functioning wrap: batteries and electronic sensitivity. While the thin-film P.V.s were readily available and inexpensive, the thin-film battery manufacturer was unable to provide us with the quantity of working batteries needed. We kept the duds in the panel to fill out the design and to keep the intention represented. The problem of O.L.E.D. sensitivity came up the week prior to the exhibit opening. It seems the P.V.s we had purchased created the potential of frying the O.L.E.D.s. No one was willing to risk damaging the most visually dynamic component of the wrap so close to our deadline. Once again, scale was our nemesis: Everything which we wanted to do was already in existence, but at the much smaller size of microelectronics.

CONSTRUCTION: ON-SITE

Despite our attention to technology and the potential benefits of seamless computer-to-fabrication production processes, the exhibit would have many of the messy construction aspects which were in direct opposition to the concept of prefabrication. Anchoring your building to the Earth is an unavoidable and inherently messy enterprise. C.V.M. had calculated the amount of mass needed to keep the pavilion from sailing down Fifth Avenue

above: Silkscreening the substrate.
Image by ILC Dover, Inc.

right: Laminating the components.
Image by ILC Dover, Inc.

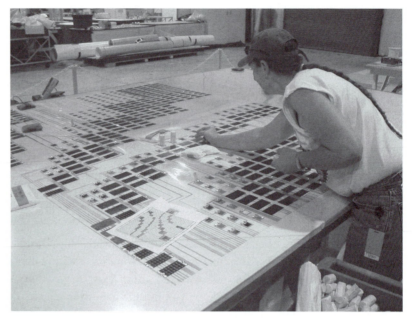

and it translated into 5 yards of dirt. Unfortunately, we could only fit a small bobcat and a wheelbarrow brigade through the garden gate. As if we hadn't made things difficult enough on ourselves, we wanted the pavilion to glow at night. An array of sixteen fluorescent lights below a translucent polypropylene floor, while the perfect design compliment to the ethereal vision of SmartWrap, required the excavation of an additional 7 yards of dirt, all of which had to be stored on site and replaced at the end of the exhibit.

Many calluses later, the dirt was in place, the foundation cured, and we were ready to erect the frame. This portion of the exhibit assembly more closely paralleled our aspirations for construction reform. Following the Ikea ideal of assembling everything with a single hex-key, the Bosch system required only a single socket size for all the connections. Finding the correct piece for the frame was only a matter of knowing the last three numbers on the barcode. The frame was erected in a day.

The simulated wraps were installed next, and the need for onsite improvisation arose. The tension bars used to restrain the orthogonal wraps needed a custom fastener not supplied by Bosch-Rexroth. We fashioned our own by customizing one of their standard parts with a 5-inch bolt, nut and washer, a strip of cardboard, and duct tape. The thought of such a homely assemblage acting as a key detail was absorbed into an evolving poetry of contrasts concealed within the building envelope of the future.

Our next task was the 100-foot simulated wrap which enclosed the entire pavilion in a helix. There had been a number of proposals calling for tools such as a scissor lift, cherry-picker lift, a 24-foot-long pole and ball-bearing assembly, and an army of pulleys. In the end, the scissor lift won out. Using a board and clamp, a spindle was fashioned to hold the 8-foot-tall roll of material to the lift. Over a two-hour period, we drove the wrap around the pavilion and secured it to the frame.

Initially we used screw clamps to hold the wrap to the outriggers to account for the slack needed for installation. After unwinding the full length of the helical wrap, we gradually added tension by winding up slack at the bottom of the pavilion and shimming the bottom of each outrigger about an inch out of the vertical plane. In the end, the tension generated was sufficient that we removed the majority of the clamps and were left supporting the entire 100-foot length from two attachment points. Over the course of the exhibit, the P.E.T. would relax and we would return to the site a couple of times to wind up the slack.

The active wrap was fully assembled and mounted to a small frame at I.L.C. Dover's Delaware facility. After unloading in New York, the plan was to hand carry it through the museum and out to the garden. However, a last-minute change in the routing and mounting of wires had added an extra 2 inches to the panel's height. This difference was significant enough that we had to unfold the panel to move it through the building. It worked out fine but was the source of last-minute sweating and improvisation. Once at the site, mounting the active panel to the pavilion proceeded smoothly, the control board was hooked up and our first prototype was turned on.

CRITIQUE: ADJUSTMENTS

How can design utilize the opportunities of current industrial production so that the practice of architectural representation is neither independent of nor subjugated to the domination of technology?[5]

Even with the exhibit's conclusion, it is probably more accurate to say that we are still in SmartWrap's programming phase. This realization as an architectural folly is the first step in our research into an open-ended product development spectrum. The promise that wrapping might hold for construction processes seems supported by our onsite experience. Ironically, the greater installation difficulty came from the elements that as architects, we are more accustomed to. The issues of excavation, existing conditions, structural shimming, scaffolding, modifying, and improvising details represent embedded technical and cultural hurdles equal to the difficulties in SmartWrap's future evolution. While it is extreme in its cultural and performative expectations, it was the provocation necessary to attract corporate collaboration. Currently KieranTimberlake Associates is engaged in incremental product development research with DuPont and, while the program guidelines for component parts and production aspects have been realigned to currently available industrial capabilities, the ultimate goal

5 David Leatherbarrow and Mohsen Mostafavi Surface Architecture (Cambridge, Mass.: M.I.T. Press, 2002), 6.

is still to achieve a printable, mass-customizable wall system. As a first prototype, there are many places to criticize SmartWrap, but the initial goal of promoting provocation and speculation through physical investigation was achieved. We had challenged ourselves to look at architecture through the lens of product development and had seen a new world of potential processes and outcomes worthy of further exploration.

As a viable building product, SmartWrap has many issues which need resolution: attachment details, weatherproofing and sealing, energy consumption, adjustability, let alone the technical hurdles of large-scale printing. While we pushed the technical attributes of walls by prefabricating electrical components right into an enclosure system, the need for large displays and patterns of color on buildings may be limited to Times Square and Las Vegas. Illumination is another matter; by locating the O.L.E.D.s to the interior, the P.V.s in concert with thin-film batteries present a viable and complementary night/day marriage. There is even further potential for O.L.E.D.s to operate in dual capacity. They may one day be built with a switch enabling them to oscillate between consuming energy to generate light and collecting light to generate energy.[6]

The idea of a film enclosing a building is asking a lot in terms of durability, weather, and cultural expectations. Such a thin skin may not satisfy our personal sense of architectural enclosure. SmartWrap confronts our traditional notions of edge, line, and its relationship to structure when considered for its spatial potential. While it is important to pursue the resolution of attachment issues as it pertains to our common understanding of building envelopes, the question for architects should be: How is interstitial space collapsed, expanded, or reoriented when we consider deployment? What if there were multiple planes of enclosure: a rainscreen rather than a hermetic enclosure? Perhaps the line of enclosure is sometimes perpendicular to edge conditions rather than parallel. The demarcation (lines) of shelter can be many and oblique, some parallel, some perpendicular. A line can have depth. The interstitial can be occupied. Layers of mediating material mark an agitation of the membrane with thin skins that oscillate between representing mass and plane. The wall is dematerialized through multiplicity rather than minimalism. Instead of reducing presence through planarity, the edge between inside and outside is rendered indistinct through an amplification of surfaces. Rather than wondering how SmartWrap becomes reoriented to our accustomed notions of enclosure, it might also be productive to consider how enclosure is reoriented to SmartWrap.

The balance between craft and technology is similar to the tension between art and commodity.[7] This has been a constant struggle for us in the pursuit of not just the design of a building product, but more importantly the reform hoped for in the processes at the core of architecture and construction that led to the development of this research project in the first place. With SmartWrap, we have attempted to embrace and elevate that tension. Is the

6 Speculation based on remarks by Dr. Alan Heeger, one of the creators of O.L.E.D. technology, at the Innovation Conference in New York City, October 2003.

Reorienting the skin. Image by author.

7 Stephen Kieran and James Timberlake Refabricating Architecture: How Manufacturing Methodologies Are Poised to Transform Building Construction (New York: McGraw-Hill, 2004).

232

hope of utilizing printing processes a too literal reframing of the maker's hand? First the architect draws the design and then prints the object. This architecture is not in conflict with representation; it is representation. We had an idea and the construction is the drawing: a virtual and physical tattoo.

Originally published in the Proceedings of the 93rd Annual Meeting of the Association of Collegiate Schools of Architecture, 2005.

QUILTING WITH GLASS, CEDAR AND FIR
A workshop and studio in Rossland, BC
ROBERT BARNSTONE

It is unusual to think about architecture in the same terms as we would think about making a quilt—sewing together patches of unrelated materials, often scrap, in a collage-like juxtaposition—but quilting describes the ways in which the Workshop/Studio project in British Columbia was designed and constructed.

The project took a ramshackle, collapsing old truck workshop and transformed it into a winterized, habitable artist's studio. The original structure was a wooden post and beam, wooden clad shed with 14-foot high ceilings, a flat roof, mostly dirt floors, and two plywood panel barn doors on the front. Many of the rafters and much of the exterior wood siding were rotten; the entire building was leaning at a 10-degree angle to one side! The first challenge was to decide what could be salvaged from the mess, and then

decide how to incorporate new construction into the existing structure. The technique was, from the start, the sewing together of old and new; collaging of found and salvaged materials with pre-existing ones. The concrete foundation walls, the large supporting posts and the ridge beam were all in fine condition and could be saved. After closer inspection, we discovered that the rafters were rotting at their outer edges. We realized that if we removed the rotten ends, we could use most of their length. We also realized that the rot was being caused by the excessive amounts of moisture rolling off the flat roof during the spring melt. By stitching rafter extensions onto the ends of the old rafters, we made the roof overhangs much longer so that when the snow melts, the water does not fall against the shed.

The front façade was composed of surplus windows purchased from a local custom window fabricator and recycled glass. Both the steel frame for the two glass doors and the façade were designed like a quilt whose outer dimensions and component parts were fixed. The challenge was to make a coherent looking design from disparate parts. The deep red color used both on the steel and a wood frame helps stitch the pieces together visually. Because the façade is facing southwest, it acts as a passive solar collector.

The side and rear façades were constructed using salvaged cast-glass doorfronts from old Herman Miller furniture with occasional cedar lattice inserts. The glass and cedar panels are wrapped around the supporting building volume like a large blanket suspended a distance from the tar paper underneath, forming an air pocket that heats up during the day and helps keep the building warm at night. The cedar was used for visual relief and in places where cutting the glass would have been difficult—around the beam/wall connections for instance. The patchwork pattern developed here, as on the solar façade, out of necessity. Although the panels had originally been one uniform size, some had broken, chipped or cracked, and had to be cut down. Even the application method is reminiscent of quilting techniques; strips of

Douglas fir form the seams onto which the glass and cedar is fastened. As on quilts, the seams are visible. Furthermore, the glass, cedar and battens are layered spatially like woven cloth.

Even the interior was made using sewing and collage techniques. The building was designed to function as both a sculptor's workshop and living quarters. The columns march down the center of the interior space, making a natural division into two. We inserted one new volume housing the bathroom, a closet, the water heater, and supporting a kitchenette. Atop this box is a loft sleeping area separating the one side of the workshop into two smaller spaces. We mounted the barndoor tracks from the ceiling, next to the columns, and fabricated a 6×12 foot gypsum wall to suspend from the tracks. By moving the wall forward or backwards along the tracks it is possible to alter the spatial configuration of the studio to accommodate different uses. The hanging wall therefore is simultaneously a stitching device and spatial divider.

Originally published in the Proceedings of the 91st Annual Meeting of the Association of Collegiate Schools of Architecture, 2003.

NAVY DEMONSTRATION PROJECT
ROBERT BARNSTONE

The Navy Demonstration Project is a collaborative research project between architects, material scientists, and structural engineers whose end product is a 5,400 square foot demonstration building for the U.S. Navy designed and built by architecture students at the Wood Materials Engineering Laboratory (W.M.E.L.) on the campus of Washington State University. The project is a unique combination of design and science; it engages a series of experiments with new material development in the field of plastic wood composites, building envelope design and structural engineering. On the one hand, the Navy Demonstration Project was an exploration into design possibilities inherent in engineered products such as wood plastic composites, oriented strand board (O.S.B.), laminated veneer lumber (L.V.L.) and I-joists; on the other hand, the project was an exploration of the engineering potentials in these same materials. The building is possibly the first in the world to use wood plastic composites so extensively and for such a wide variety of applications.

The project was initiated by the W.M.E.L. to facilitate a wood plastic composites production line for a new commercialization center for the U.S. Navy. The Navy recently awarded $1.6 million to W.M.E.L. to build full-scale production facilities to demonstrate and assess new products, prove production rates, and attract U.S. manufacturers to the wood-composite marketplace.[1] This project stands as an example of how to use wood composites: in the foundation piers and the building envelope, both as a rain screen and as typical siding products.

The Navy has a keen interest in reducing deterioration from environmental and mechanical damage to their large stock of timber structures. The marine environment in which most navy structures are situated is exposed to extreme weather and environmental conditions like salt water and harsh winds that wreak havoc on buildings in general, and on wooden structures in particular. The Navy is seeking environmentally friendly means to increase building durability and thereby reduce the costs to the Navy for replacing the structures.[2]

Wood composites have been manufactured for several decades, but they have only found significant acceptance in the building products market in the past five years and predominantly as deck products.[3] Only recently has the Strandex Corporation (Madison, Wisconsin) developed extrusion technology that can create complex finished profiles in a single process out of thermoplastics with a high wood fiber content.[4] W.M.E.L. has been working with Strandex technology for the Navy, under a number of research grants.

The program for the Navy Demonstration Project called for the design of an annex building for the W.M.E.L. to be used to warehouse machinery, store

1 See <http:www.wmel.wsu.edu/news/NavyComm.html>.

2 See <http:composites.wsu.edu.Navy/index.html>.

3 Craig M. Clemons, "Woodfiber-plastic Composites in the U.S.A.: History and Current and Future Markets," U.S.D.A. Forest Service, Forest Products Laboratory, Madison, Wisconsin, 2002.

4 Ibid.

manufactured and test products, and as a depot for nonflammable raw materials to be used in the laboratory. Furthermore, the brief required an awning to use as a covered workspace for lab technicians in the summer and for vehicle parking in the winter.

In one innovative application, we used wood plastic for the piers that attach the portal arches to the concrete foundations. Typical of our collaborative method, the engineers tested the wood plastic for its load-bearing and stress-bearing potential, while the architects and engineers worked together to design the proper size and shape of the profiles. We also used a wood plastic composite profile as a sill plate, yet another experimental application. The rain screens will be used simultaneously as cladding for the structure and as removable test panels for new materials as they are developed. The screens are entirely constructed out of colored wood plastic composites. Again, in a collaborative effort, the designers and wood engineers have explored various add-mixtures for coloring the wood plastic, UV inhibitors to prevent discoloration of the siding over time, different profile designs for the siding, and various attachment possibilities.

Besides being a vehicle for new material experimentation, the building is a place for the architects to explore the plastic possibilities of wood-construction and composite-construction techniques. In fact, one of the mandates for the building was to design a unique, memorable structure. We were inspired to explore the potential in dynamic form using the wood-plastic composite precisely because of its nature. As a material that is manmade, completely invented, and has no predetermined color or form.

Published in the Journal of Architectural Education, *60: 2 (November 2006).*

MODERNISM REDUX
A study in light, surface, and volume
GRACE LA AND JAMES DALLMAN

This design project demonstrates the transformation and reinhabitation of a 1960s multi-family high-rise, and a study of some of the fundamental principles within dwelling involving light, surface, and volume. Introducing a more fluid and sensual approach, the project confronts the doctrinaire modernism highly prevalent within this era's building type. The intentionally ambiguous and hybrid spatial sensibility offers a distinct contrast to the mathematical rigidity of the existing building form.

The high-rise, located along Lake Michigan in Milwaukee, is a familiar and common example of many multi-family projects produced throughout the 1950s to 1970s—a concrete-frame building characterized by banal conditions of low ceilings, rabbit-warren units, undifferentiated apertures, expedient (often poor) material choices, and enclosed by a uniform façade of grid-structure and infill. And Milwaukee, like many typical Midwestern cities, has lost thousands of inhabitants to the draws of suburban sprawl—a movement which inherently critiques not only the cultural desires of Americans in a broad sense, but also the livability and availability of the poor housing stock comprising much of the urban fabric. In light of the rapid trend toward depopulation, this project represents a commitment to urban dwelling and provides a venue to explore material options, lighting strategies, and formal devices that directly challenge the neutral and purely utilitarian spatial strategies of the many buildings produced during this period. The program of the project called for the consolidation of three small apartments. The southeastern unit, already in use by the owners as a kitchen, informal living space, and guest quarters, was to remain relatively unaltered. The remaining two units, forming the southwestern corner of the building footprint, were to be completely renovated into a formal entry, entertaining spaces, and the owners' bedroom suite.

The fundamental need for light produced by the cellular nature of embedded rooms within the unit's existing plan, suggested the removal of eighteen walls to significantly alter the basic size and proportion of spaces and to accommodate the desire for a more open living space. While the concept of an open plan is not unusual in architecture discourse (recalling the movements of the 1920s modern era) and despite the façade's plethora of ribbon windows intimating a broad expanse of space beyond, the existing plan was instead comprised of a conventional arrangement of distinct, separate rooms. The initial removal of these eighteen walls provided not only the necessary *tabula rasa* condition to allow light and view to enter, but also the unique opportunity to examine and reinsert the program within an open-plan concept. Accordingly, one of the formal strategies for the unit's reconfiguration relied on the design of controlled elements of furniture, both fixed and movable, to more subtly divide the space without compromise to the newfound luminosity. And the use of bamboo as the new floor surface, chosen for both its light value and sustainable properties, assisted in creating a reflective surface upon which light bounces deep into the interior. At the darkest zones, adjacent to the core, electrified light pockets were designed to wash light across wall surfaces, creating a lighting gradient which maximizes the use of these walls.

right: View of wooden wall and table from Music Room, with panorama of city slipping beyond. © 2003 Dong Wong.

bottom left: View from bathroom into bedroom. © 2003 Dong Wong.

bottom right: View of stone sculpture shelf, and folding of the wooden soffit into the transitional space between Music Room, Bedroom, and Bathroom. © 2003 Dong Wong.

Because the footprint of the unit wraps three sides of the building, the residence commands spectacular views of Lake Michigan and the cityscape, including the Milwaukee Art Museum. Embracing these visual opportunities, the new plan unifies the segmented ribbon windows by placing a series of remnant skins in the foreground of the existing window wall's rigid structural order. These spatial foils are considered a new surface, taking the form, for example, of a combined wooden curtain/table. The newly layered surface allows the view to slip seamlessly beyond the foreground, elongating the landscape beyond into a single wrapping horizon encompassing the residence's perimeter. The new surface integrates the existing mechanical equipment and coalesces the previously disjointed windows into a unified aperture.

To accentuate the newfound continuity of the window wall, additional attenuated wooden surfaces—a tongue-and-groove soffit, walls of tall cabinet doors, and benches—create partial and complete volumes wrapping the living, bath, wardrobe, and bedroom. The wooden surfaces are multidirectional, comprising horizontal and vertical planes in order to accentuate the spatial volumes and their connection to one another. The joints between these wooden surfaces and the plaster *poche* articulate spatial thresholds, creating varying degrees of privacy while maintaining functional continuity. Doors

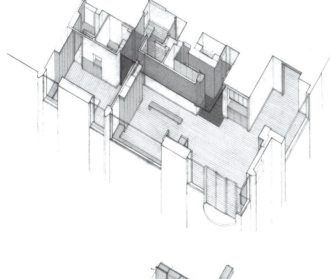

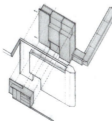

top: View of entry wood screen. © 2003 Dong Wong.

left: Axonometric drawing of residence and exploded axon of layered bedroom/Music Room wall. © La Dallman Architects Inc.

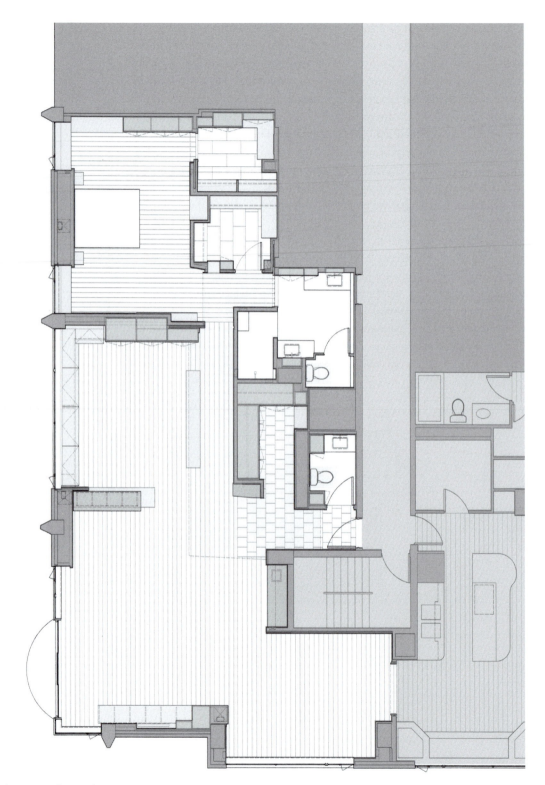

Floor Plan. © La Dallman Architects Inc.

slip into pockets within layered walls of millwork and conventional framing that reconcile the need for lighting, storage, and art display on both sides of the wall. This fluid play of surface and volume counteracts the constraining effects of the 8-foot floor-to-ceiling height by intensifying the long views, both within the porous depth of the functional interior and exploding out to the panoramic exterior. The wooden soffit, alternately volumetric and planar, and folding from the horizontal to the vertical plane, suggests readings of space extending beyond the confines of the unit. This plasticity of surface at the volumes surrounding the building core infuse the plan with intimacy, warmth, and shadow that, by contrast, allow the luminous and expansive living spaces to extend and connect with the urban context beyond.

In a transformative critique of the gridded and cellular spatial composition of the existing building, this project attempts to weave together light, surface, and volume—to provide a sensual and phenomenological response which broadens and articulates the space all the while maximizing the potentially positive characteristics of this building type such as its relentless façade of disjointed windows. Within the dominant plan-driven design of this high-rise, the project proposes the insertion of sectional devices to challenge the "pancake" quality of space produced by the low and undifferentiated ceilings. In this way, the design offers opportunity to test a material palette of cork, bamboo, and other woods in a multidirectional fashion, as well as to compose space contoured by immovable and fixed furniture rather than by conventional means through wall partitions alone. The transformation of this 1960s unit re-engages fundamental design principals such as light, volume, and surface. Enlisting the found conditions of a doctrinaire modernism, the project creates a tactile translation of space not typically found within the predictable uniformity of this building's spatial pattern, and provides an alternative reading of space and dwelling.

Originally published in the Proceedings of the 93rd Annual Meeting of the Association of Collegiate Schools of Architecture, 2005.

SOLAR SAILS AND THE TRIAD OF SUSTAINABILITY

MAHESH SENAGALA

1 Jean-Paul Sartre, quoted in Gabriel Marcel, The Philosophy of Existentialism (New York: Carol Publishing Group, 1995), 50.

2 It is the author's contention that an overt and myopic focus on energy efficiency, recycling, and other such issues of ecological significance tend to sidestep the fundamental issues of existential and institutional sustainability. There have been numerous so-called "green" projects that have either gone out of commission or fell into the lap of neglect due to their institutional unsustainability. Just because an installation or a building produces renewable energy does not mean it is sustainable. Even a zero-energy, L.E.E.D.-certified building that does not house a sustainable institution is fundamentally unsustainable. For further discussion of this issue, see Mahesh Senagala, "The Absurd Self and The Naked City: An Existential Redefinition of Sustainable Urbanism and the Case of Banaras," (Proceedings of the A.C.S.A. International Conference, Rome, 1999).

3 One hundred and fifteen entries were submitted by various professional firms and individuals. The jury included architects Bart Prince and Ralph Johnson of Perkins and Will among others. The first prize went to a proposal from Solomon Cordwell Buenz & Associates of Chicago in partnership with Ove Arup & Partners of New York. The first-prize winning entry is slated to be built with the $20 million funding approved in April 2005 through a congressional amendment. For more information and for competition booklets, please contact U.S. D.O.E.

PREAMBLE

Objects ought not to move one, since they are not alive. They should be used and put back in their place; one lives among them, they are useful and that is all. But I am moved by them, it is unbearable. I am as frightened of coming in contact with them as if they were live beasts.[1]

(Antoine Roquentin in Jean-Paul Sartre's La Nausée)

In order for something to be truly sustainable, it has to work simultaneously at three levels: *existential*, *institutional* and *ecological*.[2] The author calls this the "triad of sustainability." This triadic approach prevents such oxymorons as "sustainable prisons," "green S.U.V.s," and "ecological torture chambers!" Architecture differs from mere building and infrastructure through its engagement of the existential and institutional dimensions. Architecture is not just about making buildings; it is about making institutions. Further, architecture needs to move us, inspire us, and ennoble our otherwise prosaic and absurd existence. It is not difficult to find architects, even those of us who claim to make sustainable architecture, who share the feelings of Antoine Roquentin, fearful of making architecture that is complex, animate, and moving. No matter how we dress it, we hesitate to make architecture that is more than utilitarian, subservient, slick, performative, and infrastructural. We hesitate to address the issues of the existential and institutional complexities of our life-world that go beyond the physical making of architecture. These are some of the critical concerns of sustainability that the Solar Sails project takes into consideration.

THIS IS NOT A WALL

Salutations to you, possessor of the lustre of refined gold, destroyer of ignorance, the architect of the universe. Salutations to the destroyer of darkness, splendour incarnate; the witness of the world.

Aditya Hridayam: 21, Ancient Hindu hymns written in praise of the Sun God)

The U.S. D.O.E. and American Institute of Architects had jointly sponsored an open architectural competition for an energy-generating "Sun Wall" in the year 2000.[3] This sun wall was to be situated on or next to the 32,000-square-foot south wall of the U.S. D.O.E. headquarters, Forrestal Building, in Washington,

D.C. The site is significant given its proximity to the Washington Mall, the Smithsonian Institution and other important public institutions. The south side of Forrestal Building currently houses a triangular parking lot, which adjoins a Pennsylvania Railroad commuter rail line. The project is anticipated to become a major landmark in the national capital and a major contribution to the sustainable design landscape. "Solar Sails," designed by the author, is a joint-second-place winning entry in this competition.

Instead of designing a "wall" that would attach to the 18-inch-thick south-facing concrete wall of the Forrestal Building, the author chose to build a series of sails that stand away from the building. The sails would create an interstitial space that bears great potential for immersive visceral experience.

The proposal consists of four sails dedicated to the four seasons: spring, summer, autumn, and winter. The sails are firmly moored according to the seasonal solar azimuth. The crucial interstitial space between the sails and the blank south wall of the Forrestal Building would contain a grand stair that ascends eastward from the street level. At the end of the climb, there would be an evergreen tree that is strategically framed by the spring sail. The existing parking lot would be moved into the basement and a solar plaza would be created in front of the Solar Sails. The plaza would also act as a solar clock through a series of carefully calculated markings and animated shadows cast by the sun and the sails.

The "wall" of sails becomes a connector and a partner (as opposed to being a graft or a parasite) with the Forrestal Building. The Solar Sails would mediate between the bureaucratic space of the Forrestal bBuilding and the fluidic space of the plaza and the commuter rail line. The Solar Sails would mediate between the visitors and the sun. The Solar Sails would bridge between the strictly striated federal space and the more fluidic smooth space of the public plaza. Chance meetings, chance discoveries, spaces with varied qualities would be promoted through a complex-adaptive approach to architecture. This approach reflects the author's belief that sustainable architecture needs to be fundamentally complex (not necessarily complicated).[4]

Solar Sails are complex in the way they stand, operate, and enable diverse connections to be made to various things at multiple levels of its existence. While the competition brief had directed the participants to make the installation "not climbable," the author was convinced of the value of experiencing the installation and the spaces from a variety of "grounds" and "distances" in all senses of those words. By making the project primarily a temple to the sun and by approaching the sun wall as a public institution that reconnects the human beings to the cosmic wonder, Solar Sails aspire to become sustainable.

THE FOURTH SAIL

The first three sails—winter, summer, and fall—feature B.P. Solarex® photovoltaic skins that contain 591 photovoltaic modules altogether. At their peak, these sails would be capable of producing 142 kilowatts of electricity.

4 Here, complexity is to be understood in the sense of systemic complexity, which is in contradistinction to mere complication. A poem is a complex construct, whereas an airplane is a complicated construct. The word complexity is a derivative of the latin root complexus, which means totality and embrace. Complexity refers to a systemic totality and the interrelationships between various subsystems. This differs from common parlance that complexity is opposed to simplicity. The word simplicity descends from latin roots sim+plec, which literally means single fold. The true opposite of simplicity is complication, which means to fold together. Complex systems can be simple or complicated. Complicated systems are not necessarily complex.

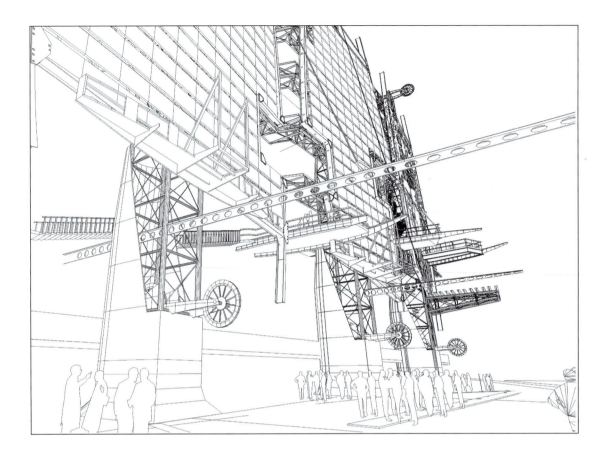

above: The solar plaza.

right: A temple to the sun.

left: View of Solar Sails from southwest.

bottom: Front and top views.

The fourth sail, dedicated to spring season, would remain as a framework that harbors seasonal vines and other vegetation. The fourth sail would spring to life during the spring and autumn seasons. It would unfurl a variegated palette of colors as the seasons pass. The fourth sail would bring into manifest existence our intrinsic connection to the sun—the life giver. The fourth sail would reframe the sun as more than a prosaic and infrastructural "source of green energy." The sun is the source and witness of life.

RE-SPATIALIZING TIME

New technologies tend to *temporalize* space. They do so by miniaturizing things and by freeing things from any sort of reliance on space. The Solar Sails, on the contrary, propose to *respatialize* time. All the processes and flows of the Solar Sail system are exposed to the discerning eyes, noses, ears, and touch of the visiting population. The Solar Sails could be understood as the temporal circle of the seasons cut open and stretched to form a jagged line.

AN OFFERING

Sing a song
or
Laugh
or
Cry
or
Go away.[5]

5 *"Please,"* Nanao Sasaki, Break the Mirror *(San Francisco, Calif.:* North Point Press, 1987), 47.

Sustainable architecture needs to be fundamentally meaningful to human beings at the existential, institutional, and ecological levels. Without such a meaningful connection that transcends a utilitarian approach, no amount of ecological consideration can ensure the sustainability of a work of architecture. Architecture that does not move us is not architecture. Architecture becomes sustainable when it is a part of our journey to understand ourselves. Architecture should "Sing a Song/or/Laugh/or/Cry" or it will "Go Away"!

Solar Sails are more than mere energy-producing infrastructures. Solar Sails are a temple to the sun. Solar Sails are not intended to be merely didactic. Solar Sails are not just for visual excitement; they form and frame a new institution where engaging the public in a meaningful manner is the primary goal. Solar Sails are not about themselves. The sails are not about technology, nor are they about the D.O.E. Solar Sails are about our relationship to the sun and the celebration of life that it enables on the earth. This project is an offering to the sun.

Originally published in the Proceedings of the 90th Annual Meeting of the Association of Collegiate Schools of Architecture, 2002.

SETTLEMENT PATTERNS

INTRODUCTION
KIM TANZER AND RAFAEL LONGORIA

Urban design is Architecture and not a separate activity mediating between planning and building. It is the physical expression of society's hopes and intentions and a means of using and developing human and architectural potential involving areas of concern which do not recognize boundaries between public and private domains.[1]

Many architectural responses to sustainability have focused on energy efficiency and healthy practices at the individual building scale, but a potent argument is crystalizing that changes at the urban scale are the essential element. Sprawl is arguably the single most detrimental characteristic of our prevailing way of building. Yet many of the emerging models of green architecture (including some featured in this publication) accept uncritically these settlement patterns.

Ken Yeang pointed out in *The Green Skyscraper* that high-rise towers may be more ecologically friendly than the proverbial little cabin in the woods.[2] While this sounds counterintuitive, there are undeniable economies of scale and proximity inherent in the denser built environments, as well as considerable social, economic, and cultural benefits associated with urban living.

While market forces, as exemplified by mushrooming L.E.E.D. practices, are slowly waking up to the profit potential of energy-efficient buildings (and even here federal regulations are playing a significant role), changes at the scale of the city are harder to stimulate without government stewardship. Curitiba, Brazil has emerged as an international role model for other cities to follow. Jaime Lerner, its enlightened architect-mayor, transformed this once provincial outpost into a successful laboratory for green initiatives that span the full gamut from transportation and education to ecology, economy, social services, and culture.

As Richard Rogers writes in *Cities for a Small Planet*, "[t]he concept of the sustainable city recognizes that the city needs to meet our social, environmental, political and cultural objectives as well as our economic and physical ones. It is a dynamic organism as complex as the society itself and responsive enough to react to its changes."[3]

The essays in this section are cautionary tales from different times and places. Racism, intolerance, politics, pollution, and profiteering are all part of these stories. Far from implying that architecture has lost relevancy because of the emphasis on the urban scale or the magnitude of the problems, in each of the three cities studied—Chicago, Sarajevo, and Los Angeles— architectural proposals are indispensable to the solution.

1 Michael Wilford "Off to the Races, or Going to the Dogs?" Architectural Design, 54, 1/2, (1984): 8.

2 Ken Yeang, The Green Skyscraper: The Basis for Designing Sustainable Intensive Buildings (New York: Prestel, 1999), 27.

3 Richard Rogers, Cities for a Small Planet (London: Westview Press, 1997), 167.

In "Economy = Ecology," Ellen Grimes uses Chicago's Lake Calumet as a vehicle to illustrate the complex problems of postindustrial environments. It is a compact case study that efficiently traces the development of a North American urban ecosystem and addresses the complex ecological, economic and political issues of industrial contamination and bio remediation. Solutions are suggested through the development of catalytic scenarios, rather than conventional design proposals.

Sarajevo is a very different city facing a completely different sort of manmade disaster. The Bosnian capital went from hosting the 1984 Winter Olympics to becoming synonymous with ethnic cleansing in a frighteningly short span of time. Srdja Hrisafovic documents a story of destruction and reconstruction that raises issues of urban ecology and collective memory. Particularly poignant is the violent clash of urban and rural cultural values. Hrisafovic introduces principles of Ottoman city planning and describes the inherent sustainability of traditional urbanisms.

Anthony Denzer's "The Suburban Critique at Mid-Century: A Case Study" brings prejudice and politics closer to home in the remarkable story of a doomed utopian neighborhood development in postwar Los Angeles. In Denzer's words, the unrealized plan for community homes is "one of the most powerful answers to what would become the 'Levittown problem.'"

The design projects in this section illustrate how architects can use specific sites and problems to construct examples that have the potential to be replicated widely. All three projects address suburban sprawl in North America. The two teams comprised by Brian D. Andrews and W. Jude LeBlanc, and Mónica Ponce de León and Nader Tehrani confront the massive waste of space and resources in our contemporary cities by proposing imaginative, and sometimes radical, uses of underutilized sites, while Stephen Luoni addresses the pervasive flooding confronting so many American cities because of thoughtless development.

Andrews and LeBlanc's housing proposals create pedestrian environments in automobile-oriented cities by placing housing units where retail and strollers are already thriving—shopping malls. Far from being a one-note project, the design of the residential units provides for natural ventilation and solar screens taking lessons from the regional vernacular.

Downtown Miami is the backdrop for Ponce de León and Tehrani's critique of the single-minded way that transportation bureaucracies have inserted freeways into city centers. Their work illustrates an array of multivalent design strategies to transform urban wastelands into vital public spaces.

Luoni's pair of plans for Eustis, Florida constitute an effective example of thoughtful development for a small lakeside town. Legislation that protects wetlands is an essential part of this proposal which carefully balances ecological and economic concerns. Perhaps not coincidentally all the design projects featured in this section happen to be located in the American

Southeast, since this is an area where booming cities encroach on extremely fragile natural environments.

Eliel Saarinen's admonition to always consider the next-larger scale when designing is particularly important when sustainability is the goal. Without critical thinking at the scale of the city and the region, sustainable buildings can become little more than a well-meaning gesture.

ECONOMY = ECOLOGY
A scenario for Chicago's Lake Calumet
ELLEN GRIMES

THE PRESENT, PART 1: JANITOR WITH A VISION

Fed up with the concrete 'boxes' being added to Chicago's storied skyline, Mayor Daley and city planners are laying down the law to developers and architects.[1]

1 Roeder, "Daley Insists Architects Think Outside Box," 10a.

On February 16 2003, the *Sunday Chicago Sun-Times* headline read: "Daley: No More Ugly Buildings." Below this command, a follow-on headline read: "Demands developers stay on the cutting edge." The same front page also told you to "Fly the Flag" under an announcement "No help at the UN," as Powell's appeal to the U.N. for cooperation in the proposed invasion of Iraq appeared to have failed.

Inside the tabloid, the article describing the Daley decree had another title, one that revealed how our mayor-for-life proposed to solve the problem: "Daley insists architects think outside box." Unnamed staff let us know that the mayor is "laying down the law," an approach characterized as "all about the message." There will be no new mandates, no new regulations, just something described as "tighter control."

What's to control? The developers' desire for ugliness? Or their desire for profit, which apparently, in Chicago, at least, means exactly the same thing? And what sort of control are we talking about? If it is not regulatory control, is it just an exercise of political power, or more mysteriously, an exertion of some other kind of force?

A year and a half later, the same mayor is profiled in *Metropolis*, a fashionable design magazine, for another sort of crusade:

2 Chamberlain.

3 First elected in 1989, Richard M. Daley was known, until recently, as Chicago's "mayor-for-life." Son of Richard J. Daley, who had reigned as mayor from 1959 to 1976, the current Mayor Daley is part of a political machine that has controlled the mayor's office and city politics for most of the twentieth century. However, recent corruption charges and federal investigations may limit or end his control of city government.

he's a janitor with a vision. It starts with him noticing the trees are all gone and having them replanted. Suddenly life springs up, and there are cafés and people where there were none before. Then it becomes, let's not just make it attractive but a healthier place. Trees reduce the heat-island effect and clean the air. Landscaping is labor intensive, so we provide a lot of jobs. That has turned into a model of economic development based on green technologies, attracting renewable-energy companies, and creating a sustainable landscaping industry.[2]

Beautification and sustainability. Both issues attractive to any politician. Putting aside the peculiar position of Chicago's current mayor,[3] this almost inevitable convergence might promise a real opportunity for designers and architects. Aesthetics and economics—pleasures and resources—are linked in the material formats created by design. As these formats range in scale from infrastructure to candy wrappers, and move through time as production and waste processes, it seems that in this mix of organization, material, and information, there's a real opportunity to invent the postindustrial metropolis.

Inevitably referred to as "an ecological disaster," this approximately 20 square mile area 15 miles south of the city's downtown that's known as Lake Calumet, contains most of the land in city available for industrial development and is the location of the "most important harbor complex in the Great Lakes."[4] These 2,500 acres of industrial land are embedded in another 4,000 acres of open land which include the only remnants of the city's presettlement landscape, habitat for a number of endangered species (including the black-crowned night heron, the snowy egret, and the occasional peregrine falcon), along with the city's only legal hunting ground, and a substantial population of subsistence fisherman. Mixed into this landscape complex are extensive brownfields, including an 87 acre Superfund site. While some remediation has been carried out, significant contamination from P.C.B.s, lead, chromium, arsenic, and volatile organic compounds remains throughout the region and continues to affect both the local groundwater and Lake Michigan, the city's source of drinking water.

After the precipitous decline of Calumet's dominant business, the steel industry, in the 1970s and 1980s, the area had existed in a toxic state of suspended animation. Years of political stalemate, a series of utopian development proposals (for a world's fair, a new airport, a national park, etc.), and

4 *Mayer,* Chicago: Growth of a Metropolis, *186.*

5 City of Chicago, "Calumet Initiative."

continuing dumping and contamination, resulted in a familiar situation: a standoff between the area's remnant industry and the largely working-class and minority stewards of the area's remnant wilderness. Fearful of a decline in property values that would accompany an attempt to seek federal government funding for clean-up, the city's mayor and the remaining manufacturers resisted approving large-scale remediation for years.

However, by June 2006, something had changed. There was a federally funded plan for remediating the most contaminated site (a toxic-waste incinerator that exploded in the 1980s), the city had prepared a land-use plan, an open-space plan, and an ecological plan, and was beginning to implement a series of new initiatives in the area, including an environmental center that would support research and education and infrastructure improvements that would support industrial development. Called the Calumet Initiative, the mayor described the project as a demonstration of "economic and ecological rehabilitation in a complementary process."[5] It sought to preserve most of the existing open land, bringing it under a "new ecological management strategy." The idea was to maintain and support the existing industrial uses and clean up and preserve the existing open land. The result: Government policy and funding would support fragments of an unstable and declining industrial economy and create and maintain unstable fragments of the area's original ecology.

In many ways Lake Calumet is the ultimate postindustrial landscape. It is an outmoded, artificial topography publicly produced to serve the industrial economy that had fueled the city's development. The presettlement landscape has been extensively and intensively manipulated: Glacial ridges and dunes have been flattened out, new mountains of waste have been built, and the region's hydrology has been engineered in so many ways that no one is certain whether the local rivers drain into or out of the lake. The city's most complex biological systems sit side by side with its most toxic industrial ruins. Rusting coke ovens are framed by dense thickets of grasses and reeds. And it's a place where, during a perfect summer day, a cop stops to tell a bicyclist to "clear out now. We find a lot of dead bodies around here," because the wastelands have become a favorite site for gang executions.

THE PAST, PART 1: HISTORIES OF EXCHANGE

Close to 100 million years ago glaciers scoured out a gently varying topography of shifting sand dunes where the balance between water and dry land changed with the seasons. The complex gradients of the area's ecotone (a meeting point of northern boreal forest, western prairie, eastern deciduous forest, with shore line dune and swale wetlands) produced a some of the highest levels of biodiversity on the continent and an intensely complex ecosystem where arctic species are found alongside southwestern desert species and formed the largest wetland complex in the United States.[6]

6 *U.S. Department of Interior, 6, 7.*

Starting around 1400, indigenous nomads—first the Miami, and then Potowatami—established a series of trails on the glacial ridges that formed the sags, and created at least one canal linking local waterways. The Potowatamis, who managed to coexist with European traders and merchants through the 1830s, built a burial ground at the mouth of a river that connected Lake Calumet with the larger Lake Michigan. A swampy, grassy area, this savanna landscape held little attraction for the European eye. In 1823, shortly after the new United States of America had established a military installation at the mouth of a the river 10 miles north of the Calumet, a European traveler would write of the region, "The appearance of the country near Chicago offers but few features upon which the eye . . . can dwell with pleasure."[7] That same year, however, perhaps in a typical display of the difference between the emerging culture of the new nation and the habits of perception of the old world, Henry R. Schoolcraft predicted that the place will become "a depot for the inland commerce, between the northern and southern sections of the union, and a great thoroughfare for strangers, merchants, and travelers."[8]

7 *Mayer, 3.*

8 *Ibid.*

Indeed, the city was first and foremost a thoroughfare that became the commercial center of the nation, a creature of an investment boom fueled by the construction of a canal linking the Great Lakes and the Mississippi River basin. Close to forty years after the city had been incorporated and twenty years after the opening of the original canal southwest of the Loop, commercial water traffic had grown to such an extent that a second port needed to be established at Chicago. In 1869, after the close of the Civil War, federal funds were appropriated for the improvement of a small harbor near the site of the old Indian burial grounds, 15 miles directly south of the city's central business district, and large-scale industrialization of Lake Calumet began. Like much of the city's development during the nineteenth century, "The growth of the Calumet Harbor area was quick and unplanned, the result of the decisions of many people and corporations."[9]

9 *Ibid., 186.*

Two years later, in 1871, despite a fire which decimated the city's commercial core, the first cargo vessels arrived in the new port. In 1875, Brown Steel and Iron, the first steel plant at Lake Calumet, opened alongside a small residential settlement called "Irondale," founded as housing for steelworkers.[10] By 1881, George Pullman had built his sleeper car factory on the banks of Lake Calumet. The first products of the new factory were not railroad cars, however. Determined to protect his workers and their families from urban vices, Pullman put his assembly line to work manufacturing the materials for the village of Pullman, his utopian workers' community, just south of the sleeper-car works, west of Lake Calumet. The factory town became both an important attraction for visitors to the 1893 World's Columbian Exposition, and a year later, the location of a massive strike.

Calumet's location, topography, and ecology were particularly suitable for industrial development. "Well equipped with the prerequisites for heavy industry, (Lake Calumet) quickly became one of the most important industrial centers in the world."[11] The undeveloped, swampy land was cheap, and the river and lake complex meant ready access to water for waste disposal, shipping, and manufacturing. Calumet's location at the southern edge of Lake Michigan sat at an intersection point of the continental's primary transportation systems, providing immediate access to raw materials and global markets through the Great Lakes waterways and the meeting point of the eastern and western continental railroad systems.

By 1920, the area had become the largest steel producer in the world.[12] Through the 1930s and 1940s, Calumet's industrial businesses and working-class neighborhoods prospered. At the end of World War II, despite a

10 *Pacyga,* Chicago, City of Neighborhoods.

11 *Mayer, 234.*

12 *U.S. Department of Interior, 16.*

remarkable slowdown in growth in the city at large (once the world's fastest growing city at the turn of the nineteenth century, Chicago's population began to decline by 1950), the Calumet area continued to expand. In 1955, in anticipation of the opening of the St. Lawrence Seaway, which would bring oceangoing ships through Lake Michigan to the port at Lake Calumet, the Calumet Sag channel, which connected Lake Calumet to the Mississippi waterway, was enlarged to a scale that significantly exceeded the new Suez Canal.

When the first transatlantic vessel docked at the Calumet Harbor in 1959, the region was the site of some of the most intensive industrial production and exchange in the world. In less than a century, a complex ecology had evolved into a new type of economic niche, creating an industrial economy that extended Chicago's resource web around the globe. But the same dynamic that drove the development of the steel mills changed the scale of global shipping, and the port failed. New oceangoing ships were too large to make it through the St. Lawrence locks, and the new harbor complex never saw significant international traffic, declining from the one of the busiest ports in the world to the twenty-eighth largest U.S. port by the close of the twentieth century.[13]

13 *Department of Planning and Development,* Calumet Area Land Use Plan, 5.

THE PRESENT, PART 2: SUCCESSION OR STASIS

Some historians of science believe that modern ecology—particularly theories describing the evolution of species and landscapes—started in Calumet with the studies of the region by Henry Cowles at the turn of the nineteenth century. Cowles formulated a theory of ecological succession that explained how change worked in ecosystems; ironically, his work coincided with the rapid succession of industrial production over biological processes in the region. Later on, as ecologists sought to understand whether ecologies work on a cooperative or competitive model during the 1930s, and then, fully developed the notion of the ecosystem in the 1940s, research in the Calumet region continued to inform ecological thought—both scientific inquiry and the conservation management practices.[14]

14 *Examples include Aldof Leopold's writings on conservation in the 1950s.*

The area's unstable economic monoculture, following a trajectory that could have been predicted using Cowles's theories of ecological succession, reached a limit in the 1970s and exhausted itself. Advances in management systems generated by new uses of information for quality and cost control realized in cultures with less management/labor conflict, changes in the global distribution of demand, and the aging of the area's century-old production facilities, combined to make the region's "keystone" industry, steel, increasingly less competitive in global markets. By 1985, most of the region's steel plants had been shut down. When the last steel plant closed in the early 1990s, the region went from being the city's largest employer to the site of its highest unemployment rates. Over 40 percent of all employment in the area had disappeared.[15] At this point approximately 3,689 acres of wetland had been filled in, and slag covered 60 square miles at depths of 5 to 60 feet.[16] Indeed,

15 *Jones, "From Steel Town to 'Ghost Town.'"*

16 *U.S. Department of Interior,* 9.

throughout the development of the area, industrial dumping was considered a means of 'improving' the region—disease-breeding swamps were replaced with income-producing real estate. Now, all at once, the contamination carried by the slag was a financial liability. At this point, both the ecological system and the economic system had fragmented and atrophied, and the question was: What would succeed them?

As the twenty-first century began, a generation after the mill closings, it seemed that Calumet was just another example of an urban industrial site where the solution to short-term economic problems conflicted with long-term environmental issues, and local minority and working-class communities paid the price for the standoff. Big ideas for redeveloping the area failed, one after another, victims of politics and financing. Public initiatives and the private market both failed to find a way to produce value out of the region. But we can't pretend that these two choices—between big utopian ideas and market freefall—exhaust the possibilities.

There is another sort of potential in what remains that constructs a new species of design opportunity connecting events across time, building alignments between the flows of resources through economies and ecologies. Just as surprising alliances between biological systems and technology emerged as industry rose to dominance, why wouldn't there be equally unexpected reciprocities or convergences between the economic and the ecological emerging from the life of postindustrial cities? Out of necessity, we are left to speculate about a form of urbanism where the relations between environment, human collectivities, and economic flows become a source of materials and opportunities rather than resistance and stasis.

There is "the curious role played by architecture in ecological thought"[17] and the equally curious but less examined role economics plays in ecology. The extensive and complex history of the role of the natural, organic, wild, and biological in design and urban discourse is in strong contrast to the rather limited role played by economic theory, and is especially curious given the obvious relation between *oikos-nemein* (house-law, or economy) and *oikos-logos* (house-knowledge, or ecology). Classical notions of mimesis would support a long and varied relationship between architecture and biological systems, but appeared to have pushed aside the notion of economy. Even though Vitruvius speaks of *distribuio* or *oikos-nemein* in his descriptions of design and construction, his desire to follow the laws of the "cosmos" became more influential in architectural discourse. Alberti, in an attempt to explain how beauty is attained in architecture, would equate the laws of nature with the laws of beauty, and in turn, with the laws of architecture. Particularly, "throughout the nineteenth century, architects made frequent reference to the rapidly developing biological sciences."[18] These borrowings occasionally yielded new concepts "seminal for architectural practice,"[19] including the notion of structure and ideas about the relationship of process and form.

17 Wigley, "Recycling Recycling," 39.

18 Picon, "Architecture, Science, Technology," 294.

19 Ibid.

Contemporary discourse on the relation between architecture and biological systems either echoes nineteenth-century practices (e.g., Lynn's use of the idea of genetic recombination to generate form) or becomes a substitution of postmodernist "biological" technologies for the modernist machine technologies. Sometimes this is a weak rhetorical device—such as James Wines's affection for the Earth as the '"ultimate machine."[20] In other instances, this contemporary mimetic impulse generates new practices and concepts, typically focused on techniques and processes. Yeang's systems approach to ecological design yields an emphasis on "the interdependencies and interconnectedness in the biosphere and its ecosystem. Here the crucial property of ecological design is the connectedness between all activities, whether man-made or natural."[21] D.I.R.T. Studio's proposal for a World Trade Center memorial engages social systems with biological processes in a similar vein, using the cycles of seasonal change in the landscape to activate new civic forms of mourning and renewal.

However provocative and productive these approaches are, there is a limit to working in imitation of nature. That limit appears in situations like Calumet because designers are asked to participate in the manipulation of an environment with an intensive mix of human and nonhuman processes, a situation where classical mimesis is useless. The "natural" in a place like Calumet is a construct, and has no stability or essential character. Mimetic approaches depend upon a distinction between design interventions and the "nature" they imitate. Situations like Calumet can't be directly engaged if we respect that limit.

In classical thought, the analogy appears as a mode of combinatorial invention, distinct from linear computational problem-solving and different—less "regulated" and more inventive—than mimesis.[22] The analog, as a heuristic, finds a resemblance of relations, directing a focus on types, qualities,

20 *Wines*, Green Architecture, 9.

21 *Yeang*, The Green Skyscraper, *12.*

22 *Stafford*, Recombinancy.

263

and effects of forms of interconnection rather than formal correspondence. These analogical approaches to design offer particularly resilient and fertile methodological frameworks because they direct attention to the potential for convergence between various systems and processes. And, in particular, they offer a means of constructing elisions between economics, ecology, and their shared term, the *oikos* or household, the human environment. In a practice which relies upon an understanding of the biological as an analogic rather than mimetic reference, attention opens toward the relation between design work and biological systems, rather than issues internal to design discourse.

When Ernst Haechel, a German zoologist, first described the new science of ecology in 1866, he characterized this new form of inquiry as an understanding of the "economy of animals and plants."[23] Now, as the design of urban environments begins to benefit from the informational and computational power of digital technologies, it becomes possible to think of urban design as, in Yeang's terms, an "applied ecology."[24] However, the execution of an applied ecology requires an equally hardy "applied economy" because the analog between ecology and design operates through the economies which structure the flows of value and resources in a given context. The potential affiliation of these two types of systems through design has typically been limited by an understanding of economy as a merely practical technical process produced by the relentlessly rationalizing machine of late capitalism.

Economics makes it into architectural education only occasionally in the form of cost-estimating. In architecture's theoretical discourse, Colin Rowe's opposition between "ideas" and economics described in his "Chicago Frame" essay is normative: He complains that Chicago architects "frankly accepted the conditions imposed by the speculator" and limited themselves to producing buildings which were no more than the logical instruments of investment absent of ideas.[25] Likewise, recent attempts by contemporary theorists recapitulate the notion that the economic erases thought, by elevating market logics over theoretical discourse. The recent embrace of the

23 *Wigley, 42.*

24 *Yeang.*

25 *Rowe, "The Chicago Frame,"* 102.

"entrepreneur" or of "triple top line" decision-making[26] is nothing more than the product of a naïve appropriation of outdated business theory masquerading as the embrace of a new pragmatism. This failure misses the potential that economies have to use difference to create value and catalyze exchange and manage complex information across many scales, in networks of relation that easily affiliate themselves with nonhuman biological systems.[27]

Recent research on the "new" economy of postindustrial production demonstrates that markets often work as directed networks, where reciprocity and reliance over time brings more sustainable rewards than short-term optimization.[28] This conception of the new economy reflects a "fundamental shift in business thinking—and behavior—today: the economy is not a mechanism, businesses are not machines. They are co-evolving, unpredictable organisms with a constantly shifting business ecosystem that no one controls."[29]

Like economies and ecologies, cities are complex systems: Most interactions are nonlinear; there are multiple decision-makers, time scales, layers of organization, and exchanges across space.[30] Even in a city like Chicago, which has been run by a small group of Irish-American men for the most of the last century, hierarchical command and control organizations survive at a very high cost. Technocratic problem-solving, that simplifies in order to optimize, works against the vitality and potential embedded in urban environments. Unfortunately, until quite recently, most economic theory relied upon analytic frameworks that disengaged small-scale interactions (micro-economics) from large-scale interactions (macro-economics), and split short-term effects from long-term effects.

Similarly, systems theorists that study sustainable environments find that command and control relationships fail to produce the consumption patterns necessary to long-term viability.[31] As a number of urban theorists and historians have observed, industrial "cities are unstable ecosystems far from

26 *See various discussions of "entrepreneurial" practice by Michael Speaks, including "Design Intelligence, Part 1: Introduction." A + U: Architecture and Urbanism, 12 (December 2002): 10–18.*

27 *A number of Fuller's projects in the 1960s, most notably the World Game, are an exception.*

28 *Baribasi.*

29 *deGeus,* The Living Company, *quote by Dyson.*

30 *Pulselli, "Self-organization as a resource."*

31 *Ibid.*

32 DeLanda, 28.

33 Pusselli, 111.

equilibrium"[32] plagued by the risks of oversimplified, homogeneous resource webs (think of Lake Calumet and steel production). A "soft" model of urban planning,[33] designed to produce intelligence about the multitude of interacting feedback loops in urban environments, could produce the sort of non-planned adaptive processes that reconfigure forms of consumption and produce more self-sustaining and self-regulating environments. This is hardly a fantastic notion. A look at historical instances of radical changes in consumption patterns, such as the rise of suburban life in postwar America, is instructive. As Easterling demonstrates in her book, *Organization Space: Landscapes, Highways, and Houses in America*, suburban subdivision development produced a particular pattern of consumption, sustained by networks of exchange that linked specialized forms of financing, ownership, and construction, and reconfigured resource webs and landscapes.

FUTURES, PART 1: GRAY CITY TO WHITE CITY TO GREEN CITY

The city's current land use plan for Calumet maintains a substantial amount of available land zoned for industry, about 2,500, of which 1,500 acres are occupied by existing industries, and 1,000 acres are vacant brownfield sites abandoned by manufacturers who shut down operations in the 1970s and 1980s. This 1,000 acres is "the largest amount of vacant industrial land in the city."[34] The city believes that the area remains an attractive site for industrial development because the "same attributes that attracted former occupants still exist in these properties: good transportation and accessible, buildable locations."[35] The area continues to support significant business activity. It is the third largest intermodal center in the world after Hong Kong and Singapore, producing twice as much traffic as any other U.S. metropolitan area.[36] And despite a 40 percent of reduction in capacity since the 1970s, the region remains the largest steel manufacturer in the United States.

34 Department of Planning and Development, 10.

35 Ibid., 13.

36 Ibid., 5.

The remaining 10,500 acres include 4,600 acres devoted to streets, alleys, waterways, and other infrastructure, and 4,000 acres of vacant land that will become part of an open space reserve.[37] This open space reserve, however, is highly fragmented.

37 Ibid., 14.

The Calumet Initiative development plan is a typical municipal planning document overlaid with an imaginative and utopian desire to "preserve" rare and precious examples of wilderness. The reality, readily acknowledged by city officials, is that the plan to maintain a significant industrial presence in the area effectively reduces the "wild" open land to intensive garden plots of indigenous plantings and habitat. While there is a genuine ambition to develop something described as an "industrial ecology," planning and environmental officials admit that they don't know what that term means.[38]

38 Wesphal, Public discussion.

Calumet persists as a fertile site for the convergence of ecology and economy. The three big issues for the region—dealing with hazardous wastes, returning vacant land to productivity, and connecting fragments of open space—need an intelligence that combines an obsessive attention to the minutia of everyday city life with the speculative force of a vision that moves without hesitation between large and small events.

As part of an exhibit on future visions of Chicago exhibited at the Art Institute of Chicago in 2006, we[39] proposed a scenario for simultaneously remediating the brownfields at Calumet and constructing a new, sustainable economy in the area. Presented as a short film, we proposed the scenario as a theoretical experiment that becomes an argument for design's role as a mediator between economies and ecologies and helps reframe or reprogram our understanding of the possibilities for postindustrial urban environments.

39 See project credits at the end of the article.

These scenarios operated as provisional structures for making new possibilities material and knowable. By devising scenarios, instead of conventional architectural representations, we could demonstrate the operations of catalytic processes, the transformative events which change the operation of systems, in time, with the force of a real proposition. Rather than propose a utopian project, or declare a critique, we constructed an open-ended, propositional narrative that suggested tactics for catalyzing change, and designed an installation for broadcasting these simultaneously real and fantastic stories. We used the installation as an opportunity to discover, experiment with, materialize, and engage the surprising logics operating in postindustrial cities. These authorless and unauthorized constructions of possibilities sought to combine the generative intensity of Hejduk's masques and with the plausibility of a management consultant's strategic plan.

Our narrative starts with Chicago's "janitor-with-a-vision," Mayor Daley, and uses the janitor's job, clean-up and trash collection, as the catalyst for the construction and restoration of Calumet's landscape and infrastructure. This revaluation of waste occurs through the deployment of biological processes—

40 Carmen, "From laboratory to landscape."

namely bio- and phytoremediation processes—that cost less than 20 percent of conventional "remove and contain" remediation practices.[40] A revival of nineteenth-century American homesteading policies, reinvented as an "ecosteading" program, becomes a new means of managing the city's waste products. Much as in a healthy ecosystem, a species of "decomposers" evolves to reprocess waste into valuable resources. Presented as a purely local phenomenon, the city institutes the ecosteads in the largest expanse of vacant land in Chicago, the Lake Calumet region.

An adaptive process, the ecosteads start as parasitical occupations of abandoned industrial infrastructure, including both built structures and the engineered waterways in the area. The reoccupation of both water and structure complement each other and become a classic example of a "succession" ecology. The water-based industrial infrastructure (barges and port facilities) become launching platforms for landscape remediation, as barges bring phytoremediating plant materials (poplars, various prairie grasses, sunflowers, and other plants with the capacity to harvest toxins from contaminated soils) from restored prairies south of the industrial zone. The new water transport relieves highway and road congestion, complements dune and swale restoration, and integrates emerging residential and commercial development with the rest of the city.

The occupation of structures, particularly large-scale structures, occurs as they are "reprogrammed" as bioremediation facilities. Some of the new programs include smelting processes that recover the metals harvested through phytoremediation, organic waste-composting facilities, inorganic waste sorting and processing facilities, biodomes which contain non-native photoremediation plantings, and enterprises that develop and research biological remediation processes. All programs are processes constructed as ecologies and economies: All new postindustrial infrastructure evolves out of remediation of existing infrastructure, and all new residential and economic development evolves out of existing communities and resources. Monoculture is impossible; old and new infrastructure, old and new communities are mixed. Residential zones begin to grow from existing neighborhoods, as the scale of the Victorian workers' village of Pullman extends across the site, integrating local residential communities with the landscape. Finally, all local remediation efforts evolve into global remediation networks, linking the ecosteads to local and global processes of exchange.

We'd like to suggest that designers can be hopeful monsters devising intricate multiscaled material organizations which support and sustain successors to industrial culture. As Pulselli puts it, "If we do not hazard a project, if we cannot imagine 'hopeful monsters' to drop in the river of human evolution, we won't get anywhere."[41]

41 Pulselli.

Originally published in the Proceedings of the 93rd Annual meeting of the Association of Collegiate Schools of Architecture, 2005.

ACKNOWLEDGMENTS

This article is derived from research produced to support an installation, Chicago Scenarios, exhibited at the Art Institute of Chicago in 2005. The author wishes to acknowledge the tremendous contribution to the work by the project team, below.

REFERENCES

Barabasi, A. *Linked*, London: Plume, 2002.

Carman, E. "From Laboratory to Landscape: A Case History and Possible Future Direction for Phyto-Enhanced Soil Bioremediation," in *Manufactured Sites, Rethinking the Post-Industrial Landscape*, edited by N. Kirkwood, London and New York: Spon, 2001.

Chamberlain, L. "Mayor Daley's Green Crusade," *Metropolis*, July 2004.

City of Chicago "Calumet Initiative," <http://egov.cityofchicago.org/city>.

City of Chicago Department of Planning and Development *Calumet Area Land Use Plan*, Chicago, Ill., 2001.

Cronon, W. *Nature's Metropolis, Chicago and the Great West*, New York: W.W. Norton, 1992.

de Geus, A. *The Living Company: Habits for Survival in a Turbulent Business World*, Boston, Mass.: Harvard Business School Press, 1997.

Easterling, K. *Organization Space: Landscapes, Highways, and Houses in America*, Cambridge, Mass.: M.I.T. Press, 1999.

Jones, E. L. "From Steel Town to 'Ghost Town': A Qualitative Study of Community Change in Southeast Chicago," unpublished master's thesis, Loyola University, Chicago, Ill., 1998.

Lydersen, K. "Your Mayor Could Clean Up this Mess," *Chicago Reader*, June 18, 2004, 1.

Mayer, H., and R. Wade *Chicago: Growth of a Metropolis*, Chicago, Ill.: University of Chicago Press, 1969.

Roeder, D. and F. Speilman "Daley Insists Architects Think Outside Box," *Chicago Sun Times*, February 16, 2003, 10a–11a.

Pacyga, D. and E. Skerrett *Chicago, City of Neighborhoods: Histories and Tours*, Chicago, Ill.: Loyola University Press, 1986.

Picon, A. "Architecture, Science, Technology and the Virtual Realm," in *Architecture and the Sciences: Exchanging Metaphor*, edited by A. Picon, Princeton, N.J.: Princeton Architectural Press, 2003.

Pulselli, R., S. Bastianoni and E. Tiezzi "Self-Organization as a Resource for a Sustainable City Planning," in *The Sustainable City II: Urban Regeneration and Sustainability*, edited by C. A. Brebbia, J. F. Martin-Duque, and L. C. Wadhwa, Boston, Mass.: W.I.T. Press, 2002.

Rowe, C. "The Chicago Frame," *The Mathematics of the Ideal Villa* Cambridge, Mass.: M.I.T. Press, 1982.

Stafford, B. *Recombinancy: Binding the Computational "New Mind" to the Combinatorial "Old Mind" Visual Analogy*, Cambridge, Mass.: M.I.T. Press, 1999.

U.S. Department of Interior, National Park Service Midwest Region, *Calumet Ecological Park Feasibility Study*, 1998.

Project credits:

Design team: Elva Rubio, Ellen Dineen Grimes, Jana Fiester, Carolyn Young, Linnea Oliver

Contributors: Joshua Cooper, Deeg Snyder, Jay Longo, Ananth Sampathkumar, Lina Lee, Ricardo Nabholz, Gerould Wilhelm, David Yocca, Chris Whelan, Siddarth Ramakrishnan, George Miller-Ramos, Karl Gustafson, Patty Mayle, Susan Hickey

Photo credits: Jordi Guillumet, Monica Rosello

Sponsors: School of Architecture—University of Illinois at Chicago, Gensler, Holopro, Conservation Design Forum

Wesphal, L., and S. Melk. Public discussion at the Calumet Research Summit, Hammond, Ind., January 10–11, 2006.

Wigley, M. "Recycling Recycling," in *Eco-Tec Architecture of the In-Between*, edited by A. Marras, New York: Princeton Architectural Press, 1999.

Wines, J. *Green Architecture*, Cologne: Taschen, 2000.

Yeang, K. *The Green Skyscraper: The Basis for Designing Sustainable Intensive Buildings*, Munich: Prestel Verlag, 1999.

SARAJEVO
Ecological reconstruction after the "urbicide"

SRDJA HRISAFOVIC

INTRODUCTION

The reality of *urbicide*[1] (in parallel to the notion of genocide) was perpetuated in Sarajevo during the recent war and brought the world's attention to the destruction of the city. During that time, Sarajevo, strangled deep in the bottom of a valley, surrounded by mountains and the Serbs' guns, was receiving thousands of shells daily. Like the rest of the world, I was appalled by the atrocities, the force, and the destructive energies pounded on that city.

Being a native of the city, often I kept thinking: Was it a military and territorial strategy that dictated the rules of the city's destruction, or was it an attempt to nullify the culture of urbanity and cosmopolitan atmosphere for which the Bosnian capital was famous?

In asking the above question, it is tempting to think that it is perhaps the second alternative that should be considered. There is enough evidence to suggest that throughout history urban centers frequently became the target of nonurban destructive powers. But to think that in modern times the same pattern still applies, that buildings, centres of culture and civilization could be erased because of their urban connotation, is troublesome, to say the least.

The aim of the paper is to pay a tribute to Sarajevo which has had an urban identity for five centuries, where various cultures and religions have lived together, then to debate the above thesis and initiate a discussion pertaining to the themes of destruction and reconstruction. Special attention will be paid to possible strategies for the renewal of Sarajevo's cultural urbanity and eco-development heritage.

CONSTRUCTION, OR THE GROWTH OF SARAJEVO

Scanning Sarajevo from mountain we can discern two formations, the oriental and European town. The oriental town is made of lovely houses surrounded by gardens. The structure are low, horizontal, unpretentious, placed in layers all over the adjacent slopes. Here and there a minaret or poplar breaks the pattern. The view is marvellously harmonious, calm, and comprehensive—the very image of an old civilisation.[2]

Sarajevo has always been an important crossroads of different cultures of the world. Since ancient times, it has acted as a gateway for the peoples of Greece and Asia Minor migrating towards the midwest of Europe and as a link between the Mediterranean and northern Europe. Thanks to its geographical position, it has been influenced by a great number of different cultures and

1 *Marshall Berman invented a word, "urbicide," the murder of a city, in the early 1980s. The term was also used during the war by a group of architects from Sarajevo to refer to the atrocities committed against the urban life of the city.*

2 *Dusan Grabrian,* The Bosnian Oriental Architecture in Sarajevo *(Ljubljana: D.D.U. Universum, 1984), 136.*

271

The City. All photos by Professor Momir Hrisafovic, University of Sarajevo.

civilizations which came together, struggled against one another, but then mixed and stayed together on this same land.

The urban structure of Sarajevo originates from the middle of the fifteenth century. In that period the Ottomans occupied Bosnia and founded the settlement of *Saray-ovasi*, i.e., "the palace in the field." The name "Sarajevo" was mentioned for the first time in a letter written by Firuz Beg in 1507. Influenced by the traditional Oriental-Islamic concept of urban place, Sarajevo shared several common elements which are characteristic to every Islamic town. The most important one is that commercial and residential areas are kept strictly apart. The market is the vital part of a city, usually located at an important junction on the main road. The housing areas are situated outside and around the market, and the houses are detached with courtyards and enclosed by a wall facing the street.

The city was built on five postulates of urban design. By today's standards this could be called ecological urbanism: "The road is the spine and the valley its shape, the slopes are the body, the Charshija (business centre) its heart; the vegetation its lungs, and the river its soul."[3] For centuries Sarajevo was developed using these metaphors for the body to zone the city.

3 Juraj Neidhart and Dusan Grabrian, Arhitektura Bosne i Put u Savremeno *(Ljubljana: CZP, 1957), 50.*

The Charshija, i.e., the business centre, was laid out in the valley and contained all the public buildings important to the city: prominent prayer houses, hotels, public baths, schools, covered markets, and artisans. The business district as the heart of the city had the regular urban pattern of typical oriental cities and was characterized by a very pronounced separation of administration and official buildings from the residential areas. This type of town planning is characteristic of Islamic culture which favours urban life.

Charshija (left) and Mahala (right).

The Ottomans always retained the existing urban structure of the places they colonized and frequently imposed this concept of zoning on them.

The mahala, i.e., the residential areas, called the body of the city, were developed on the slopes of the valley. Separated from the *charshija*, the residential area followed a more irregular urban pattern. The street pattern followed the configuration of the ground, and at every streetcrossing some public buildings could be found: a mosque and school, market or drinking-water fountain. Houses developed according to unwritten architectural laws based on two major postulates: access to sun and access to view with respect to the neighbourhood. To achieve what we would call today an excellent base for ecological design, Sarajevo developed a major longitudinal east–west axis, widely open toward the sun and views.

Whenever it was possible, the houses were placed at street crossings where a picturesque view could be obtained. If the house was erected on the street leading to the market place, attempts were made to give it such a position that the market place with its life could be overlooked. The neighbour who built his house later, placed it in such a manner that he, too, had a fine view but at the same time he took care that his house did not obstruct the sun and the view from the neighbouring house.[4]

4 *Dusan Grabrian*, The Bosnian Oriental Architecture in Sarajevo, *170.*

Over the centuries, Sarajevo became a cosmopolitan city where many religions and nationalities took root and learned how to live together. From the Ottoman-inspired eastern end of the city, narrow and steep, Sarajevo gradually spread to the west, under the influence of the Austro-Hungarian

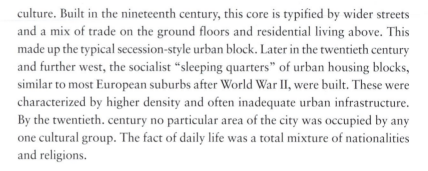

Ottoman (left), Austro-Hungarian (center) and Socialist (right).

culture. Built in the nineteenth century, this core is typified by wider streets and a mix of trade on the ground floors and residential living above. This made up the typical secession-style urban block. Later in the twentieth century and further west, the socialist "sleeping quarters" of urban housing blocks, similar to most European suburbs after World War II, were built. These were characterized by higher density and often inadequate urban infrastructure. By the twentieth. century no particular area of the city was occupied by any one cultural group. The fact of daily life was a total mixture of nationalities and religions.

DESTRUCTION

What I sense deep in the city destroyers, panic-ridden souls is a malicious animus against everything urban, everything urban that is, against a complex semantic cluster that includes spirituality, morality, language, taste, and style.[5]

5 Bogdan Bogdanovic, "Murder of the City," The New York Review, May 27, 1993, 20.

In this paper we will not discuss the political, nationalistic, or religious reasons that triggered the war in Bosnia. What interests us is the devastation of Sarajevo on such a large scale and to what extent the urban form and the urbanity enabled and provoked such a long and painful destruction.

How can it be that such excellent bases for urban and architectural design were also contributors to such destruction? Access to the sun and views opened up Sarajevo like the palm of a hand. The defenceless city was exposed to brutal shelling from the relatively safe and comfortable positions in the mountain strongholds above. Such open urban form that promoted the value of good neighbours plainly did not serve the city in a time of war!

Another reason for the city's destruction may not have been that it was merely defenceless but that it was *a city* at all. "From the fourteenth century onward, the word urbanity in most European languages stood for dignity, sophistication, the unity of thought and word, word and feeling, feeling and action."[6]

6 Ibid., 20.

The ferocious power with which Serbs pounded the city suggested an enormous hatred of this urbanity. Their military strategy was the old Mediterranean strategy of siege, one that employed long suffocation rather than the rapid gaining of territory which was practically so possible with Sarajevo in the early stage of the war. Ed Vulliamy, journalist of *The Guardian*, described the siege of Sarajevo as "a piece of violent theatre," an operation that was designed to destroy the morale of a country by removing its heart. It is widely known that the Serbian army comprised many rural Serbs. Serb leaders exploited their mistrust for urbanity with a siege strategy that gained momentum to become a massive and relentless insult to a civilian urban population. Thirty-five thousand of Sarajevo's Serbs stayed inside the city during the war experiencing shelling, humiliation, and death from nonurban Serbs. As a journalist said:

Sarajevo was a sophisticated, urban, modern city quite unlike the villages and small towns of the rest of the country. This difference has had an awful consequence. Many of those shelling the city from the hills are Serbs from surrounding villages or Serbs who had migrated to Sarajevo from the countryside. No one, including the urbanised Serbs of Sarajevo, has any time for them.[7]

This suggests that this conflict was also about rural vs. urban values. Lebbeus Woods argues that the growth of a cosmopolitan environment in the city generated hostility from the rural areas which had remained sectarian and xenophobic. This view is also supported by Bogdan Denitch who argues that: "The war in Bosnia was an 'urbicide', an act of revenge on the part of the 'local rednecks', who had always hated the city community."[8]

Throughout history, urban centres were frequently targeted by nonurban destructive powers (Huns, Tartars, Vandals, etc.). To be specific, wild tribes destroyed cities because they didn't understand them, couldn't use them, couldn't live in them. The historian Ibn Khaldun, for one, highlighted this fact

7 *Belgrade correspondent,* "Requiem for Sarajevo," The Economist, *August 21, 1993, 57.*

8 *Bogdan Denitch,* Ethnic Nationalism: The Tragic Death of Yugoslavia *(Minneapolis, Minn.: University of Minnesota Press, 1994), 27.*

City Centre 1992 (left), Olympic Hall Zetra 1992 (center), and Magribija Mosque 1992 (right).

in his famous *Prolegomena*, in referring to the dynamic of power between the Bedouins and the citydwellers in North Africa and the Near East. But to think that in modern times the same pattern still applies, that buildings, centres of culture and civilization could be erased because of their urban connotation is very disturbing.

Conveniently positioned on the mountains overlooking the city, the Serbs were killing the body of Sarajevo, by destroying the buildings, but also the spiritual base and the intellectual fundaments which are the very soul of the city. The physical damage is reparable, but to repair the damage to the soul of Sarajevo is a much more difficult task. Eleven thousand citizens of Sarajevo were killed, 62,000 were wounded and more than 120,000 fled the city.[9]

The cultural heritage of Bosnia-Herzegovina suffered major destruction. The result is what a Council of Europe Report has called "a cultural catastrophe." Historic architecture including 1,200 mosques, 150 churches, four synagogues and over 1,000 other monuments of culture, works of art, as well as cultural institutions, including major museums, libraries, archives and manuscript collections, have been systematically targeted and destroyed. The losses include not only the works of art, but also crucial documentation that might aid in their reconstruction.

Bosnia's National and University Library, a handsome pseudo-Moorish building, and a recognisable symbol of Sarajevo since 1896, was shelled by incendiary grenades and burned for three days. Most of its irreplaceable contents were reduced to ashes. Before the fire, the library held 1.5 million volumes, including over 155,000 rare books and manuscripts. Three months earlier, Sarajevo's Oriental Institute, home to one of the largest collection of Islamic and Jewish manuscript texts and Ottoman documents in southeastern Europe, was shelled with incendiary grenades and burned. In each case, the library alone was targeted; adjacent buildings stand intact.[10]

What we are trying to stress here is that Serb forces did not target the destruction of militarily important buildings and districts but systematically destroyed all urban structures. A spiritual, cultural genocide occurred by targeting the places where people gathered to live out their collective lives and where their collective memory was stored. This is why reparation of the damage cannot be limited just to reconstruction but also to the comprehensive renovation of the social structures in the urban area.

RECONSTRUCTION

Yet again and again the positive forces of co-operation and sentimental communion have brought people back to the devastated urban sites, to repair the wasted cities, the desolation of many generations. Ironically, yet consolingly, cities have repeatedly outlived the military empires that seemingly destroyed them forever. Damascus, Baghdad, Jerusalem, Athens still stand on the sites they originally occupied, alive though little more than fragments of their ancient foundations remain in view.[11]

9 See *Zavod za Planiranje i Razvoj Grada*, Strategija Obnove I Razvoja *(Sarajevo, 1998), 17–20.*

National and University Library 1992.

10 See Andras Riedlmayer *(61st I.F.L.A. General Conference, Harvard University, 20–25 August, 1995).*

11 Lewis Mumford, The City in History *(London: Secker & Warburg, 1961), 54.*

European cities destroyed in World War II generally followed two trends of reconstruction. The first one is the "nostalgic approach": the recapturing of the past by faithfully reconstructing the historic fabric of the area; Warsaw is a good example of this. The second one is the "brave new world alternative," where an entire new city is built, like Coventry for example.

Both examples offer some similarities to Sarajevo, in that the cities' centres received extensive bombing, and entire cultural-historical areas suffered comprehensive damage. These cities, however, did not experience civil war. Besides, they were united against a common enemy. Reconstruction did not have to solve the complicated problem of multicultural coexistence within the city. In this sense, the right approach to Sarajevo will not be a simple one. The damage done to the city was not caused by the typical random shelling of an ordinary war, aiming at military and economic targets, but the systematic destruction of all urban installations, cultural and symbolic targets. The result was not only the devastation of architectural heritage, but also the cultural and spiritual fundaments of the city. Therefore, reparation cannot be limited to the usual reconstruction activities of wartorn cities.

Lessons for the reconstruction of Sarajevo could also be drawn from yet another example. Beirut suffered from ethnic and religious differences for almost a decade. Like Sarajevo, the level of destruction of urban structures and architecture was extensive and focused around the central district and the historic core. Multicultural coexistence in the city also suffered a similar fate.

The reconstruction program for Beirut, according to Angus Gavin,[12] recognized that the city had become socially and psychologically split. The preliminary plans for reconstruction were based on encouraging the city to celebrate its heritage but also to look forward to the future. Surviving buildings and spaces were integrated within a new environment of modern architecture and new infrastructure that replaced the old inefficient systems. The central district became the focus of the healing process: Redesign of the public domain, establishing areas around the city to which people were drawn and encouraged to mix. This has produced a large pedestrian-friendly environment and diverse cultural heritage attractions, which helped rebuild the national and pluralistic identity of Beirut. Most importantly, the plan recognized the special qualities of place and exploited the features that had originally brought people to the area.

Beirut went for a compromise, opting for a balance between new development and the restoration of the older city structure. The "nostalgic approach" was combined with the "brave new world" approach of building a new environment. For the citizens of Beirut, a very significant part of the healing process was the references made to their different cultures and history. It was expected that these references should happen in the public realm, in the open-space network within the city to provide locations that would promote multicultural coexistence by encouraging the community to mix.

12 *See Angus Gavin*, Beirut Reborn *(London: Academy Edition, 1996).*

277

This method of reconstruction provides principles that could be applied to the reconstruction program of Sarajevo. Learning from the Beirut experience Sarajevo should:

First and foremost focus on the reconstruction of all common, centralised and decentralised urban structures permitting a normal co-existence of various cultures. Furthermore, the material expressions of the different ways of life must not be sacrificed in favour of some forced kind of uniformity. Even though all districts have suffered damage to a greater or lesser extent, the aim of the reconstruction activities should be to simply repair the damage while retaining the specific features of the corresponding district. The multi-cultural co-existence should also find an expression in the various urban life-forms.[13]

A more radical theory for the reconstruction of Sarajevo is the one advanced by Lebbeus Woods. His theory is based on the nature of the relationship between war and architecture. War acts as an aggressive stimulant to the design profession. It exposes the need for a response to the changing social and political climate, revolutionizing design concepts for the urban environment. The natural reaction of the public, according to Woods, is to restore the city by introducing a copy of the original fabric. But that is also an attempt to deny that war ever existed by wiping out all traces of its occurrence, erasing the memories of destruction and loss that linger in the old city.

Important civic and cultural monuments no doubt should be restored to their undamaged condition, as tokens of past coherence that might serve as models of civilized thought and activity, though never as re-affirmations of a past social order that ended in war. The attempt to restore the fabric of old cities to their former condition is, however, a folly that not only denies present conditions, but impedes the emergence of an urban fabric and a way of life based upon them. Wherever the restoration of war-devastated urban fabric has occured in the form of replacing what has been damaged or destroyed, it ends as parody, worthy only of the admiration of tourists.[14]

Woods' concept design sketches for a new Sarajevo honored the scars of bomb damage on the city's structures, exhilarating the healing process through confrontation and constant reminders of the effects of the war. I found this concept, of scars and scabs left behind by war, too brutal. It is more likely that the citizens of Sarajevo require a more subtle approach to commemorate the war. This multiethnic community is too fragile to accept such a bold statement which could possibly obstruct reconciliation. Stability of the community must be re-established to contrive a city that fosters multiculturalism to the degree that was present before the outbreak of the war.

13 Raymond Rehnicer, "Muslims, Serbs, Croats and Jews Used to Live Together in Peace" (Documentation of the 4th International Conference on Architectural Heritage, Graz, 1993), 51.

14 Lebbeus Woods, War and Architecture (New York: Princeton Architectural Press, 1993), 10.

To renew Sarajevo means to simultaneously renew its body and its soul. This can be achieved only if the process of rebuilding its architecture is accompanied by the process of restoring its social structure, simultaneously with the totality of its environment, its ecology, and its landscape. In the case of Sarajevo, it is precisely this unity of the local landscape, the regional ecosystem, and the city's architecture that has been so characteristic of the way of building and living in the city through the centuries of its existence. This is what I previously referred to as Sarajevo's centuries-long tradition of ecological urbanism. It is therefore my position that the most appropriate model for Sarajevo's postwar reconstruction is the eco-city model. But, there is no need to import an eco-city model, the eco-urbanist principles have been a basic ingredient of Sarajevo's vernacular urban design from its beginnings in the sixteenth century.

Sustainable urban development and the ecological design and planning of cities are concepts which are well researched and established in contemporary theory.[15] One particularly interesting version of the theory of the sustainable city has been developed by architect Richard Rogers. It could be very relevant to Sarajevo, as a bold and new approach, but one which citizens could identify with. According to Rogers:

The concept of the sustainable city recognises that the city needs to meet our social, environmental, political and cultural objectives as well as economic and physical ones. It is a dynamic organism as complex as the society itself and responsive enough to react swiftly to its changes. The sustainable city is a city of many facets . . . [One of them is] An ecological city, which minimises its ecological impact, where landscape and built form are balanced and where buildings and infrastructure are safe and resource-efficient.[16]

Future sustainable development of Sarajevo, understood in Rogers' terms, should be based on the creation of the compact city. Rejection of single-function development and the dominance of the car, the compact city should depend on a clean transport system and streets which belongs to the pedestrian and the community. Public-transport nodes should be developed around the centres of social and commercial activities, to provide focal points around which neighbourhoods should be developed. A network of these neighbourhoods, each with their own public spaces, should accommodate a diversity of overlapping private and public activities.

Sustainable Compact Cities could, I contend, reinstate the city as the ideal habitat for a community-based society. It is an established type of urban structure that can be interpreted in all manner of ways in response to all manner of cultures. Cities should be about the people they shelter, about face-to-face contact, about condensing the ferment of human activity, about generating and expressing local cultures.[17]

15 *See in particular the works of:* M. Breheny, Sustainable Development and Urban Form; H. Girardet, Cities, S. Van der Ryn and P. Caltrope, Sustainable Communities; S. Van der Ryn and S. Cowan, Ecological Design; R. Rogers, Cities for a Small Planet; L. Arkin, Sustainable Cities.

16 *Richard Rogers,* Cities for a Small Planet *(London: Faber and Faber Limited, 1997), 167.*

17 *Ibid., 40.*

In Sarajevo's case, the eco-city model is one that can provide a meaningful and healthy environment by involving the citizens in reconstructing their city in accordance with the principles which both revive the past and build a better future. It is through respect for the ecological principles of city building that Sarajevo can recover both its body and its soul. Eco-city Sarajevo is the project which all ethnic and religious groups in the city should embrace in their effort to restore a multicultural and tolerant society. Ecological urbanism is the very core of their common heritage. Restoring these principle will declare the final defeat of the perpetrators of *urbicide*.

The aim of the present paper is not to debate the detailed technicalities of this view, however. Future studies will hopefully carry on this task.

Originally published in the 1999 Association of Collegiate Schools of Architecture International Conference Proceedings.

THE SUBURBAN CRITIQUE AT MID-CENTURY
A case study
ANTHONY DENZER

In January 1946 in Los Angeles, a group of motion-picture cartoonists began to discuss forming a housing cooperative in response to the city's housing emergency. They could not have anticipated that they were in fact beginning a political odyssey that would last nearly four years and would become cited as a nationally prominent example of discrimination by civil-rights activists. Nor could they have predicted that the project, as it evolved, would come to constitute an early critique of the postwar suburban pattern in the United States, and one of the most powerful answers to what would become the "Levittown problem."

The group called itself "Community Homes." Within weeks eighty-eight families subscribed, the group drew up a prospectus and by-laws, and they bought 100 acres of land in a rural area of Los Angeles. They forecasted a community of 280 families, and they were fully subscribed in a matter of months. The group began working with architect Gregory Ain, who assembled a "dream team" of other architects, landscape architects, planners, and local housing officials. Because of this concentration of critical activity, Community Homes may be seen as the first fully conceived social and aesthetic solution to the city's postwar emergency, and certainly one of the first in the country.

The project was not initiated as a political or architectural provocation; it was a collaboratively developed solution to an urgent problem. Immediately after World War II, the national housing shortage was experienced especially strongly in Los Angeles. The city's housing supply was already stretched thin; first, due to migration from the "dust bowl" during the 1930s and, second, because of a disproportionately African American influx that relocated during the war to work in defense industries. With a third wave, the resettlement of veterans, came a true emergency. For each of the next five years, according to market analyses, 100,000 units of new housing would be needed to satisfy demand. As a stop-gap measure, the city erected "villages" of temporary housing in public parks, such as Rodger Young Village, which consisted of 750 war-surplus Quonset huts in Griffith Park.[1]

A crippling shortage of materials intensified the housing emergency. How could war veterans and their families hope to find housing in the midst of such a crisis? Ain the architect found "veteran after veteran turned up in his office for advice about building a home." He told them all the same thing: "Trying to build one small house today is next to hopeless. Small builders can't get materials. Big builders won't take small jobs. But if a group of veterans pool

1 *Dana Cuff* The Provisional City: Los Angeles Stories of Architecture and Urbanism *(Cambridge, Mass.: M.I.T. Press, 2001), 55, 172.*

2 Mary Roche, "Group Living for Veterans," New York Times Magazine, August 4, 1946, 34.

3 For Disney, Hurtz drew the dancing mushroom sequence in Fantasia. He was a founding member of the United Productions of America (U.P.A.), where he won an Academy Award in 1951. He later directed the "Rocky and Bullwinkle Show" for over twenty years. See "In Memoriam: Bill Hurtz," Peg-Board, Animation Guild Local 839 monthly newsletter, November 2000.

4 Of the eleven original board members, at least two were publicly accused of communist activities, animators David Hilberman and John Hubley. David Hilberman was identified as a communist by Walt Disney to the House Un-American Activities Committee, October 24, 1947. For a discussion of Hubley's communist affiliation, see Michael Barrier, Hollywood Cartoons: American Animation in Its Golden Age (New York: Oxford University Press, 2003), 533–535. Frank Wilkinson, who joined the board in 1947 as its public relations officer, was also publicly accused of communist activities. See Cuff, The Provisional City, 291–294.

5 Ain's second wife, Josephine Ain Chuey, told me that Ain attended Communist Party meetings during their marriage in 1937, in an interview in Los Angeles, July 16, 2000. Ain was listed as having participated in communist activities in the third and fifth reports Un-American Activities in California, California Legislature, 1947, 1949.

6 The connection between Ain's politics and his architecture is the subject of my doctoral dissertation, "Gregory Ain and the Social Politics of Housing Design" (U.C.L.A. Department of Architecture, 2005).

their plans and finances they might interest a big builder and stand some chance of getting new homes."[2] This atmosphere of emergency and scarcity foregrounded all the critical activity at Community Homes.

Significantly, the project had an explicitly political character from the beginning. The original fifteen members were not only cartoonists, but also active union members. Bill Hurtz, who was elected the cooperative's president, had made his name as the animator who led the strike against Walt Disney in 1941.[3] As the cooperative grew to an eventual size of 280 families, a majority of the new members also came from Hollywood unions and political friendships; many were socialists or communists.[4]

The project's political character was affirmed when Ain was selected to be the architect, for he was recognized as a radical. He participated in Communist Party meetings in the 1930s; he was also publicly named as a Communist by the California Un-American Activities Committee while Community Homes was being designed in 1947.[5] Because many of Ain's private houses were completed for clients who were active in the party (and indeed many of these buildings functioned as meeting houses), there is an extensive unreported history of a Communist architecture in Los Angeles that was organized around Gregory Ain.[6] Community Homes, at least to an extent, shared in this identity.

Ain developed a sophisticated critique of the planning of American suburbs, even before the explosive growth of suburbia was engineered by merchant-builders beginning in 1946. While architects awaited the end of the war and the inevitable acceleration of the postwar housing market—"a desperate need for homes"—Ain began to foresee the problems of suburban planning like a storm cloud gathering on the horizon. In 1945 he stated:

Tens of thousand of families, now compelled by circumstances to occupy substandard dwellings, will be in a position to start building as soon as priorities are lifted. For obvious practical reasons, they will be unable to wait for an industrially manufactured product, or for the saner kind of land subdivision which we hope will eventually appear.[7]

In effect, he was a critic of the Levittown pattern before Levittown even existed.

In 1945 the suburban critique was not novel—figures such as Lewis Mumford and Christine Frederick had begun to question this planning model in the early 1920s[8]—but as the war ended the issue was newly urgent. In February 1945 Ain argued: "The problem is a problem in planning, which, if not well solved now by the architects, will be badly solved later by the jerry-builders."[9] In fact, his prediction came true sooner than he might have expected. In May 1945, Fritz Burns and Henry Kaiser, who Ain certainly would have regarded as "jerry-builders," announced Kaiser Community Homes, prefabricated plywood houses which would be deployed in a repetitive grid pattern in several locations in Los Angeles.[10] Ain further insisted: "Most contemporary work is done in a fever of ruthless money-making. That attitude must be replaced by an entirely different set of values,"[11] underscoring the point that his critique was not only directed at the unimaginative architectural planning of the new suburbs, but also at the larger political and socio-economic assumptions that served as the foundations for those tracts.

For Community Homes, Ain chose to collaborate with designers who shared his critical position towards the merchant-builders. Simon Eisner, a planner for the City of Los Angeles Housing Authority, designed the site plan. Eisner, like Ain, argued that designers should resist the priorities of the real-estate industry: "If architects have learned anything during the past lean years it certainly should have been the need to consider housing in terms of an overall pattern instead of on the basis of a single unit."[12] At Community Homes, the interrelationships between units would become the primary design problem.

Reginald Johnson, who was considered "the eminent dean" of local architects, also took notice of the project and agreed to serve as a consultant to help secure Federal Housing Association (F.H.A.) financing.[13] Johnson led the design of Baldwin Hills Village (1942), a project considered a landmark in the history of American housing planning. Ain remembered Reginald Johnson as "a most extraordinary man, somewhat like Thomas Jefferson: civilized, cultivated, and [having a] great social responsibility."[14] In fact, Johnson admired the preliminary plans for Community Homes to such a degree that he consequently arranged for his son Joseph to join Ain's team in late 1946.[15] Alfred W. Day also joined Ain at this time, and Community Homes was completed under the name Ain, Johnson, and Day.

Ain also worked in collaboration with landscape architect Garrett Eckbo, and beginning with this project the two of them developed strategies to integrate the buildings and landscape, struggling with the aesthetic and spatial problem of repetition and homogeneity. As Eckbo later recalled, "the houses had a repetitive clarity with subtle variations. They challenged me to exploit variations in garden design for smaller spaces, and variations in street front treatment within overall unity."[16] On close reading, it is possible to infer from Eckbo's statement of the problem that the designers faced a difficult balancing act, encompassing: First, the need for repetition of a few house types for economic efficiency; second, variations, to ameliorate the problem of homogeneity; and again, third, social unity, to make space that engendered a feeling of community.

These progressive design considerations stood in contrast to the priorities of typical private housing tracts of the time, where the physical planning emphasized the individual unit, the privatization of land, and automobile traffic. William Levitt would soon perfect this pattern, and it was a pattern he understood as having conservative political connotations. "No man who

7 Gregory Ain, "Jury Comments," Arts and Architecture 62 (February 1945): 30.

8 For a summary of these critiques, see Rosalyn Baxandall and Elizabeth Ewen, Picture Windows: How the Suburbs Happened (New York: Basic Books, 2000), xviii–xix.

9 Ain, "Jury Comments," 30.

10 See Cuff, The Provisional City, 253–263.

11 Ain, quoted by Esther McCoy in Contemporary Architects, ed. Muriel Emanuel (New York: St. Martin's Press, 1980), 19–20. Original date of quotation unknown (probably 1945).

12 Simon Eisner, "Future Cities: A Challenge," Arts and Architecture, January 1945, 31, 50–52.

13 Appellation of "eminent dean" from Max and Rita Lawrence, interview by Esther McCoy, 8 March 1977, Esther McCoy Papers, Smithsonian Institution, Archives of American Art (A.A.A.), Washington, D.C.

14 Gregory Ain, interview by David Gebhard and Harriette Von Breton, June 19, 1973, transcribed notes, David Gebhard Papers, Architecture and Design Collection (A.D.C.), University Art Museum, University of California, Santa Barbara, 5.

15 Joseph L. Johnson had graduated from the Harvard Graduate School of Design under Walter Gropius in 1937 and worked for William Wurster's San Francisco office.

16 Esther McCoy "Garrett Eckbo: The Early Years," Arts and Architecture [The Perception of Landscape] 1, 4 (1982): 39–40.

Gregory Ain, Community Homes,
typical block showing relationship
to backyard "finger-park" and
greenbelt at upper left (1946).

18 Eunice Grier and George Grier,
Privately Developed Interracial
Housing: An Analysis of
Experience (Berkeley, Calif.:
University of California Press,
1960), 145.

19 Roche, "Group Living for
Veterans," 35.

20 Esther McCoy, handwritten
drafts for The Second Generation,
Esther McCoy Papers, Smithsonian
A.A.A.

21 Sidonie M. Gruenberg, quoted
in Crabgrass Frontier, 30.

owns his own house and lot can be a communist," Levitt famously said.[17] The
families who were invested in Community Homes, some of them communist,
might have responded to Levitt's charge by answering that they were interested in *more* than merely owning their own house and lot.

In contrast to Levittown, the plan that Eisner and Ain developed for
Community Homes gave precedence to public space over private. Sixteen
acres of the 100 total were given over to common space that was owned by
cooperative for the use of all the residents. Included were greenbelt parks,
pocket recreation spaces, and what they called "finger-parks," which were
located at the center of each block, connecting each family's backyard. These
finger-parks, in combination with the plan's "ingenious street design,"
allowed children to play in protected areas separate from traffic.[18] A *New
York Times* journalist noted that "it will be possible to go from one spot to
another in any part of the property, on foot, tricycle or roller skates, without
having to cross a street."[19] Although this statement was technically inac-
curate, it correctly highlighted the fact that separation of traffic was an
important feature of the design.

In his intention to zone vehicular and pedestrian traffic for the safety of
children, Eisner found precedent in landmark projects such as Radburn, New
Jersey (1929), where Clarence Stein and Henry Wright treated the residential
streets as service roads rather than traffic ways, and oriented the houses
towards rear communal gardens with pedestrian paths leading to continuous
"greenbelt" park space. Stein later served as a consulting architect on Baldwin
Hills Village, the landmark Los Angeles housing project designed by Reginald
Johnson and Robert Alexander and completed in 1942. Organized around a
large "village green," this low-density project contained automobile traffic
and parking on the periphery. Ain recognized Baldwin Hills Village as "one
of the best [housing projects] ever done in the country," and it was an obvious
stimulus to Community Homes.[20]

Ain and his collaborators also paid great attention to the need for spatial
and aesthetic variety in tract housing, and this represented another way in
which Community Homes embodied a critical resistance to the dominant
pattern. One of the common complaints about postwar tract housing in
general was that the uniformity of the suburbs, with people of almost exactly
the same age, background, and income, seemed to deny individuality. "Mass-
produced, standardized housing breeds standardized individuals, too—
especially among youngsters," warned one psychologist in the *New York
Times*.[21] These critiques culminated in John Keats' *The Crack in the Picture
Window* (1956), which satirically described men, returning from work, who
couldn't identify their own house among the repetitive suburban pattern.

Ain directly addressed these worries by developing a system for
Community Homes which began with six basic house types. Ain insisted on
repetition of a few floorplan types in order to standardize the construction.
He understood the economies of scale and the efficiencies of repetition that

284

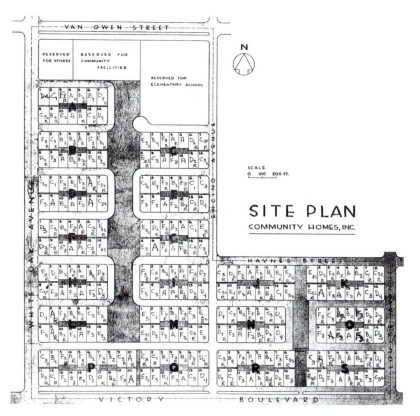

Gregory Ain, Community Homes, site plan showing house types (1948).

made tract housing successful. However each type also included variant expansion plans, and each could be mirrored or rotated, in effect producing twenty-six different houses which would be deployed throughout the neighborhood for variety. By treating the geometrical figures of the houses almost like pieces in a mathematical game, he was able to propose a new synthesis, balancing the opposing compositional principles of repetition and difference.

Despite all of this skillful manipulation of the house types, Ain wanted to be certain that he would alleviate problems of repetition and placelessness, and so he turned to landscape design as a means of creating a greater degree of spatial variety. Taking the existing spatial system, defined by the grid pattern of lot lines and Ain's patterning of houses, Eckbo overlaid a distinctly different set of forms in his landscape design. He did so by making space and borrowing from the spatial techniques of modernist painters. He used trees to expand blocks across the suburban pattern the way that Mondrian would construct space beyond the frame of the picture. He wrapped the landscape continuously around corners, a reinterpreted treatment of the three-dimensional relationship between front and side, as in Picasso's human figures. According to Dorothée Imbert: "The planting schemes for Community Homes used trees to form linear spines or allées through the

right: Garrett Eckbo. Community
Homes, aerial perspective (1947).

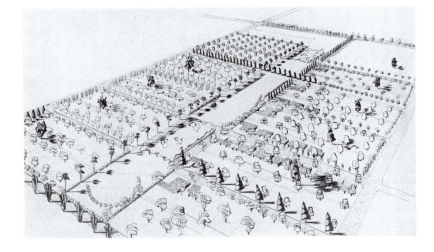

right: Garrett Eckbo. Community
Homes, landscape plan (1947).

below: Garrett Eckbo. Community
Homes, street tree diagram
showing influence of modern
painting techniques (1947).

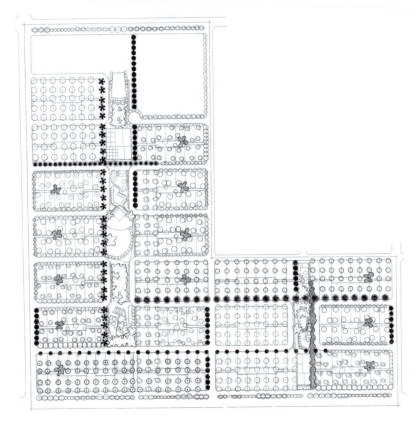

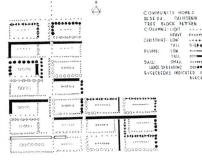

22 Dorothée Imbert, "The Art
of Social Landscape Design," in
Garrett Eckbo: Modern Landscapes
for Living (Berkeley, Calif.:
University of California Press,
1997), 154.

residential neighborhood and even to subvert its order."[22] When Eckbo's tree
plan was overlaid on Ain's distribution of houses, the resultant interference
pattern meant that not one of the 280 houses would be alike.

The houses themselves were designed in a modernist idiom of flat roofs and
glass walls, and their floor plans included several innovations which Ain had

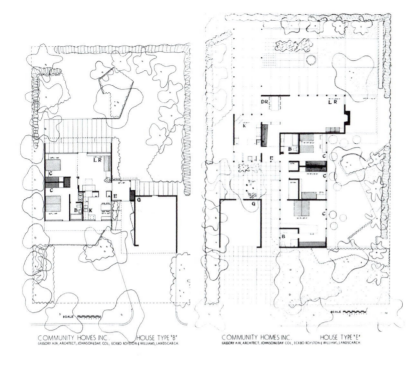

COMMUNITY HOMES INC. HOUSE TYPE "B"
GREGORY AIN, ARCHITECT, JOHNSON&DAY, COL., ECKBO ROYSTON & WILLIAMS, LANDSCA&CH.

COMMUNITY HOMES INC. HOUSE TYPE "E"
GREGORY AIN, ARCHITECT, JOHNSON&DAY, COL., ECKBO ROYSTON & WILLIAMS, LANDSCA&CH.

Gregory Ain, Community Homes, house plan types "B" and "E", the smallest and the largest (1947).

pioneered, based on feminist ideals and progressive theories of parenting. He advocated placing the kitchen at the center of the house and "opening" it, which would allow the housewife to watch her children in the living room or backyard while she worked. He also employed movable partition walls, which allowed the house to be reconfigured according to changing needs. Ain called his houses "flexible," and he argued that they would give older children a "greater independence and responsibility."[23]

All of the houses shared a common orientation, with the livingroom oriented to the rear garden for privacy. Whereas a traditional American home would address the public realm through the use of a front porch or picture window, Ain considered it a "sacrifice of privacy" to place the living room facing the street. "The large picture window which frames a picture of the house interior to be seen from the street is always a poor solution . . . Windows must be placed for looking out and not for looking in."[24] Typical postwar tract houses, such as those at Levittown, followed the traditional pattern. (Levittown's 1947 models had the living room facing the street with a picture window. Their 1949 ranch house had the living room facing the rear, suggesting that this new orientation was quickly adopted by the mainstream.)

Ain also implicitly criticized the typical tract-house pattern of the time by placing the garage in front and pulling it forward from the main body of the house, which was one of his typical techniques, because a shorter driveway would save construction costs and reserve more of the site for landscaping. "Most front yards are just so much waste space," one journalist noted. But

23 Ain, *"The Flexible House Faces Reality,"* Los Angeles Times Home Magazine, *April 15, 1951, 4–5, 23.*

24 Ain, *"Some Notes on the Contemporary House,"* n.d., Ain Papers, A.D.C., University Art Museum, University of California, Santa Barbara.

25 Mary Davis Gillies, "A right-about-face house," McCall's, April 1949, 90.

Ain reduced the front yard "to its legal minimum . . . That leaves a generous back yard for months of warm-weather expanded living."[25] Like the rear-facing living room, Ain's placement of the garage in front would later become adopted by tract homebuilders as part of the suburban vernacular, although these techniques were initially quite revolutionary.

Community Homes was also economically structured to promote a diversity of residents. While most privately developed suburban tracts consisted of a few house types of similar size and price, projecting a relatively homogeneous community of middle-class young families with children, the cooperative would offer a greater variety. For example, the smallest house (Type B), would be a two-bedroom model at 784 square feet, while the largest (Type D) would measure 2,016 square feet. Total costs for the units would run from $6,000 to $12,000, which was a rather astonishing range in the context of new suburban housing. In effect, the cooperative projected a mixed community of (relatively) rich and (relatively) poor residents, single or married with children, young or old.

Community Homes also projected a highly participatory social life for its residents and again sought to construct a different type of subjectivity from that which was projected in the Levittown model. The cooperative's Articles of Incorporation, adopted in March 1946, expressed the intent of the project as to provide "facilities for housing, feeding, transporting, maintaining, and providing professional care, education, and means of communication for its members and others and otherwise to provide for the welfare and accommodation of its members and others."[26] Most provocatively, the cooperative planned for social structures oriented to the liberation of housewives. "Sitters will be superfluous," the New York Times reported, "since each mother will take her turn at watching all the pre-school children of her neighborhood group."[27] In similar vein, Ain placed "two-family drying yards" between pairs of homes, offering the opportunity for shared work.

26 "Articles of Incorporation of Community Homes, Inc., A Non-Profit Corporation," March 11, 1946, Helen Gahagan Douglas Collection, Carl Albert Center, Norman, Okla.

27 Roche, "Group Living for Veterans," 35.

The project's community building was intended for social, cultural, and educational activities, including lecture programs, the content of which can only be imagined. The maintenance shop would be outfitted with craft equipment for the teenagers, and the cooperative formed a credit union for its members. In other words, the group defined its task in the social terms of service and welfare in addition to the merely physical terms of buildings and infrastructure. Although Levitt's projects did provide some public amenities, these innovations were largely motivated by profit, not social welfare; they were treated as marketing tools for the ultimate aim of private consumption and thus his developments projected fundamentally conservative social relationships.

28 Correspondence between Ruth Jaffee, Executive Secretary, Community Homes Inc., to Helen Gahagan Douglas, July 11, 1947, Douglas Collection.

Executive Secretary Ruth Jaffee described Community Homes as a "struggle for better housing in a truly democratic community," and thus political participation was viewed as an essential ingredient to the community's success.[28] Each of the 280 members would have one equal vote; the voting rules were spelled out specifically in the cooperative's by-laws.[29] Even design decisions such as the species of street trees, Garrett Eckbo recalled, needed to be approved by the cooperative members through "a thoroughly democratic process."[30]

If the democratic structure of decision-making set Community Homes apart from privately developed tracts like Levittown, one feature that they shared was a lengthy set of property restrictions. At Community Homes, rules were established "for the greatest degree of health, safety, architectural beauty, and amenity for the property-owners and inhabitants." Some of these regulations addressed typical zoning issues, such as those prohibiting industrial and agricultural uses and those requiring that only one family could live on each lot. More specifically, however, the rules sought to "preserve the attractiveness" of Ain's architectural intent by restricting changes and additions to the structures. Even altering a house's exterior color would require the approval of the cooperative's board of directors. Like Levittown, Community Homes would prohibit the hanging of laundry in areas visible from the street.[31]

The cooperative's most radical aspect was that it was racially integrated from the beginning, and this, in fact, proved to be the project's fatal flaw. In the context of postwar housing, to be organized as a cooperative was a fundamentally political act, but to be racially integrated was truly radical. When the cooperative completed their purchase of land, a local Race Restrictions Board asked them to place restrictive covenants on a portion of the property, but they refused.[32]

The project's leaders understood their historical pioneering role in proposing a planned interracial community. Raymond Voigt, Community Homes' financial consultant, spoke of "spearheading the movement here on the west coast" and he found "the assignment is [as] inspiring as it is challenging."[33] The only earlier example of a similar project that Community Homes could consult for encouragement was Parklawn, a public housing project built in Milwaukee in 1936–1937 and integrated despite bitter protest. Because of its success, Parklawn became a touchstone for Community Homes. "For the first time in the history of public housing in the U.S.A.," Voigt claimed, "an interracial community was established . . . It did work out, and with no damage or harm to anyone, and with no depreciation or jeopardy of property values."[34] Community Homes, Voigt believed, would follow in the footsteps of Parklawn.

Community Homes's policy of racial integration ultimately caused the F.H.A. to reject the project. After reviewing the project's site plan, the same plan that city officials had determined to be the finest ever submitted, local F.H.A. officials surprisingly rejected it in mid-1947 after learning that the cooperative was racially integrated.[35] F.H.A. Commissioner Raymond M. Foley said that, if the project's racial makeup significantly increased the financial risk, "we are not warranted in accepting the risk, regardless of

29 "By Laws of Community Homes, Inc., A Non-Profit Corporation Organized under the Laws of the State of California," n.d., Douglas Collection.

30 Imbert, "Art of Social Landscape Design."

31 "Community Homes, Inc., Declaration of Establishment of Restrictions," September 17, 1946, Douglas Collection.

32 Grier and Grier, Privately Developed Interracial Housing.

33 Raymond A. Voigt, Financial Representative, Community Homes, Inc., to Catherine Bauer Wurster, May 29, 1947, Catherine Bauer Wurster Papers, Bancroft Library, University of California, Berkeley.

34 Ibid.

35 H. H. Thompson, Chief Underwriter for the Los Angeles F.H.A. office, first rejected the project. This decision was appealed to John E. McGovern, the Director of the Los Angeles F.H.A. office, who deferred the decision to the national office. See Voigt to McGovern, June 3, 1947, Douglas Collection.

36 Raymond M. Foley, F.H.A.
Commissioner, to Community
Homes, Inc., July 3, 1947, Douglas
Collection.

the nature of the cause producing that effect."[36] In fact the risk was minimal at that time, since Community Homes was fully subscribed: 280 families had made $1,500 down-payments for houses that did not yet exist. After a heartbreaking period of nearly four years of planning, stops and starts, good news and bad news, during which time members simply waited through one delay after another, some living in trailers or other temporary accommodations, the cooperative was finally disbanded and the land was sold in late 1949. None of the houses were built. Ain, the architect, later recalled that the project failed simply because F.H.A. considered it "a bad business practice"[37] to provide mortgage insurance to integrated projects.

37 Ain, quoted in Esther McCoy
The Second Generation (Salt Lake
City, Utah: Peregrine Smith Books,
1984), 121.

F.H.A. opposed the project, according to cooperative member Max Lawrence, in part because "they thought we were all crazy radicals."[38] Certainly this political identity was encoded in the architecture itself. F.H.A. was commonly hesitant to insure mortgages for houses with flat roofs, refusing to consider them sound, long-term investments, perhaps in part because modern architecture was beginning to be associated with socialism and communism at the dawn of the McCarthy era. Ain and other progressive architects frequently found difficulty with restrictions they found capricious. At one of Ain's other housing projects, which was designed in a similar architectural style, the F.H.A. repeatedly asked that colonial, Cape Cod, Italian, and Spanish-style houses be included—styles that represented political conservatism.[39] "Most 'modern' architects who have encountered F.H.A. processing," *Architectural Forum* reported, "agree that the most disheartening aspect of the situation is official insistence on routine planning with which they are familiar and a complete unwillingness to try anything new."[40]

38 Max Lawrence, interview by
the author, June 15, 2004, Bel Air,
Calif.

39 "One Convertible Plan,"
Architectural Forum (April 1949):
126–128.

40 "Apartment Boom,"
Architectural Forum (January
1950): 104–105.

By February 1949, the story of the group's plight made it all the way to the desk of President Truman. In a twenty-one-page letter to the President on the subject of F.H.A.'s racism, Thurgood Marshall, working for the N.A.A.C.P., used the case of Community Homes to illustrate the bureaucracy's resistance to integration. Marshall concluded: "The achievement of racial residential segregation is the purpose and the effect of F.H.A.'s policy."[41] The long-term social implications of F.H.A.'s policies during this period are staggering to consider.

When Lewis Mumford reflected on the American urban pattern in 1961, he was justifiably preoccupied with the powerful influence of Levittown. He described the pattern as:

41 Thurgood Marshall,
"Memorandum to the President
of the United States Concerning
Racial Discrimination by the
Federal Housing Administration,"
February 1, 1949, Library of
Congress, Manuscripts Division,
N.A.A.C.P. Collections, 14.

a multitude of uniform houses, lined up inflexibly, at uniform distances, on uniform roads, in a treeless communal waste, inhabited by people of the same class, the same income, the same age group, witnessing the same television performances, eating the same tasteless prefabricated foods, from the same freezers, conforming in every outward and inward respect to a common mold.[42]

42 Lewis Mumford The City
in History: Its Origins, Its
Transformations, and Its Prospects
(New York: Harcourt, Brace &
World, Inc., 1961), 486.

Clearly Community Homes—through its financial organization, through its political character, through its policies of racial inclusion, and through its physical planning—was developed in a mood of critical resistance to the problems Mumford would describe with such wit. In fact, Ain and his collaborators *anticipated* these problems before they were manifest in American society, and thus offered a powerful critique of Levittown before it even existed.

far left: Garrett Eckbo (c. 1945).

left: Gregory Ain (date unknown). Author's collection, courtesy Emily Ain.

Originally published in the Proceedings of the 93rd Annual Meeting of the Collegiate Schools of Architecture, 2005.

I-10 THE GULF COAST STATES/
MALL HOUSING
BRIAN D. ANDREWS AND W. JUDE LEBLANC

The proposals included here are part of a larger project of research and speculation which we've named "I-10 the Gulf Coast States." This body of work explores the question of how to better create an architecture that has the capacity to respond to particular cultural circumstances. Interstate 10, the east–west highway which links the Gulf Coast states, provides the framework, both literally and figuratively, which organizes these proposals. All of the projects are thematically related in support of a single thesis that explores the obligation of architecture to contribute to particular geographic places. In the words of Flannery O'Connor, that meticulous craftsman of the short story, "Someplace is better than anyplace."

DESCRIPTION
Highway Housing consists of dwelling units sited in proximity to an overpass. The housing is of a light steel frame and steel stud and sheathed in galvanized

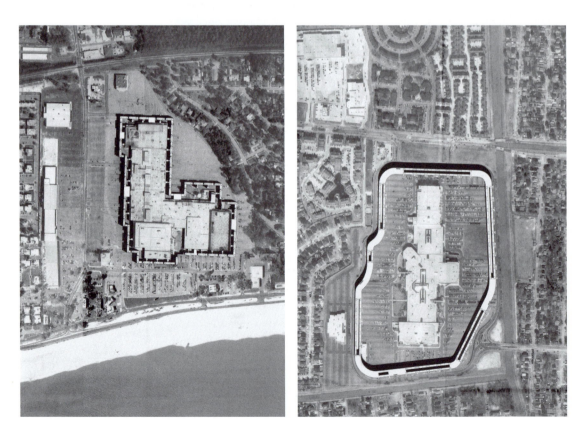

sheet metal with standing seams. The south elevation is covered with a bleached cypress *bris soleil*. Elevated entry porches are made of poured-in-place concrete and are designed to support cypress trees. But for the addition of these green trees, the dwellings are silver-gray monochrome. The structures are supported by long-span trusses with tension ring connections, fitted with heavy spring dampeners, at the existing concrete columns.

A bridge is proposed which would offer an alternate pedestrian route to the Gulfgate Mall, the first covered shopping center in Houston. The bridge would be made as an habitable box beam and would house a gymnasium. Also proposed in the site development is a daycare center, the roof of which connects the shopping mall with the bridge from the housing development.

The units are disposed to create front doors which face either a street or a common yard, and rear doors which face semi-public alleyways with parking. The common yard includes a swimming pool and a community house. The site plan includes drop-off points for recycling, a community garden and a grove of cypress trees, which in 100 years time could be used to replace the large south-facing *bris soleil*.

CONTRIBUTIONS TO PARTICULAR GEOGRAPHIES

The diminishment of species diversity in the natural environment has its corollary in the built environment. Current building continues to result in loss, as building practices diminish desirable differences and nuances in neighborhoods and cities as well as natural environments across the globe. Building construction in the United States, over the past several decades, has tended to level differences across geographic locales. Numerous factors such as gains in global production, distribution, and information have resulted in a building industry characterized by these strong generalizing trends.

We imagine our design projects as contributions to the evolving life of the cultural geographies of particular settlements. To the degree that settlements are understood historically, architecture is a component of narrative construction. The particular disposition of a settlement in time is a cross section of its history, or *histories*, a static diagram of the ongoing construction of its stories.

EXPERIMENTAL PROPOSITIONS TO LOCATE NEW SITES FOR BUILDING: THE SHOPPING MALL AND HIGHWAY INTERCHANGE COUPLED

The Gulfgate Housing scheme is one of three projects recently undertaken which look to the highway and to the shopping mall, infra-structure, and quasi-public space, as a site for architectural speculation. The choice of such generic nonplace specific contexts is a test of our thesis that architecture might respond in relation to particular locales. These prototypes offer new infill sites, the utilization of which will decrease suburban sprawl. These housing strategies would be accessible to automobile traffic and would also produce small-scale pedestrian districts.

While not replicating the form of traditional urban spaces, these housing types used individually or in combination, would result in organic social overlaps common to urban environments. Similar ends, the invention of new spaces coupled and the resurrection of lost desirable environmental characteristics are sought at all scales. Spatial types and precedents, careful proportions, and indigenous planting, are common to all three proposals.

TOWARD A SUSTAINABLE ENVIRONMENT

The practical obstacles to such as a proposal as this are numerous, but several options present themselves. Noise near freeways is problematic but the most quiet areas around an elevated roadway is the area directly beneath it.

The air-borne toxins produced by automobile exhaust are probably the most serious obstacle. Housing types such as this one, which attempt to claim dormant land in areas already populated may have to wait until the inevitable mandate of less environmentally destructive vehicles, such as the electric car.

The harsh tropical climate of Houston results in massive air-conditioning usage nearly all year round. If air-conditioning could be produced by photovoltaic panels, charcoal filters could result in a clean interior environment.

FLEXIBLE HOUSING PLANS WHICH CAN ACCOMMODATE NEW SOCIAL REALITIES AND A VARIETY OF OCCUPATIONAL USAGES

The floor plans are configured in response to current changes in households and the evolving idea of what constitutes a family or family life. Each unit has two entries, a primary entry off a street or a common lawn and a secondary entry off a semi-public alleyway. Each unit has two equal-sized bedrooms on the top floor and a bathroom which can be compartmentalized and used by several persons at once. Located on the main floor, in addition to the living area and kitchen, is a studio-type area which can be used as a home office, a bedroom, or a semi-autonomous dwelling for another family member or group.

What happened to all that talk a few years ago about repairing the American "infrastructure"—getting people out to rebuild the roads and bridges that are falling apart? A lot of good ideas just seem to fade away.

Andy Warhol, America, *1985*

Originally published in the Proceedings of the 85th Annual Meeting of the Association of Collegiate Schools of Architecture, 1997.

COMMUNITY REDEVELOPMENT FOR A SMALL TOWN IN FLORIDA
STEPHEN LUONI

Our planning efforts for a small town in Florida suggests that the viable sustainable design approaches to community development are inherently bound up in the linkage of those technical practices with the cultural logic of a place. Through the investigation of a planning project and its mission to revitalize marginalized zones of the community, we hope to illustrate two important forces in community development. The first concerns how the physical landscape and environment might instruct one in the management and development of a place. Successful planning efforts are not completely organized by a compositional logic, but rather a technological one as well. Indeed, the physical context encourages certain technologies of development which constitutes its very regionalism. The second idea concerns the difficult proposition of a public realm and the possibility now that its destiny is tied to the utilitarian yet performative logic of infrastructure.

All community development in Florida must confront the politics of water management. In East Eustis, the lowest point is a small town with a 100-foot variation in topography, the channeling of stormwater runoff coupled with the prohibition of new building construction on protected local wetlands presents an opportunity to create new public spaces in a community that desires redevelopment of existing scattered resources. A proposed linear

Proposed storm water management infrastructure for Eustis, Florida.

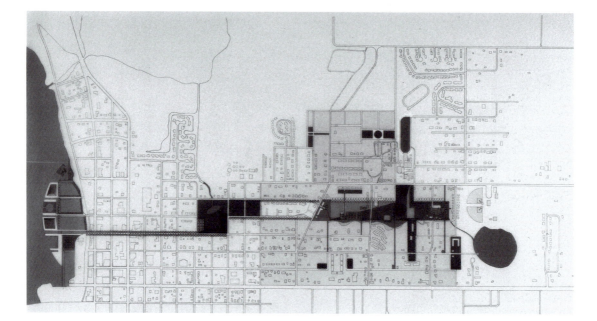

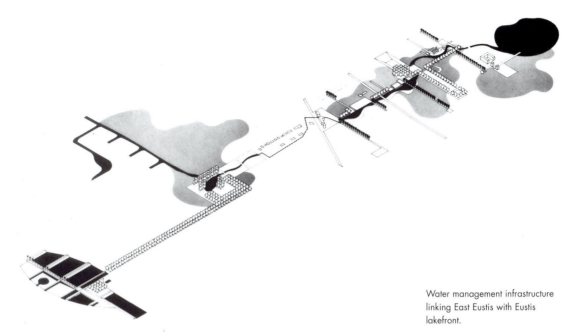

Water management infrastructure linking East Eustis with Eustis lakefront.

public park on the wetlands will connect existing scattered development with new peripheral institutional, commercial, and residential development in the establishment of a connected neighborhood for East Eustis. In the obligation to protect existing wetlands and to manage the flow of water, the new park utilizes the water as a resource in the creation of public space.

On the downtown lakefront in Eustis the proposed public park provides four municipal stormwater treatment ponds in the city's existing lake. Rather than construct a costly new mechanical treatment facility on the lakefront,

Lakefront storm water park.

the stormwater runoff would be aerated by fountains and naturally treated through the construction of a miniature ecosystem in the new ponds. The public park would organize future downtown development.

Originally published in the Proceedings of the 82nd Annual Meeting of the Association of Collegiate Schools of Architecture, 1994.

DRIFTING URBANISM
STEPHEN LUONI

Typical area lakefront.

This proposed waterfront redevelopment for Eustis, Florida is the second phase of a redevelopment masterplan prepared for this small town of 14,000 people. A distinctive feature organizing the masterplan is the integration of ecological concerns with transportation and new development. In this current phase, the primary objective is to coordinate the redevelopment initiatives of various downtown commercial interest with those of the lakefront in a comprehensive design that promotes economic revitalization yet respects the endangered ecology of the lake's edge.

As a seam binding land and water, the design attempts to negotiate the conflicting interests that operate throughout four linear networks: (1) a proposed pedestrian and boat docking infrastructure; (2) the riparian ecology of the lake edge; (3) two proposed anchoring civic landscapes; and (4) a band of abandoned commercial building slated for adaptive reuse. These four layers combine with the existing railroad to establish an intermodal transportation facility connecting local and regional travel between land and water by boat, train, automobile, small marine airplane, and foot. This diversification of transit expands the options of a car-based culture and its exclusive patterns of attraction across this expanding region.

Fifteen percent of Lake County's surface is covered by a network of 1,400 lakes, and home to a large and growing population of avid boaters. Our proposal could be likened to a *protean urbanism* inspired more by ecology, water, and the local patterns of movement that it favors, than by a tradition

Protean Urbanism.

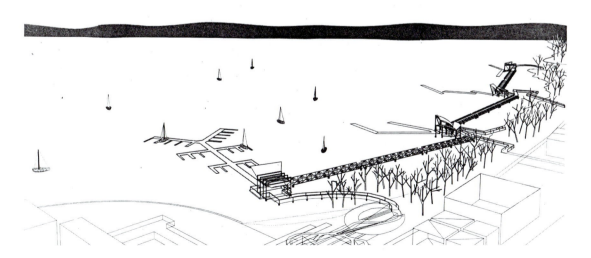

299

of proper urban form. The low-impact, flexible, floating transportation infrastructure proposed is better equipped than a heavy, permanent, land-based system in responding to fluctuating demographic concentrations and the attendant stress that such shifts place on local resources. Like most early American urban waterfronts, the Eustis urban-riparian seam is organized by the isotropic rationality of land speculation and its road networks. This indifference to place, history, and identity stems from their single-purpose logic—efficiency in resource allocation. Local history, a sense of place, and the body then, are consciously inscribed values in the tectonic and spatial organizations of the proposed redevelopment infrastructure.

The four development networks: transit, ecology, landscape, and building.

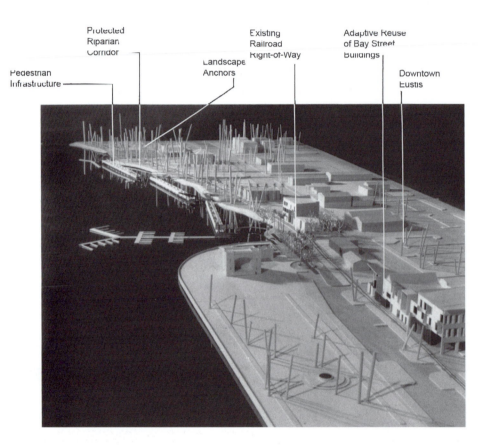

Pedestrian Infrastructure

Protected Riparian Corridor

Landscape Anchors

Existing Railroad Right-of-Way

Adaptive Reuse of Bay Street Buildings

Downtown Eustis

Originally published in the Proceedings of the 84th Annual Meeting of the Association of Collegiate Schools of Architecture, 1996.

THE ROLE OF INFRASTRUCTURE IN THE PRODUCTION OF PUBLIC SPACES FOR THE CITY OF MIAMI

MÓNICA PONCE DE LEÓN AND
NADER TEHRANI

The presence of massive infrastructure elements, such as highways, metrorail systems, or commuter stations, is a reality of the contemporary city. Contrary to the infrastructure of the nineteenth and early twentieth century—the Berlin Stadtbahn, Otto Wagner's Stadtbahn and locks in Vienna, the 1930s works of Robert Moses in New York City, etc.—one finds few examples in recent history (the case of Barcelona is quite exceptional) where their colossal presence has been addressed in urbanistic or architectural terms. After World War II, the realm of infrastructure has all too often been relegated to the domain of the civil and traffic engineer, whose disciplines do not have the means to fully address the complexities—architectural, urbanistic, social— involved in planning the large city.

As a result, while cities' infrastructures have developed a great deal in the past three decades, they have often done so to the detriment of the urbanistic and public aspects of the city. For instance, even though many highways have successfully connected the city's districts at a regional level, they have failed to account for the relationship between neighboring communities through (and over) which they have intervened. Furthermore, since they have been

designed for the automobile (inevitably resulting in colossal dimensions), they have rarely been scaled to accommodate other forms of transportation, such as the pedestrian. This has resulted in the vast expanse of wasted space under, around, and between most major infrastructure interventions in the city.

In this context, our modern proposal—developed between 1991 and 1993—for the Road 836 overpass near downtown Miami is the opportunity to explore some of the programmatic, urbanistic, and architectural potentials of public infrastructure. The proposal also operates at a general planning level and aims at reorienting the development and the life of the city towards one of its main natural resources, the Miami River. The 836 overpass constitutes a unique moment on one of the Miami's most traveled freeways. As it crosses the Miami River, the highways dramatically rises to great heights to allow for the masts of sailboats to pass below it. The space created underneath it is of monumental dimensions and bears an uncanny resemblance to what could be called a "hypostyle hall." The crossing of the highway also maintains an important adjacency between two significant public institutions on both sides of the river: the Orange Bowl Stadium and the Dade Country Courthouse.

The proposal for the overpass uses the existing highway infrastructure as a means of connecting both these public buildings to the river. On the north bank, the unusual height of the highway becomes an opportunity for the creation of a public hall. This screened space which holds activities associated with the water, such as a public market and boat storage, serves to define a public plaza facing the existing courthouse. Similarly, on the south bank of the river, the underbelly of the highway is programmed with a parking garage and recreational facilities. These new programs open into a sport complex of playing fields and athletics buildings, working in conjunction with the existing stadium.

The iconographic specificity of this proposal was seen as rhetorically crucial to create a link with Miami's history, but also to give an air of reality and a sense of cultural immediacy to schemes that may otherwise remain utopian.

Originally published in the Proceedings of the 81st Annual Meeting of the Association of Collegiate Schools of Architecture, 1993.

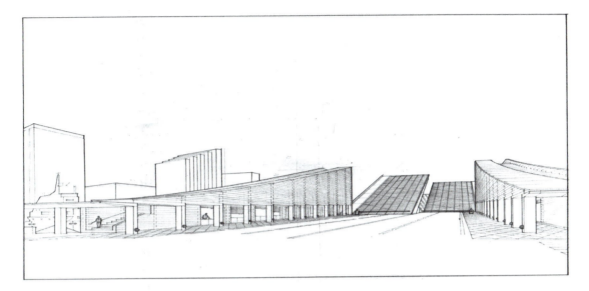

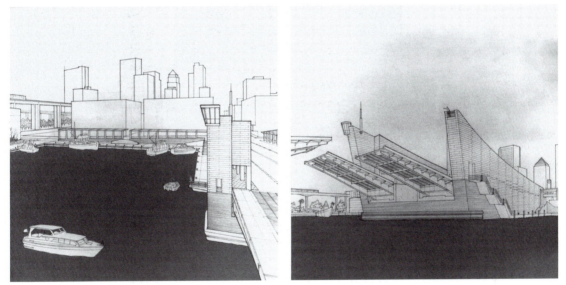

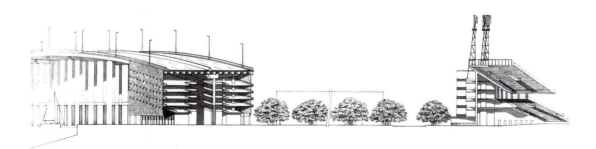

THE SHARED REALM

INTRODUCTION

KIM TANZER AND RAFAEL LONGORIA

Culture is capital; it is the thing which gives knowledge of life.[1]

1 *Jean-Marie Tjibaou, as quoted by Findley in this volume.*

In a number of ways the concept of sustainability implies what will be characterized in this section as the behavior called "sharing." Sharing might be described as a willingness to equalize resources, an acknowledgment of the phenomenon of interdependence, or the enactment of empathy with others. In the parlance of sustainability, sharing occurs when networked thinking replaces hierarchy with equality, in that all elements necessarily contribute to the network's effectiveness. Behaviors that account for long-term viability recognize that immediate individual gain often shortchanges the future.

While the Gaia hypothesis and the school of thought known as deep ecology suggest that the concept of sharing, or interconnecting, is applicable to all elements of the planet Earth, as they are all equally alive and contributing to the planet's health, this section will focus specifically on sharing within the human realm.[2]

2 *The Gaia hypothesis, articulated by James Lovelock and Lynn Margulis, proposes that there is a comprehensive system regulating all life of the planet, involving the cooperation of everything on the planet. See James Lovelock, "Gaia: A Model for Planetary and Cellular Dynamics," in* Gaia A Way of Knowing: Political Implications of the New Biology, *ed. William Irwin Thompson (Great Barrington, Mass.: Lindisfarne Press, 1987).*

Here, at its essence, sharing refers to the sharing of power. Among human beings, power manifests itself in currencies as diverse as knowledge, wealth, landownership, legal rights, and tangible goods as diverse as jewelry, electronics, architecture, and sneakers. The act of sharing moves to equalize one or several of these power currencies among individuals or cultures. The essays and projects in this section demonstrate a variety of transfers or transformations of power, all with the intention of equalizing resources and opportunities.

Occasionally the sharing or equalizing of power begins with an act or attitude of generosity on the part of the individual or group holding more power. This, it has been argued, is the promise of human intelligence. In these cases, hierarchy is flattened from above, so to speak. More often, however, power is equalized through subversion or violence, two tools that have been historically useful to the disenfranchised. In some cases power is redistributed through global forces apparently beyond the reach of individual or groups strategies. As articulated in the recent book *The World is Flat*, global economic forces—acting through a complex set of mechanisms including international finance and multinational corporations, nations' policies, and cultural and environmental predispositions—are redistributing global power in ways apparently both unpredictable and uncontrollable.[3]

3 *Thomas Friedman* The World is Flat: A Brief History of the Twenty-First Century *(New York: Farrar, Straus & Giroux, 2005).*

A number of mechanisms of power equalization can be discerned in the essays in this section. Lisa R. Findley, in "Architecture and the Representation of Culture: The Tjibaou Cultural Center of New Caledonia," demonstrates several. This essay describes the process of building the Tjibaou Cultural

Center, from its inception, through the selection of the architect, the design process and the construction process, and ends by citing reactions by members of the Kanak cultural group to the completed project. Woven through this thoughtfully documented process are a number of transfers of power. For instance, power is granted by those in control when the French government under François Mitterand includes the Kanak Cultural Center in New Caledonia among its list of *Grands Projets*. Similarly, whether for strategic or ethical purposes, architect Renzo Piano granted power to the Kanak people with whom he worked by facilitating a highly participatory design process. But, as Findley describes, the French did not choose to "grant" power to the Kanaks until they had, in fact, wrested it from their French occupiers through a lengthy period of protest, some of it violent. In fact, the center was named for one of the movement's leaders, the nonviolent Jean-Marie Tjibaou, who was, ironically, assassinated by a Kanak extremist.

The Women Suffrage Memorial Project, by Raveevarn Choksombatchai and Ralph Nelson, honors the wresting of political power from Minnesota's male-only electorate in the nineteenth century. This design, a proposal for a public memorial set in St. Paul, Minnesota's state capital, takes advantage of the sloping landscape, key historic narratives, and the framing of symbolically powerfully vistas to communicate crosscurrents of power. Whereas the Kanak people, though oppressed for centuries, achieved their political goals quickly, the memorial compares the suffragists' slow and steady efforts to the glaciation of the Minnesota landscape over the course of geological time.

Carlos Martín, in "Global Constructions, Or Why Guadalajara Wants a Home Depot while Los Angeles Wants Construction Workers," paints a fascinating picture of power subverted. He identifies formal globalizing practices, such as construction industries' corporate tendencies to utilize global labor inequities to maximize efficiency and profit working with the complicity of governments that develop policies to reinforce these inequities in the name of nationalism and juxtaposes them to informal practices that more effectively globalize knowledge and capital.

Similarly, Mildred Howard, an African American artist cited by Jeanine Centouri in "Unmasking Urban Traces," demonstrates the tradition of reframing everyday objects to draw the collective power of memory and community into focus, but only for those who are looking carefully. Here power is subverted through objects with double meanings, while Martín argues that power is subverted through actions invisible to those in formal control. Both mechanisms of subversion rely on the arrogant blindness of those in power to behaviors seemingly beneath their status.

James Rojas, of the Metropolitan Transportation Authority, describes the subversion of Anglo-American cultural capital through appropriation of the Anglo-American housing typology in eastern Los Angeles to suit Mexican living practices. As another example of Centouri's urban traces unmasked, he argues that the expression of identity through ritualistic actions serves to redirect the formal and symbolic persuasiveness of the American dream toward a hybridized and more inclusive America.

On occasion architects, through their programmatic and spatial decisions, can assist in brokering power, in order to revitalize a disenfranchised or marginalized community. "A Raptor Enclosure for the Zuni Pueblo," by Donna Cohen and Claude Armstrong, describes the role their project played in reinforcing cultural traditions in the face of well-intentioned government restrictions regarding the collection of ceremonial eagle feathers. Through a sensitive understanding of the tribe's needs and the Government's requirements, the project facilitates a true win-win scenario by equally protecting two endangered groups, the eagles and the Zuni. Though more ephemeral, Dean Sakamoto's Progess Wall, also cited by Centouri, demonstrated to the New Haven community the power of ethnic diversity and reminded community members of its disappearance.

Systems theory teaches us that change is a constant.[4] Thus, if power is seen as a kind of currency, it should not be surprising that, over time, power changes hands. Transformations in local cultural circumstances reflect such global readjustments. This story is told most clearly through "Weaving the Urban Fabric: Transformations in the Traditional Housing Form of Chanderi, India," by Jyoti Hosagrahar. She carefully describes the home of one extended family in the weaving town of Chanderi, and outlines the historic changes in technological, political, economic, and social elements that impact the community's physical environment. Without rendering judgment she explains, for instance, how women's entry into the work environment had the inadvertent effect of diminishing street life and increasing the use of electric light over daylight.

The projects and essays in this section make clear the complexity of relationship between what theorists describe as the self and the other. Findley, as described above, recounts the irony surrounding the French adoption of the Kanak Cultural Center as a national *Grands Projet* and the tragedy wherein the Kanaks' nonviolent leader Jean-Michel Tjibaou was assassinated by a Kanak extremist. Centouri, by highlighting a series of urban traces specific to certain ethnic groups demonstrates the variety of overlapping others found in vital urban centers. She leaves open questions regarding these groups' relationships with each other. Hosagrahar, by describing the role women play in modern Chanderi, makes it clear that changes benefiting women come at the expense of other desirable aspects of sustainable urban life. And Martín, by separating formal strategies for globalization from informal strategies, suggests that official ideas of the other do not track with those of individuals who participate within these cultures.

Centouri also identifies another key aspect of self/other distinction of importance to architects. She suggests that the collection of designers whose work she spotlights "makes a connection between the world of design and the world of the vernacular." Architects and other professionals are often

4 *The theme of inevitable change also runs through some of the world's major religions.*

309

implicated in, if not in charge of, the exchanges Martín describes as formal exchanges. Members of the architecture profession are particularly well placed to make and reinforce the connections that, quoting Centouri, reveal "our common history and our common bonds to the landscape which we commonly inhabit." Indeed, the flattening of this hierarchy, giving voice to all cultures and equal access to all cultures' capital, suggests a key role to be played by design professionals in the future.

Finally the work included in the section entitled "The Shared Realm" is consistently non-nostalgic. While there is a tendency to fix vernacular or popular cultures in an eternal, unchanging present, these essays and projects firmly fight this inclination. They advocate respect for living, changing traditions without negating either the inevitability of change or the thematic qualities of cultures studied. Hosagrahar most precisely records the nature of change in the weavers' microcluster in Chanderi. Choksombatchai and Nelson, using the metaphor of slow change through glaciation, celebrate cultural transformation symbolically. Martín, perhaps to the chagrin of some readers, challenges romanticized notions of appropriate cultural responsiveness with the convenience of Home Depot. In these cases and others, a careful, respectful understanding, often based on the authors' long-standing interaction with cultures under discussion, reveals cultures far richer and more dynamic than those too often reduced to folk caricatures.

"The Shared Realm" offers the hope that globalization might help us understand and appreciate the riches of the world's diverse cultural capital, that we might recognize the value in knowledge unlike our own and that our built world might increasingly reflect the intelligence of all members of our human community. It also provides examples for those who seek to equalize resources and opportunities in order to design this promise.

ARCHITECTURAL INVENTION AND THE POSTCOLONIAL ERA
The Tjibaou Cultural Center in New Caledonia by the Renzo Piano Building Workshop

LISA R. FINDLEY

This is a case study of an architectural project caught in a complicated historical moment.

In this post-Cold War, postcolonial era, the Asia Pacific region is one of many places worldwide undergoing profound cultural change. Indigenous peoples who have been systematically marginalized in their own lands, are regaining their voices as the totalizing colonial or conquering cultures become either embarrassed by their own arrogance in the face of global condemnation of colonial practices, or confronted with indigenous people who refuse, sometimes violently, to see themselves as "primitive" any longer. The Maori of New Zealand, the Orang Asli of Malaysia, the Dayak of Borneo, the rich array of tribal groups in the Yunnan Province of China, and many, many other indigenous peoples will no longer remain on the cultural fringes of their countries.

In their struggle to be recognized as legitimate players in their national cultures, many indigenous people have formed new institutions to represent their ways of being in the world—often in the form of cultural preservation and development agencies. While recognized as essential to cultural autonomy and advancement, these institutions present many new problems. For some it forces a singularizing view of indigenous cultures that had great variety even within a small geographical sphere. For others, the size and structure of these institutions are anathema to traditional practices. And finally, for most, these institutions require physical facilities of a size and nature for which there is no precedent within the indigenous culture.

The architectural questions this situation raises are messy and difficult. There is no way to avoid the fact that whatever structure is to house such a cultural institution will be symbolic on many levels. Its mere existence is political, much less its form and expression. Such a building project will exist in huge tension and ambiguity. It must embody many things for many people—and must avoid being patronizing or sentimental. While there certainly cannot be a singular way or formula for navigating through the design and construction of such a project, there are important lessons to be learned from an examination of a recently completed cultural center for the Kanak people of the French South Pacific territory of New Caledonia. Here the Renzo Piano Building Workshop (R.P.B.W.) faced these issues explicitly and directly, and used their capacity for technological invention to answer some of the perplexing symbolic difficulties of the Kanak situation.

THE TJIBAOU CULTURAL CENTER

A line of mysterious alien forms quietly occupy a tree-covered peninsula on a South Pacific island. Surreal and beautiful, they can be seen from the surrounding hills, with the tallest rising from the landscape to a height of 28 meters. Upon approaching, they continue to be breathtaking and strange. They meet the sky not with strong silhouetted solid edges, but rather with feathered fingers that appear to fade into the sky in certain light. This makes them seem a distant kin of the columnar pine trees that share the lush site.

The Tjibaou Cultural Centre from across the Bay. (All images are by the author except as noted.)

This is the Jean-Marie Tjibaou Cultural Center in New Caledonia. Designed by the Renzo Piano Building Workshop it is the last of François Mitterand's *Grand Projets*. The $34 million project sits on a narrow 8 hectare peninsula that protects a placid lagoon edged with mangrove trees from the sometimes fierce prevailing winds and waves of the bay beyond. The building reinforces the natural role of the peninsula with a 755-foot long open-air circulation allée that follows the gently curving line of a pre-existing footpath along the small ridge. The allée divides the building into two distinct architectural vocabularies: On the slightly sloping lagoon side, just off the ridge and protected from the weather, four horizontal flat-roofed glass and steel pavilions dock along the allée with landscape in between. Strung like pearls along the other, steeper bay side of the allee, ten soaring circular iroko

312

mahogany *cases* (an early European word for traditional South Sea huts) turn their curved slatted backs to the wind and stretch structural ribs into the sky.

In June 1998, while Renzo Piano was in Washington D.C. to receive the Pritzker Prize, his newly completed Tjibaou Cultural Center opened to the public half the world away. The project for the indigenous Kanak people of New Caledonia had been much anticipated by the international architectural community since the R.P.B.W. had won the commission in a 1991 competition. The competition and the development of the project were the subject of numerous articles in international architectural journals through the early and mid-1990s. Upon its completion, a steady stream of architectural journalists and photographers made the pilgrimage to New Caledonia to document and report on the building. And the resulting steady stream of articles worldwide in the journals, including my own for New York-based *Architecture* magazine, praise the project from the usual formal perspectives for its startling invention, its skillful siting, its refined construction, and its unabashed beauty. Due to the setting, history, and nature of the building program, many of these articles step beyond the usual analysis of building-as-formal-product to praise Piano's dedication to working with the Kanak people throughout the design of the project to ensure that their culture would be embodied in the result. In fact, it is quite clear that the project could never have taken on its distinctive form if it were not for its cultural and political context.

Despite the unanimous international acclaim, it is these particular cultural and historical circumstances that call into question the technology and means of production of the project. At second glance these appear to be willful and fraught with environmental, cultural, and postcolonial difficulties. Is this, as one of Mitterand's *Grand Projets*, only a new, passive-aggressive extension of 150 years of colonialism? Is it postcolonial patronizing? What purpose do Piano's technological innovations serve in this context? Why did he not use local building materials and technology? What, after all, are the implications of designing a project that requires, for example, mahogany cut from forests in Africa to be shipped to France for intensive shaping, gluing, and forming, then to be shipped again half way around the world to New Caledonia where it is moved by truck to the site of a building whose purpose is to house the continuing cultural development of a people whose culture was severely injured by the French in the first place?

THE CONDITION OF THE KANAK SPIRIT

New Caledonia sits on the western edge of Oceania, about 620 miles off the eastern coast of Australia. It is a French overseas territory that consists of a main island, Grande Terre, over 300 miles long, and several outlying islands. When Europeans first arrived, at least twenty-seven distinct languages were spoken among the indigenous Melanesian peoples of the islands, the Kanak.

313

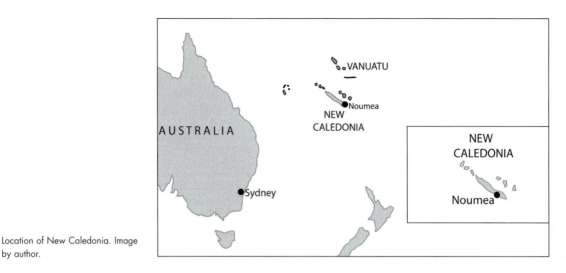

Location of New Caledonia. Image by author.

The history of the Kanak people after initial contact with Europeans in 1774 is shamefully similar to the stories of indigenous peoples worldwide. Early curiosity on the islanders' part quickly gave way to hostility when the presence of foreigners led to decimation of the population through introduced diseases, occupation of and removal from ancestral lands, desecration of sacred sites, political disenfranchisement, confinement to reservations, destruction of cultural artifacts and traditions, and insistence on the superiority of the introduced culture.

The Kanak, with a warrior tradition, did not always accept this treatment peacefully. Many armed, bloody conflicts and revolts occurred, especially after the island group became a French colony in 1853. While the plight of the Kanak became somewhat better when the world began to decolonialize after World War II, history, racism, and lack of educational and economic opportunity continue to plague their position in the modern life and prosperity of New Caledonia. They remain a predominantly rural people, working as farmers, miners, and laborers. In the capital, Noumea, they are exposed to the latest in international technology: imported B.M.W. convertibles, the fastest computers, and domestic conveniences of every description. However, due to economic stratification and the high prices on imports, these things are almost categorically out of reach.

In the course of the development of international discourse about civil rights in the 1960s, certain Kanak leaders became quite articulate about their place not only on the political margins of New Caledonian life, but also its cultural margins. As was the case in most eighteenth- and nineteenth-century European colonies, New Caledonia had been transformed during its 150 years of colonial rule to reflect France as much as possible in the remote, rugged, and sub-tropical locale.[1] This transformation of the landscape, imposition of the French language, and imitation of the cultural spaces, activities, and behaviors of the colonizing nation made the urbanized parts

1 *This observation is developed in response to ideas articulated by Said,* Culture and Imperialism, *225–226.*

314

of New Caledonia completely foreign to the Kanak. Their own landscape, languages, and cultural spaces were systematically devalued in the process—held to be "primitive" in the terms of the imposed French culture. As a key leader of the Kanak Liberation movement, Jean-Marie Tjibaou put it, "While I can share what I have of French culture with a non-Kanak in this country today, it is impossible for him to share with me the universal aspects of my culture."[2] The majority of the local white population of French descent, known as the Caldoche, remain to this day highly defensive of their version of French culture and particularly resistant to and threatened by Kanak enfranchisement.

In 1988, the most recent outbreak of violence between the Kanak and the French threatened the territory with outright civil war. This was averted by the signing of the Matignon Accord in the same year. The leader who negotiated the accord for the Kanak was Jean-Marie Tjibaou who argued unrelentingly that cultural presence was essential to political inclusion. "For me," Tjibaou said, "culture is capital; it is the thing which gives knowledge of life."[3] The accord included, at the insistence of the Kanak, the explicit support and development of Kanak culture as an integrated part of the overwhelmingly French New Caledonian culture. This was to be achieved through the establishment and funding of the Agency for the Development of Kanak Culture (A.D.C.K.). Tjibaou was adamant that this agency should have a cultural center, and that it must be located in Noumea, the mostly white capital, and not in some remote rural location. The center would not only present and preserve traditional Kanak culture, dance, art, and language, but would allow for its development and interaction with other Pacific Islanders and the world.[4] A former priest, the nonviolent Tjibaou, was assassinated one year after the signing of the accord by a Kanak extremist.

This assassination demonstrated the need for an immediate gesture to secure peace. In 1989, the French government committed to the cultural center, which appropriately bears Tjibaou's name. In a move that might be interpreted either as a masterful public-relations pseudo-apology, as cynical postcolonial grandstanding, or perhaps as both, François Mitterand included the Kanak Cultural Center on the list of major building projects that would serve as a legacy of his government. It was the only one of the so-called *Grand Projets* to be located outside of France. And so the colonizers coopted the project that the Kanak had to threaten violence in order to achieve. The building could appear to the outside world to be a gift from the kindly, paternalistic French to exhibit their generous enlightened postcolonial attitudes.

The condition of the human spirit that Piano was compelled to address with this building, then, was one of an exhausted, cynical, and angry people. Marginalized for generations in their own land to the point of taking up weapons in order to make themselves heard, the Kanak had little reason to believe that this project was going to serve their best interests. It must have

Jean Marie Tjibaou. Photo courtesy of James Clifford.

2 *R.P.B.W. Press Kit.*

3 *Tjibaou Exhibit.*

4 *The text of the Matignon-Oudinot Accord of 1988 states that the role of the Agency for the Development of Kanak Culture is "to accord full value to the Kanak cultural heritage in all its forms: archeological, ethnographic and linguistic; to encourage contemporary forms of Kanak culture; to promote cultural exchange, especially within the South Pacific region; to define and conduct research programs of value to Kanak culture."*

been hard to accept this French gesture, no matter how large, when it was made under duress, was motivated by guilt, and seemed so small in comparison to the size, duration, and brutality of colonial offenses—the most recent one a massacre of some twenty rebels in 1988. "Ambiguity haunted this facility," writes Alban Bensa, the anthropologist who worked with Piano throughout the project.[5]

5 *Bensa*, Architecture d'aujourd'hui.

WORKING WITH AMBIGUITY

Before Renzo Piano committed the Building Workshop to enter the competition, he visited New Caledonia and spent time with Octave Tonga, the director of the center, then located in temporary quarters in central Noumea. At Piano's request, Tonga left him alone for several hours on the beautiful site which separates a quiet lagoon from the more active bay. Piano was moved by the fact that the place had served as the location of Melanesia 2000, a festival organized by Jean-Marie Tjibaou and his followers in 1975 which was the first cultural festival in New Caledonia explicitly celebrating Kanak heritage.

Upon returning to Europe, Piano assembled his Building Workshop team, which included Paul Vincent, his associate in Paris, and Alban Bensa, the noted anthropologist with specialized knowledge of the Kanak people. The inclusion of the articulate and politicized Bensa on his team assured from the outset that Piano, already sensitized to the issues, had an understanding of the highly politicized situation he was entering. There was no way to avoid the fact that the building would be taken symbolically: For better or worse. "I had to create a symbol," says Piano, "a cultural center devoted to Kanak civilization, the place that would represent them to foreigners and that would pass on their memory to their grandchildren. Nothing could have been more loaded with symbolic expectations."[6]

6 *Piano*, Logbook.

It is clear from Piano's writings about the project that the past as well as this particular historical moment were foremost in his mind as he began to work on his competition entry. He was self-conscious of his position as an outsider, and perhaps was aware of the postcolonial contradictions of how the project came to be. While I am still researching his attitudes on the adoption of the center by Mitterand, Piano does hint at his awareness of the issue when he writes in his Logbook:

It has to said that, quite apart from good intentions, from the rejection of any form of colonialism, and from the respect due other cultures, there was no alternative. A proposal based upon our own models would simply not have worked in New Caledonia. It was not feasible to offer a standard product of Western architecture, with a layer of camouflage over the top: it would have looked like an armored car covered with palm leaves.[7]

7 *Ibid.*

With this, Piano entered a difficult terrain in today's poststructuralist, hyper-politically correct world—he committed himself to a politicized and symbolic

316

project. I think the story of how the project came to be what we see here, and why, demonstrates that Piano sought at every possible juncture to return the building to the Kanak. The Kanak people hold Piano in continued respect for the way that he approached the project. Emmanuel Kasarherou, Cultural Director of the Center said, "From the beginning, Renzo Piano had a deep understanding of the need for a unique building. He understood the Kanak spirit in a way that the other competitors did not. He was open-minded and could admit when he needed help."[8] After years of coping with colonial arrogance, Piano's approach must have indeed been refreshing for the Kanak people.

8 *Kasarherou, author interview.*

CREATING A LEGIBLE LANDSCAPE

The site for the project, the Tina Peninsula, is on the outskirts of Noumea— New Caledonia's unsentimental and unremarkable capital of 70,000 people. The agency had initially wanted the project in Noumea proper as a forceful cultural presence in the midst of the very French city, and were at first dismayed at the relative remoteness of the site. The finger of land divides a tranquil lagoon from a bay connected to the ocean. The quiet lagoonside is lined with dense mangroves rising out of the water's edge. Originally, other native trees covered the peninsula, with the exception of a well-worn path along the small ridge that ran the length of the peninsula, and a clearing off the path near the center of the site. The bay side of the small ridge was more windswept and showed signs of having survived fierce storms. On his first visit to the site, Piano sketched three ideas that were woven with a number of Kanak traditions about nature and the landscape throughout the site development: (1) the intense heat of the sub-tropical sun; (2) the almost constant presence of wind; and (3) an image of the cross-section of the site in which the building would reinforce the natural barrier the ridge provided for the ecology of the lagoon—giving the site two very different faces. In addition, Piano saw the many existing trees as a site asset and strove to retain them. This suggested that the building should keep to the path and clearing.

Alban Bensa helped the Workshop to understand that the Kanak had no built history. With the mild subtropical climate of New Caledonia, there was little need to develop elaborate buildings. Instead the Kanak developed a deep and subtle relationship with the landscape. They have extensive knowledge of native vegetation; using it not only for food and medicine, but as cultural markers of boundary, entrance, greeting, and occupation as well. For instance, the towering thin columnar pine, the male symbol, is planted alongside the female symbol, the coconut tree, wherever there is a household, thus marking human occupation in an otherwise low-growing landscape. Another plant, with red coloring on its leaves, marks the threshold of land that is occupied.

While the Kanak had no permanent buildings, they did have a building tradition—one of small wood-frame buildings erected on earthen bases and topped with thatch roofs. Due to the subtropical climate and the temporary

Piano's first site response sketch. Courtesy of RPBW.

9 Miyake, A+U.

nature of available building materials, these structures had to be renewed periodically. The form of the buildings differed from island to island; on Grand Terre they were round in plan with tall conical roofs.[9] The Kanak also had a tradition of making buildings in groups, with the headman's house at the end of a long, open public allée formed by other buildings clustered along either side. Often the allée was planted with trees, providing a shady central gathering place. Buildings were seldom placed close together, and the landscape always slid between them. Due to the nature of the buildings and the lush vegetation, the village was always being created, and was never completed. As long as this tradition of inhabiting a place was unbroken, there was little need for a heritage of permanent buildings. The activity itself served as the cultural link to the past.

Before European intrusion, a Kanak's particular geographical place was a defining quality of his or her being. With a rugged landscape and a culture that incorporated suspicion of strangers, Kanak language groups grew up isolated from one another and confined and identified by geographical enclosure. This attachment to place, and the language that went with it, made the displacement imposed by the French particularly devastating for Kanak identity. People were removed from the valley or mountain shoulder that was the center of their world and placed on reservations with strangers. However, the embedding of the culture in the landscape, a way of living primarily outside of buildings, and the use, appreciation, and cultural signification of plants, has survived beyond forced removal into the present day.

This landscape focus of the Kanak people, overlaid with Piano's experience and reading of the site, became the place where the Building Workshop began its design. First they had to devise a strategy for a building program of 8,550 square meters, that would incorporate in a deep, rather than superficial, way the landscape traditions and habitation sensibilities of the Kanak, while answering the demands of a state-of-the-art cultural center. Piano wrote, "The link between nature and the built structure must be so close that they exude the same smells, breathe the same wind, form a unique, semi-built, near-complete space."[10] To achieve this, the team began investigating how to break down the scale and bulk of the building and connect its pieces to the landscape, to create a place that would seem familiar to the Kanak who would be using it. "As an expression of a link with nature," Piano wrote, "which constitutes age-old tradition the Centre is not, could not be, enclosed in a monumental form. For this reason, it is not about a unique edifice: it is an ensemble of villages and of stands of trees, of functions and paths, full and empty spaces."[11]

10 R.P.B.W. Press Kit.

11 Ibid.

This attitude led to a site strategy of using the existing path along the peninsula ridge as an allée, not unlike the open allées in Kanak villages. This one, however was exceedingly long and narrow by comparison and would need to be covered to protect people from the intense sun and frequent rain. The program elements, then, were be strung along the allée, with space in between them to allow the inhabitants of the building to always be connected to the landscape and the elements. Service and storage areas were pushed into the ground to reduce building bulk and leave much of the site unbuilt. Parking was moved off the peninsula toward the mainland. People would approach the building on foot through the landscape.

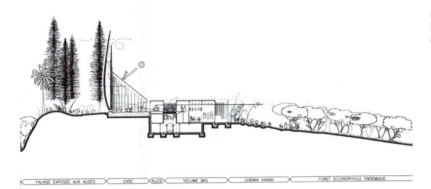

Project pushed into the ground to keep the site as free as possible. Courtesy of RPBW.

Further refinements were made to these landscape ideas after Piano won the competition, and began including Octave Tonga, the Director of the Center, Marie-Claude Tjibaou, President of the Agency for the Development of Kanak Culture and Jean-Marie's widow, and other Kanak people on the workshop team. The deeply embedded relationship to nature is further cultivated at the center in the Kanak Path, an interpretive landscape path which ties local vegetation to the Kanak creation myth by organizing a series of landscapes along a wandering walkway between the building and the lagoon. During the opening days of the center, the Kanak Path was crowded with Kanak people clearly excited by the recognition of their well-known myth and their landscape at this new place. For non-Kanak people, it unveils and makes more legible the rural New Caledonian landscape.

Ways of moving through the landscape were also incorporated. Kanak tradition holds that an indirect path is the proper way to approach a building, especially the dwelling of an important person. As a result of this, the entry to the building is not at the end of the allée, where conventional Western architectural logic would have it. Instead one follows a path that approaches the end of the building, then swings away from it toward the lagoon, up a small rise, then turns toward the building to enter it under a wide porch along the side. Alternately, one can take the Kanak Path, which wanders three-quarters of the way around the building, allowing entry mid-way along the bay side, under the café porch. While first-time non-Kanak visitors search in goal-oriented confusion for an entrance, Kanak visitors wander calmly toward it.

Emmanuel Kasarherou states, "It was very intelligent to use the landscape to introduce the building. This is a way the Kanak people can understand."[12]

12 *Kasarherou, author interview.*

319

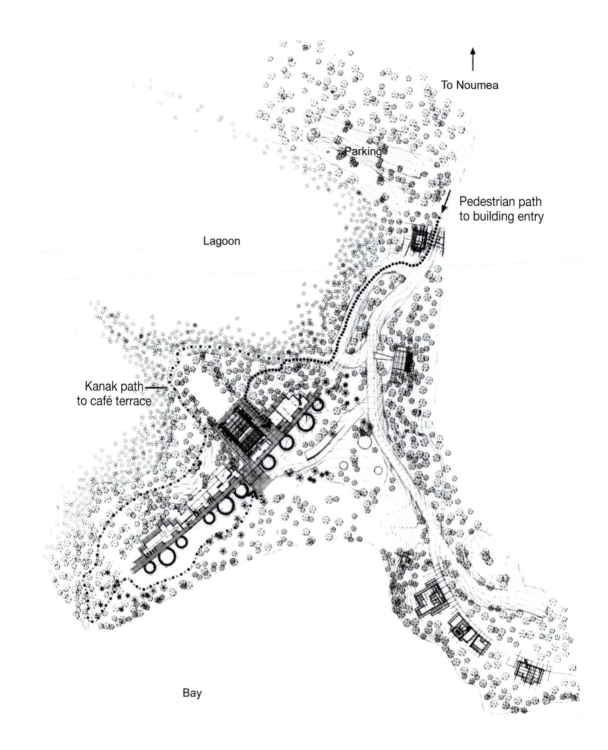

To Noumea

Parking

Pedestrian path
to building entry

Lagoon

Kanak path
to café terrace

Bay

Site plan showing alternate paths
into the building. Base plan
courtesy of RPBW.

N

Entry porch. Photo courtesy of RPBW.

This sort of embedding of the project in the landscape would not have been possible on a site in the center of Noumea. In the end, the peninsula has turned out to be the ideal site—rural enough to be comfortable for the Kanak who come to it from small towns and villages, yet close enough to Noumea to attract visitors and participants in cultural activities, and to provide access to urban infrastructure and services.

TRANSFORMING SYMBOLS

So Piano seems to have gotten the site strategy right. However, the site strategy as stated does not yet hold anything that would suggest building form or technology—except for the suggestion that passive strategies for ventilation should be used to help maintain connection to the landscape. Much more difficult was discovering the form and materials the building should take.

It should be noted here that the local building industry in New Caledonia seems to have a quite limited repertoire of material experience: Almost every building is reinforced concrete frame with block infill. Local steel fabrication is limited primarily to the rough functional work needed by the huge nickel-mining industry of the territory. The only refined building craft tradition found locally is fine carpentry and cabinet-making. It is easy to imagine, given Piano's obvious dedication to elegant buildings, that local skills and technology were not up to making any building he would design. It was almost a foregone conclusion that much of the building materials and technology

321

would have to be imported, especially if the building was to live up to its French role as the last of the *Grand Projects*.

While both Piano and the center were dedicated to using as much local labor as possible for the project, the local builders had limited skills with technologies other than concrete frame. This did not create an obstacle for Piano—instead it points to another reason his selection as architect for this project was so appropriate. The R.P.B.W. commonly uses a kit-of-parts approach for its projects. This comes in part from a refined modernist sensibility about repetition and pattern, as well as a concern about quality of construction. With the kit-of-parts approach, the pieces could be fabricated overseas, then shipped to the site, where local labor could put it all together. This is the very practice that was used by Gustav Eiffel for his many train station projects in South America. It allowed the latest in building technology to be used to create great buildings in parts of the world where the technology would not otherwise be available.

It might be argued that this view of technology and building is a type of colonialism: That it universalizes a place and a people, ignoring their own sensibilities. In the case of Eiffel and the trains that were populating South America at the turn of the century, there was no local tradition of building that could possibly contain the huge machines. This is also the case, in a different sense, for the Tjibaou Cultural Center: There is no precedent in the Kanak building tradition for the accommodation of computers, large works of art, studio space for visiting international artists, telephone and fax service, or contemporary dance performances.

At this point in time, the Kanak culture has already been irretrievably altered—it exists right now in an international condition. It would be patronizing to expect these people to return to their precolonial era way of life or technology; to not share in the material prosperity their land has created. "The return to tradition is a myth," said Jean-Marie Tjibaou, "No people has ever achieved that. The search for identity, for a model, I believe lies before us."[13] And so forward is where Piano searched for architectural and tectonic expression free of what was available in the locale. Alban Bensa suggests that he accomplished even more than that: "Local traditions are not copied but transfigured by contemporary architecture, which draws its substance from what is specific in Kanak culture, giving it universal legibility and thus turning towards other civilizations and the future."[14]

As Piano has proven over and over in his career as an architect, there is no line for him between design and the technical manifestation of the design. The modification and invention of building technology and detail is part and parcel of how he works as an architect, and of how he runs his practice as a building workshop. It has been written about Piano that for him, "Technique means knowing how to integrate the most sophisticated technology with the creative, manual, and intellectual input of the individual; from the architect to whoever participates in the construction and, if possible, also he for whom

13 *R.P.B.W. Press Kit.*

14 *Bensa.*

the architecture is intended."[15] With a commitment made to making a symbolic building, Piano turned again to the Kanak for hints about what to do.

Throughout New Caledonia, one can locate a Kanak house or a village by looking for the great columnar pines that they plant upon occupation of a site. These rise as distinctive vertical markers of inhabitation in the sometimes rugged landscape. Likewise, particularly on Grande Terre, traditional Kanak buildings are capped by a tall conical thatched roof many times the height of the building. Piano takes the pine tree and the *case* as a point of departure for what came to be the iconic forms of the project. He found in the modernist notion of material and structural expression a place where the old might become new. Traditionally the *cases* are circular wood-framed structures that rise from a built-up earthen base. Pole rafters rest on exterior walls and meet at the top of a towering central pole. Crosspieces are then lashed between wall posts and between rafters to support the deep thatch of the exterior. The structural dynamics and methods of making are revealed in the unfinished interior.

Through a series of disciplined study models the R.P.B.W. transformed the *cases*. They stripped off the thatch and refined the crosspieces as battens with rhythmic spacing. They removed the central pole, opened the pole rafters like petals of a flower to become vertical structures with their tips no longer meeting, and changed the rafters into curved glulam ribs that step down in height as they form the circle with the tallest opposite the circulation allée. The resulting interior space is a circular room opening onto the allée and roofed with a flat disc tilted up from the entrance toward the high point of the ribs.

Once this general form was achieved, the R.P.B.W. further refined this form in response to the tropical climate and widely varying wind conditions of the site. They developed a double skin system on the walls of the *cases* to allow the exterior wall to shade the interior wall and leaving a space for a thermal chimney in between. Their wind tunnel tests demonstrated that all the *cases* should be oriented with their highest sides toward the prevailing wind which gave them both structural and ventilation advantages and provided the logic for the spacing of the exterior battens. They tied the glulams together with galvanized steel bracing to form a three-dimensional circular truss designed to withstand hurricane-force winds. After criticism from the Kanak working on the team, the workshop made other revisions to make the tectonic forces and counterforces of the cases more legible. Finally, the interior skin consists of louvered panels operated by computer to maximize natural cooling.

In the end, the *cases* have a deep reference to their traditional predecessors, yet become something equally authentic while completely new. They have lost their earthbound sensibility and their solid silouette. Now they soar up from the ground, and like the pines, the tops feather out against the sky. The

Building Workshop's study of traditional Kanak *Case*. Courtesy of RPBW.

15 Franco Zagari, "The Piano Effect," quoted in Kenneth Frampton, "Renzo Piano."

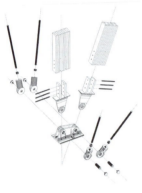

top: Bracing detail in the new *cases*. Photo courtesy of RPBW.

above: Kit-of-parts construction of *case* bracing system. Courtesy of RPBW.

16 *Piano*, Logbook.

edge of building and sky seem to shift over the course of the day and in different light: Sometimes making a distinct lace-like pattern, sometimes appearing to blend almost seamlessly.

The transformed *cases* by themselves were not sufficient to contain the symbolic and the programmatic demands of the center. There needed to be something else, something of the world beyond the shores of New Caledonia—beyond the specific history of this particular colonial occupation. For this, Piano chose a clear international vocabulary of horizontally proportioned glass and steel flat-roofed boxes, modified for the climate. These provide a visual and cultural foil for the soaring curving shapes of the *cases*— and perhaps suggest the distance still to be traversed in Kanak healing and cultural visibility.

The contrast between the two structural vocabularies and their technological demands did not trouble Piano. In fact, their coexistence became a further symbolic gesture of the project: he says, "Above all, (it was) to be a project synonymous with peace, enabling valuable dialogue to be established with the other communities in the territory and throughout the Pacific. It should," he continues, "enable the Melanese to express their cultural roots and to empress upon this magical location their identity and their open-mindedness with regard to the future. The strength of the building and of its setting must be inherent in the gentle but clearly affirmed transition between the earliest Kanak culture and the innovative demands of modernity. Indeed," says Piano, " we must bear in mind that we are at the threshold of the 21st century and that we can use a certain type of technology, advanced but kind, compatible with the notion of memory, not opposed or unsuited to it. We have to reconcile modernity and technology with nature and tradition."[16]

End porch of project where it is easy to see the vocabulary of the soaring *cases* meeting the pragmatics of the flat-roofed portions of the centre. Image by author.

MAKING IT RIGHT

Having determined that minimal construction and fabrication skills and technology existed in New Caledonia, R.P.B.W. began looking globally for the best materials possible. For the *cases* they needed a type of wood that was farmed, was unusually stable and therefore could be laminated in large pieces, had natural insect-repelling qualities and would require little maintenance. They found iroko, a kind of mahogany grown in Guinea which is insect and moisture resistant and ages to a silvery gray over time.

The fabrication of the wood into the giant glulam ribs used for the cases could only be accomplished at five fabricators worldwide. Piano's Paris-based team chose to work with a fabricator in France. After the ribs were fabricated they were slung onto the deck (as they could not fit into the opening of the hold) of the only ship large enough to take them that plied the waters to New Caledonia. The cast-steel connectors and footings of the *cases* as well as all of the other major building components were likewise prefabricated and shipped to the islands. One doesn't need much experience with building-site glitches to imagine the continuous headaches the remote fabrication and shipping schedules created on the construction site.

The running of the construction site is the final place where Piano's sensitivity to the historical and cultural context of the project played out. He sent as his site architect a Frenchman named William Vassal, who had worked closely on the design of the project for years. Vassal set the tone for the site when on the first day he insisted on walking the heavy equipment operators over the site before they started clearing and grading to explain the project and why certain trees should be maintained. This was so effective in getting the operators to work carefully with the existing vegetation of the site, that he later had to negotiate with them to remove a tree or two for aesthetic reasons. Vassal continued this interactive mode of supervision of crews not used to the daily presence of an architect on the site or to reading drawings prepared for unique building systems: Explaining, demonstrating, collaborating, providing unconventional drawings, and always insisting on the best work possible under the circumstances. He says in retrospect, "Everyone was proud to work on the project. They all went the extra distance to make sure it was a good building."[17]

17 Vassal, author interview.

So this is how the project looks. It nestles into the subtle topography of the small peninsula. The experience of the place is of a series of small buildings clustered together in the landscape. Ten of the transformed cases line the bay side of the central allée. They clearly symbolize the Kanak—radically changed from their precolonial past and looking toward the future. The allée itself and the pieces that line up on the lagoon side of it, are a blatantly international style assembly of steel and glass, with interior floors and finishes of wood, except in the galleries, where white walls are the rule. The double-layered flat roofs of these pieces are held even, with the bulk of the spaces pressed underground so that the cases can soar above them. The flat roofs extend beyond

Aerial view over lagoon. Image by author.

the building to make great shaded porches on the northwestern side of the building. The galleries inside are great high clean Renzo Piano galleries, full of filtered daylight and bringing to mind his galleries for the de Menil Collection in Houston. Clearly this part of the building symbolizes the international community which the Kanak are entering.

The project is remarkable for the fact that it avoids both international arrogance and picturesque sentimentality, both dangers in designing for indigenous communities. Instead it walks the delicate line between tradition and international culture.

William Vassal tells the following story:

We were showing the building site to a group of Kanak people, with (Director of the Center) Octave Tonga, and I was explaining to them the work of Piano and the team, and we arrived in front of a case. I said, "here is a hut." The Kanak said nothing and spoke together in the Kanak language, and Tonga translated that they were asking where the hut was. I tried to explain in place of Renzo that this was the remembering of a hut. He wanted to do the transition between modernity and tradition. Also he uses this sentence from the South American writer, Borges, that the work of the creators, like architect, is just on the border between memory and oblivion. When Piano explained that it was the remembering of a hut, it was just what you remember of a hut before you begin to forget it and you begin to do something else. So this is what I said to the Kanaks, and they talked together again, and the oldest one said, "This hut is like ours, before we put the thatched roof on it." He stopped speaking and started again, "This is not us anymore, but it's still us."[18]

18 Vassal, A+U *interview.*

326

It is obvious from this story and from the project as you see it here that the Tjibaou Cultural Center sits outside of easy politically correct condemnations, either cultural or environmental. It exists in the swirling cross-currents of our postcolonial, post-Cold War, world. Piano accepted this flickering condition and strove with all of his immense ability to make the building he and his collaborators were making as a container for the fragile, battered, but optimistic spirits of the Kanak people as they move forward. This seems to me a most human way to use technological ability and innovation, even in our slippery, messy world.

Alban Bensa, with characteristic clarity, sums it up this way:

For Kanaks, the cultural center is like the sculpted prow of a canoe heading for independence. But while it projects an ultra-modern image of "custom" for the purposes of international media, it also unsettles a population still composed mainly of farmers and workers, and thus figures the deep social and ideological currents that are changing the Kanaks. As for the public authorities, they seem intent on making this monumental facility (which Mitterand had already foreseen on a postage stamp design) the flagship for the new role France hopes to play in a Pacific at long last nuclear free and calm. Cutting across anti-colonial feeling and continued French presence in New Caledonia, midway between a tribute to Kanak civilization and progressive European architectural thought serving our modernity, and amidst the difficult coming together of living traditions and those that are represented, the Jean-Marie Tjibaou Cultural Center focalizes the tensions of its own ambiguity.[19]

Image by author.

19 Bensa.

ACKNOWLEDGMENTS

The outline of the Kanak history and many of the facts presented here are the result of a series of interviews with William Vassal, R.P.B.W. site architect, over a three-day period in June 1998 in Noumea. I am indebted to his generosity and patience.

REFERENCES

Bensa, Alban "Piano: Noumea," *Architecture d'aujourd'hui* 308 (December 1996).

Buchanan, Peter *Renzo Piano Building Workshop*, Vols 1 and 2, London: Phaidon Press, 1993 and 1997.

—— "Pacific Piano," *Architectural Review*, March 1992.

—— "Pacific Rim and Planetary Culture," *Architectural Review*, August 1991.

Campbell, I. C. *A History of the Pacific Islands*, Berkeley, Calif.: University of California Press, 1996.

Findley, Lisa "Piano Nobile," Review of Tjibaou Cultural Center, *Architecture*, October 1998.

Frampton, Kenneth "Renzo Piano: The Architect as Homo Faber," *GA Architect*, 14.

Hart, Sara "Double Indemnity," Technology Report on Tjibaou Cultural Center, *Architecture*, October 1998.

Miyake, Riichi. "From the Vernacular to the Universal," *A+U*, August 1998.

Piano, Renzo, "Jean-Marie Tjibaou Cultural Center, Construction: 1995–1998," *Renzo Piano Logbook*, London: Thames & Hudson, 1997.

—— "Project Background," Monument #3 1994.

R.P.B.W. Press Kit. Centre Culturel Tjibaou, Noumea, New Caledonia. Renzo Piano Building Workshop, 1998.

Said, Edward *Culture and Imperialism*, New York: Alfred A. Knopf, 1993.

Smith, Stephanie "Phoenix," Review of Tjibaou Cultural Center, *Architecture Australia*, 1998.

Tjibaou, Jean-Marie, quotes from exhibition on Tjibaou at the Cultural Center.

Vassal, William Interview by the author, *A+U*, August 1998.

Originally published in the Proceedings of the 88th Annual Meeting of the Association of Collegiate Schools of Architecture, 2000. This paper is an early version of research and writing that resulted in the book Building Change: Architecture Politics and Cultural Agency *(Routledge 2005). Some portions of this text appear in Chapter 2 of the book.*

HISTORY, TRADITION, AND MODERNITY
Urbanism and cultural change in Chanderi, India

JYOTI HOSAGRAHAR

The story of Chanderi is an oft-repeated tale of a place that has stood still in time—or had until its recent "discovery." The distinctive built form of a place that seems exotic and timeless. Signs of engagement with modernity seem threatening to those eager to romanticize and preserve its uniqueness. Yet, change is apparent—and inevitable. It is a living town. The historic, medieval fabric has remained continuously inhabited. The remarkable character of Chanderi seems fragile and threatened by development and modernization. How can we consider sustainability in the context of change in such a settlement?

This chapter is an ethnographic study of the changing urban fabric in an apparently tradition-bound, medieval settlement, Chanderi, India. My fieldwork among the weavers of Chanderi revealed the intricate relationship between the economic, social, and spatial organization of weaving, and that of dwelling.[1] Through a study of the historical development of building and weaving as well as the interactions and activities around the weavers' housing, I hold that transformations taking place in the built form are intricately linked to social and economic changes in the organization of weaving and family structure. Such an approach to studying the built environment as a cultural landscape is in contrast to a majority of studies that have examined such historic towns as "traditional settlements" and as culturally determined artifacts or as forms determined by climate, and geography. Studying the cultural landscapes of Chanderi demands an understanding of the structures and spatial configurations but also of their social, economic, and cultural significance and changes over time. This approach is particularly important in places where the distinctions between work and home are much more closely interrelated and overlapping than in a typical industrial or urban housing. In Chanderi, the entire family is involved in the production process and the division of labor is across age and gender.

Rather than view Chanderi as an exotic and "traditional" settlement, a cultural landscape approach reveals that the distinctive architecture and urbanism are fundamentally cultural processes that are intricately connected to a place, its natural and social context. If change is central to an apparently changeless identity, then resolving the residents' aspirations to become "modern" without losing their rich heritage would contribute to sustainable architecture and urbanism.

1 The author gratefully acknowledges the support of the Madhya Pradesh government, and the Indian National Trust for Art and Cultural Heritage. The study was part of a redevelopment proposal for Chanderi.

329

CHANDERI: AN INTRODUCTION

Chanderi is a historic town in Madhya Pradesh, in central India. According to available records, the city was first established in the thirteenth century. While handloom weaving was always a significant activity in Chanderi, since the past 400 years it has been the primary occupation of the town's residents. Today Chanderi has a population of over 20,000, 60 percent of whom are involved in the production of hand-woven fabrics. The textiles produced by the weavers of Chanderi are gossamer silks and brocades of very fine quality. Most of these are produced as *sari* and dress materials sold in boutiques and *sari* showrooms both within the country and overseas.[2]

Historically, at the settlement level, the king, along with his architects and planners, made decisions regarding building and layout of the town in Chanderi. The walled town of Chanderi had been laid out on the *prastara* planning principles.[3] These ancient codes and scriptures informed the layout of key features such as the main streets, the location of the royal palace and the seats of government and administration, the location of neighborhoods, and the overall form of the town. The king and other members of the royal family constructed water bodies such as *talaab* (ponds or lakes) and *baoli* (stepped wells), temples and mosques as well as the town wall.

2 *The* sari *is the customary garb of a majority of women in India. Typically, it is a piece of unstitched cloth that is 1 yard wide and 6 yards long. Colors, intricate patterns, and decorations are also typical.*

3 Prastara *principles are ancient Hindu town-planning principles based on the* mandala *or a cosmic scheme.*

Layout of Chanderi, India. Shows an incrementally developed built form with separate neighborhoods. The dark line shows an asphalt road that connects the town to a highway.

330

Neighborhoods were often based on caste, and occupation, and sometimes on religion (although I often found Hindu and Muslim families living next to each other).

DWELLING AND WEAVING IN THE ANSARI FAMILY

The Ansari family offers a valuable window into the cultural and spatial patterns of a typical weaver's family in Chanderi. The Ansari family lived in what I call a 'microcluster'—a compound where several branches of a large family lived together in separate dwellings.[4] An historical perspective on the use and significance of spaces in a single microcluster is revealing.

FAMILY AND SPACE

Shakurullah Ansari (Shakur), patriarch of the Ansari household, was a weaver in Chanderi. The Ansari household lived in a neighborhood or community of weavers in the western part of Chanderi. He lived with his wife Tasneem, eight unmarried children, three married sons, and their families. Shakur had two looms, and each of his married sons owned one. Shakur, Tasneem, and their unmarried children lived in the rooms around the eastern courtyard. The married sons, Salim, Abdul, and Ali lived with their wives and children in the units around the western courtyard. The families of Abdul and Ali inhabited different floors of the same structure. Each of the family units also had a goatshed attached to it. In a sense, they were four families living together as one extended family. While all these nuclear families lived in contiguity within the same larger compound and shared a common block of facilities, they did not cook and eat together. Each family had its own cooking arrangements and food-storage areas, an area for the loom and a multipurpose area. All the micro-families shared the open courtyards as well as the entrances. However, Shakur's sons and their families used the western courtyard and entrance

4 *A microcluster indicates a common type of dwelling arrangement among weavers in Chanderi. It consists of a group of dwellings and workplaces grouped around courtyards. A number of related nuclear families living and working together form an extended family that inhabit a microcluster.*

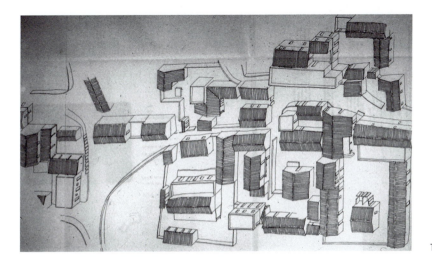

The Ansari neighborhood.

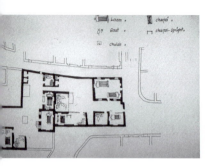

Spatial organization of activities in the Ansari microcluster.

Narrow street with courtyard of microcluster behind the street front.

more than the eastern one while Shakur, his wife, and younger children used the latter more frequently. The interior spaces for cooking and storage were "territories" of the women in the families. Women also generally took care of the goats and their sheds.

Entering the Ansari microcluster into the eastern courtyard, the loom room was to the right, its windows overlooking the street, and a semienclosed goatshed to the left. At the far end of the courtyard was a semienclosed cooking and storage area. Another goatshed, a recently constructed toilet and bathing area were also around the same courtyard. The western courtyard had two entries—one from the street and another from the eastern courtyard. A double-storied structure inhabited by the families of Abdul and Ali, a single-storied dwelling of Salim and his family, attached goatsheds for each, and a toilet block were all located around the eastern courtyard.

This microcluster is Shakur's ancestral home and one he lived in as a child, so he could recall the previous arrangement of the units around the eastern courtyard from his childhood. The structures of the cooking and storage areas and the goatsheds had been there as long as he could recall. However, the goatshed at the far end of the courtyard used to be a cooking area and the present cooking and storage areas were once the loom areas. About forty years ago he remembered helping his father build the new loom room. In those days, Shakur said, his married brothers did not have separate cooking or storage spaces, nor did they each work on separate looms. For one thing, the earlier looms required two people to operate and for another, there was a single cooking arrangement and the entire joint family ate out of a single pot. Now his sons and their families were more independent.

Semiprivate platform in another neighborhood.

After Shakur's father died, his mother lived in the room at the far end of the western courtyard. When Salim married, the newly-weds moved in there. For Shakur's second son, Abdul, and his family, Shakur decided to build an additional unit a few years ago. Recently, they pulled down the sloping roof of the single-storied structure, laid stone slabs and put up a second floor to the unit for their third son, Ali. He wished he could have afforded to build a flat-roofed cement and concrete structure since it was easier to add to. Shakur said that the next time they add a structure they would have a mason come from one of the nearby towns to put up a flat concrete roof instead of the usual sloping frame one. He said that many of his neighbors had done that as it was easier to build a second floor on top.

SPATIAL IMPLICATIONS OF WEAVING

Weaving in Chanderi is a complex process with many operations preparatory to actually working the loom. In the Ansari family, Shakur got the yarn, both silk and cotton, from the Chanderi Weavers' Cooperative, a government organization to support handloom weaving in Chanderi. The yarn came in long hanks. Officials of the cooperative also specified the design, colors, and quantities of saris and dress materials to be woven. The cooperative worked with designers in large cities to decide the different colors and designs for different markets both national and international.

The yarn in hanks was first dyed the appropriate colors before turning on to the looms. Dying the yarn was a skillful process as the threads are very delicate. Shakur and his sons usually bought chemical dyes in the open market (rather than the dyes provided by the cooperative). They prepared the dye solution in vats in the courtyard of the microcluster. The two court-yards of the Ansari microcluster were stone paved. While neither had running water, washing areas were clearly designated. The dying was usually done in the larger of the two courtyards and the excess dyes poured into the open, stone-lined drain in the courtyard or thrown over the stone paving and allowed to seep into the earth. The whole process of dying took four or five hours. Drying the freshly dyed yarn required four to six people and a linear space. For this reason drying was often done in the street either by men or women of the family. They stretched out the yarn, often 30 to 40 feet in length on the streets and then swung the threads gently or lay them across bamboo stands.

Preparing the warp of the loom was a tedious task that required the help of neighbors. Each thread had to be tautly secured and rolled on the beam. Shakur and his sons usually did this with the help of neighbors in the cluster open space or in the length of the street. It took almost a whole day to join the threads. This done, the warp was now ready. The thread for the weft needed to be on fly shuttles which moved across the loom. Women filled shuttles by laying hanks of thread on spinning wheels and rolling thread onto the shuttles by hand-spinning the wheel. I observed women, and sometimes

A woman spinning thread in the courtyard of the microcluster while watching over a young child.

5 *Customarily, men were the primary weavers in a family while the women engaged in many tasks preparatory to weaving as well as the finishing of the woven material in addition to household chores and caring for the young and the elderly. In recent years women have increasingly taken to working looms if the family is able to afford additional ones.*

even children, carrying on this task constantly: on the platforms, in the court-yards, or within the rooms around.[5]

The head of a microcluster, the patriarch of the extended family in the Ansari household, took decisions about building or adding to an existing dwelling. They had extended and added units to their microcluster over time. The first expansion had been horizontal addition of units around the courtyards. When the main courtyards had been more or less surrounded by units, the family chose to make additions to the top of existing ones. Growth in the city's population, and a growing demand for land made vertical expansion of dwelling units a convenient alternative for the weavers. The other, less popular option was to leave the neighborhood altogether and build a new unit in the periphery of the city. In the Ansari cluster I noted that whatever the mode of development, the expansions and additions were such that they maintained the privacy of the women in the household and the social and functional character of the courtyards so essential to the households.[6]

6 *Women in Chanderi follow the purdah or the custom of seclusion (or veiling) from men outside the immediate family. Although this practice is more pronounced among Muslims in Chanderi, the spatial movements of Hindu women, too, is restricted by it.*

TEXTILE PRODUCTION AND SOCIO-SPATIAL TRANSFORMATIONS

Historically, the region was fertile and grew good cotton. Chanderi was well known for producing simple cotton textiles. In the early sixteenth century the local king brought some renowned weavers of Dacca to train local weavers the art of weaving fine cotton muslin. About 100 years later silk was introduced. From then on the weavers of Chanderi have produced cotton, cotton-silk, and pure silk textiles.

Until the nineteenth century the yarn was all hand-spun. The British introduced mill-spun thread to Chanderi in the late nineteenth century. Its advent resulted in the extinction of an entire occupation and community, the *katiya*. The ancestral occupation of the *katiya* community of Chanderi had been hand-spinning threads from raw cotton and silk. The spinning of the threads was done in Chanderi itself. The mill-spun threads introduced by the British were found to be tougher and finer and were adopted for weaving in the preference to the hand-spun ones.

For a long time, the fabrics woven by the weavers were for the pleasure of the kings and the nobility. The items woven were intended for the attire of nobility and included *dupatta* (long scarf), *saffaa* (cloth wrapped as turban for men), and *peti* (cloth draped on elephants for ceremonial occasions). The nobility sought to wear fabrics that were unique and exquisite in their design and rewarded these qualities in the weavers. Master weavers competed to produce the most artful and unique designs with intricate brocadework of fine gold wire for royalty and the elite. With changes in the social structure and lifestyle, these items of traditional attire were no longer in demand.

In the 1940s, weavers switched to weaving the *sari*. Innocuous as this change may sound, the impact of weaving the *sari* on the weaving process was immense. The width of the handlooms is designed according to the item that a particular weaver specializes in weaving. Hence, the width of the traditional looms, designed for the narrower width of the *dupatta* and the *saffaa*, were inadequate for weaving the *sari*. New looms that accommodated the *sari* were wider and occupied more space in the loom rooms than the previous looms. In addition, the changes made obsolete the structure of traditional looms. Since the organization of the household and its activities were closely related to the functioning of the loom, changes in the size, shape, and usage of the looms implied changes in the sizes of the loom rooms and the organization of the activities around the loom areas. Looms today have been standardized to suite the weaving of the *sari*. I also observed a corresponding standardization in the sizes and construction of loom rooms. This homogeneity in construction and size was not characteristic of the older houses of Chanderi in part because the weaving of numerous different items meant that looms and hence, the loom rooms, varied greatly in size and proportion.

Another technological change in weaving that affected the architecture of the loom room was the introduction of the fly shuttle in the 1950s. Before this time, three shuttles were used and traditionally, two people worked one loom. With the innovation of the fly shuttle, only one person was needed to work one loom. This in turn, altered dramatically the size and the arrangement of the loom rooms.

In 1946, in a new environment of democracy and independence, the state government started the Chanderi Weaver's Cooperative. The cooperative helped to replace or provide an alternative to the *sahukar* or merchant on

A typical layout of loom rooms. Shows the position of the looms during the day and string beds (*charpoys*) at night. Many loom rooms may have only one loom in them.

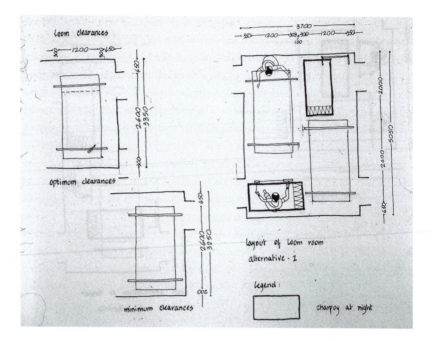

whom the weavers had once been dependent. Wealthy merchants had served as the middlemen or intermediaries between the weavers and the nobility. It was they who gave orders to the weavers and provided them material, and they who inspected the quality of the products before making payments. Weavers were invariably caught in a cycle of debilitating debt with the *sahukar* who wielded complete power over them.

Through the cooperative, the weavers received orders for the fabrics including specifications of colors and quantity. Once they wove the cloth, the weavers brought it back to the cooperative for sale. The cooperative provided them yarn, loans to buy or repair looms, and paid weavers for their labor by yard of woven cloth. While the new system released the weavers from the crippling burden of debt and helped to revive the craft, the system also provided the weavers an incentive to produce more—an emphasis different from that of earlier times when the stress was not on quantity but on quality and uniqueness of fabrics. This trend in the increasing commodification of labor has led some merchants and entrepreneurial weavers to employ other poorer weavers as labor. Large "factories" have started to come up where hand-looms are already set up, the yarn provided, and the design dictated. Even those with no looms of their own could be employed as weavers and receive wages in return for length of cloth woven. Hence, recently there has been a proliferation of sweatshops. In this way, despite Chanderi's apparent preindustrial character, modernity, industrialization, and capitalism have influenced the development of both the town and the handicraft.

The simple designs and motifs of the contemporary Chanderi *sari* (in comparison to those of the nineteenth and early twentieth centuries) require less skill and practice to weave. The support of the Textile Center and the current mass demand for the Chanderi *sari* has meant that the quantity of *saris* produced becomes more important than the quality of the fabric woven. Today each family seeks to acquire more and more looms. Since the textiles are delicate and need to be protected from dirt, moisture, insects, and harsh light, each additional loom demands a protected space. An increase in the number of looms and the persons weaving directly changes the organization of the microcluster and the rooms. The "simplified" craft has also enabled economic independence for weavers, facilitating the proliferation of extended and nuclear families in contrast to the old, joint families. This, in turn has meant that microclusters are now designed to include self-contained units with separate kitchens, toilets, goatsheds and access to the streets.

The emphasis on producing large quantities of fabric has put pressure on the weavers to weave increased quantities to bring home a higher income. More members in the family now spend their time indoors at the loom than in other tasks in the courtyards as before. The tasks associated with weaving themselves have become more specialized and commodified. Recent innovations in weavers' houses in the periphery of the city did not allot much space for courtyards and platforms. The design of windows to the loom room was an interesting and unique architectural feature in the older houses. The windows were tall with low sills and faced shaded streets to allow a constant diffused light on the weaving area. The sill was designed to be low so that a weaver seated at the pit-loom could interact with passersby on the street or even with a weaver at a loom in the building across the street.

With the introduction of the Weavers' Cooperative, its training facilities and payment for labor, more women now work the loom. Loom rooms had once been exclusively male areas with windows overlooking the street while women did many of the secondary tasks including dying, spinning, embroidery, and finishing in the making of the Chanderi textiles. With more women weaving, they had either to compromise their privacy and sit by public windows or work their looms from inadequately lit interior rooms. To protect women's privacy, increasingly, loom rooms had the windows to the street shut and used electric lamps instead. The quality of the streets and the nature of community interactions have all been redefined by these shut windows. Streets that were once filled by the rhythmic sound of clicking looms are silent. Electric lighting has further reduced the significance of the customary window designs. Sunrise and sunset no longer provide rhythms for the work day. It is no surprise that some of the more recent constructions show no respect for age-old windows favoring instead, standardized, small, high windows.

BUILDING TECHNOLOGY AND TRANSFORMATIONS IN THE BUILDING PROCESS

Vernacular building processes in Chanderi had demanded a close connection between the master builders, masons, and the residents shared a cultural understanding of space and building techniques. The role of the master builder in the construction of a dwelling depended to a large extent on the social and economic status of the families. The nobility and wealthy merchants had houses constructed of well-cut stone with fine carvings and *jail* (lattice work on fenestrations). *Chinkari* stonework was used with stone pillars, wooden trusses and regular stone shingles.[7] Such houses needed the skills of a master builder, who commanded stone carvers and masons, to innovate using a limited palette of technological and material possibilities. But the decisions of what to build and how much, and at what expense, remained with the owners.

In contrast, the dwellings of the weavers were built of rough-cut masonry blocks often set without mortar. The flooring was of packed earth. As the structures and forms of the dwellings were relatively simple, a skilled mason and a stone cutter could help the family put the structure together. The family members helped with whatever tasks they could to keep the costs down. The structures were unique and 'custom-made' for each circumstance and owner. Some communities were more particular about private courtyards within the microclusters, others had more subtle distinctions between public and private with semi-private spaces and platforms. The advent of standardized brick, concrete, and industrially produced doors and windows has rendered the distinctions between the different house-types in recent years less visible.

The British rule saw the decline of Chanderi's traditional nobility and with it the loss of patrons for the construction of palaces, forts, and elaborate, monumental buildings. By the turn of the twentieth century, master builders and stone-carvers no longer found their skills in demand. Many sought alternative employment and the skills themselves have almost disappeared. The introduction of new materials such as cement and concrete has often meant that masons are brought from the larger cities for construction work.

Among the weavers, the decisions of where to build and what to build were taken by the head of household. Each family participated actively in all stages of the building process. Not only members of the family, but neighbors and friends also helped out. In the building process the mason would cut and lay the stone while the men worked on the roof frame. A family's savings toward the house would often be building materials. Families stacked stone slabs and beams in courtyards as and when they could. Women, too, participated. They built platforms, plastered the walls and the floors and decorated the house with art of symbolic and ritual significance. Changing technologies, the use of industrially manufactured brick, cement and concrete, give no room for such participation making building the purview of paid masons.

7 Chinkari *was the local name for a type of stone masonry typical of the older structures in the region.*

If political changes in Chanderi have resulted in transformations in spatial patterns where the neighborhoods of weavers are more significant than erstwhile mansions, the introduction of new technologies have rendered traditional occupations and occupational groups such as the thread-spinners, potters, and the stone carvers obsolete. Architectural features, house-forms and enclaves in the city identified with these groups are dated and much transformed today.

Changes seemingly peripheral to building construction have influenced transformations in the building process. The traditional building material, buff-colored sandstone, is now in short supply. In the outskirts of Chanderi there used to be stone quarries. However, in the past twenty-five years, two of the stone quarries have been closed resulting in a shortage in the supply of building stone. As a consequence people have pilfered stones from the historic structures to construct their own dwellings. The historic structures, including the palace complex and the town wall, were built of a very special kind of dressed-stone masonry called *chinkari* work. I observed that many houses of weavers and other common folk had additions and extensions of *chinkari* stonework. The city administration has taken measures to police this "stealing," and the gradual destruction of historic monuments. Despite all the policing however, all that remains now of the city walls now are the massive gateways. Citizens, for their part, saw no reason to revere a town wall which serves them no purpose today. Concomitant changes in technology such as reinforced concrete roofing has reduced further the need for traditional construction skills. As a result, the master builders of the yesteryear are only masons today working under builders who come in from towns nearby.

INVENTING TRADITIONS: THE CONSERVATION DEVELOPMENT DILEMMA

In a globalizing world threatened by corporate homogeneity and complicated by transnationalism, Chanderi offers a window into a place that is deeply connected to its social, cultural, and natural environment. In the efforts to preserve the distinctive built environment of Chanderi, and places like it, the tendency of architectural professionals has often been to imagine a static and unified building character and process. In the process, building traditions are invented and then preserved. Building regulations and development norms sought to construct and create a static tradition in a dynamic environment. Neither the people of Chanderi, nor their buildings have been unified and static. Different groups of people in different parts of the city built in different ways that was suitable for the organization of their work and family life. Among the weavers, I observed that the use and significance of spaces and structures was linked clearly to the social and economic organization of dwelling and weaving. Changes and developments in weaving and the family have transfigured customary spatial relationships and architecture. Moreover, since weaving has been the primary economic activity in Chanderi, alterations in the social, political, and economic structures have implied changes in the building processes in addition to the introduction of new technologies. Examining the urban fabric in a larger context of home, work, society, and economy reveal that neither the culture of Chanderi nor its spontaneous, and apparently traditional, built form have ever been static, and major transformations have occurred in the traditional building process to affect the built form. The "traditional" architecture of Chanderi is not a timeless building form that is ahistorical and unchanging. Many observers regard innovations in the contemporary building forms as "untraditional," and "unauthentic." As architects and planners, we have perceived these forms as aberrations and merely as evidence of "disappearing skills," which need to be conserved.

As residents seek development and change and the right to identify themselves as "modern," policies, plans, and building regulations that do not include the varied views of the residents and their aspirations are doomed for failure. Chanderi teaches us instead that we should view the creation of buildings and urban environments as fundamentally cultural processes that are intricately connected to a place, its natural and social context. If the settlement form is seen in its context rather than as teleological, perhaps then the goal would no longer be to seek an unattainable "authenticity" in an invented "traditional" architectural and urban form. Despite its apparent exotic "otherness," Chanderi had too had seen changes and the influence of modernity. Enhancing and enriching the connections between builders, inhabitants, and designers in the building process allows greater opportunities for creating places rich with meanings. Enhancing and enriching connections to place contribute to sustainable architecture and urbanism everywhere.

Originally published in the Proceedings of the 82nd Annual Meeting of the Collegiate Schools of Architecture, 1994.

GLOBAL CONSTRUCTIONS, OR WHY GUADALAJARA WANTS A HOME DEPOT WHILE LOS ANGELES WANTS CONSTRUCTION WORKERS

CARLOS MARTÍN

INTRODUCTION

The first time I heard the term "global practices" used was in a graduate course on the international construction industry, a course devoted almost entirely to analyzing economic opportunities more than anything else. Questioning how the means and methods of design services would shape the social, political, and stylistic relations between the developing and developed nations—or even between designers and users—was a distant concern. That monetary profit was a central focus in that class is not so remarkable, nor was it particularly enlightening. But, one set of course discussions struck me then and continues to be mulled over in my mind.

The professors devoted a few days to talking about how doing work in foreign countries would change the materials of construction, the types of technology to be implemented, and, in turn, the ultimate design choices. "For example," they would say, "if you're doing work in the Third World you wouldn't use heavy construction equipment because you'd have hundreds of cheap construction workers. Then, your design would depend on how precise and uniform the construction would be because of that, too." Students were shown slides of construction sites teeming with poorly protected workers hauling bags of dirt out of trenches. We were told that bamboo was the world's most widespread construction material, with the hope that we would all be surprised at the pervasiveness of such "primitive" methods. We even calculated how many workers it would take to equal the power of a back hoe, and compare their respective costs.

Introducing new construction technology and methods to the Third World was purportedly less viable because of those nations' poor economic state. New designs that required new physical techniques or that were predicated on alternative technologies were similarly improbable. So, my professors and presumably most international designers and construction engineers were very conscious of the correlations between design, construction, and economic and social difference. Despite the racial, class, and nationalist overtones of these lessons, I do believe that these professors and the course did get one thing right: Design necessarily implicates techniques, form, and labor. As such, certain people would surely benefit from design choices, while others would be put at a disadvantage.

What they were dead wrong about, though, was how those benefits would play out. While global development projects are traditionally studied for their symbolic and political import, their physical construction demonstrates design's uniqueness in perpetuating and, at times, subverting formal politics. The means and methods of building in many sites certainly point to the assumptions about labor, technology, and industrial achievement that determine the politics and form of design interventions. But exchanges in design and construction knowledge are also inscribed in these practices in ways that subvert those same assumptions. We studied *formal* design globalization when, in fact, globalization is transpiring *informally* to a much larger extent. Increased accessibility to design tools and products across national borders and the acquiring of construction skills through immigration and labor, for example, are insuring more prevalent changes in design than formal and heavy-handed projects in both the First and Third World.

GLOBAL CONSTRUCTIONS

In this paper, I track these contemporary formal assumptions and informal exchanges. By retelling a series of personal, professional, and historical stories set in Mexico, the U.S. Southwest, and the border region at large, I point out the authority held by Western architects and engineers, and that authority's nationalization, racialization, and classing of construction labor and design skill. But I also point to the ways in which informal practices are shifting the lines between developed and developing nations and between design producers and users. These informal transformations, I argue, will ultimately change the terms of design globalization.

Specific choices made by designers in one location not only determine the construction methods and materials at another, but are also informed by assumptions regarding the latter's social and industrial achievement. Many of the social inequities that have been linked with transnational design exchanges in the past reproduce broader injustices: Assumptions regarding lack of technological capacity; purported labor surpluses and subsequent skill and wage disparities; and an ostensible need for guidance into modern environments. If "technological maximization . . . is often antithetical to the creation and maintenance of the place-form," as Kenneth Frampton suggests, then the design and technical choices made in building here and elsewhere are inextricably linked to how we perceive and imagine these places.[1] These links are that much more critical when we think about how designers and builders in the developed world think about places, people, and skills in the developing world.

In this paper I would like to present a few stories—some set in Mexico and some in the U.S. Southwest—that illustrate the discrepancy in architectural production between First World design and building circles and Third World interventions in the built landscape. I especially look at the technological authority assumed by Western architects and engineers; the effect of that authority on the nationalizing, racializing, and classing of construction labor and design skill; and the symbolic use of design and construction as a sign of

1 Kenneth Frampton, *introduction to* Technology, Place, and Architecture: The Jerusalem Seminar in Architecture, *ed. Kenneth Frampton (New York: Rizzoli, 1998), 14.*

modernization. Rather than looking at specific buildings or projects as canonical examples of transnational and transcultural exchanges, though, I am more curious about broader changes in the economic and cultural transactions that are design and construction.

What is particularly interesting about these cases is that they are shaped both by formal institutional practices with regard to building and design and by informal exchanges. As such, they are all tales about social inequities and cultural transformations despite the purported geographic and political distance between the United States and Mexico. Interestingly, the actors in both stories are not only related metaphorically or even politically, but by blood as well. Building practices are becoming more entangled, more insidious, and more complex. In short, people from all sides of all borders negotiate modernization and modern design through formal projects and informal practices—both of which are influenced by changing politics, technology, and design methods. Here are some stories.

LOCAL CONSTRUCTIONS: MEXICO

A few years ago, my cousin Tarcicio was visiting my family in San Francisco from his home near Guadalajara, one of Mexico's emerging centers for post-N.A.F.T.A. manufacturing and information technology work. As a practicing architect and contractor, we knew that Tarcicio would be particularly interested in looking at different buildings. Though he did marvel at downtown skyscrapers and timber construction, he reacted more to what was meant to be a quick purchase at the local Home Depot.

Tarcicio was overwhelmed not by the variety or quantity of design and construction goods on the store's shelves. While he did leave the store with stacks of catalogues, brochures, and samples, he was already well acquainted with the proliferation of products involved in his own work, including many of the same ones he found here. Rather, he was excited by the limitless access to them. The very ability to get information and goods for his small practice easily and directly represented a departure from his usual work. Aside from his own potential benefit, Tarcicio also commented on how desperately Mexico needed such stores. They could provide small-scale architects and contractors with new building ideas and techniques, and they would provide both professionals and ordinary consumers with the chance to pick the best solution for their particular problem from a wealth of choices. He was so taken, in fact, that he approached the store manager to ask whether Home Depot had plans to globalize, especially in Mexico. So, not only did he leave the store with product propaganda, but he also left with the hope of seeing this instant and open access back home.

While a possible Home Depot in Guadalajara seemed to validate the Americanization of commerce and design in developing nations to me, for my cousin it was much more positive. Home Depot was a democratizing of goods, an economic opportunity not just for individual enterprise, but for collective progress. Home Depot stored a kit of tools that would both aid his design skill and capacity, and simultaneously aid in national development. Tarcicio's visit to the Home Depot ultimately reaffirmed many conceptions I had about the high value placed on design and construction in the developing world. But, it also brought out a few new twists.

The professors in my international construction-industry course had advocated tailoring design services and construction techniques to local social contexts like labor skill, material availability, and technological capacity in ways that, I felt, assumed poor achievement on all those fronts. For Tarcicio, understanding and working within that local context was central to his enthusiasm about Home Depot. The goods and services available there could be tailored for his practice and his community in ways that broader, national development efforts could never approach. So, while international-development institutions have repeated the importance of making practices and technologies *appropriate* over the past few decades, Tarcicio believed that the Home Depot was, in fact, appropriate due to its institutional subversion.

While my cousin's fascination with Home Depot certainly provided me with some interesting fodder for study (along with giving my family some funny stories), it reflected a much broader change in international trade which further tied the developed United States and developing Mexico this past decade. In fact, appropriate growth in design, construction, and technology became an explicit means for social, economic, and political change in Mexican development policies. It also became a symbol for that change.

Appropriateness and its related designs and technologies took on a particularly nationalist form in Mexico from 1988 to 1994, the years of President Carlos Salinas de Gortari's administration. In addition to the North American Free Trade Agreement (N.A.F.T.A.), the Harvard-trained Salinas implemented a major developmental policy for improving national economics and individual circumstance: the *Programa Nacional de Solidaridad*, more commonly known as *Solidaridad*, or Solidarity. Design and construction were specific targets for the national government, as they have been in developing nations for quite some time.[2] *Solidaridad*, however, suggested a change in the interactions between developed and developing people through informal design exchanges.

Begun in December of 1988, *Solidaridad* was described as a way to combine foreign (particularly, American) knowledge with Mexican know-how and human capital for local development projects. As such, the program would create a new and appropriate exchange of design and construction services and technologies. Contrary to traditional governmental interventions, *Solidaridad* required the formation of local committees to assess the social and economic needs of their respective regions. They would suggest possible development projects and then serve as labor on those projects. Four "basic principles" would guide these projects: respect for community decisions;

2 For historical readings of the Mexican design and construction industry, see Dimitrios A. Germidis The Construction Industry in Mexico *(Paris: Organization for Economic Cooperation and Development, 1972), and* Labour Conditions and Industrial Relations in the Building Industry in Mexico *(Paris: Organization for Economic Cooperation and Development, 1974).*

collective participation; mutual responsibility between the government and communities; and the honest management of tasks.[3]

Within a few years, over 100,000 *Solidaridad* committees were established in urban, rural, and indigenous communities throughout the country. Each was organized in such a way that its community's members would be enlisted to work cooperatively on construction projects.[4] In so doing, the national government believed it could "avoid the dependence and paternalism" of the past by both increasing employment and incorporating local citizens into the design choices and technological decisions that would affect their surroundings.[5] As such, *Solidaridad* would create a uniquely Mexican design and technology development program, one that formally provide for informal exchanges.

For new design and construction to be "more in line with our resources," the government and *Solidaridad* committees would transform "all technical decisions into sociopolitical ones."[6] The building and construction industry was viewed as the most viable sector for this negotiation because of its history as a strong employer, its reliance on manual work, and its explicitly social importance. Analysts pointed out past evils in governmental projects to demonstrate the need for *Solidaridad* designs. Among the most infamous examples of badly conceived architecture included the specification of aluminum roofs for housing in the Mexican tropics (which, of course, rusted immediately) and of cement block buildings in the middle of interior forests (where timber construction would have been less costly and material intensive).

Architects and engineers were called on to research materials like adobe brick and passive heating and cooling systems as part of the environmentally, socially, and economically "appropriate" goals of the project. More directly, Mexican architects and engineers were called upon to accommodate their traditional practices and tools to make them more national: "Engineers must participate in this . . . national process of design and construction." The new professional skill was even given the label "rural engineering and design."[7] *Solidaridad*, however, failed in part because of this. While architects and engineers were asked to change their practices, they were not asked to change their social positions. Designers and engineers maintained the same authority over their design and construction knowledge rather than sharing them with the committees. In fact, each committee's projects were headed by an engineer who was to lead the committees and workers, and to "explain to them how they were to organize as well mention some of the project's characteristics."[8] Their authority was unquestioned. Traditional social hierarchy was combined with the full-scale importation of design work and technology provided under N.A.F.T.A.'s plans.

Throughout all of this, N.A.F.T.A. further undermined attempts at local self-reliance in design. Even before the United States officially approved the trade agreement, U.S. designers and contractors were heading south in record

3 Raúl Salinas de Gortari, Tecnología, Empleo, y Construcción en el Desarrollo de México, Segunda Edición (Mexico City: Editorial Diana, 1993), 126. Note that this book's author is ex-President Carlos Salinas de Gortari's brother and is currently serving a prison sentence in Mexico for embezzling and murder. I rely on this text both because of its relation to design and construction services and, particularly, because of this telling connection. All translations were performed by the paper's author.

4 Ibid., 34.

5 Ibid., 36.

6 Ibid., 38.

7 Ibid., 118 and 144. Design (diseño) and engineering (ingeniería) are terms with almost identical meaning in Spanish, and the architectural and civil engineering professions are closely alligned in Mexico.

8 Ibid., 141–143.

9 See, for example, Gary Tulacz
and Debra Rubin "Mexico Blooms
as N.A.F.T.A. Looms," Engineering
News-Record, November 1, 1993,
or "Booming Mexican market
may flourish with free trade,"
Engineering News-Record,
September 27, 1993. In the former,
one contractor is quoted as saying
"Mexico is going to happen with
or without N.A.F.T.A."

10 Richard Korman and Steven
Setzer "Engineers Seeking
Licenses," Engineering
News-Record, November 1, 1993.

11 See Tim Grogan and Tom
Ichniowski "Mexico: Still
Recovering from Crisis,"
Engineering News-Record,
December 22, 1997, or Michael
A. Moore "Mexican Firms Are
Coping," Engineering News-
Record, March 6, 1995.

12 Michael Flagg "Southland is
Hooked in Cheap Immigrant
Labor . . ." Los Angeles Times,
September 7, 1992.

13 Leonel Sanchez, "Drywallers'
Strike: Confrontations Multiply;
500 Workers, Mostly Latino," San
Diego Union-Tribune, August 23,
1992.

14 Harry Bernstein "The
Drywallers—An Ironic Tale,"
Los Angeles Times, September 29,
1992.

numbers.[9] Besides being awarded major infrastructure and housing projects, U.S. designers and contractors were also assured that their Mexican counterparts would not make many inroads outside.[10] By the 1993 devaluation of the peso and the political scandals following President Salinas' departure from office, *Solidaridad* was dead, N.A.F.T.A. was alive and kicking, and the lay communities of Mexico were left with little of the design education and technological skills to which they were meant to have access.[11]

Unfortunately, such failed developments to institutionalize informal exchanges in knowledge and design are far too common in the history of developing nations. Despite its significant attempts to reconsider design and construction for popular ends, *Solidaridad* proved ineffective because of the same formal political and knowledge structures that it sought to dismantle. Only certain people on both sides of the border had the skills and insight that could have transformed the Mexican social and built landscape. They also retained the power for applying them.

LOCAL CONSTRUCTION: UNITED STATES

During the early years of N.A.F.T.A., Mexican architects and contractors actively sought joint ventures with U.S. firms for projects in the United States at the same time that U.S. firms were building all over Mexico. But, a more interesting and, in fact, more profound exchange was occurring across the border: immigration. A significant fraction of Mexican rural folk—including a substantial percentage of the townspeople from my and my cousin's hometown—were and are continuously crossing the historically porous line.

While many who settle on this side of the border find work in agriculture and other fields traditionally taken by immigrants in the U.S. Southwest, many who have arrived in the past two decades find jobs in construction. A trip to any construction site in the greater Los Angeles area—and in the entire U.S. Southwest for that matter—bears witness to these changing labor demographics. Though exact numbers are not known, it has been estimated that the majority of construction workers in southern California—especially in open-shop residential construction—are Latino immigrants. The construction industry is one of the ten largest employers of Latinos in the state of California, and this labor change happened over the span of only one decade.[12]

Drywall construction is a particularly interesting case. Nine out of ten drywallers in southern California today are Latino, and many of them are undocumented.[13] Only two decades ago, the majority of construction workers in the area were white and union-affiliated. As the design and building sector dried up in the mid-1970s, drywall contractors began hiring undocumented laborers to replace union trades. In 1982, after a heated strike, the contractors broke the union and Latino immigrants soon filled the labor supply.[14]

The work became piecemeal, routine, and thoroughly nonunion through-out the 1980s as the design and construction industry tried to come to terms with a depressed housing market.[15] The workers' plight was further exacerbated by low wages, no healthcare, and fear due to their precarious immigration status. The work itself was increasingly consigned and referred to as "Mexican" work or, as one observer noted, was not even acknowledged at all.[16] The previous drywallers settled into commercial construction, taking the union with them. The traditional building trades were so averse to the new workers that they refrained from any attempts at organizing the new work.

Despite such lack of support and even resistance, the drywallers chose to organize themselves—an act that would be regularly compared to the early union organizing of the largely immigrant United Farm Workers in the 1960s. With the assistance of local Latino aid agencies, Catholic clergy, and the "workers' family and geographical ties to Mexico," drywallers walked off construction sites throughout the Southland in June of 1992. The strike broke many contractors, who were already feeling the crunch of the California building recession. With freeway blockades, caravans, and public demonstrations in open defiance of building, police, and immigration authorities, the drywallers made themselves and their work known. Five months later, thirty-nine builders signed an organizing agreement with the approximately 4,000 drywallers.[17]

The success of the strike was seen as a wake-up call for the building trade unions, and the design and construction industry as a whole. After establishing explicit characteristics for construction work (including so-called low skill tasks and meager salaries) that could only be filled by an implicit labor group (that is, geographically close undocumented immigrants), builders were faced with the very real possibility of addressing a classed and racialized labor union. The strikes and the ensuing conflict were especially fueled by the scare of California's most recent anti-immigrant episode. Immigration officials launched major raids and deportations against southern California drywallers just two years after those same workers gained union recognition.[18] Union leaders publicly denounced these attacks, claiming that the Immigration and Naturalization Service was targeting drywallers solely because of their recent and successful organizing campaign.[19] The next year, further, California's Governor Pete Wilson selected the head of the world's largest land developer (the Irvine Land Company) to serve as the chief fundraiser for his presidential bid.[20]

One month after Wilson's announcement, carpenters and framers throughout the Los Angeles area began picketing residential building sites.[21] Confrontations between the workers, contractors, and land developers became commonplace. Even more telling is that these confrontations usually took place on the quintessentially Californian design development: the Angelino suburban residential tract. With the economic boom of the past

15 Rick Burnham "Union Wants Role in House Building Industry," Riverside Press-Enterprise, May 7, 1995.

16 Mike Clements "Drywallers' Strike Nails Down a Principle . . . Workers, Especially Immigrants, Need a 'Public Dace' to Win Justice . . .," Los Angeles Times, November 16, 1992.

17 Michael Flagg "A 'Landmark' Victory for Drywall Union; Labor: Mexican Immigrants Outlast Builders . . .," Los Angeles Times, November 11, 1992.

18 Sandy Stokes "Over 400 Drywallers Deported," Riverside Press-Enterprise, March 15, 1994.

19 Sandy Stokes "I.N.S. Trying to Punish Drywallers," Riverside Press-Enterprise, March 22, 1994.

20 David Bacon "Shutting Down Homebuilding in LA Basin; Immigrants Lead New Surge of Labor Activism," Pacific News Service, May 9, 1995.

21 Pacific News Service, May 9, 1995.

half-decade, however, labor disputes have been ignored as architects and builders have found themselves inundated with new work.

Immigrant construction labor, however, has most surely not ended. Just last spring, Latino workers struck a Kaufman and Broad job site in Las Vegas, Nevada.[22] Two related articles came out in the *Engineering News-Record* this past summer, as well. The first reported the hearings of a panel of architects and contractors on "future trends" in building, the most notable of which was the "shortage of skilled, motivated, and loyal employees at levels throughout the construction industry [that was] threatening its survival."[23] The second article—titled "Let in More Mexicans Legally"—called on all design- and building-affiliated professionals to push for expanded visa programs for Mexican nationals during "peak times of construction activity" since, in the past, "many illegals who sneaked by [immigration officials] ended up on construction sites."[24]

That the premier journal for project announcements and construction information would print such articles speaks volumes about how design and building professionals see themselves in relation to the skills, capacities, and personal characteristics of their workforce. That the same journal, further, would name *nations* in a manner that opposed recent popular sentiments reveals much more about how race, class, and national status both determine conceptions of design and building practices and perpetuate these across political and cultural boundaries.

In fact, the drywallers' skills and knowledge—or more accurately, the assumptions made regarding their skills and knowledge—were predicated on these social and political categories. Such decisions and professional border-drawing parallel the relations that Mexico's *Solidaridad* and N.A.F.T.A. established between U.S. design and construction firms and their Mexican counterparts, and between Mexican designers and engineers and the general populace. What is more, this tension between informal exchanges in design from laborers and regular folk and formal claims over design knowledge and policy by professional and governmental bodies will most likely continue throughout future globalization projects.

CONSTRUCTING THE GLOBE

In many ways, the local stories I describe here are not new. Institutional attempts to transform building practices have a long history in both developed and developing nations. Informal exchanges have an even longer one. Linking certain kinds of work (particularly design and construction occupations) to specific class, race, and gender groups is also an unfortunate truism. The most critical difference in these stories, though, is the fact that neither could be told without incorporating the loose affiliations between people on both sides of geographic and cultural border. Global practices in design and construction can no longer be simply described in terms of Western design and technology exports to the developing world, nor in terms of tailoring that technology

22 Nancy Cleeland "Las Vegas Labor Protests Brought to LA Builder," Los Angeles Times, April 2, 1999.

23 Nancy Cleeland "Work Force," Engineering News-Record, May 24, 1999, 44.

24 Alan Goozner "Let in More Mexicans Legally" Engineering News-Record, August 16, 1999, 99.

appropriately to the local developing context. The increasing complexity of global economies and cultural exchanges prohibits such simple readings of contemporary architectural design and construction.

As with most challenges, however, the problem is the solution. *Solidaridad* and other modernization projects in the developing world persist in remaking the class hierarchies that translate into castes of knowledge, skill, and authority. In *Solidaridad*, authority still rested with Mexican engineers and architects and ultimately, with the federal government and foreign (that is, U.S.) design and technology exporters. The Mexican people might have been the formal beneficiaries of these works, but did not retain informal authority over them. Similarly, the exploitation of undocumented immigrant exploitation and the disavowal of their informal skill and contributions remakes skill and information borders along similar motives. In both cases, conceptions of the design and technological *other* serve as the means for reproducing authority and defining formal control—be it the authority of the developed world over the developing, of the building professional over the laborer, or of the building industry over common folk.

Formally constructing the designed *other*, the construction *other*, and the technological *other* prohibits the incorporation of the more liberatory informal knowledge exchanges. Providing design and technology services or even employment is insufficient for remedying global inequities. Rather, programs that question *who* retains knowledge and skill in design and technology more effectively subvert traditional boundaries between the developed and developing world, between the design and building professional and workers, and between the producers and recipients of building exchanges.

As economics and politics obscure geographic borders, culture and technology are blurring traditional lines between design and construction. We are already witnessing these transformations with our own design and construction practices both here and abroad, though we often choose to overlook them. The daily and ubiquitous transacting of design skills and construction products serve more to break down geopolitical and professional borders. The catalogues that Tarcicio took back to Guadalajara and the methods learned by Los Angeles' drywallers will negotiate global design and construction practices in more equitable and less heavy-handed ways. In short, we already practice global practices right here.

Ultimately, my cousin was right in many ways about the Home Depot. Now, I am not saying that Home Depot *should* open up in Guadalajara. But I no longer think that it is an altogether bad idea. As scholars of design and building, we should devise ways to support such informal yet strategic interactions. When we speak of globalization, we usually speak about knowing that what is *here* is linked to what is *there* in subtle ways; the study of specific and bounded design projects usually masks that subtlety. We talk about Western designers and multinational contractors working in the Third World, rather than the immigrant adding a room to her home. So, when we speak of global design practices, we must understand that global links are based on assumptions of and authority over design and technological knowledge—that is, we know that what is *there* was designed and constructed by what is *here*, and vice versa.

Originally published in the Proceedings of the 88th Annual Meetinig of the Association of Collegiate Schools of Architecture, 2000.

A RAPTOR ENCLOSURE FOR THE ZUNI PUEBLO
Construction and reconsideration

CLAUDE E. ARMSTRONG AND
DONNA L.COHEN

above: Golden Eagle in raptor enclosure (photo credit Claude Armstrong).

UNDER CONSTRUCTION 1999

Eagle feathers play a central role in the ritual observances of many Native Americans. In the past, tribal members were free to keep eagles for religious and ceremonial use. Today however, application must be made to the Federal Government to receive feathers. High demand for feathers results in waits of several years, and feathers may arrive in damaged condition.

The leaders of the Zuni Pueblo asked us to work with them to design a structure to hold eagles unsuited to the wild. This raptor enclosure is essentially a flight area and cages for eagles; when the birds molt, the tribe will collect the feathers. We expect the building to take on a ceremonial character, and the ritual of gathering feathers here to become a way of life. This new program makes this the first building of its kind.

The intention is to use material from the pueblo lands for the construction. The highly skilled Zuni stone masons lay the reddish sandstone walls in Chaco style. Younger members of the tribe are being trained to learn this skill. Some lumber comes from the Zuni mountains and is being milled in the newly acquired sawmill. The overall dimensions of the building are 43 feet wide × 110 feet long × 18 feet high. Orientation is east–west with protection from the winds on the ends. The structure is sited to face the mesa Dowayalanee, which has sacred connections to the eagles and the tribe.

bottom left: Dowayalanee seen through enclosure (photo credit Claude Armstrong).

bottom right: Light in raptor enclosure (photo credit Claude Armstrong).

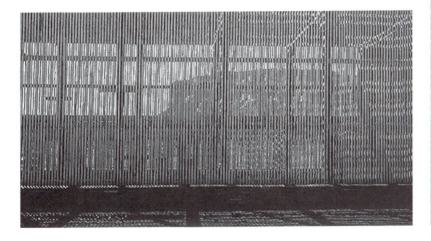

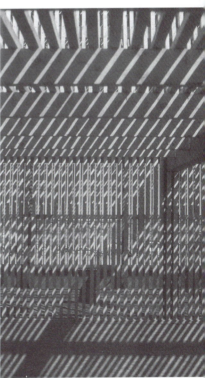

351

right: Construction crew
(photo credit Steve Albert).

The initial aviary project is a bold reinvention of a traditional Zuni pro-gram, the result of generations of artistic vision, and of the Zuni commitment to excellence in craft.

NATURAL RESOURCES COMPOUND 2002

The Zuni Eagle Aviary is a place of practical purpose and spiritual presence. One building, designed to hold birds and their caregivers, has expanded in significance as people from Zuni and elsewhere discover the power of the space inhabited the eagle.

The project is recognized both for sustaining Zuni cultural and religious practices, and for its architectural integrity. As a result of its success, over

bottom: Aerial view of compound

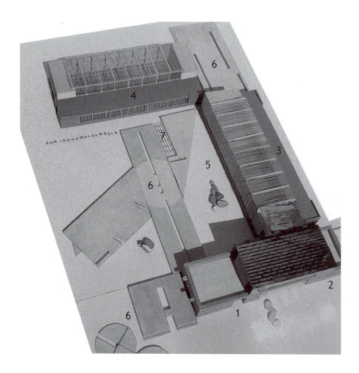

1. Entry to compound

2. Rammed earth meeting room

3. Raptor enclosure east

4. Raptor enclosure north

5. Interior courtyard

6. Land maps

7. Waffle garden

the course of several years, a natural resources compound is designed as an addition to the site, envisioned as demonstration ground where visitors gain an understanding of the Zuni relationship to the natural world.

The compound is to include:

- sister sanctuary, a new eagle breeding facility;
- portals, visitor orientation with portals for eagle viewing;

below: Compound—raptor enclosures, meeting room, Dowayalanee, view to East

bottom: Raptor enclosure, south-east corner elevation

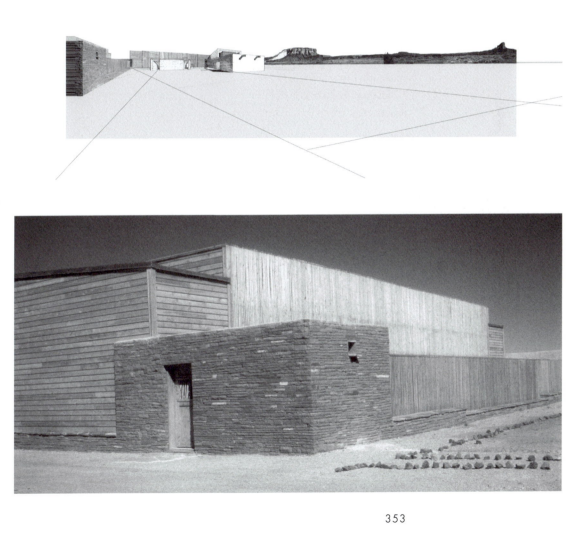

Project credits:

Client: Pueblo of Zuni, Governor Malcolm Bowekaty, Department of Fish and Wildlife

Directors: Jim Enote, Steve Albert

Construction: Members of the Zuni Pueblo

Funding: Phase 1 significant in-kind funds from the Bureau of Indian Affairs and generous contributions from The Lannan Foundation, The Christopher Reynolds Foundation, The Fund of Four Directions, The Angelica Foundation, and the Chamiza Foundation

Phase 2 design funded by the National Endowment for the Arts

- speaking or listening room, a community meeting room, constructed of rammed earth, with acoustic panels in walls and ceiling to modulate voices, with cool areas to store peaches;
- map garden, including a solar array, and marks in the land, which allude to the significance of outlying sites.

NEW DIRECTIONS 2005

Tourism increases at the Zuni pueblo, due in part to interest in the aviary, and the tribe reconsiders the role of visitor orientation. A delicate balance is sought: What does the tribe want to share, and what does the tribe want to protect? Although proud of its history of connection with natural resources, the consensus is that the aviary is part of religious tradition and will remain a quiet place. As the community conversation unfolds, tourist orientation shifts from the eagle sanctuary and proposed natural resources compound to the A:shiwi A:wan Museum and Heritage Center. The careful use of natural resources is considered to be part of the Zuni heritage, and will be demonstrated at the Heritage Center. The raptor enclosure assumes a more private position in pueblo life.

Originally published in the Proceedings of the 87th Annual Meeting of the Association of Collegiate Schools of Architecture, 1999.

GARDEN OF TIME, LANDSCAPE OF CHANGE
Women Suffrage Memorial, St. Paul, Minnesota, 1996
RAVEEVARN CHOKSOMBATCHAI
AND RALPH KIRK NELSON

The design proposal is based on a fundamental assumption that human history and natural history are intertwined.

The Women Suffrage Memorial Garden gives presence to the spirit of individuals and collective organizations that brought about monumental change in the political, social, and cultural landscape of Minnesota. It acknowledges the context of the greater Capitol Mall and the state landscape it embraces. The Memorial Garden is considered a microcosm of these broad landscapes, a revelation of natural and cultural forces.

CHANGE

A vision of monumental, positive change lay at the core of the Women Suffrage Movement; the Nineteenth Amendment is a change to the constitution. Seeking to extend the depth of interpretation and educate through local analogy, the garden is articulated by another forceful movement of geological transformation. Glaciation had the most profound influence on the landscape of Minnesota and the *process* of glaciation parallels the slow, steady, and forceful changes brought about by the suffragist movement. In this way the project seeks to join human events with natural events, each illuminating and enriching the other.

TIME

The garden registers marks of time related to selected natural, cultural, and political conditions of Minnesota. The garden articulates time through physical form and phenomena. The dominant landscape of the memorial reflects the kettles and kames so indiginous to the natural landscape of the state. This landscape, formed by the last major glacier to recede from Minnesota, is evidenced by striations of movement recorded in the face of the limestone bedrock. These marks of time are revealed on the site as stone garden edges. The connection is further reinforced by the joining together of a native prairie and a native woodland landscape by a *woven trellis*. This trellis is composed of vertical elements that correspond to the years in which the suffragists struggled for their cause; each interval between posts mark *one year*. The stepped bench at the base of the trellis registers intervals in

1848
SENECA FALLS CONVENES

1920
19TH AMENDMENT RATIFIED

INDIVIDUAL LIFE LINES

years; each rise occurring at pivotal moments in history. The woven horizontal bands of the trellis correspond to the lifeline of specific individuals and pivotal events. In this way the linear, compressed time of history is connected to the real time of site experience. Both ends of the trellis are open, implying extension back in time (downhill) or forward in time (uphill, toward the capitol). Each stone striation from the glacial marking on the ground plane is woven through each decade marker on the trellis. Entry can occur at either end or in the middle but begins chronologically on the lower end. Entry here brings the visitor to a segment of time from 1840 to 1850. Selected quotations on wide bands reflect upon the injustices faced by suffragists and their impending

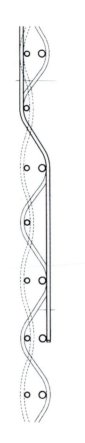

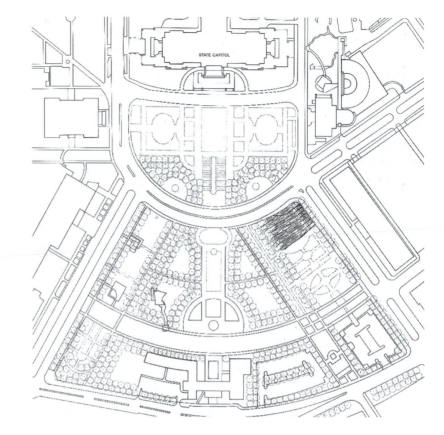

Project credits:

Drawings/Design: LOOM,
Raveevarn Choksombatchai,
Ralph Nelson

Photographic Work: Christian Faust

Written Description: Ralph Nelson

struggle. Also noted are the names and birthdates of selected suffragists born in this decade who may or may not have lived to experience the Nineteenth Ammendment. The middle segment of the trellis covers the years 1850 through 1920 and is devoted to pivotal women, organizations, and events that affected positive change or deeds in Minnesota. Sunlight casting through the cut-out band of each name can be cast onto the body of each visitor.

CONTEXT

The garden responds directly to site-specific scale, context, material, and local orientation. The major space of the garden is scaled to the open space and view shed extending from the capitol to the city. The garden embraces the east side and northeast corner of the site along Cedar Street as a logical area in which to draw visitors or passerbys into the garden. The sloped walkway is to provide easier wheelchair movement on this part of the site. If a visitor is moving uphill toward the capitol, along the trellis, the view of the capitol is hidden through the grove of trees untill the 1920 trellis mark near the corner, at which point it is revealed.

Originally published in the Proceedings of the 85th Annual Meeting of the Association of Collegiate Schools of Architecture, 1997.

360

UNMASKING URBAN TRACES

JEANINE CENTOURI WITH CRAIG BARTON, MILDRED HOWARD, JAMES ROJAS, AND DEAN SAKAMOTO

The title "Unmasking Urban Traces" refers to a mode of operation on the city where everyday signs of life, culture, and tradition are unmasked in meaningful ways. The urban environment is largely being designed through incremental patterns of use and adaptation. "Unmasking" or exposing is a kind of urban archeology where latent mysteries of the city are unearthed. While architectural discourse has been developing its own language and concerns within the discipline, the built environment has been largely shaped by the decisions of people who are not architects. Methods should be forged so those trained in the art of designing spaces can be empowered to address the mundane problems facing our cities today. We need to see advocacy and education as an equal part of our architectural mission, parallel to the development of methods for using new materials and form generation.

Urban Traces can be tracked at many different scales. Large-scale patterns can be found in communities of immigration who adapt built fabric to their everyday needs such as Latino East Los Angeles. Cultural groups often bring their own spatial divisions and everyday rituals to existing environments—sometimes these patterns layered over the existing create new cultural forms of expression. The city as a palimpsest is one which is written and rewritten many times, with each new layer augmenting, adapting, or erasing from its previous histories. Marginalized aspects of our history can be unmasked and reconstituted. Unmasking the traces of history of a building or site can also reveal contested terrain with regard to ownership and the public realm. Uncovering signs of repression or struggle for territory in the city is another means by which to consider traces.

"Unmasking Urban Traces" describes a genre of work in the built environment from different fields and perspectives which attempts to pay close attention to cultural traces which are informing the vitality of our cities. The strategies of this work range from exposing latent histories in order to empower marginalized groups, to strengthening the democratic use of public space within the city, to political activism expressed in built form. This vision of the city makes a connection between the world of design and the world of the vernacular. The act of unmasking graces is a way of revealing our common history and our common bonds to the landscape which we commonly inhabit.

MEMORY NARRATIVE AND IDENTITY, MILDRED HOWARD

> *Prophetic thought and action is a preservative in that it tries to keep alive certain elements of a tradition bequeathed to us from the past and revolutionary in that it attempts to project a vision and inspire a praxis which fundamentally transforms the prevailing status quo in light of the best of the tradition and the flawed yet significant achievement of the present order.*[1]

1 Cornel West, Prophetic Fragments *(Trenton, New Jersey: African World Press, Inc., 1988) p. 11*

The use of memory, place, history, family, and identity are used to stimulate creativity. Using objects to comingle past and present, a model of the world is created; to stir emotions, to question beliefs and misconceptions about how different people view their environment. Everyday objects are used beyond their original purposes to express connection to and respect for ancestors personally and collectively.

The circumscribing of space can be seen as evoking a centrality of location. The work is inspired by the spatial presence and feeling of congregation—a group, a choir, or an idea about issues of race, gender, culture, and religion. Often the anticipation of these groups is not present in the real world but (exists) as a memory of the past or an anticipation of the future.

UNMASKING LATINO URBANISM, JAMES ROJAS

Every place and people have history. Sometimes these histories are shared, but many times they are not as in the case of East Los Angeles. The history of the built environment of East Los Angeles is American and the history of the residents is Mexican.

East Los Angeles was not built by Mexicans but by many ethnic groups that came before them. Mexicans have retrofitted the existing landscape to fit their needs, thus creating a new hybrid. To fully understand and appreciate this urban hybrid one must examine the two histories: one of place and one of people.

There are many different disciplines which unmask the physical environments and social characteristics of people. The sociologist examines people's behavior. The urban planner analyzes data and numbers. The anthropologist examines artifacts. While all are excellent methods of comprehending place, a more comprehensive approach is needed in order to truly understand the complex nature of East Los Angeles. This approach advocates drawing upon techniques from several disciplines in order to read patterns evolving within urban communities.

Patterns can be deciphered amongst the traces within this community. Ritualistic activities are brought to this place and superimposed onto the existing architecture. Activities such as hanging out, talking to a neighbor, and decorating your house add dimension and meaning to our public realm.

EVOLUTION OF EAST LOS ANGELES VERNACULAR

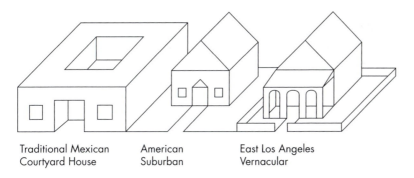

Traditional Mexican
Courtyard House

American
Suburban

East Los Angeles
Vernacular

Adaptation of the existing urban fabric creates vernacular hybrid forms. The city is being designed incrementally by cultural groups expressing their identities—becoming sensitive to these traces perhaps can yield a more realistic approach to urbanism.

NATIONAL VOTING RIGHTS INTERPRETIVE CENTER AND MEMORIAL PARK, RBGC ARCHITECTS, CRAIG BARTON, AND CHRISTOPHER FANNIN

The National Voting Rights Interpretive Center and Memorial Park, located on Alabama State Highway 80 at the foot of the Edmund Pettus Bridge, overlooks the site of the "Bloody Sunday" confrontation. Bloody Sunday (March 7, 1965) proved to be one of the most significant battles of the voting rights movement, pitting the local voting rights activists led by John Lewis (then a representative of the Student Nonviolent Coordinating Committee, currently a member of the U.S. Congressional delegation from Georgia) attempting to march to the state capital *against* members of the Alabama state police and other law enforcement officials mobilized by Governor George C. Wallace. The troopers violently prevented Lewis and the other marchers from crossing Pettus Bridge, and forced them back into the city of Selma.

The project helps to interpret the site's significance by providing a destination for the annual bridge-crossing jubilee, which commemorates the events of Bloody Sunday. This history comes alive with a series of methods designed to connect thought to emotion. Architectural, landscape, and graphic features link history with phenomenological experiences. Through didactic and associative means, visitors and motorists are connected to this powerful landscape.

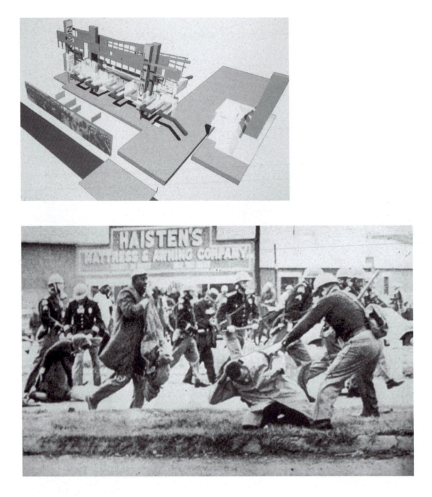

THE PROGRESS WALL, DEAN SAKAMOTO

The Progress Wall at 1156 Chapel Street is a temporary public space project that reveals the forgotten traces of history of an urban landmark, its near death as a vacant property, and questions its future impact on a diverse section of the city. The Progress Wall speculates upon the real meaning of progress by serving as an interactive surface, a record and collector of individual responses to the specific site or the city in general. As a public space, this project investigates the possibility of creating an interim site that informs and empowers its everyday users, regardless of race, class, occupational, or political position, in influencing the direction of urban development.

From 1954 to 1986, 1156 Chapel Street was the site of a vital Jewish Community Center (J.C.C.) designed by Louis I. Kahn in consultation to Abramovitz & Weinstein, a local architectural firm. The JCC's closing mirrored the demise of New Haven's downtown and heightened its division from Yale University, which today is the city's largest employer and landowner. For over twelve years the vacant JCC structure stood symbolic of a brief but

lively postwar period of multiethnic comingling and urban prosperity. In reality, however, this architectural carcass represented the failure of New Haven as a model city of federally funded urban renewal forty years ago that created radical changes in the urban landscape by exclusive decision-making and without sensitivity to the existing fabric. In contrast to the bare chainlink fences and bulldozers more typical to periods of redevelopment, the Progress Wall is an example of how an interim urban space project can excavate meaning, sensitize future development to what already exists, and provide an open venue for participation in the public realm.

Originally published in the Proceedings of the 88th Annual Meeting of the Association of Collegiate Schools of Architecture, 2000.

365

INDEX

Also available from Routledge…

Housing and Dwelling

Perspectives on Modern Domestic Architecture

Edited by Barbara Miller Lane

Housing and Dwelling collects the best in recent scholarly and philosophical writings that bear upon the history of domestic architecture in the nineteenth and twentieth centuries. Lane combines exemplary readings that focus on and examine the issues involved in the study of domestic architecture. The extracts are taken from an innovative and informed combination of philosophy, history, social science, art, literature and architectural writings. The readings address, among other issues, the relation between the public and the private sphere, the gendering of space, notions of domesticity, the relation between domesticity and social class, the role of builders and prefabrication, and the relationship between architects and the inhabitants of dwellings.

Uniquely, the readings in *Housing and Dwelling* underline the point of view of the user of a dwelling and assess the impact of varying uses on the evolution of domestic architecture.

Housing and Dwelling is a valuable asset for students, scholars, and designers alike. The book explores the extraordinary variety of methods, interpretations and source materials now available in this important field. For students, it opens windows on the many aspects of domestic architecture. For scholars, it introduces new, interdisciplinary points of view and suggests directions for further research. It acquaints practising architects in the field of housing design with history and methods and offers directions for future design possibilities.

ISBN: 978–0–415–34655–9 (Hb)
978–0–415–34656–6 (Pb)

For ordering and further information please visit:

http://www.routledge.com/builtenvironment

Narrating Architecture

A retrospective anthology

Edited by James Madge and Andrew Peckham

The Journal of Architecture is jointly published by The Royal Institute of British Architects (RIBA) and Routledge. An international journal committed to advancing architectural discourse in its widest sense, its aim is to seek diverse views of the past, present and future practice of architecture, and to attract a wide variety of perspectives from the architectural and related professions, as well as from academics.

This anthology brings together in one volume a selection of papers that stand out after ten years of publication. The editors give readers access to international contributions in a carefully structured book, bringing coherence to a wide range of topics. The book is divided into seven parts: Architects and the practice of design; Architecture and the discourses of science; Issues of materiality; Narratives of domesticity; Problems of building; The sociology of architectural practice and Identity and the appropriation of place. It offers those teaching or running seminars in this subject area a readily available collection of recent research in several key areas.

ISBN: 978–0–415–37435–4 (Hb)
978–0–415–38564–0 (Pb)

For ordering and further information please visit:

http://www.routledge.com/builtenvironment

Rethinking Technology

A reader in architectural theory

Edited by William Braham and Jonathan Hale

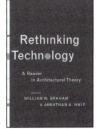

Rethinking Technology is an essential reference for all students of architecture, design and the built environment; providing a convenient single source for all the key texts in the recent literature on architecture and technology.

The essays included are chronicles, manifestos, reflections, and theories produced by architects and architectural writers. Arranged in chronological order of original publication, these essays allow comparisons to be made between writings produced in a similar historical context and reveal the discipline's long and close attention to the experience and effects of new technologies, from the early twentieth century to the present day.

The editors preface each text with a short introduction explaining the significance of the essay in relation to the broader developments charted by the book. Cross-references are also made between individual texts in order to highlight important thematic connections across time.

ISBN: 978–0–415–34653–5 (Hb)
978–0–415–34654–2 (Pb)

For ordering and further information please visit:

http://www.routledge.com/builtenvironment

eBooks – at www.eBookstore.tandf.co.uk

A library at your fingertips!

eBooks are electronic versions of printed books. You can store them on your PC/laptop or browse them online.

They have advantages for anyone needing rapid access to a wide variety of published, copyright information.

eBooks can help your research by enabling you to bookmark chapters, annotate text and use instant searches to find specific words or phrases. Several eBook files would fit on even a small laptop or PDA.

NEW: Save money by eSubscribing: cheap, online access to any eBook for as long as you need it.

Annual subscription packages

We now offer special low-cost bulk subscriptions to packages of eBooks in certain subject areas. These are available to libraries or to individuals.

For more information please contact webmaster.ebooks@tandf.co.uk

We're continually developing the eBook concept, so keep up to date by visiting the website.

www.eBookstore.tandf.co.uk